PAPER 5

ACCOUNTING

First edition August 1985
Reprinted September 1986
Revised and reprinted September 1987
Revised and reprinted July 1988
Second edition August 1989

ISBN 0 86277 114 5

A CIP catalogue record for this book is
available from the British Library

Published by

BPP Publishing Ltd
BPP House, Aldine Place
142-144 Uxbridge Road
London, W12 8AA

Printed and Bound in England
by Watkiss Studios Limited
Biggleswade, Beds. SG18 9ST

We are grateful to the Association of Accounting Technicians, the London Chamber of
Commerce and Industry and the Institute of Chartered Secretaries and Administrators
for permission to reproduce past examination questions. The suggested solutions have
been prepared by BPP Publishing Ltd.

©

BPP Publishing Limited
1989

CONTENTS

CONTENTS

SECTION 3: FINAL ACCOUNTS

SECTION 4: INTERPRETATION OF FINANCIAL STATEMENTS

PREFACE

This study text is designed to provide comprehensive coverage of the syllabus for the Intermediate Examination Paper 5: Accounting. There have now been seven sittings of the examination under the new syllabus introduced in 1986. Taken in conjunction with the syllabus itself, which is set out on page (vi), the papers set give students a reasonable guide on what to expect in the examination and this study text covers everything you need to know to pass.

Paper 5 is an important step in your examination structure because you will later have to build on the knowledge gained here in order to attempt papers 9 and 10 of the Final Examination. A thorough understanding of the subject at Intermediate level will be an invaluable aid to your future examination and career success.

BPP Publishing
August 1989

INTRODUCTION

Syllabus

Aims

To develop

   (a)   an understanding of accounting concepts and methods.
   (b)   competence in the relevant skills of collecting and processing accounting data.
   (c)   a base for more advanced technical studies.

Content

10%   *Accounting concepts*
The entity - distinction between the entity and its owner. Monetary measurement, going concern, consistency, conservatism and matching, and their application to the recording of transactions and drafting of accounting statements.

25%   *Accounting records*
The nature of the more usual forms of business transactions and their documentation. The techniques of double entry book-keeping to record transactions and process entries through to trial balance. The location of errors and the use of suspense accounts, adjustments to correct errors, internal control, bank reconciliations, the purpose and operation of control accounts.

50%   *Accounting statements*
The significance of the capital/revenue distinction. The accounting treatment of stocks, fixed assets, depreciation and VAT. The adjustment of the trial balance for accruals, prepayments, provisions for depreciation, doubtful debts and stock profits; the production of manufacturing, trading, profit and loss and appropriation accounts and balance sheets for sole traders, partnerships and companies.

Partnership accounts: entries on the formation of a partnership, the appropriation of partnership profits, current and capital accounts. Partnership and company compared and contrasted as forms of business structure.

Preparation of accounts from incomplete records, and the use of incomplete records techniques to calculate stock losses and defalcations. Receipts and payments accounts and the accounting statements of non-commercial undertakings.

15%   *Interpretation of financial statements*
The significance and limitations of financial ratios, the definition and application of basic financial ratios and the selection and application of appropriate accounting concepts and methods to simple business problems.

A knowledge of the disclosure requirements of the Companies Acts will not be required at this level.

INTRODUCTION

Structure of the exam paper

The paper consists of seven questions, carrying 25 marks each. The two questions in Section A are compulsory; Section B involves a choice of any two from five.

The questions set almost exclusively involve computational work, although a brief discussion section has appeared in one of the optional questions in each paper.

When the pilot paper was published in 1985 it was accompanied by the following introduction to the syllabus.

'Introduction

This paper concentrates on the foundations of practical accounting which are fundamentally important to the accounting technician.

Whilst the major part of the syllabus is concerned with how business transactions are recorded and how to prepare various accounting statements for sole traders, partnerships and limited companies as well as non-commercial undertakings, emphasis is also placed on basic accounting concepts which must be understood if meaningful accounting material is to be produced. The syllabus is completed by a reference to the interpretation of financial ratios.

At this stage, candidates should be able to prepare and process accounting entries for transactions covering records of prime entry (eg journal) and the ledger. It is necessary for them to be able to prepare and adjust trial balances and then to produce manufacturing, trading, profit and loss and appropriation accounts and balance sheets. Although questions will usually require computational answers, there may occasionally be an analytical section while some questions (for example, on the interpretation of financial statements) may need essay or report type answers.

At least one of the two compulsory questions will be concerned largely with the accounting statement section of the syllabus.

In answering examination papers, candidates must pay particular attention to layout and supporting workings.'

Past papers

A brief analysis of the subjects covered by recent papers is given below.

		Marks	Compulsory (c)/ Optional (o)
June 1989			
1.	Income and expenditure accounts	25	c
2.	Write up purchase ledger control account and compute gross profit	25	c
3.	Report on two businesses to a potential purchaser	25	o
4.	Trial balance and accounts	25	o
5.	Stock valuations using FIFO and LIFO	25	o
6.	Journals and ledger accounts	25	o
7.	Partners' appropriation account and balance sheet	25	o

INTRODUCTION

SECTION 1

INTRODUCTION TO ACCOUNTING

Chapter 1

THE PURPOSE
OF ACCOUNTING

The purpose of this chapter is:

- to explain the terms 'accounting' and 'accounts'
- to explain the reasons why businesses prepare accounts
- to discuss the categories of people who use accounts and their information needs
- to identify the characteristics of useful information and the extent to which accounting statements display such characteristics.

Introduction

1. In this study text we will be looking in detail at the way in which accounting records are maintained and at the presentation of accounting information in the form of financial statements. But before doing so, we must first explain what is meant by 'accounting' and 'accounts'.

   Accounting could be defined as the process of collecting, recording, summarising and communicating financial information.

   Accounts are the records in which this information is recorded.

   Keeping the most basic records is described as *bookkeeping* and the profession responsible for the summarising and communicating of financial information is the *accountancy* profession.

Why keep accounts?

2. Accounts have been kept for thousands of years because they help to keep track of money, by showing where it came from and how it has been spent.

   Another reason is that the production of accounting information can itself play an important role in the efficient running of a business. For example, a business needs to pay bills in respect of the goods and services it purchases. It must, therefore, keep a record of such bills so that the correct amounts can be paid at the correct time. Similarly a business needs to keep track of cash and cheques received from customers. Such records form one part of a basic accounting system. Additionally, keeping records of a business's assets (eg its motor vehicles or computers) makes it easier to keep them secure.

3. Another reason arises from the complexity of most modern businesses. Centuries ago, a business enterprise might consist of a single venture with a limited life. For example, a merchant might charter a ship to purchase goods from abroad for sale in his own country. In such cases it was easy to ascertain the merchant's profit: it was simply the amount of cash he had left at the end of the venture. Similarly, a small shop needs to generate enough money to pay for all its proprietor's personal expenses and occasional large purchases (eg replacement till or van). The proprietor can quite easily check that this aim is being met by counting the cash in the till.

4. However, modern businesses are often much more complicated. They seldom have a single owner (in fact, some very large enterprises, such as British Telecom, may be owned by millions of shareholders). Frequently the owners are not involved in the day-to-day running of the business but appoint managers to act on their behalf. In addition, there are too many activities and assets for the managers to keep track of simply from personal knowledge and an occasional glance at the bank statement. It is therefore desirable that businesses should produce accounts which will indicate how successfully the managers are performing.

5. In 1975 a committee established by the UK accountancy bodies published a discussion paper called *The corporate report*. (A corporate report is a report, including accounts, prepared by a business enterprise). One of the questions which the committee attempted to answer was why businesses produce accounts. They concluded that the fundamental objective of a corporate report is:

> ". . . to communicate economic measurements of, and information about, the resources and performance of the reporting entity useful to those having reasonable rights to such information".

6. In other words, a business should produce information about its activities because there are various groups of people who want or need to know that information. This sounds rather vague: to make it clearer, we should look more closely at the classes of people who might need information about a business. We need also to think about what information in particular is of interest to the members of each class. Because large businesses are usually of interest to a greater variety of people than small businesses we will consider the case of a large public company whose shares can be purchased and sold on the Stock Exchange.

Users of accounting information

7. The people who might be interested in financial information about a large public company may be classified as follows.

(a) *Managers of the company*. These are people appointed by the company's owners to supervise the day-to-day activities of the company. They need information about the company's current financial situation and what it is expected to be in the future. This enables them to manage the business efficiently and to take effective control and planning decisions.

(b) *Shareholders of the company*, ie the company's owners. They will want to assess how effectively management is performing its stewardship function. They will want to know how profitably management is running the company's operations and how much profit they can afford to withdraw from the business for their own use.

(c) *Trade contacts*, including suppliers who provide goods to the company on credit and customers who purchase the goods or services provided by the company. Suppliers will want to know about the company's ability to pay its debts; customers need to know that the company is a secure source of supply and is in no danger of having to close down.

(d) *Providers of finance to the company*. These might include a bank which permits the company to operate an overdraft, or provides longer-term finance by granting a loan. The bank will want to ensure that the company is able to keep up with interest payments, and eventually to repay the amounts advanced.

(e) *The Inland Revenue*, who will want to know about business profits in order to assess the tax payable by the company.

(f) *Employees of the company*. They should have a right to information about the company's financial situation, because their future careers and the size of their wages and salaries are dependent on it.

(g) *Financial analysts and advisers* need information for their clients or audience. For example, stockbrokers will need information to advise investors in stocks and shares; credit agencies will want information to advise potential suppliers of goods to the company; and journalists need information for their reading public.

Management accounting and financial accounting

8. To a greater or lesser extent, accountants aim to satisfy the information needs of all the different groups mentioned above. Managers of a business need the most information, to help them take their planning and control decisions; and they obviously have 'special' access to information about the business, because they are in a position to organise the provision of whatever internally produced statements they require. When managers want a large amount of information about the costs and profitability of individual products, or different parts of their business, they can arrange to obtain it through a system of *cost and management accounting*. The preparation of accounting reports for external use is called *financial accounting*.

9. Management accounting systems produce detailed information often split between different departments within an organisation (eg sales, production, finance etc). Although much of the information necessarily deals with past events and decisions, management accountants are also responsible for preparing budgets, helping to set price levels and other decisions about the future activities of a business.

10. Financial accountants, however, are usually solely concerned with summarising historical data, often from the same basic records as management accountants, but in a different way. This difference arises because external users have different interests from management and have neither the time nor the need for very detailed information, but also because financial statements are prepared under constraints which do not apply to management accounts produced for internal use.

11. Different types of financial statements are produced for each external user group, reflecting their different needs and the legal and professional constraints in operation.

(a) Shareholders receive annual accounts prepared in accordance with the Companies Act 1985 and *Statements of standard accounting practice* (SSAPs) issued jointly by the professional accountancy bodies. In addition, companies listed on the Stock Exchange have to comply with regulations in the Stock Exchange's *Yellow Book.*

(b) The accounts of limited companies must be filed with the Registrar of Companies (under the Companies Act 1985) and are available for public inspection. In addition, the company itself will often distribute these accounts on request to potential shareholders, the bank and financial analysts. These accounts are all that is usually available to suppliers and customers.

(c) Employees may receive the company's accounts and/or may receive *employee reports*, summarising and expanding on the matters of greatest interest to them.

(d) The Inland Revenue will receive the published accounts and as much supplementary detail as the Inspector of Taxes needs to assess the corporation tax payable on profits.

(e) Banks frequently require more information than is supplied in the published accounts when considering applications for loans and overdraft facilities. They may be given cash flow and profit forecasts and budgets prepared to show management's estimates of future activity in the business.

Characteristics of useful information

12. In the next chapter we will look at the most common accounting statements which companies produce. Before that, it will be worthwhile to look at some of the general characteristics which information must possess if it is to be useful. Our particular interest is in accounting and financial information but the characteristics below are relevant to other kinds of information as well.

13. The following characteristics of useful information have been identified.

(a) *Relevance*. The information provided should be that which is required to satisfy the needs of information users. In the case of company accounts, clearly a wide range of information will be needed to satisfy the interested parties identified earlier in the chapter.

(b) *Comprehensibility*. Information may be difficult to understand because it is skimpy or incomplete; but too much detail is also a defect which can cause difficulties of understanding.

(c) *Reliability*. This will be enhanced if information is independently verified. The law requires that the accounts published by limited companies should be verified by an auditor, who must be a person independent of the company and the holder of an approved qualification.

(d) *Completeness*. A company's accounts should present a rounded picture of its economic activities.

(e) *Objectivity*. The usefulness of information will be enhanced if it contains a minimum of subjective judgement. This is particularly the case where conflicting interests operate and an unbiased presentation of information is needed. In the context of preparing accounts, where many decisions must be based on judgement rather than objective facts, this problem often arises. Management are often inclined to paint a rosy picture of a company's profitability to make their own performance look impressive; while the auditor responsible for verifying the accounts is inclined to take a more prudent view so that he cannot be held liable by, say, a supplier misled into granting credit to a shaky company.

(f) *Timeliness.* The usefulness of information is reduced if it does not appear until long after the period to which it relates, or if it is produced at unreasonably long intervals. What constitutes a long interval depends on the circumstances: management of a company may need very frequent (perhaps daily) information on cash flows to run the business efficiently; but shareholders are normally content to see accounts produced annually.

(g) *Comparability.* Information should be produced on a consistent basis so that valid comparisons can be made with information from previous periods and with information produced by other sources (eg the accounts of similar companies operating in the same line of business).

Internal control

14. To produce the necessary accounting information, the management of a business must establish an adequate accounting system. The system should incorporate controls to ensure that the information produced is reliable, complete and objective. The system of controls instituted by management is referred to as the *internal control system* of the business.

15. It is worth thinking about the kind of controls which management might decide to implement.

(a) *Arithmetical controls.* For example, when a business receives a bill (invoice) from one of its suppliers it would be normal to check that the supplier has charged for the correct quantity of goods supplied at the correct prices, and that the multiplication and addition on the invoice are correct. Otherwise, the business might pay more than it really owed.

(b) *Authorisation controls.* For example, a business might instruct its bank not to cash cheques on the business bank account except when signed by the managing director. This would mean that no payments could be charged to the business account unless authorised at the highest level. To limit the power of authorisation to the managing director in this way would be an extreme example of an internal control, but the same principle could be applied at lower levels of the organisation.

(c) *Internal check.* This refers to a procedure whereby the work of one person is checked by another. Obviously this reduces the chance that an error will go undetected.

16. There are many other types of internal control which you will come across both in your professional work and in your later studies of auditing. No organisation will institute every possible type of internal control. Small businesses, in particular, may rely on very limited controls. But internal controls of some sort are present in every organisation and the efficiency with which they operate is an important consideration in assessing the reliability of the accounting information produced.

The audit of accounts

17. It was stated earlier that one of the desirable characteristics of accounting information is objectivity. Accounts may be more objective if they are subject to review by an independent person, ie by a person not involved in their preparation. An independent review of this kind is called an *audit* of the accounts.

18. Independence is an essential characteristic of an audit. A finance director who prepares a set of accounts may check his own work for accuracy or he may request a fellow director or subordinate to check it. This would not count as an audit of the accounts because the element of independence is absent. But if the finance director engaged an outside firm of accountants to review his work and express an opinion on the accounts, the external accountants would be performing an audit.

19. Any organisation might engage a firm of accountants to conduct an audit, but in some circumstances an audit is obligatory. The most important case is that of the annual accounts published by limited companies. It has already been mentioned (paragraph 9 above) that companies are obliged to publish annual accounts and a further requirement of the Companies Act 1985 is that these accounts should be audited.

Auditors' qualifications

20. The auditor of a company must have certain qualifications. With a few exceptions, only members of the following bodies are permitted by the Companies Act 1985 to act as company auditors:

    (a) the Institute of Chartered Accountants in England and Wales;

    (b) the Institute of Chartered Accountants of Scotland;

    (c) the Chartered Association of Certified Accountants;

    (d) the Institute of Chartered Accountants in Ireland.

The objectives of an audit

21. The auditor of a company is required by law to express an opinion on whether the accounts show a true and fair view of the company's results and its financial position and comply with the Companies Act 1985. The main objective of the auditor is therefore to do sufficient checking and review of the accounts so that he can form an opinion on them.

22. It is important to be clear about the limitations in the work carried out by an auditor of a company.

    (a) The auditor is *not* responsible for the preparation of the accounts. It is the directors of the company who are obliged to prepare accounts complying in form and content with the requirements of companies legislation. Some small companies have no staff with accounting expertise and may require the services of a firm of accountants to prepare their accounts. Frequently such companies engage the same firm of accountants as their auditors. But the preparation of the accounts and their subsequent audit are still two completely separate functions which ideally should be carried out by different members of the accountancy firm.

(b) The auditor is *not* required to certify that the accounts are correct in every particular. Indeed this would not be possible: as we shall see in later chapters, many of the figures which appear in accounts are only best estimates arrived at by judgement rather than established facts. He only needs to say whether, in his opinion, the accounts give a *true and fair view*.

23. The concept of a true and fair view is very difficult to define, and in fact no satisfactory definition exists. This is surprising because, according to the Companies Act 1985, the requirement that a company's accounts should show a true and fair view is of overriding importance. Any detailed accounting provision of the Act may be ignored if compliance with it would mean that a true and fair view was not given.

24. The concept is bound up with the idea of *materiality*. Consider the case of a large company which undertakes millions of transactions in a year. If one small-value transaction is wrongly recorded, or overlooked altogether, it could be said that the company's accounts were inaccurate. But the error would be trivial. Nobody reading the accounts could be seriously misled by the inaccuracy. If an omission or misstatement in a set of accounts is too trivial to affect anyone's understanding of the company's results or financial position, the error is described as immaterial or not material.

25. Auditors are not concerned with immaterial items because the omission or misstatement of such an item would not affect the true and fair view given by the accounts.

26. Perhaps the best way of thinking about the 'true and fair' concept is to consider circumstances in which accounts would *not* show a true and fair view.

    (a) Certain accounting principles or concepts are taken for granted in preparing accounts. These are discussed in the next chapter. If a company prepared accounts on the basis of principles different from those generally accepted the accounts would not show a true and fair view. Users of the accounts would assume that the usual principles had been adopted and could be seriously misled.

    (b) There are areas where a number of possible methods might be applied in arriving at a figure for inclusion in the accounts. For example, there are several ways in which a value could be attributed to a physical, non-monetary asset such as a factory building. Statements of standard accounting practice (SSAPs) issued by the professional accountancy bodies attempt to define which of these methods are acceptable and which are not. If the method adopted by a company was not one of those sanctioned by an SSAP, the accounts might not show a true and fair view.

27. When the auditor has completed his work he must prepare a report explaining the work that he has done and the opinion he has formed. In simple cases he will be able to report that he has carried out his work in accordance with approved auditing standards and that, in his opinion, the accounts show a true and fair view and comply with the Companies Act 1985. This is described as an unqualified audit report.

28. Sometimes the auditor may disagree with the directors on a point concerned with the accounts. If he is unable to persuade the directors to change the accounts, and if the item at issue is material, it is the auditor's duty to prepare a qualified report, setting out the matter(s) on which he disagrees with the directors.

29. The auditor's report is included as a part of the company's published accounts. It is addressed to the owners of the company, ie the shareholders.

Summary of the chapter

- Businesses produce accounts in order to satisfy the information needs of certain groups of people. These include the managers of the business, the owners of the business, trade contacts, providers of finance, the Inland Revenue, employees and financial advisers and analysts.

- Accounting information should possess the general characteristics of useful information: relevance, comprehensibility, reliability, completeness, objectivity, timeliness, comparability.

- The reliability of accounts is enhanced if they are audited. An audit is a review of accounts carried out by an independent person in order to express an opinion on them. Any business *may* have its accounts audited; the published accounts of limited companies *must* be audited.

TEST YOUR KNOWLEDGE

Numbers in brackets refer to paragraphs of this chapter

1. What, according to *The corporate report*, is the fundamental objective of a corporate report? (5)

2. List seven categories of people who might be interested in the financial information contained in a set of accounts. (7)

3. List seven general characteristics of useful information. (13)

4. List three types of internal control. (15)

5. What is the objective of an audit? (21)

6. Explain the term 'material' in the context of accounts. (24)

Chapter 2

THE THEORETICAL BASIS
OF ACCOUNTING

The purpose of this chapter is:

- to describe the main financial statements prepared by accountants
- to introduce the principal concepts which underlie the preparation of accounts

---

The main financial statements

1. The two principal financial statements drawn up by accountants are the *balance sheet* and the *profit and loss account.*

2. The balance sheet is simply a list of all the assets owned by a business and all the liabilities owed by a business as at a particular date. It is a snapshot of the financial position of the business at a particular moment. Assets are the business's resources so, for example, a business may buy buildings to operate from, plant and machinery, stock to sell and cars for its employees. These are all resources which it uses in its operations. Additionally, it may have bank balances, cash and amounts of money owed to it. These provide the funds it needs to carry out its operations. On the other hand, it may owe money to the bank or to suppliers. These are *liabilities.* The sum of the assets will always be equal to the sum of the liabilities. You will see why this is so in Chapter 3.

3. A profit and loss account is a record of income generated and expenditure incurred over a given period. The period chosen will depend on the purpose for which the statement is produced. The profit and loss account which forms part of the published annual accounts of a limited company will be made up for the period of a year, commencing from the date of the previous year's accounts. On the other hand, management might want to keep a closer eye on a company's profitability by making up quarterly or monthly profit and loss accounts. The profit and loss account shows whether the business has succeeded in generating more income than expenditure (a profit) or vice versa (a loss). Organisations which are not run for profit (charities etc) produce a similar statement called an *income and expenditure account* which shows the *surplus* of income over expenditure (or *deficit* where expenditure exceeds income).

11

4. It is very important to grasp the principle which is applied in nearly all businesses' accounts that accounts are not prepared on a *cash* basis but on an *accruals* (or earnings) basis. This is important because most businesses, even if they do not sell on credit, make purchases on credit. If cash accounting is used, then accounts do not present a true picture of the business's activities in any given period. Accountants call this convention an application of the *accruals concept*. This is discussed in more detail later in this chapter.

Example

5. Brenda has a business importing and selling model Corgi dogs. In May 19X9, she makes the following purchases and sales.

    Purchases

Invoice date	Numbers sold	Invoiced cost £	Invoice paid
7.5.X9	20	100	1.6.X9

    Sales

8.5.X9	4	40	1.6.X9
12.5.X9	6	60	1.6.X9
23.5.X9	10	100	1.7.X9

    What is Brenda's profit and loss account for May?

Solution

6. *Cash basis*

	£
Sales	-
Purchases	-
Profit/loss	-

    Accruals basis

Sales (£40 + £60 + £100)	200
Purchases	100
Profit	100

7. Obviously, the accruals basis gives a truer picture than the cash basis. Brenda has no cash to show for her efforts until June but her customers are legally bound to pay her and she is legally bound to pay for her purchases.

    Her balance sheet as at 31 May 19X9 would therefore show her assets and liabilities as follows.

	£
Assets: Debtors (£40 + £60 + £100)	200
Liabilities: Creditors	100
Net assets	100
Proprietor's capital	100

8. *Capital* is a special form of liability, representing the amount owed by the business to its proprietor(s). In Brenda's case it represents the profit earned in May, which she, as sole proprietor of the business, is entitled to in full. Usually, however, capital will also include the proprietor's initial capital, introduced as cash and perhaps equipment or other assets.

9. For example, if Brenda had begun her business on 30 April 19X9 by opening a business bank account and paying in £100, her balance sheet immediately after this transaction would look like this:

	£
Assets	
Bank	100
Proprietor's capital	100

10. On 31 May 19X9, the balance sheet would look like this.

	£
Assets	
Debtors	200
Bank	100
	300
Liabilities	
Creditors	100
Net assets	200
Proprietor's capital	
Brought forward	100
Profit for the period	100
Carried forward	200

11. This simple example shows that both the balance sheet and the profit and loss account are summaries of a great many transactions.

    In the later chapters of this text we will look in detail at the ways in which these transactions are recorded and financial statements prepared. Before doing that, however, it will be useful to examine some of the concepts which underly accounting practice.

Accounting concepts

12. Accounting practice has developed gradually over a matter of centuries. Many of its procedures are operated automatically by people who have never questioned whether alternative methods exist which have equal validity. However, the procedures in common use imply the acceptance of certain concepts which are by no means self-evident; nor are they the only possible concepts which could be used to build up an accounting framework.

13. Our next step is to look at some of the more important concepts which are taken for granted in preparing accounts. A statement of standard accounting practice (SSAP2 *Disclosure of accounting policies*) describes four concepts as *fundamental accounting concepts:* they are going concern, prudence, accruals and consistency. These four are also identified as fundamental by the

Companies Act 1985, which adds a fifth to the list (the separate valuation principle). But there is no universally agreed list of fundamental concepts, and others besides these have been described as fundamental by various authors.

---

14.   In this chapter we shall single out the following concepts for discussion:

    (a)   the entity concept;
    (b)   the money measurement concept;
    (c)   the accruals or matching concept;
    (d)   the prudence concept;
    (e)   the going concern concept;
    (f)   the consistency concept.
    (g)   the separate valuation principle;
    (h)   the materiality concept.

The entity concept

15.   This will be discussed more fully in the next chapter. Briefly, the concept is that accountants regard a business as a separate entity, distinct from its owners or managers. The concept applies whether the business is a limited company (and so recognised in law as a separate entity) or a sole proprietorship or partnership (in which case, the business is not separately recognised by the law). So, in the previous example of Brenda, the money she transferred to her business bank account becomes, in accounting terms, a *business* asset (but legally remains a *personal* asset).

16.   Acceptance of this concept has important practical consequences. Particularly in the case of a small business run by a single individual, the owner's personal affairs and business affairs may appear to be inextricably linked; for example, Brenda may conduct her business from home. But in preparing the business accounts it is essential to distinguish her private transactions and keep them separate.

17.   Suppose that Brenda withdraws a number of Corgis from her stock to give to friends, the correct accounting treatment is to regard her as having purchased the goods from the business, which is a completely separate entity; the subsequent gift to her friends is then a private transaction and is not recorded anywhere in the books of the business. Brenda should pay for the Corgis by taking money from her own purse and putting it into the till or she should regard the withdrawal as a repayment of capital. Otherwise, the business accounts will give a misleading picture.

The money measurement concept

18.   This concept states that accounts will only deal with those items to which a monetary value can be attributed. For example, in the balance sheet of a business monetary values can be attributed to such assets as machinery (eg the original cost of the machinery; or the amount it would cost to replace the machinery) and stocks of goods (eg the original cost of the goods, or, theoretically, the price at which the goods are likely to be sold).

19. The money measurement concept introduces limitations to the subject-matter of accounts. A business may have intangible assets such as the flair of a good manager or the loyalty of its workforce. These may be important enough to give it a clear superiority over an otherwise identical business, but because they cannot be evaluated in monetary terms they do not appear anywhere in the accounts.

The going concern concept

20. The going concern concept implies that the business will continue in operational existence for the foreseeable future, and that there is no intention to put the company into liquidation or to make drastic cutbacks to the scale of operations.

21. The main significance of the going concern concept is that the assets of the business should not be valued at their 'break-up' value, which is the amount that they would sell for if they were sold off piecemeal and the business were thus broken up.

22. Suppose, for example, that Brenda acquires a Corgi making machine at a cost of £60,000. The asset has an estimated life of six years, and it is normal to write off the cost of the asset to the profit and loss account over this time. In this case a depreciation cost of £10,000 per annum will be charged. (This topic will be covered in more detail in later chapters.)

23. Using the going concern concept, it would be presumed that the business will continue its operations and so the asset will live out its full six years in use. A depreciation charge of £10,000 will be made each year, and the value of the asset in the balance sheet will be its cost less the accumulated amount of depreciation charged to date. After one year, the *net book value* of the asset would therefore be £(60,000 - 10,000) = £50,000, after two years it would be £40,000, after three years £30,000 etc, until it has been written down to a value of 0 after 6 years.

24. Now suppose that this asset has no other operational use outside the business, and in a forced sale it would only sell for scrap. After one year of operation, its scrap value might be, say, £8,000.

The net book value of the asset, applying the going concern concept, would be £50,000 after one year, but its immediate sell-off value only £8,000. It might be argued that the asset is over-valued at £50,000 and that it should be written down to its break-up value (ie in the balance sheet it should be shown at £8,000 and the balance of its cost should be treated as an expense). However, provided that the going concern concept is valid, so that the asset will continue to be used and will not be sold, it is appropriate accounting practice to value the asset at its net book value.

Example

25. A retailer commences business on 1 January and buys a stock of 20 washing machines, each costing £100. During the year he sells 17 machines at £150 each. How should the remaining machines be valued at 31 December if:

(a) he is forced to close down his business at the end of the year and the remaining machines will realise only £60 each in a forced sale; or

(b) he intends to continue his business into the next year?

Solution

26. (a) If the business is to be closed down, the remaining three machines must be valued at the amount they will realise in a forced sale, ie 3 x £60 = £180.

(b) If the business is regarded as a going concern, the stock unsold at 31 December will be carried forward into the following year, when the cost of the three machines will be matched against the eventual sale proceeds in computing that year's profits. The three machines will therefore appear in the balance sheet at 31 December at cost, 3 x £100 = £300.

The prudence concept

27. This is the concept that where alternative procedures, or alternative valuations, are possible, the one selected should be the one which gives the most cautious presentation of the business's financial position or results. For example, you may have wondered why the three washing machines in paragraph 24(b) were stated in the balance sheet at their cost (£100 each) rather than their selling price (£150 each). This is simply an aspect of the prudence concept: to value the machines at £150 would be to anticipate making a profit before the profit had been realised.

28. The other aspect of the prudence concept is that where a *loss* is foreseen, it *should* be anticipated and taken into account immediately. If a business purchases stock for £1,200 but because of a sudden slump in the market only £900 is likely to be realised when the stock is sold the prudence concept dictates that the stock should be valued at £900. It is not enough to wait until the stock is sold, and then recognise the £300 loss; it must be recognised as soon as it is foreseen.

29. A profit can be considered to be a realised profit when it is in the form of:

(a) cash; or
(b) another asset which has a reasonably certain cash value. This includes amounts owing from debtors, provided that there is a reasonable certainty that the debtors will eventually pay up what they owe.

30. SSAP2 describes the prudence concept as follows. 'Revenue and profits are not anticipated, but are recognised by inclusion in the profit and loss account only when realised in the form either of cash or of other assets the ultimate cash realisation of which can be assessed with reasonable certainty; provision is made for all known . . . expenses and losses whether the amount of these is known with certainty or is a best estimate in the light of the information available.'

31. Some examples might help to explain the application of the prudence concept:

    (a) A company begins trading on 1 January 19X5 and sells goods worth £100,000 during the year to 31 December. At 31 December there are debts outstanding of £15,000. Of these, the company is now doubtful whether £6,000 will ever be paid.

    The company should make a *provision for doubtful debts* of £6,000. Sales for 19X5 will be shown in the profit and loss account at their full value of £100,000, but the provision for doubtful debts would be a charge of £6,000. Because there is some uncertainty that the sales will be realised in the form of cash, the prudence concept dictates that the £6,000 should not be included in the profit for the year.

    (b) Samson Feeble trades as a carpenter. He has undertaken to make a range of kitchen furniture for a customer at an agreed price of £1,000. At the end of Samson's accounting year the job is unfinished (being two thirds complete) and the following data has been assembled:

	£
Costs incurred in making the furniture to date	800
Further estimated costs to completion of the job	400
Total cost	1,200

    The incomplete job represents *work in progress* at the end of the year which is an asset, like stock. Its cost to date is £800, but by the time the job is completed Samson will have made a loss of £200.

    The full £200 loss should be charged against profits of the current year. The value of work in progress at the year end should be its *net realisable value*, which is lower than its cost. The net realisable value can be calculated in either of two ways:

(i)		£	(ii)		£
Eventual sales value		1,000	Work in progress at cost		800
Less further costs to completion in order to make the sale		400	Less loss foreseen		200
Net realisable value		600			600

The prudence concept and your examination

32. Although the accruals concept is the concept you will be mainly concerned with in your examination, you should expect an occasional question which tests your ability to recognise a situation which calls for some consideration of the prudence concept. There is no hard-and-fast rule about what 'prudence' is in any particular situation. However, the types of situation in which you might need to discuss prudence and how it should affect the accounts (trading, profit and loss account or balance sheet) are:

    (a) deciding when revenue should be 'realised' and brought into the trading, profit and loss account (and so deciding when profits are realised);

    (b) deciding how to put a value to assets in the balance sheet.

    Attempt your own brief solution to the following example.

Example: prudence concept

33. It is generally agreed that sales revenue should only be 'realised' and so 'recognised' in the trading, profit and loss account when:

   (a) the sale transaction is for a specific quantity of goods at a known price, so that the sales value of the transaction is known for certain;

   (b) the sale transaction has been completed, or else it is certain that it will be completed (eg in the case of long-term contract work, when the job is well under way but not yet completed by the end of an accounting period);

   (c) the *critical event* in the sale transaction has occurred. The critical event is the event after which either:

      (i) it becomes virtually certain that cash will eventually be received from the customer, or

      (ii) cash is actually received.

34. Usually, revenue is 'recognised' either:

   (a) when a cash sale is made; or
   (b) the customer promises to pay on or before a specified future date, and the debt is legally enforceable.

The prudence concept is applied here in the sense that revenue should not be anticipated, and included in the trading, profit and loss account, before it is reasonably certain to 'happen'.

Required:

Given that prudence is the main consideration, discuss under what circumstances, if any, revenue might be recognised at the following stages of a sale.

   (a) Goods have been acquired by the business which it confidently expects to resell very quickly.
   (b) A customer places a firm order for goods.
   (c) Goods are delivered to the customer.
   (d) The customer is invoiced for goods.
   (e) The customer pays for the goods.
   (f) The customer's cheque in payment for the goods has been cleared by the bank.

Solution

35. (a) A sale must never be recognised before the goods have even been ordered. There is no certainty about the value of the sale, nor when it will take place, even if it is virtually certain that goods will be sold.

   (b) A sale must never be recognised when the customer places an order. Even though the order will be for a specific quantity of goods at a specific price, it is not yet certain that the sale transaction will go through. The customer may cancel the order, or the supplier might be unable to deliver the goods as ordered.

(c) A sale will be recognised when delivery of the goods is made only when:

    (i)   the sale is for cash, and so the cash is received at the same time; or

    (ii) the sale is on credit and the customer accepts delivery (eg by signing a delivery note).

(d) The critical event for a credit sale is usually the dispatch of an invoice to the customer. There is then a legally enforceable debt, payable on specified terms, for a completed sale transaction.

(e) The critical event for a cash sale is when delivery takes place and when cash is received; both take place at the same time.

It would be too cautious or 'prudent' to await cash payment for a credit sale transaction before recognising the sale, unless the customer is a high credit risk and there is a serious doubt about his ability or intention to pay.

(f) It would again be over-cautious to wait for clearance of the customer's cheques before recognising sales revenue. Such a precaution would only be justified in cases where there is a very high risk of the bank refusing to honour the cheque.

The accruals concept or matching concept

36. This concept states that, in computing profit, revenue earned must be matched against the expenditure incurred in earning it. This is illustrated in the example Brenda; profit of £100 was computed by matching the revenue (£200) earned from the sale of 20 Corgis against the cost (£100) of acquiring them.

If, however, Brenda had only sold eighteen Corgis, it would have been incorrect to charge her profit and loss account with the cost of twenty Corgis, as she still has two Corgis in stock. If she intends to sell them in June she is likely to make a profit on the sale. Therefore, only the purchase cost of eighteen Corgis (£90) should be matched with her sales revenue, leaving her with a profit of £90.

Her balance sheet would therefore look like this.

	£
Assets	
Stock (at cost, ie 2 x £5)	10
Debtors (18 x £10)	180
	190
Liabilities	
Creditors	100
	90
Proprietor's capital (profit for the period)	90

37. If, however Brenda had decided to give up selling Corgis, then the going concern concept would no longer apply and the value of the two Corgis in the balance sheet would be a break-up valuation rather than cost. Similarly, if the two unsold Corgis were now unlikely to be sold at more than their cost of £5 each (say, because of damage or a fall in demand) then they should be recorded on the balance sheet at their *net realisable value* (ie the likely eventual sales price less any expenses incurred to make them saleable, eg paint) rather than cost. This shows the application of the prudence concept.

38. In this example, the concepts of going concern and matching are linked. Because the business is assumed to be a going concern it is possible to carry forward the cost of the unsold Corgis as a charge against profits of the next period.

The accruals concept defined

39. The 'accruals' or 'matching' concept is described in SSAP2 as follows: 'revenues and costs are accrued (that is, recognised as they are earned or incurred, not as money is received or paid), matched with one another so far as their relationship can be established or justifiably assumed, and dealt with in the profit and loss account of the period to which they relate ... Revenue and profits dealt with in the profit and loss account of the period are matched with associated costs and expenses by including in the same account the costs incurred in earning them (so far as these are material and identifiable)'.

40. The Companies Act 1985 gives legal recognition to the accruals concept, stating that: 'All income and charges relating to the financial year to which the accounts relate shall be taken into account, without regard to the date of receipt or payment.' This has the effect, as we have seen, of requiring businesses to take credit for sales and purchases when made, rather than when paid for, and also to carry unsold stock forward in the balance sheet rather than to deduct its cost from profit for the period.

The consistency concept

41. Accounting is not an exact science. There are many areas in which judgement must be exercised in attributing money values to items appearing in accounts. Over the years certain procedures and principles have come to be recognised as good accounting practice, but within these limits there are often various acceptable methods of accounting for similar items.

42. The consistency concept states that in preparing accounts consistency should be observed in two respects:

    (a) similar items within a single set of accounts should be given similar accounting treatment;

    (b) the same treatment should be applied from one period to another in accounting for similar items. This enables valid comparisons to be made from one period to the next.

The separate valuation principle

43. The Companies Act 1985 recognises the same four fundamental accounting concepts as SSAP2, although it describes them not as concepts but as *accounting principles*. The Act also mentions a fifth principle, which may be called the separate valuation principle. Although it is not described by SSAP2 as a fundamental accounting concept it has long been recognised as good accounting practice.

44. The separate valuation principle states that, in determining the amount to be attributed to an asset or liability in the balance sheet, each component item of the asset or liability must be determined separately. These separate valuations must then be aggregated to arrive at the

balance sheet figure. For example, if a company's stock comprises 50 separate items, a valuation must (in theory) be arrived at for each item separately; the 50 figures must then be aggregated and the total is the stock figure which should appear in the balance sheet.

The materiality concept

45. The concept of materiality was mentioned briefly in the previous chapter. In the context of the audit of accounts it was stated that an error which is too trivial to affect anyone's understanding of the accounts is referred to as *immaterial*. In preparing accounts it is important to assess what is material and what is not, so that time and money are not wasted in the pursuit of excessive detail.

46. Determining whether or not an item is material is a very subjective exercise. There is no absolute measure of materiality. It is common to apply a convenient rule of thumb (for example to define material items as those with a value greater than 5% of the net profit disclosed by the accounts). But some items disclosed in accounts are regarded as particularly sensitive and even a very small misstatement of such an item would be regarded as a material error. An example in the accounts of a limited company might be the amount of remuneration paid to directors of the company.

47. The assessment of an item as material or immaterial may affect its treatment in the accounts. For example, the profit and loss account of a business will show the expenses incurred by the business grouped under suitable captions (heating and lighting expenses, rent and rates expenses etc); but in the case of very small expenses it may be appropriate to lump them together under a caption such as 'sundry expenses', because a more detailed breakdown would be inappropriate for such immaterial amounts.

48. In assessing whether or not an item is material, it is not only the amount of the item which needs to be considered. The context is also important.

   (a) If a balance sheet shows fixed assets of £2 million and stocks of £30,000 an error of £20,000 in the depreciation calculations might not be regarded as material, whereas an error of £20,000 in the stock valuation probably would be. In other words, the total of which the erroneous item forms part must be considered.

   (b) If a business has a bank loan of £50,000 and a £55,000 balance on bank deposit account, it might well be regarded as a material misstatement if these two amounts were displayed on the balance sheet as 'cash at bank £5,000'. In other words, incorrect presentation may amount to material misstatement even if there is no monetary error.

Costs and values

49. Accounting concepts are a part of the theoretical framework on which accounting practice is based. Before we proceed to the sections which discuss accounting practice in detail, it is worth looking at one further general point, the problem of attributing monetary values to the items which appear in accounts.

50. A basic principle of accounting (some writers include it in the list of fundamental accounting concepts) is that resources are normally stated in accounts at historical cost, ie at the amount which the business paid to acquire them. An important advantage of this procedure is that the objectivity of accounts is maximised: there is usually objective, documentary evidence to prove the amount paid to purchase an asset or pay an expense.

51. In general, accountants prefer to deal with costs, rather than with 'values'. This is because valuations tend to be subjective and to vary according to what the valuation is for. For example, suppose that a company acquires a machine to manufacture its products. The machine has an expected useful life of four years. At the end of two years the company is preparing a balance sheet and has to decide what monetary amount to attribute to the asset.

52. Numerous possibilities might be considered:

    (a) the original cost (historical cost) of the machine;
    (b) half of the historical cost, on the ground that half of its useful life has expired;
    (c) the amount the machine might fetch on the secondhand market;
    (d) the amount it would cost to replace the machine with an identical machine;
    (e) the amount it would cost to replace the machine with a more modern machine incorporating the technological advances of the previous two years;
    (f) the machine's economic value, ie the amount of the profits it is expected to generate for the company during its remaining life.

53. All of these valuations have something to commend them, but the great advantage of the first two is that they are based on a figure (the machine's historical cost) which is objectively verifiable. (Some authors regard objectivity as an accounting concept in its own right). The subjective judgement involved in the other valuations, particularly (f), is so great as to lessen the reliability of any accounts in which they are used. As we will see in later chapters, method (b), or a variation of it, is the one which would normally be used.

54. The method chosen has important consequences for the measurement of profit, as the following example will show.

Example

55. Brian sets up in business on 1 January 19X5 selling accountancy text books. He buys 100 books for £5 each and by 31 December 19X5 he manages to sell his entire stock, all for cash, at a price of £8 each. On 1 January 19X6 he replaces his stock by purchasing another 100 books; by this time the cost of the books has risen to £6 each. Calculate the profit earned by Brian in 19X5.

Solution

55. In conventional historical cost accounting, Brian's profit would be computed as follows:

	£
Sale of 100 books (@ £8 each)	800
Cost of 100 books (@ £5 each)	500
Profit for the year	300

The purchase of the books is stated at their historical cost. Although this is accepted accounting practice, and is the method we will be using almost invariably throughout this text, it involves an anomaly which can be seen if we look at how well off the business is.

56. On 1 January 19X5 the assets of the business consist of the 100 books which Brian has purchased as stock. On 1 January 19X6 the business has an identical stock of 100 books, and also has cash of £200 (ie £800 received from customers, less the £600 cost of replacing stock). So despite making a profit of £300, measured in the conventional way, the business appears to be only £200 better off.

57. This anomaly could be removed if an alternative accounting convention were used. Suppose that profit was measured as the difference between the selling price of goods and the cost of replacing the goods sold. Brian's profit would then be computed as follows:

	£
Sale of 100 books	800
Cost of replacing 100 books sold	600
Profit for the year	200

Now the profit for the year is exactly matched by the increase in the company's assets over the year.

Summary of the chapter

58.

> • The main financial statements prepared by an accountant are the balance sheet and the profit and loss account. The balance sheet is a list of the assets and liabilities of a business at a particular time. The profit and loss account is a record of revenue earned and expenditure incurred over a defined period.
>
> • In preparing financial statements, certain fundamental concepts are adopted as a framework. From the many concepts which might be identified, we have examined eight which are of particular importance.
>
> (a) *The entity concept.* A business is an entity distinct from its owner(s).
> (b) *The money measurement concept.* Accounts only deal with items to which monetary values can be attributed.
> (c) *The going concern concept.* Unless there is evidence to the contrary, it is assumed that a business will continue to trade normally for the foreseeable future.
> (d) *The prudence concept.* Where alternative accounting procedures are acceptable, choose the one which gives the less optimistic view of profitability and asset values.
> (e) *The accruals or matching concept.* Revenue earned must be matched against expenditure incurred in earning it.
> (f) *The consistency concept.* Similar items should be accorded similar accounting treatments.
> (g) *The separate valuation principle.*
> (h) *The materiality concept.* Only items material in amount or in their nature will affect the true and fair view given by a set of accounts.
>
> These concepts may appear vague and hard to grasp at this stage. In later chapters their importance will become more apparent as they are illustrated with concrete examples.

TEST YOUR KNOWLEDGE
Numbers in brackets refer to paragraphs of this chapter

1. What are the two main financial statements drawn up by accountants? (1)

2. List five important accounting concepts. (14)

3. What is meant by:
   (a) the money measurement concept? (18-19)
   (b) the prudence concept? (27-28)

4. Suggest four possible values which might be attributed to an asset in the balance sheet of a business. (52)

Chapter 3

ASSETS, LIABILITIES AND THE ACCOUNTING EQUATION

The purpose of this chapter is:

● to describe the nature of assets and liabilities

● to illustrate the equality of assets and liabilities in a business by means of the accounting equation.

Introduction

1. In the previous two chapters we have used the terms 'business', 'assets' and 'liabilities' without looking too closely at their meaning. This has been possible because the terms are common in everyday speech and you are likely to be familiar with them. From now on we will be examining accounting practice in more detail and it is important that you should have a thorough understanding of how these terms are used in an accounting context.

What is a business?

2. There are a number of different ways of looking at a business. Some ideas are listed below.

    (a) A business is a commercial or industrial concern which exists to deal in the manufacture, re-sale or supply of goods and services.
    (b) A business is an organisation which uses economic resources to create goods or services which customers will buy.
    (c) A business is an organisation providing jobs for people to work in.
    (d) A business invests money in resources (eg it buys buildings, machinery etc, it pays employees) in order to make even more money for its owners.

3. This last definition introduces the important idea of profit which was briefly discussed in the last chapter. Business enterprises vary in character, size and complexity. They range from very small businesses (the local shopkeeper or plumber) to very large ones (ICI). But the objective of earning profit is common to all of them.

4. Profit is the excess of income over expenditure. When expenditure exceeds income, the business is running at a loss. One of the jobs of an accountant is to measure income, expenditure and profit. It is not such a straightforward problem as it may seem and in later chapters we will look at some of the theoretical and practical difficulties involved.

5. There are some organisations which do not have a profit motive.

   (a) Charities exist to provide help to the needy. However, a charity must keep its expenditure within the level of its income or it could not continue in operation.

   (b) Public sector organisations exist to serve the community rather than to make profits. Such organisations include government departments and services (eg the fire service, police force, national health service etc). But even though their purpose is not primarily to make a profit, they can only spend the money allowed to them by the government. Like charities, they must be cost-conscious.

   (c) Certain clubs and associations exist to provide services to their members. Profit is not their primary objective, but to maintain and improve the services they offer they must ensure that their income is at least as great as their expenditure.

Assets and liabilities

6. An asset is something valuable which a business owns or has the use of. Examples of assets are factories, office buildings, warehouses, delivery vans, lorries, plant and machinery, computer equipment, office furniture, cash and also goods held in store awaiting sale to customers, and raw materials and components held in store by a manufacturing business for use in production.

7. Some assets are held and used in operations for a long time. An office building might be occupied by administrative staff for years; similarly, a machine might have a productive life of many years before it wears out. Other assets are held for only a short time. The owner of a newsagent shop, for example, will have to sell his newspapers on the same day that he gets them, and weekly newspapers and monthly magazines also have a short shelf life. The more quickly a business can sell the goods it has in store, the more profit it is likely to make. That is the meaning of the phrase 'business is brisk'.

8. A liability is something which is owed to somebody else. 'Liabilities' is the accounting term for the debts of a business. Here are some examples of liabilities.

   (a) *A bank loan or bank overdraft.* The liability is the amount which must eventually be repaid to the bank.

   (b) *Amounts owed to suppliers* for goods purchased but not yet paid for. For example, a boatbuilder might buy some timber on credit from a timber merchant, which means that the boatbuilder does not have to pay for the timber until some time after it has been delivered. Until the boatbuilder pays what he owes, the timber merchant will be his creditor for the amount owed.

   (c) *Taxation owed to the government.* A business pays tax on its profits but there is a gap in time between when a company declares its profits and becomes liable to pay tax and the time when the tax bill must eventually be paid.

3: ASSETS, LIABILITIES AND THE ACCOUNTING EQUATION

The business as a separate entity

9. So far we have spoken of assets and liabilities 'of a business'. In the previous chapter, it was pointed out that in accounting terms, a business is always a separate entity; but there are two aspects to this question: the strict legal position and the convention adopted by accountants.

10. Many businesses are carried on in the form of *limited companies*. The owners of a limited company are its shareholders, who may be few in number (as with a small, family-owned company) or very numerous (eg in the case of a large public company whose shares are quoted on the Stock Exchange).

11. The law recognises a company as a legal entity, quite separate from its owners. A company may, in its own name, acquire assets, incur debts, and enter into contracts. If a company's assets become insufficient to meet its liabilities, the company as a separate entity might become 'bankrupt', but the owners of the company could not usually be required to pay the debts from their own private resources: the debts are not debts of the shareholders, but of the company. This is *limited liability:* the liability of shareholders to the company is *limited* to the amount the company asks for their shares on issue.

12. The case is different, in law, when a business is carried on not by a company, but by an individual (a sole trader) or by a group of individuals (a partnership). Suppose that Rodney Quiff sets himself up in business as a hairdresser trading under the business name 'Quiff's Hair Salon'. The law recognises no distinction between Rodney Quiff, the individual, and the business known as 'Quiff's Hair Salon'. Any debts of the business which cannot be met from business assets must be met from Rodney's private resources.

13. But the crucial point which must be understood at the outset is that the convention adopted in preparing accounts (the *entity concept*) is *always* to treat a business as a separate entity from its owner(s). This applies whether or not the business is recognised in law as a separate entity, ie it applies whether the business is carried on by a company or by a sole trader.

14. This is an idea which at first sight seems illogical and unrealistic; students often have difficulty in understanding it. Nevertheless, it is an idea which you must try to appreciate. It is the basis of a fundamental rule of accounting, which is that the assets and liabilities of a business must always be equal. A simple example may clarify the idea of a business as a separate entity from its owners.

Example

15. On 1 July 19X6, Liza Doolittle decided to open up a flower stall in the market, to sell flowers and potted plants. She had saved up some money in her building society, and had £2,500 to put into her business.

16. When the business is set up, an 'accountant's picture' can be drawn of what it owns and what it owes.

The business begins by owning the cash that Liza has put into it, £2,500. But does it owe anything? The answer is yes.

The business is a separate entity in accounting terms. It has obtained its assets, in this example cash, from its owner, Liza Doolittle. It therefore owes this amount of money to its owner. If Liza changed her mind and decided not to go into business after all, the business would be dissolved by the 'repayment' of the cash by the business to Liza. (This idea was briefly explained in Chapter 2.)

Capital as a liability

17. The money put into a business by its owners is *capital*. In accounting, capital is an investment of money (funds) with the intention of earning a return. A business proprietor invests capital with the intention of earning profit. As long as that money is invested, accountants will treat the capital as money owed to the proprietor by the business.

The accounting equation

18. When Liza Doolittle sets up her business:

     Capital invested   =   £2,500
     Cash   =   £2,500

     Capital invested is a form of liability, because it is an amount owed by the business to its owner(s). Adapting this to the idea that liabilities and assets are always equal amounts, we can state the accounting equation as follows:

     Capital   +   Liabilities   =   Assets

     For Liza Doolittle, as at 1 July 19X6:

     £2,500   +   £0   =   £2,500 (cash)

Example continued

19. Liza Doolittle uses some of the money invested to purchase a market stall from Len Turnip, who is retiring from his fruit and vegetables business. The cost of the stall is £1,800.

     She also purchases some flowers and potted plants from a trader in the New Covent Garden wholesale market, at a cost of £650.

     This leaves £50 in cash, after paying for the stall and goods for resale, out of the original £2,500. Liza kept £30 in the bank and drew out £20 in small change. She was now ready for her first day of market trading on 3 July 19X6.

20. The assets and liabilities of the business have now altered, and at 3 July, before trading begins, the state of her business is:

Capital	+	Liabilities	=	Assets	£
£2,500	+	£0	=	Stall	1,800
				Flower and plants	650
				Cash at bank	30
				Cash in hand	20
					2,500

The stall and the flowers and plants are physical items, but they must be given a money value. As explained in the last chapter, this money value will usually be their historical cost.

Profit introduced into the accounting equation

21. Let us now suppose that on 3 July Liza has a very successful day. She is able to sell all of her flowers and plants, for £900. All of her sales are for cash.

Since Liza has sold goods costing £650 to earn revenue of £900, we can say that she has earned a profit of £250 on the day's trading.

Profits belong to the owners of a business. In this case, the £250 belongs to Liza Doolittle. However, so long as the business retains the profits, and does not pay anything out to its owners, the retained profits are accounted for as an addition to the proprietor's capital.

Capital		+ Liabilities	=	Assets	
	£				£
Original				Stall	1,800
investment	2,500			Flower and plants	0
Retained				Cash in hand and	
profit	250			at bank (30+20+900)	950
	2,750	+ £0	=		2,750

Increase in net assets

22. We can re-arrange the accounting equation to get:

Capital	=	Assets - Liabilities, which is also
Capital	=	Net assets

(Net assets is simply the difference between total assets and total liabilities).

23. At the beginning and then at the end of 3 July 19X6 Liza Doolittle's financial position was as follows:

		Capital		Net Assets	
(a)	At the beginning of the day:	£2,500	=	£(2,500 - 0) = £2,500	
(b)	At the end of the day:	£2,750	=	£(2,750 - 0) = £2,750	

There has been an increase of £250 in net assets, which is the amount of profits earned during the day.

Drawings

24. Drawings are amounts of money taken out of a business by its owner.

Since Liza Doolittle has made a profit of £250 from her first day's work, she might well feel fully justified in drawing some of the profits out of the business. After all, business owners, like everyone else, need income for living expenses. We will suppose that Liza decides to pay herself £180, in 'wages'.

3: ASSETS, LIABILITIES AND THE ACCOUNTING EQUATION

25. The payment of £180 is probably regarded by Liza as a fair reward for her day's work, and she might think of the sum as being in the nature of wages. However, the £180 is not an expense to be deducted before the figure of net profit is arrived at. In other words, it would be incorrect to calculate the net profit earned by the business as follows:

	£
Profit on sale of flowers etc	250
Less 'wages' paid to Liza	180
Net profit earned by business	70

26. This is because any amounts paid by a business to its proprietor are treated by accountants as withdrawals of profit (the usual term is *appropriations* of profit), and not as expenses incurred by the business. In the case of Liza's business, the true position is that the net profit earned is the £250 surplus on sale of flowers:

	£
Net profit earned by business	250
Less profit withdrawn by Liza	180
Net profit retained in the business	70

27. The drawings are taken in cash, and so the business loses £180 of its cash assets. After the drawings have been made, the accounting equation would be restated as:

(a)

	Capital +	Liabilities =	Assets	
	£			£
Original investment	2,500		Stall	1,800
Retained profit	70		Flowers and plants	0
			Cash (950–180)	770
Total capital	2,570 +	£0 =		2,570

(b) Alternatively

Capital +	Net assets	
£2,570 =	£(2,570 – 0) =	£2,570

The increase in net assets since trading operations began is now only £(2,570–2,500) = £70, which is the amount of the retained profits.

The business equation

28. The business equation gives a definition of profits earned. The preceding example has attempted to show that the amount of profit earned can be related to the increase in the net assets of the business, and the drawings of profits by the proprietor.

29. The business equation is:

$$P = I + D - C_i$$

where

    P   represents profit
    I   represents the increase in net assets, after drawings have been taken out by the proprietor
    D   represents drawings

C_i represents the amount of extra capital introduced into the business during the period. This is a negative figure in the equation, because when a business is given new capital, perhaps in the form of extra money paid in by the proprietor himself, there will be an increase in the net assets of the business without any profits being earned. This means, say, that if a proprietor puts an extra £5,000 into his business the profit from the transaction, according to the business equation would be P = £5,000 + 0 - 5,000 = £0.

30. In our example of Liza Doolittle's business on 3 July 19X6, after drawings have been taken:

Profit = £ 70 + £180 - £0
= £250

Example continued

31. If you think that you understand the ideas explained above, you should now attempt the following exercise yourself before reading on.

The next market day is on 10 July, and Liza gets ready by purchasing more flowers and plants for cash, at a cost of £740. She was not feeling well, however, because of a heavy cold, and so she decided to accept the offer of help for the day from her cousin Ethel. Ethel would be paid a wage of £40 at the end of the day.

Trading on 10 July was again very brisk, and Liza and Ethel sold all their goods for £1,100 cash. Liza paid Ethel her wage of £40 and drew out £200 for herself.

You are required to:

(a) state the accounting equation before trading began on 10 July;

(b) state the accounting equation at the end of 10 July, after paying Ethel:

(i) but before drawings are taken out;
(ii) after drawings have been made;

(c) state the business equation to compute profits earned on 10 July.

You are reminded that the accounting equation for the business at the end of transactions for 3 July is given in paragraph 27(a).

Solution

32. (a) After the purchase of the goods for £740:

Capital	+	Liabilities	=	Assets	£
£2,570	+	£0	=	Stall	1,800
				Goods	740
				Cash (770 - 740)	30
					2,570

(b) (i) On 10 July, all the goods are sold for £1,100 cash, and Ethel is paid £40. The profit for the day is £320.

	£	£
Sales		1,100
Less cost of goods sold	740	
Ethel's wage	40	
		780
		320

	Capital + Liabilities =		Assets	
	£			£
At beginning of 10 July	2,570		Stall	1,800
Profits earned on 10 July	320		Goods	0
			Cash (30 + 1,100-40)	1,090
	2,890	+ £0	=	2,890

(ii) After Liza has taken drawings of £200 in cash, retained profits will be only £(320 - 200) = £120.

	Capital + Liabilities =		Assets	
	£			£
At beginning of 10 July	2,570		Stall	1,800
Retained profits for			Goods	0
10 July	120		Cash (1,090-200)	890
	2,690	+ £0		2,690

(c) The increase in net assets on 10 July, after drawings have been taken, is:

	£
Net assets at end of 10 July	2,690
Net assets at beginning of 10 July	2,570
Increase in net assets	120

33. The business equation is:

$$P = I + D - C_i$$
$$= 120 + 200 - 0$$
$$= £320$$

This confirms the calculation of profit made earlier.

Tutorial note: it is very important that you should understand the principles described so far. Do not read on until you are confident that you understand the solution to this exercise.

Creditors and debtors

34. A *creditor* is a person to whom a business owes money.

A trade creditor is a person to whom a business owes money for debts incurred in the course of trading operations, and in an examination question, this term might refer to debts still outstanding which arise from the purchase from suppliers of materials, components or goods for resale.

35. A business does not always pay immediately for goods or services it buys. It is a common business practice to make purchases on credit, with a promise to pay within 30 days, or 2 months or 3 months of the date of the bill or 'invoice' for the goods. For example, if A buys goods costing £2,000 on credit from B, B might send A an invoice for £2,000, dated say 1 March, with credit terms that payment must be made within 30 days. If A then delays payment until 31 March, B will be a creditor of A Limited between 1 and 31 March, for £2,000.

36. A creditor is a liability of a business.

37. Just as a business might buy goods on credit, so too might it sell goods to customers on credit. A customer who buys goods without paying cash for them straight away is a *debtor*. For example, suppose that C sells goods on credit to D for £6,000 on terms that the debt must be settled within 2 months of the invoice date 1 October. If D does not pay the £6,000 until 30 November, D will be a debtor of C for £6,000 from 1 October until 30 November.

38. A debtor is an asset of a business. When the debt is finally paid, the debtor 'disappears' as an asset, to be replaced by 'cash at bank and in hand'.

Example continued

39. The example of Liza Doolittle's market stall will be continued further, by looking at the consequences of the following transactions in the week to 17 July 19X6. (See paragraph 32 (b)(ii) for the situation as at the end of 10 July.)

    (a) Liza Doolittle realises that she is going to need more money in the business and so she:

        (i)   decides to invest immediately further capital herself of £250;

        (ii) persuades her Uncle Henry to lend her £500 immediately. Uncle Henry tells her that she can repay the loan whenever she likes, but in the meantime, she must pay him interest of £5 per week each week at the end of the market day. They agree that it will probably be quite a long time before the loan is eventually repaid.

    (b) She is very pleased with the progress of her business, and decides that she can afford to buy a second hand van to pick up flowers and plants from her supplier and bring them to her stall in the market. She finds a car dealer, Laurie Loader, who agrees to sell her a van on credit for £700. Liza agrees to pay for the van after 30 days' trial use.

    (c) During the week before the next market day (which is on 17 July), Liza's Uncle George telephones her to ask whether she would be interested in selling him some garden gnomes and furniture for his garden. Liza tells him that she will look for a supplier. After some investigations, she buys what Uncle George has asked for, paying £300 in cash to the supplier. Uncle George accepts delivery of the goods and agrees to pay £350 to Liza for them, but he asks if she can wait until the end of the month for payment. Liza agrees.

    (d) The next market day approaches, and Liza buys flowers and plants costing £800. Of these purchases £750 are paid in cash, with the remaining £50 on 7 days' credit. Liza decides to use Ethel's services again as an assistant on market day, at an agreed wage of £40.

(e)   For the third market day running, on 17 July, Liza succeeds in selling all her goods earning revenue of £1,250 (all in cash). She decides to take out drawings of £240 for her week's work. She also pays Ethel £40 in cash. She decides to make the interest payment to her Uncle Henry the next time she sees him.

(f)   We shall ignore any van expenses for the week, for the sake of relative simplicity.

Required:

(a)   State the accounting equation:

   (i)   after Liza and Uncle Henry have put more money into the business after the purchase of the van;
   (ii)   after the sale of goods to Uncle George;
   (iii) after the purchase of goods for the weekly market;
   (iv)   at the end of the day's trading on 17 July, and after drawings have been appropriated out of profit.

(b)   State the business equation showing profit earned during the week ended 17 July.

Solution

40.   There are a number of different transactions to account for here. This solution deals with them one at a time in chronological order. (In practice, it would be possible to do one set of calculations which combines the results of all the transactions, but we shall defer such 'shortcut' methods until later.)

(a)   The addition of Liza's extra capital and Uncle Henry's loan.
      An investment analyst might define the loan of Uncle Henry as a capital investment on the grounds that it will probably be for the long term. Uncle Henry is not the owner of the business, however, even though he has made an investment of a loan in it. He would only become an owner if Liza offered him a partnership in the business, and she has not done so. To the business, Uncle Henry is a long-term creditor, and it is more appropriate to define his investment as a liability of the business and not as business capital.

      The accounting equation after £(250 + 500) = £750 cash is put into the business will be:

	Capital £	+ Liabilities £	= Assets		£
As at end of 10 July	2,690		Stall		1,800
Additional capital		Loan 500	Goods		0
put in	250		Cash (890+750)		1,640
	2,940	500 =			3,440

(b)   The purchase of the van (cost £700) is on credit.

	Capital £	+ Liabilities £	= Assets		£
As at end of 10 July	2,690	Loan 500	Stall		1,800
Additional capital	250	Creditor 700	Van		700
			Cash		1,640
	2,940	+ 1,200 =			4,140

(c)   The sale of goods to Uncle George on credit (£350) which cost the business £300 (cash paid).

	Capital	+ Liabilities		= Assets	
	£		£		£
As at end of 10 July	2,690	Loan	500	Stall	1,800
Additional capital	250	Creditor	700	Van	700
Profit on sale to				Debtor	350
Uncle George	50			Cash (1,640-300)	1,340
	2,990	+	1,200	=	4,190

(d)   After the purchase of goods for the weekly market (£750 paid in cash and £50 of purchases on credit).

	Capital	+ Liabilities		= Assets	
	£		£		£
As at end of 10 July	2,690	Loan	500	Stall	1,800
Additional capital	250	Creditor		Van	700
Profit on sale to		for car	700	Goods	800
Uncle George	50	Creditor		Debtor	350
		for		Cash (1,340-750)	590
		goods	50		
	2,990	+	1,250		4,240

(e)   After market trading on 17 July. Sales of goods costing £800 earned revenues of £1,250. Ethel's wages were £40 (paid), Uncle Henry's interest charge is £5 (not paid yet) and drawings out of profits were £240 (paid). The profit for 17 July may be calculated as follows, taking the full £5 of interest as a cost on that day:

	£	£
Sales		1,250
Cost of goods sold	800	
Wages	40	
Interest	5	
		845
Profit earned on 17 July		405
Profit on sale of goods to Uncle George		50
Profit for the week		455
Drawings appropriated out of profits		240
Retained profit		215

	Capital	+ Liabilities		= Assets	
	£		£		£
As at end of 10 July	2,690	Loan	500	Stall	1,800
Additional capital	250	Creditor		Van	700
		for van	700	Stocks	0
Profits retained	215	Creditor		Debtors	350
		for goods	50	Cash (590+1250	
		Credit for		-40 - 240)	1,560
		interest			
		payment	5		
	3,155	+	1,255		4,410

41. The increase in the net assets of the business during the week was:

	£
Net assets as at the end of 17 July £(4,410 - 1,255)	3,155
Net assets as at the end of 10 July (paragraph 19 (b)(ii))	2,690
Increase in net assets	465

The business equation for the week ended 17 July is as follows.
(Remember that extra capital of £250 was invested by the proprietor).

$$P = I + D - C_i$$
$$= 465 + 240 - 250$$
$$= £455$$

This confirms the calculation of profit above in paragraph 40(e).

42. You might now wish to test your understanding of the accounting equation and the business equation by attempting the following exercises.

Example 1

43. Calculate the profit for the year ended 31 December 19X1 from the following information:

	1 January 19X1		31 December 19X1	
	£	£	£	£
Assets				
Property	20,000		20,000	
Machinery	6,000		9,000	
Debtors	4,000		8,000	
Cash	1,000		1,500	
		31,000		38,500
Liabilities				
Overdraft	6,000		9,000	
Creditors	5,000		3,000	
		(11,000)		(12,000)
Net assets		20,000		26,500
Drawings during the year				4,500
Additional capital introduced by the proprietor during the year				5,000

Solution

44. The increase in net assets during the year was £(26,500 - 20,000) = £6,500.

$$P = I + D - C_i$$
$$= £6,500 + £4,500 - £5,000$$
$$= £6,000$$

Example 2

45.   On 1 January 19X5, Patrick received a legacy of £2,000 and decided to open a shop. He paid the £2,000 into a business bank account. He paid £300 for shop fittings and £500 for a delivery van.

Detailed accounts were not kept but at the end of December 19X5 there was a stock of goods in the shop which had cost £300, credit customers owed £250 and there was £1,535 in the bank. There were creditors for supplies amounting to £200 and for rent of £30. Insurance and rates had been paid up to 31 March 19X6 at the rate of £5 per month. Patrick had drawn for himself £300. It was agreed that at 31 December the shop fittings and the van should be valued at £270 and £400 respectively.

(a)   Show the calculation of the profit for the year.
(b)   Produce the accounting equation as at 31 December.

Solution

46.   Two new ideas are introduced here.

(a)   The *prepayment* of rates and insurance for the first three months of 19X6. The business has paid cash for items of expenditure which relate to a future period of time. The £15 has been spent, but is not yet a charge against profit. It represents a right to obtain future services, ie the future services from local government rates and insurance, and as such, prepayments are accounted for as an asset of the business. Prepayments are described more fully in a later chapter.

(b)   The fall in the value of the van reduces the net assets of the business, in this case by £100, as the van is now worth only £400. This is an illustration of the effect of *depreciation* which is also described more fully in a later chapter.

(a)   CALCULATION OF PROFIT FOR THE YEAR TO 31 DECEMBER 19X5

	£	£	£
The net assets at 1 January were (cash)			2,000
Assets as at 31 December 19X5:			
Shop fittings		270	
Motor van		400	
Stock of goods		300	
Debts owed by customers		250	
Balance in the bank		1,535	
Rates and insurance paid in advance		15	
Total assets at 31 December 19X5		2,770	
Less liabilities:			
Creditors for purchased goods	200		
Creditor for rent	30		
		230	
Net assets at 31 December 19X5			2,540
Increase in net assets during 19X5			540
Add drawings by Patrick			300
			840
Further capital introduced during the year			0
Profit for the year			840

(b)   ACCOUNTING EQUATION AS AT 31 DECEMBER 19X5

	Capital	+	*Liabilities*	=	*Assets*
	£		£		£
Capital at start of year	2,000				
Retained profit for the year (=total profits less drawings)	540				Sundry assets
	2,540	+ Creditors	230	= as shown above	2,770

The usefulness of the accounting equation and business equation

47. The accounting equation and the business equation are useful introductory concepts in accounting, because:

(a) the accounting equation emphasises the equality between assets and liabilities (including capital as a liability);

(b) the business equation emphasises the inter-relationship between profits, net assets, appropriations of profit (drawings) and new capital investment.

48. You should now be aware, for example, that when business transactions are accounted for, it should be possible:

(a) to restate the assets and liabilities of the business after the transactions have taken place; and also

(b) to state the profit or loss, if any, arising as a result of the transactions.

The balance sheet and the trading, profit and loss account

49. In practice, the accounting equation and business equation are rarely used to state assets and liabilities and profit.

(a) The assets and liabilities of a business at any moment in time are shown in a balance sheet. This is very similar to the accounting equation.

(b) The profit (or loss) earned by a business during a given period of time is shown in a trading, profit and loss account.

These will be described in the following chapter.

Summary of this chapter

50. Check that you understand the following main points from this chapter.

(a) In accounting, a business is defined in terms of assets and liabilities.

(b) Total liabilities (including capital) are always equal to total assets.

(c)   In accounting, a business is treated as a separate entity, which owes capital (including retained profits) to its owner(s).

(d)   Drawings are appropriations of profits by the owner(s) of a business.

(e)   Profits are the excess of income over expenditure for a certain period of time. They can be measured as the increase in the net assets of the business over the period, plus drawings (which are profits taken out) less the amount of any additional capital put into the business. If no additional capital is put in, the increase in net assets will be equal to the amount of retained profits (ie profits earned and not drawn out by the owner(s), but kept in the business instead).

TEST YOUR KNOWLEDGE

Numbers in brackets refer to paragraphs of this chapter

1.   What is an asset? Give three examples.   (6)

2.   What is a liability? Give three examples.   (8)

3.   What is the accounting equation?   (18)

4.   What are drawings?   (24)

5.   What is the business equation?   (29)

6.   Distinguish between a debtor and a creditor.   (34, 37)

---

1. THE ACCOUNTING EQUATION

Peter Reid decides he is going to open a bookshop called Easyread, which he does by investing £5,000 on 1.1.19X7. During the first month of Easyread's existence, the following transactions occur:

(a) Bookshelves are purchased for £1,800.

(b) Books are purchased for £2,000.

(c) Half of the books are sold for £1,500 cash.

(d) Peter draws £200 out of the business for himself.

(e) Peter's brother John loans £500 to the business.

(f) Carpets are purchased for £1,000 on credit (to be paid in two months time).

(g) A bulk order of books worth £400 is sold on credit (to be paid in one month's time) for £600.

Required

Write down the accounting equation after each transaction has occurred.

2. FINANCIAL STATEMENTS

What is the difference between the balance sheet and the trading, profit and loss account? What is the difference between capital and revenue expenditure? Which of the following transactions is capital expenditure and which revenue expenditure?

(a) A bookseller buys a car for its director for £9,000.

(b) In the first year, the car is depreciated by £900.

(c) The business buys books for £1,500.

(d) The business builds an extension for £7,600.

(e) The original building is repainted, a job costing £1,200.

(f) A new sales assistant is taken on and his salary in the first year is £10,000.

SECTION 1: ILLUSTRATIVE QUESTIONS

3. PRICE LEVELS

(a) What problems does a period of changing price levels cause for:

    (i) businessmen; and
    (ii) accountants?

(b) How have accountants attempted to deal with these problems?

4. CORPORATE REPORT

(a) What is the fundamental objective of a corporate report?

(b) To whom should information contained in a corporate reported be communicated?

(c) What are the desirable characteristics of information which will satisfy the fundamental objective of a corporate report?

(d) Describe briefly the kind of information needed by two of the groups of people you mentioned in (b).

SECTION 1: SUGGESTED SOLUTIONS

1. THE ACCOUNTING EQUATION

Transaction	Capital £	+	Liabilities £	=	Assets	£
Start of business	5,000	+	0	=	Cash	5,000
(a)	5,000	+	0	=	Cash	3,200
					Shelves	1,800
						5,000
(b)	5,000	+	0	=	Cash	1,200
					Shelves	1,800
					Books	2,000
						5,000
(c)	5,000	+	0	=	Cash	2,700
Profit	500				Shelves	1,800
	5,500				Books	1,000
						5,500
(d)	5,000	+	0	=	Cash	2,500
Profit	500				Shelves	1,800
Drawings	(200)				Books	1,000
	5,300					5,300
(e)	5,000	+	Loan 500	=	Cash	3,000
Profit	500				phelves	1,800
Drawings	(200)				Books	1,000
	5,300		500			5,800
(f)	5,000	+	Loan 500	=	Cash	3,000
Profit	500		Creditor 1,000		Shelves	1,800
Drawings	(200)				Books	1,000
	5,300		1,500		Carpets	1,000
						6,800
(g)	5,000	+	Loan 500	=	Cash	3,000
Profit	700		Creditor 1,000		Shelves	1,800
Drawings	(200)				Books	600
	5,500		1,500		Carpets	1,000
					Debtor	600
						7,000

SECTION 1: SUGGESTED SOLUTIONS

2. FINANCIAL STATEMENTS

A balance sheet is a 'snapshot' of the financial position of a business. It is a statement of the liabilities, assets and capital of the business at a given moment in time. It is basically the same as the accounting equation, but written out in more detail.

The trading profit and loss account is not a static picture like the balance sheet, but is a record of income generated and expenditure incurred over the relevant accounting period.

Capital expenditure is expenditure which results in the acquisition of fixed assets (or an improvement in their earning capacity). It is not charged as an expense in the trading, profit and loss account.

Revenue expenditure is any other expenditure such as purchase of goods and expenses incurred to keep the business running (eg repairs, wages, electricity etc). It is accounted for in the trading, profit and loss account.

Capital expenditure   :   (a), (d)
Revenue expenditure :   (b), (c), (e), (f)

(Note that the value of the transactions is irrelevant.)

3. PRICE LEVELS

(a) Businessmen experience a number of problems in a period when prices are rising.

   (i)   Decision-making is more difficult when estimates of future costs and prices are affected by inflation. The difficulty is more acute when the effects of the decision extend over a long-period of time. But even short-term decisions such as price increases are affected.

   (ii) Accounting profits (at least where accounts are prepared under the historical cost convention) are an inadequate guide to the amount which may safely be distributed as dividend. This is because at least a part of the profit shown by the historical cost accounts must be ploughed back into the business just to maintain its previous capacity.

   (iii) Depreciation charged in historical cost accounts is inadequate to finance the replacement of fixed assets. (What is important is not the replacement of one asset by an identical one, something which rarely happens, but the replacement of the operating capability of an old asset.)

Problems encountered by accountants include:

(i)   Accounts are prepared in terms of a monetary unit (eg in the UK, the £). In times of rising prices the unit is not constant and comparisons over time are unrealistic.

(ii) Asset values are unrealistic. This applies even to such current assets as stocks, but is more of a problem in the case of fixed assets. For example, a freehold property may be held by a business for twenty years or more, during which time its value is likely to increase greatly over its original cost.

(iii) There are difficulties in measuring profits. In historical cost accounts, holding gains on stocks are included in the gross profit figure. Such gains merely represent the amount the business would have to spend to maintain its existing level of stocks. Conversely profits or losses on holdings of monetary items are not shown.

(b) Accountants have made many attempts to deal with the problems outlined above. One step which is commonly taken in practice is to prepare *modified* historical cost accounts. This usually means that current valuations are included in the historical cost balance sheet for some or all of a company's fixed assets, without any other adjustments being made. No attempt is made to tackle the difficulties of profit measurement.

More active measures have been taken to find alternatives to the historical cost convention. The two alternative systems which have found favour, at different times, in the UK are current purchasing power accounting (CPP) and current cost accounting (CCA). In general terms, CPP tackles the problems by attempting to express accounting values in terms of a stable monetary unit; while CCA attempts to show assets at current values, and to calculate profits after allowing for adjustments necessary to maintain a business's operating capability intact.

4. CORPORATE REPORT

(a) The fundamental objective of corporate reports (ie reports, including accounts, produced by businesses) is to communicate economic measurements of an information about the resources and performance of the reporting entity useful to those having reasonable rights to such information.

(b) The people who might be interested in financial information about a company are:

    (i) the *owners* of the company;

    (ii) the *managers* of the company, ie the people appointed by the company's owners to supervise the day-to-day activities of the company (called the stewardship function). In a small company, owners and managers might well be the same people.

    (iii) *suppliers* who provide goods to the company;

    (iv) *customers* who purchase goods or services from the company;

    (v) *providers of finance* to the company (eg a bank);

    (vi) the *Inland Revenue*;

    (vii) *employees* of the company;

    (viii) *financial experts* outside the company.

(c) There are seven characteristics which information contained in corporate report should possess - indeed, to be of any use, any information should possess them.

    (i) *Relevance*. The information provided should be that which is required to satisfy the needs of information users;

(ii) *Comprehensibility.* Information may be difficult to understand because it is skimpy or incomplete; but too much detail is also a defect which can cause difficulties of understanding.

(iii) *Reliability.* This will be enhanced if information is independently verified. The law requires that the accounts published by limited companies should be verified by an auditor, who must be a person independent of the company and the holder of an approved qualification.

(iv) *Completness.* A company's accounts should present a rounded picture of its economic activities.

(v) *Objectivity.* The usefulness of information will be enhanced if it contains a minimum of subjective judgement.

(vi) *Timeliness.* The usefulness of information is reduced if it does not appear until long after the period to which it relates, or if it is produced at unreasonably long intervals.

(vii) *Comparability.* Information should be produced on a consistent basis so that valid comparisons can be made with information from previous periods and with information produced by other sources (eg the accounts of similar companies operating in the same line of business.

(d) (i) *Employees of the company* have a right to information about the company's financial situation, because their future careers and the size of thei wages and salaries are dependent on it.

(ii) *Financial analysts and advisers* need information for their clients or audience. For example, stockbrokers will need information to advise investors in stocks and shares; credit agencies will want information to advise potential suppliers of goods to the company; and journalists need information for their reading public.

SECTION 2

ACCOUNTING PROCEDURES AND SYSTEMS

Chapter 4

AN INTRODUCTION TO FINAL ACCOUNTS

The purpose of this chapter is:

- to describe the principal features of the balance sheet and the trading and profit and loss account

- to distinguish between capital expenditure and revenue expenditure

Introduction

1. We have already mentioned that the most important financial statements are the balance sheet and the profit and loss account. We have also explained that both of these statements are summaries of many individual accounting transactions. In this text we look at the way in which such individual transactions are first recorded (in *books of prime entry*) and then follow the process by which other similar transactions are accumulated alongside them. Eventually we explain how this accumulated data is summarised to produce final accounts.

2. Before beginning on this process, it will be helpful to take an introductory look at the end-product. In this chapter we explain the purpose of a balance sheet and profit and loss account, and we set out in general terms the items which they contain and the form in which they are presented. In the following chapters the preparation of final accounts will be explained from the recording of transactions in books of prime entry through the trial balance stage.

The balance sheet

3. A balance sheet is a statement of the liabilities, capital and assets of a business at a given moment in time. It is like a 'snapshot' photograph, since it captures on paper a still image, frozen at a single moment in time, of something which is dynamic and continually changing. Typically, a balance sheet is prepared to show the liabilities, capital and assets as at the end of the accounting period to which the financial accounts relate.

4. As you should readily appreciate, a balance sheet is therefore very similar to the accounting equation. In fact, the only differences between a balance sheet and an accounting equation are:

(a) the manner or format in which the liabilities and assets are presented; and
(b) the extra detail which a balance sheet usually goes into.

Details in the balance sheet

5. A balance sheet is divided into two halves, with either:

    (a) capital and liabilities in one half and assets in the other; or

    (b) capital in one half and net assets in the other.

6. In other words, a balance sheet might be presented in either of the following ways.

    (a) Either

NAME OF BUSINESS
BALANCE SHEET AS AT (DATE)

	£		£
Capital	X	Assets (item by item)	X
Liabilities (item by item)	X		
	X		X

    (b) or

NAME OF BUSINESS
BALANCE SHEET AS AT (DATE)

	£
Assets	X
Less liabilities	X
Net assets	X
Capital	X

Method (a) puts capital and liabilities on the same side of the balance sheet, whereas method (b) shows capital on its own, and nets off liabilities against assets on the other side. Method (a) is now considered rather old-fashioned and is not much used. We will therefore only use the vertical format in this study text.

7. In either form of presentation, the total value on one side of the balance sheet (ie in one half of the balance sheet) will equal the total value on the other side. You should readily understand this from the accounting equation.

    Capital, liabilities and assets are usually shown in some detail in a balance sheet. The following paragraphs describe the sort of detail we might expect to find.

Capital

8. The proprietor's capital might well be analysed into its component parts:

	£	£
Capital as at the beginning of the accounting period (ie capital 'brought forward')		X
Add additional capital introduced during the period		X
		X
Add profit earned during the period	X	
Less drawings	(X)	
Retained profit for the period		X
Capital as at the end of the accounting period (ie capital 'carried forward')		X

('Brought forward' means 'brought forward from the previous period', and 'carried forward' means 'carried forward to the next period'. The carried forward amount at the end of one period is also the brought forward amount of the next period.)

Liabilities

9. The various liabilities should be itemised separately. In addition, a distinction is made between:

    (a) current liabilities; and

    (b) long-term liabilities.

10. *Current liabilities* are debts of the business that must be paid within a fairly short period of time (by convention, within one year). In the accounts of limited companies, the Companies Act 1985 requires use of the term 'creditors: amounts falling due within one year' rather than 'current liabilities' although they mean the same thing.

11. Examples of current liabilities are:

    (a) loans repayable within one year;

    (b) a bank overdraft (see paragraph 12);

    (c) trade creditors;

    (d) bills of exchange which are payable by the business;

    (e) taxation payable;

    (f) 'accrued charges'. These are expenses already incurred by the business, for which no bill has yet been received.

12. It is often argued that a bank overdraft is not a current liability, because a business is usually able to negotiate an overdraft facility for a long period of time. If an overdraft thus becomes a more permanent source of borrowing, it is really a long-term liability. However, you should normally expect to account for an overdraft as a current liability, since banks reserve the right to demand repayment at short notice.

13. *Long-term liabilities (or deferred liabilities)* are debts which are not payable within the 'short term' and so any liability which is not current must be long-term. Just as 'short-term' by convention means one year or less, 'long-term' means more than one year. In the accounts of limited companies, the Companies Act 1985 requires use of the term: 'Creditors: amounts falling due after more than one year'.

14. Examples of long-term liabilities are:

    (a) loans which are not repayable for more than one year, such as a bank loan, or a loan from an individual to a business;

    (b) a mortgage loan, which is a loan specifically secured against a freehold property. (If the business fails to repay the loan, the lender then has 'first claim' on the property, and is entitled to repayment from the proceeds from the enforced sale of the property);

    (c) debentures or debenture loans. These are usually found in larger limited companies' accounts. Debentures are securities issued by a company at a fixed rate of interest. They are repayable on agreed terms by a specified date in the future. Holders of debentures are therefore lenders of money to a company. Their interests, including security for the loan, are protected by the terms of a trust deed.

Assets

15. Assets in the balance sheet are divided into:

    (a) fixed assets:

        (i) tangible fixed assets;
        (ii) intangible fixed assets;
        (iii) investments (long-term);

    (b) current assets.

Fixed assets

16. A fixed asset is an asset acquired for use within the business (rather than for selling to a customer), with a view to earning income or making profits from its use, either directly or indirectly.

    Examples

    (a) In a manufacturing industry, a production machine would be a fixed asset, because it makes goods which are then sold.

(b) In a service industry, equipment used by employees giving service to customers would be classed as fixed assets (eg the equipment used in a garage, and furniture in a hotel).

(c) Factory premises, office furniture, computer equipment, company cars, delivery vans or pallets in a warehouse are all fixed assets.

17. To be classed as a fixed asset in the balance sheet of a business, an item must satisfy two further conditions.

(a) Clearly, it must be used by the business. For example, the proprietor's own house would not normally appear on the business balance sheet.

(b) The asset must have a 'life' in use of more than one year (strictly, more than one 'accounting period' which might be more or less than one year).

18. A *tangible* fixed asset is a physical asset, ie one that can be touched. It has a real, 'solid' existence. All of the examples of fixed assets mentioned above are tangible.

An *intangible* fixed asset is an asset which does not have a physical existence. It cannot be 'touched'. The idea of intangible assets might well puzzle you at the moment, and a description of them will be deferred until a later chapter. However, the expense of acquiring patent rights or developing a new product would be classified as an intangible fixed asset.

An *investment* might also be a fixed asset. Investments are commonly found in the published accounts of large limited companies. A large company A might invest in another company B by purchasing some of the shares or debentures of B. These investments would earn income for A in the form of interest or dividends paid out by B. If the investments are purchased by A with a view to holding on to them for more than one year, they would be classified as fixed assets of A.

In this chapter, we shall restrict our attention to tangible fixed assets.

Fixed assets and depreciation

19. Fixed assets might be held and used by a business for a number of years, but they wear out or lose their usefulness in the course of time. Every tangible fixed asset has a limited life. The only exception is land held freehold.

20. The accounts of a business try to recognise that the cost of a fixed asset is gradually consumed as the asset wears out. This is done by gradually writing off the asset's cost in the profit and loss account over several accounting periods. For example, in the case of a machine costing £1,000 and expected to wear out after ten years, it might be appropriate to reduce the balance sheet value by £100 each year. This process is known as depreciation.

21. If a balance sheet were drawn up four years, say, after the asset was purchased, the amount of depreciation which would have accumulated would be 4 x £100 = £400. The machine would then appear in the balance sheet as follows:

	£
Machine at original cost	1,000
Less accumulated depreciation	400
Net book value*	600

* ie the value of the asset in the books of account, net of depreciation. After ten years the asset would be fully depreciated and would appear in the balance sheet with a net book value of zero.

Current assets

22. Current assets are either:

(a) items owned by the business with the intention of turning them into cash within one year; or

(b) cash, including money in the bank, owned by the business.

These assets are 'current' in the sense that they are continually flowing through the business.

Current assets and the cash cycle

23. The definition in (a) above needs explaining further. Let us suppose that a trader, Chris Rhodes, runs a business selling motor cars, and purchases a showroom which he stocks with cars for sale. We will also suppose that he obtains the cars from a manufacturer, and pays for them in cash on delivery.

(a) If he sells a car in a cash sale, the goods are immediately converted into cash. The cash might then be used to buy more cars for re-sale.

(b) If he sells a car in a credit sale, the car will be given to the customer, who then becomes a debtor of the business. Eventually, the debtor will pay what he owes, and Chris Rhodes will receive cash. Once again, the cash might then be used to buy more cars for sale.

24. In this example:

(a) the cars (goods) held in stock for re-sale are current assets, because Chris Rhodes intends to sell them within one year, in the normal course of trade;

(b) any debtors are current assets, if they are expected to pay what they owe within one year;

(c) cash is a current asset.

25. The transactions described above could be shown as a cash cycle.

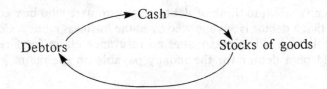

Cash is used to buy goods which are sold. Sales on credit create debtors, but eventually cash is earned from the sales. Some, perhaps most, of the cash will then be used to replenish stocks.

26. The main items of current assets are therefore:

   (a) stocks;
   (b) debtors;
   (c) cash.

27. It is important to realise that cars are current assets of Chris Rhodes because he is in the business of buying and selling them - ie he is a car trader. If he also has a car which he keeps and uses for business purposes, this car would be a fixed asset. The distinction between a fixed asset and a current asset is not what the asset is physically, but for what purpose it is obtained and used by the business.

28. There are some other categories of current assets. These are:

   (a) *short-term investments*. These are stocks and shares of other businesses, currently owned, but with the intention of selling them in the near future. For example, if a business has a lot of spare cash for a short time, its managers might decide to 'have a flutter' on The Stock Exchange, and buy shares in, say, Marks and Spencer, ICI or GEC. The shares will later be sold when the business needs the cash again. If share prices rise in the meantime, the business will make a profit from its short-term investment;

   (b) *prepayments*. These are amounts of money already paid by the business for benefits which have not yet been enjoyed but will be enjoyed within the next accounting period. Suppose, for example, that a business pays an annual insurance premium of £240 to insure its premises against fire and theft, and that the premium is payable annually in advance on 1 December. Now, if the business has an accounting year end of 31 December it will pay £240 on 1 December, but only enjoy one month's insurance cover by the end of the year. The remaining 11 months' cover (£220 cost, at £20 per month) will be enjoyed in the next year. The prepayment of £220 would therefore be shown in the balance sheet of the business, at 31 December, as a current asset.

   A prepayment might be thought of as a form of debtor. In the example above, at 31 December the insurance company still owes the business 11 months' worth of insurance cover.

Trade debtors and other debtors

29. Although it is convenient to think of debtors as customers who buy goods on credit, it is more accurate to say that a debtor is anyone who owes the business money. Continuing the example of an insurance policy, if a business makes an insurance claim for fire damage, the insurance company would be a debtor for the money payable on the claim.

30. A distinction can be made between:

   (a) trade debtors, ie customers who still owe money for goods or services bought on credit in the course of the trading activities of the business;
   (b) other debtors, ie anyone else owing money to the business.

The value of current assets in the balance sheet

31. Current assets must never be valued at more than their net realisable value, which is the amount of cash they will eventually earn the business when they are sold, minus the further costs required to get them into a condition for sale and to sell them. For example:

   (a) debtors are valued at the cash value of the debt - ie at their realisable value;

   (b) stocks of goods are usually valued at historical cost. However, if the net realisable value (NRV) of stocks is less than their cost, the stocks will be valued at NRV instead of cost. In other words, stocks of goods are valued at the lower of their cost and net realisable value. In normal circumstances, the lower of the two amounts is cost.

Balance sheet preparation: an example

32. We shall now look at how the various types of assets and liabilities are shown in the balance sheet of a business. You might like to attempt to prepare a balance sheet yourself before reading the solution which follows. You are required to prepare a balance sheet for the Sunken Arches Shoes and Boots Shop as at 31 December 19X6, given the information below.

	£
Capital as at 1 January 19X6	47,600
Profit for the year to 31 December 19X6	8,000
Freehold premises, net book value at 31 December 19X6	50,000
Motor vehicles, net book value at 31 December 19X6	9,000
Fixtures and fittings, net book value at 31 December 19X6	8,000
Long-term loan (mortgage)	25,000
Bank overdraft *	2,000
Goods held in stock for resale	16,000
Debtors	500
Cash in hand*	100
Creditors	1,200
Taxation payable	3,500
Drawings	4,000
Accrued costs of rent	600
Prepayment of insurance	300

*A shop might have cash in its cash registers, but an overdraft at the bank.

Solution

33. SUNKEN ARCHES BALANCE SHEET
AS AT 31 DECEMBER 19X6

	£	£
Fixed assets at net book value		
Freehold premises		50,000
Fixtures and fittings		8,000
Motor vehicles		9,000
		67,000
Current assets		
Stocks	16,000	
Debtors	500	
Prepayment	300	
Cash	100	
	16,900	
Current liabilities		
Bank overdraft	2,000	
Creditors	1,200	
Taxation payable	3,500	
Accrued costs	600	
	7,300	
Net current assets		9,600
		76,600
Long-term liabilities		
Loan		(25,000)
		51,600
Capital		
Capital as at 1 January 19X6		47,600
Profit for the year		8,000
		55,600
Less drawings		(4,000)
		51,600

The order of items in the balance sheet

34. By convention, a balance sheet lists liabilities and assets in a particular order. For limited companies, this order is compulsory (in most cases) under the Companies Act 1985. It is therefore worth getting into the habit of using this format from the beginning of your studies.

   (a) *Fixed assets* are listed in order of length of useful life, so that land and buildings would usually head the list.

   (b) *Current assets* are listed in descending order of *liquidity*. This means that those expected to take longest to convert into cash will be listed first (usually stocks followed by debtors).

(c) *Current liabilities* are listed in the order shown. The bank overdraft is shown first, because, as discussed in paragraph 12, it is usually a long-term source of finance in spite of being repayable on demand.

(d) *Net current assets* is equivalent to *working capital* and is an important figure in assessing a company's liquidity or ability to fund its operations in the short term. Thus, it is highlighted in the standard format.

The trading, profit and loss account

35. The profit and loss account has already been mentioned several times as a statement in which revenues and expenditure are compared to arrive at a figure of profit or loss. Many businesses try to distinguish between a gross profit earned on trading, and a net profit. They prepare a statement called a trading, profit and loss account: in the first part of the statement (the trading account) revenue from selling goods is compared with direct costs of acquiring or producing the goods sold to arrive at a gross profit figure; from this, deductions are made in the second half of the statement (the profit and loss account) in respect of indirect costs (overheads).

36. The trading, profit and loss account is a statement showing in detail how the profit (or loss) of a period has been made. The owners and managers of a business obviously want to know how much profit or loss has been made, but there is only a limited information value in the profit figure alone. In order to exercise financial control effectively, managers need to know how much income has been earned, what various items of costs have been, and whether the performance of sales or the control of costs appears to be satisfactory. This is the basic reason for preparing the trading, profit and loss account.

37. The two parts of the statement may be examined in more detail.

(a) *The trading account*. This shows the gross profit for the accounting period. Gross profit is the difference between:

(i) the value of sales (excluding value added tax); and
(ii) the purchase cost or production cost of the goods sold.

In the retail business, the cost of the goods sold is their purchase cost from the suppliers. In a manufacturing business, the production cost of goods sold is the cost of raw materials in the finished goods, plus the cost of the labour required to make the goods, and often plus an amount of production 'overhead' costs.

(b) *The profit and loss account*. This shows the net profit of the business. The net profit is:

(i) the gross profit;
(ii) plus any other income from sources other than the sale of goods;
(iii) minus other expenses of the business which are not included in the cost of goods sold.

38. Income from other sources will include:

    (a) dividends or interest received from investments;
    (b) profits on the sale of fixed assets;
    (c) bad debts written off in a previous accounting period which were unexpectedly paid in the current period (see paragraph 39 (a) below).

39. Other business expenses that will appear in the profit and loss account are as follows.

    (a) *Selling and distribution expenses.* These are expenses associated with the process of selling and delivering goods to customers. They include the following items.

        • Salaries of a sales director and sales management.

        • Salaries and commissions of salesmen.

        • Travelling and entertainment expenses of salesmen.

        • Marketing costs (eg advertising and sales promotion expenses).

        • Costs of running and maintaining delivery vans.

        • Discounts allowed to customers for early payment of their debts. For example, a business might sell goods to a customer for £100 and offer a discount of 5% for payment in cash. If the customer takes the discount, the accounts of the business would not record the sales value at £95; they would instead record sales at the full £100, with a cost for discounts allowed of £5. Discounts are described more fully in a later chapter.

        • Bad debts written off. Sometimes debtors fail to pay what they owe, and a business might have to decide at some stage of chasing after payment that there is now no prospect of ever being paid. The debt has to be written off as 'bad'. The amount of the debt written off is charged as an expense in the profit and loss account. Bad debts will be described more fully in a later chapter.

    (b) *Administration expenses.* These are the expenses of providing management and administration for the business. They include the following items.

        • Salaries of directors, management and office staff.
        • Rent and rates.
        • Insurance.
        • Telephone and postage.
        • Printing and stationery.
        • Heating and lighting.

    (c) *Finance expenses*
        • Interest on a loan.
        • Bank overdraft interest.

As far as possible, you should try to group items of expenses (selling and distribution, administration and finance) but this is not something that you should worry about unnecessarily at this stage.

Example: trading, profit and loss account

40. On 1 June 19X5, Jock Heiss commenced trading as an ice-cream salesman, selling ice-creams from a van which he drove around the streets of his town.

   (a) He rented the van at a cost of £1,000 for three months. Running expenses for the van averaged £300 per month.

   (b) He hired a part-time helper at a cost of £100 per month.

   (c) He borrowed £2,000 from his bank, and the interest cost of the loan was £25 per month.

   (d) His main business was to sell ice-cream to customers in the street, but he also did some special catering arrangements for business customers, supplying ice-creams for office parties. Sales to these customers were usually on credit.

   (e) For the three months to 31 August 19X5, his total sales were:

       (i)   cash sales £8,900;
       (ii) credit sales £1,100.

   (f) He purchased his ice-cream from a local manufacturer, Floors Limited. The cost of purchases in the three months to 31 August 19X5 was £6,200, and at 31 August he had sold every item of stock. He still owed £700 to Floors Limited for unpaid purchases on credit.

   (g) One of his credit sale customers has gone bankrupt, owing Jock £250. Jock has decided to write off the debt in full, with no prospect of getting any of the money owed.

   (h) He used his own home for his office work. Telephone and postage expenses for the three months to 31 August were £150.

   (i) During the period he paid himself £300 per month.

   Required
   Prepare a trading, profit and loss account for the three months 1 June - 31 August 19X5.

Solution

41. A trading, profit and loss account can be presented in either a horizontal format or a vertical format.

   (a) *Horizontal format*

JOCK HEISS
TRADING, PROFIT AND LOSS ACCOUNT
FOR THE THREE MONTHS ENDED 31 AUGUST 19X5

	£		£
Cost of sales	6,200	Sales	10,000
Gross profit carried down	3,800		
	10,000		10,000

Wages	300	Gross profit brought down	3,800
Van rental	1,000		
Van expenses	900		
Bad debt written off	250		
Telephone and postage	150		
Interest charges	75		
Net profit transferred to			
the balance sheet	1,125		
	3,800		3,800

Notes:

1. In a horizontal trading account, the cost of sales is shown on the left hand side and sales are shown on the right. The difference between the two amounts is the gross profit (or loss).

2. The gross profit so calculated is carried down into the profit and loss account, where it is shown on the right hand side. The various expenses are itemised on the left, and the difference between the gross profit and total expenses is the net profit. A net profit appears on the left, whereas a net loss would be shown on the right.

3. The net profit is the profit for the period, and it is transferred to the balance sheet of the business as part of the proprietor's capital.

4. Drawings are appropriations of profit and not expenses. They must not be included in the profit and loss account. In this example, the payments that Jock Heiss makes to himself (£900) are drawings.

5. The cost of sales is £6,200, even though £700 of the costs have not yet been paid for, and Floors Limited is still a creditor for £700 in the balance sheet.

Again, the horizontal format is uncommon in practice and in this text the vertical format will be used.

(b) *Vertical format*

A vertical trading, profit and loss account shows the same information, but with a different layout of figures.

JOCK HEISS
TRADING, PROFIT AND LOSS ACCOUNT
FOR THE THREE MONTHS ENDED 31 AUGUST 19X5

	£	£
Sales		10,000
Cost of sales		6,200
Gross profit		3,800
Expenses		
Wages	300	
Van rental	1,000	
Van expenses	900	
Bad debt written off	250	
Telephone and postage	150	
Interest charges	75	
		2,675
Net profit (transferred to the balance sheet)		1,125

What goes in the balance sheet and what goes in the profit and loss account?

42. You might by now be a little confused about what items appear in a balance sheet and what appears in a profit and loss account. For example, suppose that a business sells goods worth £20,000 (for cash) during one month, and during the same month borrows £10,000 from a money lender. Its total receipts for the month are £30,000.

    (a) The £20,000 of sales appear as sales in the trading, profit and loss account.
    (b) The £10,000 borrowed will not be shown in the profit and loss account, but will be shown as an asset (cash) and a liability (loan) of £10,000 in the balance sheet.

43. Suppose again that a business spends £15,000 buying some shares of a public company through the stock market. The company pays a dividend out of its profits, and the business receives a dividend of, say, £1,000 on its investment.

    (a) The cost of the shares will not be an expense in the profit and loss account. They will appear as an asset (investment) in the balance sheet.
    (b) However, the dividend of £1,000 will appear as income of the business in the profit and loss account.

44. The two illustrations above are examples of transactions where it is by no means necessarily clear whether an item should appear in the balance sheet or trading, profit and loss account. To try to make a distinction we must now turn our attention to the distinctions between capital expenditure and revenue expenditure, and capital income and revenue income.

Capital expenditure and revenue expenditure

45. Capital expenditure is expenditure which results in the acquisition of fixed assets, or an improvement in their earning capacity.

    (a) Capital expenditure is not charged as an expense in the profit and loss account but a depreciation charge will usually be made to write capital expenditure off over time. Depreciation charges are expenses in the profit and loss account.

    (b) Capital expenditure on fixed assets results in the appearance of a fixed asset in the balance sheet of the business.

46. Revenue expenditure is expenditure which is incurred either:

    (a) for the purpose of the trade of the business, including expenditure classified as selling and distribution expenses, administration expenses and finance charges; or
    (b) to maintain the existing earning capacity of fixed assets.

47. Revenue expenditure is charged to the profit and loss account of a period, provided that it relates to the trading activity and sales of that particular period. For example, if a business buys 10 widgets for £200 (£20 each) and sells 8 of them during an accounting period, it will have 2 widgets left in stock at the end of the period. The full £200 is revenue expenditure but only £160 is a cost of goods sold during the period. The remaining £40 (cost of 2 units) will be included in the balance sheet in the stock of goods held - ie as a current asset valued at £40.

Capital expenditure and revenue expenditure compared

48. Suppose that a business purchases a building for £30,000. It then adds an extension to the building at a cost of £10,000. The building needs to have a few broken windows mended, its floors polished and some missing roof tiles replaced. These cleaning and maintenance jobs cost £900.

    In this example, the original purchase (£30,000) and the cost of the extension (£10,000) are capital expenditure because they are incurred to acquire and then improve a fixed asset. The other costs of £900 are revenue expenditure, because these merely maintain the building and thus the 'earning capacity' of the building.

Capital income and revenue income

49. Capital income is the proceeds from the sale of non-trading assets (ie proceeds from the sale of fixed assets, including fixed asset investments). The profits (or losses) from the sale of fixed assets are included in the profit and loss account of a business, for the accounting period in which the sale takes place.

50. Revenue income is income derived from:

    (a) the sale of trading assets; or
    (b) interest and dividends received from investments held by the business.

51. The word 'revenue' in revenue expenditure and revenue income is perhaps a little confusing. Certainly 'revenue expenditure' can seem like a contradiction in terms.

Additional capital, additional loans and the repayment of existing loans

52. The categorisation of capital and revenue items given above does not mention raising additional capital from the owner(s) of the business, or raising and repaying loans. These are transactions which either:

    (a) add to the cash assets of the business, thereby creating a corresponding liability (capital or loan); or
    (b) when a loan is repaid, reduce the liabilities (loan) and the assets (cash) of the business.

    None of these transactions would be reported through the profit and loss account.

Why is the distinction between capital and revenue items important?

53. Revenue expenditure results from the purchase of goods and services that will either:

    (a) be used fully in the accounting period in which they are purchased, and so be a cost or expense in the trading, profit and loss account; or
    (b) result in a current asset as at the end of the accounting period (because the goods or services have not yet been consumed or made use of).

54. Capital expenditure results in the purchase or improvement of fixed assets, which are assets that will provide benefits to the business in more than one accounting period, and which are not acquired with a view to being resold in the normal course of trade. The cost of purchased fixed assets is not charged in full to the trading, profit and loss account of the period in which the purchase occurs. Instead, the fixed asset is gradually depreciated over a number of accounting periods.

55. Since revenue items and capital items are accounted for in different ways, the correct and consistent calculation of profit for any accounting period depends on the correct and consistent classification of items as revenue or capital.

Capital and revenue items: exercise

56. State whether each of the following items should be classified as 'capital' or 'revenue' expenditure or income for the purpose of preparing the trading, profit and loss account and the balance sheet of the business.

   (a) Purchase of leasehold premises.
   (b) Annual depreciation of leasehold premises.
   (c) Solicitors' fees in connection with the purchase of leasehold premises.
   (d) Costs of adding extra storage capacity to a mainframe computer used by the business.
   (e) Computer repairs and maintenance costs.
   (f) Profit on the sale of an office building.
   (g) Revenue from sales by credit card (Access or Barclaycard).
   (h) Cost of new machinery.
   (i) Customs duty charged on the machinery when imported into the country.
   (j) 'Carriage' costs of transporting the new machinery from the supplier's factory to the premises of the business purchasing the machinery.
   (k) Cost of installing the new machinery in the premises of the business.
   (l) Wages of the machine operators.

Solution

57. (a) Capital expenditure.
   (b) Depreciation of a fixed asset is revenue expenditure.
   (c) The legal fees associated with the purchase of a property may be added to the purchase price and classified as capital expenditure. The cost of the leasehold premises in the balance sheet of the business will then include the legal fees.
   (d) Capital expenditure (enhancing an existing fixed asset).
   (e) Revenue expenditure.
   (f) Capital income (net of the costs of sale).
   (g) Revenue income.
   (h) Capital expenditure.
   (i) If customs duties are borne by the purchaser of the fixed asset, they may be added to the cost of the machinery and classified as capital expenditure.
   (j) Similarly, if carriage costs are paid for by the purchaser of the fixed asset, they may be included in the cost of the fixed asset and classified as capital expenditure.
   (k) Installation costs of a fixed asset are also added to the fixed asset's cost and classified as capital expenditure.
   (l) Revenue expenditure.

Items appearing in both the balance sheet and the trading, profit and loss account

58. A few items appear in both the trading, profit and loss account and also the balance sheet.

    (a) *Net profit.* The net profit in the profit and loss account is the profit for the financial year or other period which is then added to the proprietor's capital in the balance sheet.

    (b) *Expenses incurred but not yet paid for.* The cost of goods purchased by a business and then re-sold before the business has paid for them will be included in the trading account (cost of goods sold) and in the balance sheet (as a creditor).

    (c) *The value of goods sold on credit,* for which payment is still owed. Credit sales are included in the trading account, and unpaid debts are debtors in the balance sheet;

    (d) *The cost of goods purchased but not yet sold by the business* will appear in the balance sheet as stocks held at the end of one accounting period (current assets) and will become a cost of goods sold in the trading account in a subsequent accounting period when the goods are eventually sold.

Another important item which is relevant both to the profit and loss account and the balance sheet is depreciation. Depreciation is dealt with in a later chapter.

Summary of the chapter

59.   The purpose of this chapter has been to introduce in broad outline the characteristics of the balance sheet and the trading, profit and loss account. In the next chapters, we shall go on to consider in detail some of the techniques and principles applied to prepare the trading, profit and loss account.

- A *balance sheet* is a statement of the financial position of a business at a given moment in time.

- A *trading, profit and loss account* is a financial statement showing in detail how the profit or loss of a period has been made.

- A distinction is made in the balance sheet between:
  (a) long-term liabilities and current liabilities;
  (b) fixed assets and current assets.

- *Current liabilities* are debts which are payable within one year.

- *Fixed assets* are those acquired for long-term use within the business. They are normally valued at cost less depreciation.

- *Current assets* are those which are expected to be converted into cash within a year. They are normally valued at cost less depreciation. Current assets are those acquired for conversion into cash and should never be shown in the balance sheet at a figure greater than *net realisable value.*

- *Depreciation* is the measure of the deterioration of a fixed asset over a period of time.

- A distinction can be made between *capital* and *revenue* items of income and expenditure.

Other definitions

Working capital is the amount of *net current assets*, ie current assets less current liabilities.

Gross profit is the amount of sales less the purchase cost or production cost of goods sold.

Net profit is the amount of gross profit, plus income other than from the sale of goods, minus other expenses.

TEST YOUR KNOWLEDGE

Numbers in brackets refer to paragraphs of this chapter

1. What are the component parts of the item 'proprietor's capital' in a balance sheet? (8)

2. Give two examples of long-term liabilities. (14)

3. What are the main items of current assets in a balance sheet? (26)

4. What is the 'working capital' of a business? (34)

5. What is the distinction between capital expenditure and revenue expenditure? (45, 46)

6. Describe two items which appear in both the balance sheet and the profit and loss account. (58)

Chapter 5

THE COST OF GOODS SOLD
ACCRUALS AND PREPAYMENTS

The purpose of this chapter is:

- to explain the effect of opening and closing stock on the calculation of profit

- to explain the nature of accruals and prepayments and to describe how they are calculated.

Introduction: calculating the amount of profit earned

1. Profit earned can be defined as the value of sales less the cost of sales and expenses. This definition might seem simple enough; however, it is not always immediately clear how much the costs of sales or expenses are. A variety of difficulties can arise in measuring them: some of these problems can be dealt with fairly easily, whereas others are less obvious to solve. The purpose of this chapter and the next is to describe some of these problems and their solutions.

2. In this chapter, we shall consider unsold goods in stock at the beginning and end of an accounting period, carriage costs, writing off or writing down stock values, and the accounting treatment of accruals and prepayments.

Unsold goods in stock at the end of an accounting period

3. Goods might be unsold at the end of an accounting period and so still held in stock at the end of the period. The purchase cost of these goods should not therefore be included in the cost of sales of the period.

4. Suppose that Perry P Louis, trading as the Umbrella Shop, ends his financial year on 30 September each year. On 1 October 19X4 he had no goods in stock. During the year to 30 September 19X5, he purchased 30,000 umbrellas costing £60,000 from umbrella wholesalers and suppliers. He resold the umbrellas for £5 each, and sales for the year amounted to £100,000 (20,000 umbrellas). At 30 September there were 10,000 unsold umbrellas left in stock, valued at £2 each.

What was Perry P Louis's gross profit for the year?

5: THE COST OF GOODS SOLD; ACCRUALS AND PREPAYMENTS

Solution

5. Perry P Louis purchased 30,000 umbrellas, but only sold 20,000. Purchase costs of £60,000 and sales of £100,000 do not represent the same quantity of goods.

    The gross profit for the year should be calculated by 'matching' the sales value of the 20,000 umbrellas sold with the cost of those 20,000 umbrellas. The cost of sales in this example is therefore the cost of purchases minus the cost of goods in stock at the year end:

	£	£
Sales (20,000 units)		100,000
Purchases (30,000 units)	60,000	
Less closing stock (10,000 units @ £2)	20,000	
Cost of sales (20,000 units)		40,000
Gross profit		60,000

6. > You should recognise that this is an example of the *accruals concept*, described in an earlier chapter.

Example

7. We shall continue the example of the Umbrella Shop into its next accounting year, from 1 October 19X5 to 30 September 19X6. Suppose that during the course of this year, Perry P Louis purchased 40,000 umbrellas at a total cost of £95,000. During the year he sold 45,000 umbrellas for £230,000. At 30 September 19X6 he had 5,000 umbrellas left in stock, which had cost £12,000.

    What was his gross profit for the year?

Solution

8. In this accounting year, he purchased 40,000 umbrellas to add to the 10,000 he already had in stock at the start of the year. He sold 45,000, leaving 5,000 umbrellas in stock at the year end. Once again, gross profit should be calculated in accordance with the accruals concept by matching the value of 45,000 units of sales with the cost of those 45,000 units.

    The cost of sales is the value of the 10,000 umbrellas in stock at the beginning of the year, plus the cost of the 40,000 umbrellas purchased, less the value of the 5,000 umbrellas in stock at the year end.

	£	£
Sales (45,000 units)		230,000
Opening stock (10,000 units) *	20,000	
Add purchases (40,000 units)	95,000	
	115,000	
Less closing stock (5,000 units)	12,000	
Cost of sales (45,000 units)		103,000
Gross profit		127,000

    *This is the closing stock value of the previous accounting year.

The cost of goods sold

9.

	£
To summarise, the cost of goods sold is found by applying the following formula:	
Opening stock value	X
Add cost of purchases (or, in the case of a manufacturing company, the cost of production)	X
	X
Closing stock value	(X)
Equals cost of goods sold	X

In other words, to match 'sales' and the 'cost of goods sold', it is necessary to adjust the cost of goods manufactured or purchased to allow for increases or reduction in stock levels during the period.

10. You might agree that the 'formula' above is based on a logical idea. You should learn it, because it is a fundamental principle of accounting.

Test your knowledge of the formula with the following example.

Example: cost of goods sold and variations in stock levels

11. On 1 January 19X6, the Grand Union Food Stores had goods in stock valued at £6,000. During 19X6 its proprietor, who ran the shop, purchased supplies costing £50,000. Sales turnover for the year to 31 December 19X6 amounted to £80,000. The cost of goods in stock at 31 December 19X6 was £12,500.

Required: calculate the gross profit for the year.

Solution

12.

GRAND UNION FOOD STORES

TRADING ACCOUNT FOR THE YEAR ENDED 31 DECEMBER 19X6

	£	£
Sales		80,000
Opening stock	6,000	
Add purchases	50,000	
	56,000	
Less closing stock	12,500	
Cost of goods sold		43,500
Gross profit		36,500

5: THE COST OF GOODS SOLD; ACCRUALS AND PREPAYMENTS

The cost of carriage inwards and outwards

13. 'Carriage' refers to the cost of transporting purchased goods from the supplier to the premises of the business which has bought them. Someone has to pay for these delivery costs: sometimes the supplier pays, and sometimes the purchaser pays. When the purchaser pays, the cost to the purchaser is *carriage inwards*. When the supplier pays, the cost to the supplier is known as *carriage outwards*.

14.
> * The cost of carriage inwards is usually added to the cost of purchases, and is therefore included in the trading account.
>
> * The cost of carriage outwards is a selling and distribution expense in the profit and loss account.

Example: carriage inwards and carriage outwards

15. Gwyn Tring, trading as Clickety Clocks, imports and resells cuckoo clocks and grandfather clocks. He must pay for the costs of delivering the clocks from his supplier in Switzerland to his shop in Wales.

He resells the clocks to other traders throughout the country, paying the costs of carriage for the consignments from his business premises to his customers.

On 1 July 19X5, he had clocks in stock valued at £17,000. During the year to 30 June 19X6 he purchased more clocks at a cost of £75,000. Carriage inwards amounted to £2,000. Sales for the year were £162,100. Other expenses of the business amounted to £56,000 excluding carriage outwards which cost £2,500. Gwyn Tring took drawings of £20,000 from the business during the course of the year. The value of the goods in stock at the year end was £15,400.

Required: prepare the trading, profit and loss account of Clickety Clocks for the year ended 30 June 19X6.

Solution

16.
CLICKETY CLOCKS
TRADING, PROFIT AND LOSS ACCOUNT
FOR THE YEAR ENDED 30 JUNE 19X6

	£	£
Sales		162,100
Opening stock	17,000	
Purchases	75,000	
Carriage inwards	2,000	
	94,000	
Less closing stock	15,400	
Cost of goods sold		78,600
Gross profit		83,500
Carriage outwards	2,500	
Other expenses	56,000	
		58,500
Net profit (transferred to balance sheet)		25,000

Goods written off or written down

17. A trader might be unable to sell all the goods that he purchases, because a number of things might happen to the goods before they can be sold. For example:

(a) goods might be lost or stolen;

(b) goods might be damaged, and so become worthless. Such damaged goods might be thrown away;

(c) goods might become obsolete or out of fashion. These might have to be thrown away, or possibly sold off at a very low price in a clearance sale.

18. When goods are lost, stolen or thrown away as worthless, the business will make a loss on those goods because their 'sales value' will be nil.

Similarly, when goods lose value because they have become obsolete or out of fashion, the business will make a loss if their clearance sales value is less than their cost. For example, if goods which originally cost £500 are now obsolete and can only be sold for £150, the business will suffer a loss of £350.

19.
> If, at the end of an accounting period, a business still has goods in stock which are either worthless or worth less than their original cost, the value of the stocks should be written down to:
>
> (a) *nothing* if they are worthless; or
> (b) their *net realisable value* if this is less than their original cost.
>
> This means that the loss will be reported as soon as it is foreseen, even if the goods have not yet been thrown away or sold off at a cheap price. This is an application of the *prudence concept* described in an earlier chapter.

20. The costs of stock written off or written down should not usually cause any problems in calculating the gross profit of a business, because the cost of goods sold will include the cost of stocks written off or written down, as the following example shows.

Example: stocks written off and written down

21. Lucas Wagg, trading as Fairlock Fashions, ends his financial year on 31 March. At 1 April 19X5 he had goods in stock valued at £8,800. During the year to 31 March 19X6, he purchased goods costing £48,000. The goods still held in stock at 31 March 19X6 had an original purchase cost of £7,600 but this includes fashion goods which cost £2,100 but which Lucas Wagg believes could only now be sold at a sale price of £400. Sales for the year were £81,400.

Required: calculate the gross profit of Fairlock Fashions for the year ended 31 March 19X6.

Solution

22. Initial calculation of closing stock values:

STOCK COUNT

	At cost	Revalued amount	Amount written down
	£	£	£
Fashion goods	2,100	400	1,700
Other goods (balancing figure)	5,500	5,500	-
	7,600	5,900	1,700

FAIRLOCK FASHIONS
TRADING ACCOUNT FOR THE YEAR ENDED 31 MARCH 19X6

	£	£
Sales		81,400
Value of opening stock	8,800	
Purchases	48,000	
	56,800	
Less closing stock	5,900	
Cost of goods sold		50,900
Gross profit		30,500

Accruals and prepayments

23. It has already been stated that the gross profit for a period should be calculated by matching sales and the cost of goods sold. In the same way, the net profit for a period should be calculated by charging the expenses which relate to that period. For example, in preparing the profit and loss account of a business for a period of, say, six months, it would be appropriate to charge six months' expenses for rent and rates, insurance costs and telephone costs etc.

24. Expenses might not be paid for during the period to which they relate. For example, if a business rents a shop for £20,000 per annum, it might pay the full annual rent on, say, 1 April each year. Now if we were to calculate the profit of the business for the first six months of 19X7, the correct charge for rent in the profit and loss account would be £10,000 even though the rent paid in that period would be £20,000. Similarly, the rent charge in a profit and loss account for the business in the second six months of the year would be £10,000, even though no rent payment would be made in that six month period.

25. *Accruals or accrued expenses* are expenses which are charged against the profit for a particular period, even though they have not yet been paid for. *Prepayments* are payments which have been made in one accounting period, but should not be charged against profit until a later period, because they relate to that later period. Once again, the calculation of accrued and prepaid expenses is necessary to comply with the *accruals concept*.

26. Accruals and prepayments may seem difficult at first, but the following examples should help to clarify the principle involved: expenses should be matched against the period to which they relate.

First example: accruals

27. Horace Goodrunning, trading as Goodrunning Motor Spares, ends his financial year on 28 February each year. His telephone was installed on 1 April 19X6 and he receives his telephone account quarterly at the end of each quarter. He pays it as soon as it is received. On the basis of the following data, you are required to calculate the telephone expense to be charged to the profit and loss account for the year ended 28 February 19X7.

Telephone expense for the three months ended:

	£
30. 6.19X6	23.50
30. 9.19X6	27.20
31.12.19X6	33.40
31. 3.19X7	36.00

Solution

28. The telephone expenses for the year ended 28 February 19X7 are:

	£
1 March – 31 March 19X6 (no telephone)	–
1 April – 30 June 19X6	23.50
1 July – 30 September 19X6	27.20
1 October – 31 December 19X6	33.40
1 January – 28 February 19X7 (two months: ⅔ x £36.00)	24.00
	108.10

The charge for the period 1 January – 28 February 19X7 is two-thirds of the quarterly charge received on 31 March. As at 28 February 19X7, no telephone bill has been received for the quarter, because it is not due for another month. However, it would be inappropriate to ignore the telephone expenses for January and February, and so an accrued charge should be made. (Obviously, if Horace knew that the usage of the telephone was not spread evenly over the quarter, then a simple time apportionment would be inappropriate).

The accrued charge will also appear in the balance sheet of the business as at 28 February 19X7, as a current liability.

Second example: accruals

29. Ratsnuffer is a business dealing in pest control. Its owner, Roy Dent, employs a team of eight, who were paid £12,000 per annum in the year to 31 December 19X5. In the following year 19X6 he raised salaries by 10% to £13,200 per annum per employee.

    On 1 July 19X6, he hired a trainee at a salary of £8,400 per annum.

    He pays his work force on the first working day of every month, one month in arrears, so that his employees receive their salary for January on the first working day in February, etc.

    Required:

    (a) calculate the cost of salaries which would be charged in the profit and loss account of Ratsnuffer for the year ended 31 December 19X6;

    (b) calculate the amount actually paid in salaries during the year (ie the amount of cash received by the work force);

    (c) state the amount of accrued charges for salaries which would appear in the balance sheet of Ratsnuffer as at 31 December 19X6.

Solution

30. (a) *Salaries cost in the profit and loss account*

	£
Cost of 8 employees for a full year at £13,200 each	105,600
Cost of trainee for half a year	4,200
	109,800

    (b) *Salaries actually paid in 19X6*

	£
December 19X5 salaries paid in January (8 employees x £1,000 per month)	8,000
Salaries of 8 employees for January to November 19X6, paid in February to December (8 employees x £1,100 per month x 11 months)	96,800
Salary of trainee (for July to November, paid in August to December 19X6: 5 months x £700 per month)	3,500
Salaries actually paid	108,300

    (c) *Accrued salaries costs as at 31 December 19X6*
    (ie costs charged in the P & L account, but not yet paid)

	£
8 employees x 1 month x £1,100 per month	8,800
1 trainee x 1 month x £700 per month	700
	9,500

5: THE COST OF GOODS SOLD; ACCRUALS AND PREPAYMENTS

(d) *Summary*

	£
Accrued wages cost at 31 December 19X5	8,000
Add salaries cost for 19X6 (P & L account)	109,800
	117,800
Less salaries paid	108,300
Accrued wages cost at 31 December 19X6	9,500

First example: prepayments

31. The Square Wheels Garage pays fire insurance annually in advance on 1 June each year. The firm's financial year end is 28 February. From the following record of insurance payments you are required to calculate the charge to profit and loss for the financial year to 28 February 19X8.

Insurance paid

	£
1.6.19X6	600
1.6.19X7	700

Solution

32. Insurance cost for:

	£
(a) 1 March – 31 May 19X7 ($\frac{3}{12}$ x £600)	150
(b) 1 June 19X7 – 28 February 19X8 ($\frac{9}{12}$ x £700)	525
Insurance cost for the year, charged to the P & L account	675

At 28 February 19X8 there is a prepayment for fire insurance, covering the period 1 March – 31 May 19X8. This insurance premium was paid on 1 June 19X7, but only nine months worth of the full annual cost is chargeable to the accounting period ended 28 February 19X8. The prepayment of ($\frac{3}{12}$ x £700) £175 as at 28 February 19X8 will appear as a current asset in the balance sheet of the Square Wheels Garage as at that date.

In the same way, there was a prepayment of ($\frac{3}{12}$ x £600) £150 in the balance sheet one year earlier as at 28 February 19X7.

Summary	£
Prepaid insurance premiums as at 28 February 19X7	150
Add insurance premiums paid 1 June 19X7	700
	850
Less insurance costs charged to the P & L account for the year ended 28 February 19X8	675
Prepaid insurance premiums as at 28 February 19X8	175

Second example

33. The Batley Print Shop rents a photocopying machine from a supplier for which it makes a quarterly payment as follows:

(a) three months rental in advance;
(b) a further charge of 2 pence per copy made during the quarter just ended.

The rental agreement began on 1 August 19X4 and the first six quarterly bills were as follows:

Bills dated and received	Rental £	Costs of copies taken £	Total £
1 August 19X4	2,100	0	2,100
1 November 19X4	2,100	1,500	3,600
1 February 19X5	2,100	1,400	3,500
1 May 19X5	2,100	1,800	3,900
1 August 19X5	2,700	1,650	4,350
1 November 19X5	2,700	1,950	4,650

The bills are paid promptly, as soon as they are received.

Required:

(a) calculate the charge for photocopying expenses for the year to 31 August 19X4 and the amount of prepayments and/or accrued charges as at that date;

(b) calculate the charge for photocopying expenses for the following year to 31 August 19X5, and the amount of prepayments and/or accrued charges as at that date.

Solution

34. (a) *Year to 31 August 19X4* £

	£
One month's rental ($\frac{1}{3}$ x £2,100) *	700
Accrued copying charges ($\frac{1}{3}$ x £1,500) **	500
Photocopying expense (P & L account)	1,200

* From the quarterly bill dated 1 August 19X4
** From the quarterly bill dated 1 November 19X4

There is a prepayment for 2 months' rental (£1,400) as at 31 August 19X4.

(b) *Year to 31 August 19X5*

	£	£
Rental charge for the year:		
Rental from 1 September 19X4 - 31 July 19X5		
(11 months at £2,100 per quarter or £700 per month)		7,700
Rental from 1 August - 31 August 19X5 ($\frac{1}{3}$ x £2,700)		900
		8,600
Copying charges:		
1 September - 31 October 19X4 ($\frac{2}{3}$ x £1,500)	1,000	
1 November 19X4 - 31 January 19X5	1,400	
1 February - 30 April 19X5	1,800	
1 May - 31 July 19X5	1,650	
Accrued charges for August 19X5 ($\frac{1}{3}$ x £1,950)	650	
		6,500
Total photocopying expenses (P & L account)		15,100

There is a prepayment for 2 months' rental (£1,800) as at 31 August 19X5.

Summary of year 1 September 19X4 - 31 August 19X5

	Rental charges £	Copying costs £
Prepayments as at 31.8.19X4	1,400	
Accrued charges as at 31.8.19X4		(500)
Bills received during the year		
1 November 19X4	2,100	1,500
1 February 19X5	2,100	1,400
1 May 19X5	2,100	1,800
1 August 19X5	2,700	1,650
Prepayment as at 31.8.19X5	(1,800)	
Accrued charges as at 31.8.19X5		650
Charge to the P & L account for the year	8,600	6,500

Balance sheet items as at 31 August 19X5

Prepaid rental (current asset)		1,800
Accrued copying charges (current liability)		650

Summary of the chapter

35. This chapter has illustrated how the amount of profit is calculated when:

   (a) there are opening or closing stocks of goods in hand;

   (b) there is carriage inwards;

   (c) stocks are written off or written down in value;

   (d) there are accrued charges;

   (e) there are prepayments of expenses.

36.
   - The *cost of goods sold* is calculated by adding the value of opening stock in hand to the cost of purchases and subtracting the value of closing stock.

   - Carriage inwards may be added to the cost of purchases.

   - Accrued expenses are expenses which relate to an accounting period but have not yet been paid for. They are a charge against the profit for the period and they are shown in the balance sheet as at the end of the period as a current liability.

   - Prepayments are expenses which have already been paid but relate to a future accounting period. They are not charged against the profit of the current period, and they are shown in the balance sheet as at the end of the period as a current asset.

   - Accruals and prepayments are aspects of the accruals concept which is one of the fundamental concepts in accounting.

TEST YOUR KNOWLEDGE

Numbers in brackets refer to paragraphs of this chapter

1. What is the formula for calculating the cost of goods sold?   (9)

2. How is the cost of carriage inwards treated for accounting purposes?   (14)

3. How is a reduction in stock value treated for accounting purposes?   (19)

4. Define accruals and prepayments.   (24)

Chapter 6

DISCOUNTS, BAD DEBTS AND PROVISIONS

The purpose of this chapter is:

- to explain the accounting treatment of discounts allowed to customers and discounts received from suppliers

- to describe the accounting treatment of bad and doubtful debts

---

Introduction

---

1.   As a general rule, for the purpose of accounting (as distinct from the legal aspects of the law of contract) a sale or purchase of goods or services by a business (ie recognition of revenue) takes place at one of two points in time.

- *Cash sales*: if the sale is for cash, it occurs when the goods or services are given in exchange for an immediate payment, in notes and coins, or by cheque or credit card.

- *Credit sales*: if the sale is on credit, it occurs when the business making the sale sends out an invoice for the goods or services supplied. (An invoice is a letter from a supplier to a customer, showing details of the goods or services supplied, the amount of money owed by the customer, and the terms of payment – eg payment requested immediately, or within 30 days etc).

- *Purchases for cash*: if the goods are paid for promptly (ie in cash) the purchase occurs when the goods and cash exchange hands.

- *Purchases on credit*: if the goods are bought on credit, the purchase normally occurs when the business receives the goods, accompanied by an invoice from the supplier.

---

2.   The accounting problems discussed in this chapter are concerned with *sales or purchases on credit*. With credit transactions, the point in time when a sale or purchase is recognised in the accounts of the business is not the same as the point in time when cash is eventually received or paid for the sale or purchase. There is a gap in time between the sale or purchase and the eventual cash settlement, and it is possible that something might happen during that time which results in the amount of cash eventually paid (if any) being different from the original value of the sale or purchase on the invoice.

3. We shall consider three such 'happenings':

    (a) *discounts allowed by the supplier* for goods purchased by the business;
    (b) *discounts allowed to customers* for goods sold by the business;
    (c) *bad debts*, which arise when the business decides that a credit customer will never pay the money he owes.

Discounts

4. A discount is a reduction in the price of goods below the amount at which those goods would normally be sold to other customers of the supplier. A distinction must be made between:

    (a) *trade* discount; and
    (b) *cash* discount, or *settlement* discount.

5. *Trade discount* is a reduction in the cost of goods owing to the nature of the trading transaction. It usually results from buying goods in bulk. For example:

    (a) a customer might be quoted a price of £1 per unit for a particular item, but a lower price of, say, 95 pence per unit if the item is bought in quantities of, say, 100 units or more at a time; or

    (b) important or regular customers might be offered a discount on all the goods they buy regardless of the size of each individual order, because the total volume of their purchases over time is so large.

6. *Cash discount* is a reduction in the amount payable to the supplier, in return for immediate payment in cash, rather than purchase on credit. For example, a supplier might charge £1,000 for goods, but offer a discount of, say, 5% if the goods are paid for immediately in cash.

7. *Settlement discount* is similar to cash discount. It is a discount on the price of the goods purchased for credit customers who pay their debts promptly. For example, a supplier might charge £1,000 to a credit customer for goods purchased, but offer a discount of, say, 5% for payment within so many days of the invoice date.

Accounting for trade discount

8. Trade discount is a reduction in the amount of money demanded from a customer.

    (a) If trade discount is received by a business for goods purchased from a supplier, the amount of money demanded from the business by the supplier will be net of discount (ie it will be the normal sales value less the discount).

    (b) Similarly, if a trade discount is given by a business for goods sold to a customer, the amount of money demanded by the business will be after deduction of the discount.

9.
> Trade discount should therefore be accounted for as follows.
>
> (a) Trade discount *received* should be deducted from the gross cost of purchases. In other words, the cost of purchases in the trading account will be stated at gross cost minus discount (ie it will be stated at the invoiced amount).
>
> (b) Trade discount *allowed* should be deducted from the gross sales price, so that sales for the period will be reported in the trading account at their invoice value.

Cash discounts and settlement discounts received

10. When a business is given the opportunity to take advantage of a cash discount or a settlement discount for prompt payment, the decision as to whether or not to take the discount is a matter of *financing* policy, not of *trading* policy.

11. Suppose that A buys goods from B, on the understanding that A will be allowed a period of credit before having to pay for the goods. The terms of the transaction might be as follows:

    (a) date of sale: 1 July 19X6;
    (b) credit period allowed: 30 days;
    (c) invoice price of the goods: £2,000 (the invoice will be issued at this price when the goods are delivered);
    (d) cash discount offered: 4% discount for prompt payment.

12. A has a choice between holding on to his money for 30 days and then paying the full £2,000 or paying £2,000 less 4% - ie £1,920 now. This is a financing decision about whether it is worthwhile for A to save £80 by paying his debts sooner, or whether he can employ his cash more usefully for 30 days, and pay the debt at the latest acceptable moment.

13.
> The cash discount received are accounted for in what might seem like an unusual way.
>
> (a) In the *trading account*, the cost of purchases will be at the invoiced price (or 'full trade' price). When the invoice is received, it will be recorded in his books of account at that price, and the subsequent financing decision about accepting the cash discount is ignored.
>
> (b) In the *profit and loss account*, the cash discount received is shown as though it were income received. There is no expense in the P & L account from which the cash discount can be deducted, and so there is no alternative other than to show the discount received as income, odd though this may seem to you.

14. In our example, we would have:

	£
Cost of purchase from B by A (trading account)	2,000
Discount received (income in the P & L account)	(80)
Net cost	1,920

Settlement discounts are accounted for in exactly the same way as cash discounts.

Cash discounts and settlement discounts allowed

15. The same principle is applied in accounting for cash discounts or settlement discounts allowed to customers. Goods are sold at a trade price, and the offer of a discount on that price is a matter of financing policy for the business and not a matter of trading policy.

16. Suppose that X sells goods to Y at a price of £5,000. Y is allowed 60 days' credit before payment, but is also offered a settlement discount of 2% for payment within 10 days of the invoice date.

    X will issue an invoice to Y for £5,000 when the goods are sold. At this point in time, X has no idea whether or not Y will take advantage of the discount. In trading terms, and in terms of the amount charged in the invoice to Y, Y is a debtor for £5,000. If Y subsequently decides to take the discount, he will pay £5,000 less 2% - ie £4,900 - ten days later.

17. The discount allowed (£100) is accounted for as follows.

    (a) In the *trading account*, sales will be valued at their full invoice price.

    (b) In the *profit and loss account*, the discount allowed will be shown as an expense (either as a selling expense or as a finance expense, although it was listed as a selling expense in an earlier chapter of this text).

18. In our example, we would have:

	£
Sales (trading account)	5,000
Discounts allowed (P & L account)	(100)
Net sales	4,900

Cash discounts allowed are accounted for in exactly the same way as settlement discounts.

Discounts: example

19. You are required to prepare the trading, profit and loss account of Seesaw Timber Merchants for the year ended 31 March 19X6, given the following information.

	£
Goods in stock, 1 April 19X5	18,000
Purchases at gross cost	120,000
Trade discounts received	4,000
Cash and settlement discounts received	1,500
Goods in stock, 31 March 19X6	25,000
Cash sales	34,000
Credit sales at invoice price	150,000
Cash and settlement discounts allowed	8,000
Selling expenses	32,000
Administrative expenses	40,000
Drawings by proprietor, Tim Burr	22,000

Solution

20.

SEESAW TIMBER MERCHANTS
TRADING, PROFIT AND LOSS ACCOUNT
FOR THE YEAR ENDED 31 MARCH 19X6

	£	£
Sales (note 1)		184,000
Opening stock	18,000	
Purchases (note 2)	116,000	
	134,000	
Less closing stock	25,000	
Cost of goods sold		109,000
Gross profit		75,000
Discounts received		1,500
		76,500
Expenses:		
Selling expenses	32,000	
Administrative expenses	40,000	
Discounts allowed	8,000	
		80,000
Net loss transferred to balance sheet		(3,500)

Note 1   £(34,000 + 150,000)
Note 2   £(120,000 - 4,000)
Note 3   Drawings are not an expense, but an *appropriation* of profit.

Bad debts

21. Customers who buy goods on credit might fail to pay for them, perhaps out of dishonesty or perhaps because they have gone bankrupt and cannot pay. Customers in another country might be prevented from paying by the unexpected introduction of new foreign exchange control restrictions by their country's government during the credit period.

For one reason or another, a business might decide to give up expecting payment and to write the debt off as a 'lost cause'.

Writing off bad debts

22. When a business decides that a particular debt is unlikely ever to be repaid, the amount of the debt should be 'written off' as an expense in the profit and loss account.

23. For example, if Alfred's Mini-Cab Service sends an invoice for £300 to a customer who subsequently does a 'moonlight flit' from his office premises, never to be seen or heard of again, the debt of £300 must be written off. It might seem sensible to record the business transaction as:

    Sales £(300 - 300) = £0.

24.
    > However, bad debts written off are accounted for as follows.
    >
    > (a) Sales are shown at their invoice value in the trading account. The sale has been made, and gross profit should be earned. The subsequent failure to collect the debt is a separate matter, which is reported in the P & L account.
    >
    > (b) Bad debts written off are shown as an expense in the profit and loss account.

25. In our example of Alfred's Mini-Cab Service:

	£
Sales (invoice in the trading account)	300
Bad debts written off (expenses in the P & L account)	300
Net value of sales	0

26. Obviously, when a debt is written off, the value of the debtor as a current asset falls to zero. If the debt is expected to be uncollectable, its net realisable value is nil, and so it has a zero balance sheet value.

Bad debts written off and subsequently paid

27.
    > A bad debt which has been written off might occasionally be unexpectedly paid. The only accounting problem to consider is when a debt written off as bad in one accounting period is subsequently paid in a later accounting period. The amount paid should be recorded as additional income in the profit and loss account of the period in which the payment is received.

28. For example, a trading profit and loss account for the Blacksmith's Forge for the year to 31 December 19X5 could be prepared as shown below from the following information:

	£
Stocks of goods in hand, 1 January 19X5	6,000
Purchases of goods	122,000
Stocks of goods in hand, 31 December 19X5	8,000
Cash sales	100,000
Credit sales	70,000
Discounts allowed	1,200
Discounts received	5,000
Bad debts written off	9,000
Debts paid in 19X5 which were previously written off as bad in 19X4	2,000
Other expenses	31,800

BLACKSMITH'S FORGE
TRADING PROFIT AND LOSS ACCOUNT FOR THE YEAR ENDED 31.12.19X5

	£	£
Sales		170,000
Opening stock	6,000	
Purchases	122,000	
	128,000	
Less closing stock	8,000	
Cost of goods sold		120,000
Gross profit		50,000
Add: discounts received		5,000
debts paid, previously written off as bad		2,000
		57,000
Expenses:		
Discounts allowed	1,200	
Bad debts written off	9,000	
Other expenses	31,800	
		42,000
Net profit		15,000

A provision for doubtful debts

29. When bad debts are written off, specific debts owed to the business are identified as unlikely ever to be collected.

A business might well be aware, however, of the risks involved in selling goods on credit, and it might accept that a certain percentage of its outstanding debts at any time are unlikely to be collected. But although it might be estimated that, say, 5% of debts will turn out bad, the business will not know until later which specific debts are bad.

30. Suppose that a business commences operations on 1 July 19X4, and in the twelve months to 30 June 19X5 makes sales of £300,000 (all on credit) and writes off bad debts amounting to £6,000. Cash received from customers during the year is £244,000, so that at 30 June 19X5, the business has outstanding debtors of £50,000.

	£
Credit sales during the year	300,000
Add debtors at 1 July 19X4	0
Total debts owed to the business	300,000
Less cash received from credit customers	244,000
	56,000
Less bad debts written off	6,000
Debtors outstanding at 30 June 19X5	50,000

Now, some of these outstanding debts might turn out to be bad. The business does not know on 30 June 19X5 which specific debts in the total £50,000 owed will be bad, but it might guess (from experience perhaps) that 5% of debts will eventually be found to be bad.

31. When a business expects bad debts amongst its current debtors, but does not yet know which specific debts will be bad, it can make a provision for doubtful debts.

32.

> A 'provision' is a 'providing for' and so a provision for doubtful debts provides for future bad debts, as a *prudent* precaution by the business. The business will be more likely to avoid claiming profits which subsequently fail to materialise because some debts turn out to be bad.
>
> (a)   When a provision is first made, the amount of this initial provision is charged as an expense in the profit and loss account of the business, for the period in which the provision is created.
>
> (b)   When a provision already exists, but is subsequently increased in size, the amount of the *increase* in provision is charged as an expense in the profit and loss account, for the period in which the increased provision is made.
>
> (c)   When a provision already exists, but is subsequently reduced in size, the amount of the *decrease* in provision is recorded as an item of 'income' in the profit and loss account, for the period in which the reduction in provision is made.

33. The *balance sheet,* as well as the profit and loss account of a business, must be adjusted to show a provision for doubtful debts. The value of debtors in the balance sheet must be shown after deducting the provision for doubtful debts. This is because the net realisable value of all the debtors of the business is estimated to be less than their 'sales value'. After all, this is the reason for making the provision in the first place.

> The net realisable value of debtors is the total value of debtors minus the provision for doubtful debts.

34. In the example above in paragraph 30 the newly created provision for doubtful debts at 30 June 19X5 will be 5% of £50,000 = £2,500. This means that although total debtors are £50,000, eventual payment of only £47,500 is expected.

(a)   In the P & L account, the newly created provision of £2,500 will be shown as an expense.

(b)   In the balance sheet, debtors will be shown as:

	£
Total debtors at 30 June 19X5	50,000
Less provision for doubtful debts	2,500
	47,500

Example: provision for doubtful debts

35. Corin Flakes owns and runs the Aerobic Health Foods Shop in Dundee. He commenced trading on 1 January 19X1, selling health foods to customers, most of whom make use of a credit facility that Corin offers. (Customers are allowed to purchase up to £200 of goods on credit but must repay a certain proportion of their outstanding debt every month.)

This credit system gives rise to a large number of bad debts, and Corin Flake's results for his first three years of operations are as follows:

Year to 31 December 19X1
Gross profit	£27,000
Bad debts written off	£ 8,000
Debts owed by customers as at 31 December 19X1	£40,000
Provision for doubtful debts	2½% of outstanding debtors
Other expenses	£20,000

Year to 31 December 19X2
Gross profit	£45,000
Bad debts written off	£10,000
Debts owed by customers as at 31 December 19X2	£50,000
Provision for doubtful debts	2½% of outstanding debtors
Other expenses	£28,750

Year to 31 December 19X3
Gross profit	£60,000
Bad debts written off	£11,000
Debts owed by customers as at 31 December 19X3	£30,000
Provision for doubtful debts	3% of outstanding debtors
Other expenses	£32,850

Required: for each of these three years, prepare the profit and loss account of the business, and state the value of debtors appearing in the balance sheet as at 31 December each year.

Solution

36.
AEROBIC HEALTH FOOD SHOP
PROFIT AND LOSS ACCOUNTS
FOR THE YEARS ENDED 31 DECEMBER

	19X1		*19X2*		*19X3*	
	£	£	£	£	£	£
Gross profit		27,000		45,000		60,000
Reduction in provision for doubtful debts*						350
						60,350
Expenses:						
Bad debts written off	8,000		10,000		11,000	
Increase in provision for doubtful debts*	1,000		250		–	
Other expenses	20,000		28,750		32,850	
		29,000		39,000		43,850
Net(loss)/profit		(2,000)		6,000		16,500

*At 1 January 19X1 when Corin began trading the provision for doubtful debts was nil. At 31 December 19X1 the provision required was 2½% of £40,000 = £1,000. The increase in the provision is therefore £1,000. At 31 December 19X2 the provision required was 2½% of £50,000 = £1,250. The 19X1 provision must therefore be increased by £250. At 31 December 19X3 the provision required is 3% x £30,000 = £900. The 19X2 provision is therefore reduced by £350.

VALUE OF DEBTORS IN THE BALANCE SHEET

	As at 31/12/X1 £	As at 31/12/X2 £	As at 31/12/X3 £
Total value of debtors	40,000	50,000	30,000
Less provision for doubtful debts	1,000	1,250	900
Balance sheet value	39,000	48,750	29,100

Other provisions

37. A provision for doubtful debts is not the only type of provision you will come across in accounting. The Companies Act 1985 defines a provision as 'any amount written off or retained by way of providing for depreciation, renewals or diminution in value of assets or retained by way of providing for any known liability of which the amount cannot be determined with substantial accuracy'.

38. For most businesses, by far the largest provision in their accounts is the provision for depreciation which is described in the next chapter.

Exercise: preparing a trading, profit and loss account and balance sheet

39. You should now try to use what you have learned to attempt a solution to the following exercise.

The financial affairs of Newbegin Tools prior to the commencement of trading were as follows:

NEWBEGIN TOOLS
BALANCE SHEET AS AT 1 AUGUST 19X5

	£	£	£
Fixed assets			
Motor vehicle		2,000	
Shop fittings		3,000	
			5,000
Current assets			
Stocks		12,000	
Cash		1,000	
		13,000	
Current liabilities			
Bank overdraft	2,000		
Trade creditors	4,000		
		6,000	
Net current assets			7,000
			12,000
Financed by			
Capital			12,000

At the end of six months the business had made the following transactions.

(a) Purchases of goods were made on credit at a gross amount of £10,000.

(b) Trade discount received was 2% on this gross amount and there was a settlement discount received of 5% on settling debts to suppliers of £8,000. These were the only payments to suppliers in the period.

(c) Closing stocks of goods were valued at £5,450.

(d) Cash sales and credit sales together totalled £27,250.

(e) Outstanding debtors balances at 31 January 19X6 amounted to £3,250 of which £250 were to be written off.

(f) A further provision for doubtful debts is to be made amounting to 2% of the remaining outstanding debtors.

(g) Cash payments were made in respect of the following expenses:

(i)	stationery, postage and wrapping	£500
(ii)	telephone charges	£200
(iii)	electricity	£600
(iv)	cleaning and refreshments	£150

(h) Cash drawings by the proprietor, Alf Newbegin, amounted to £6,000.

(i) The outstanding overdraft balance as at 1 August 19X5 was paid off. Interest charges and bank charges on the overdraft amounted to £40.

Alf Newbegin knew the balance of cash on hand at 31 January 19X6 but he wanted to know if the business had made a profit for the six months that it had been trading, and so he asked his friend, Harry Oldhand, if he could tell him.

Required: prepare the trading, profit and loss account of Newbegin Tools for the six months to 31 January 19X6 and a balance sheet as at that date.

6: DISCOUNTS, BAD DEBTS AND PROVISIONS

Solution

40. The trading, profit and loss account should be fairly straightforward.

NEWBEGIN TOOLS
TRADING AND PROFIT AND LOSS ACCOUNT
FOR THE SIX MONTHS ENDED 31 JANUARY 19X6

	£	£
Sales		27,250
Opening stocks	12,000	
Purchases (note 1)	9,800	
	21,800	
Less closing stocks	5,450	
Cost of goods sold		16,350
Gross profit		10,900
Discounts received (note 2)		400
		11,300
Expenses		
Sales and distribution:		
Electricity	600	
Stationery, postage and wrapping	500	
Bad debts written off	250	
Provision for doubtful debts (note)	60	
Administration:		
Telephone charges	200	
Cleaning and refreshments	150	
Finance charges:		
Interest and bank charges	40	
		1,800
Net profit		9,500

Notes:
1. Purchases at cost £10,000 less 2% trade discount.
2. 5% of £8,000 = £400
3. 2% of £3,000 = £60.

The preparation of a balance sheet is not so easy, because we must calculate the value of creditors and cash in hand.

(a) *Creditors as at 31 January 19X6*
The amount owing to creditors is the sum of the amount owing at the beginning of the period, plus the cost of purchases during the period (net of all discounts), less the payments already made for purchases. If you think carefully about this, you should see that this calculation is logical. What is still owed is the total amount of costs incurred less payments already made.

	£
Creditors as at 1 August 19X5	4,000
Add purchases during the period, net of trade discount	9,800
	13,800
Less settlement discounts received	(400)
	13,400
Less payments to creditors during the period*	(7,600)
Creditors as at 31 January 19X6	5,800

* £8,000 less settlement discount of £400.

90

(b) *Cash at bank and in hand at 31 January 19X6*
This too requires a fairly lengthy calculation. You need to identify cash payments received and cash payments made.

		£
(i)	*Cash received from sales*	
	Total sales in the period	27,250
	Add debtors as at 1 August 19X5	0
		27,250
	Less unpaid debts as at 31 January 19X6	3,250
	Cash received	24,000

(ii)	*Cash paid*	
	Trade creditors (see (a))	7,600
	Stationery, postage and wrapping	500
	Telephone charges	200
	Electricity	600
	Cleaning and refreshments	150
	Bank charges and interest	40
	Bank overdraft repaid	2,000
	Drawings by proprietor	6,000
		17,090

Note: it is easy to forget some of these payments, especially drawings. When you have to work through a mass of information like this, it helps to tick each item off as you go along.

(iii)	Cash in hand at 1 August 19X5	1,000
	Cash received in the period	24,000
		25,000
	Cash paid in the period	(17,090)
	Cash at bank and in hand as at 31 January 19X6	7,910

(c) When bad debts are written off, the value of outstanding debtors must be reduced by the amount written off. This is because the debtors are no longer expected to pay, and it would be misleading to show them in the balance sheet as current assets of the business for which cash payment is expected within one year. Debtors in the balance sheet will be valued at £3,000 less the provision for doubtful debts of £60 - ie at £2,940.

(d) Fixed assets should be depreciated. However, in this exercise depreciation has been ignored.

NEWBEGIN TOOLS
BALANCE SHEET AS AT 31 JANUARY 19X6

	£	£
Fixed assets		
Motor vehicles	2,000	
Shop fittings	3,000	
		5,000
Current assets		
Stocks	5,450	
Debtors	2,940	
Cash	7,910	
		16,300
		21,300
Current liabilities		
Trade creditors		(5,800)
		15,500
		£
Financed by		
Capital at 1 August 19X5		12,000
Net profit for the period		9,500
		21,500
Less drawings		6,000
Capital at 31 January 19X6		15,500

The bank overdraft has now been repaid and is therefore not shown.

Conclusion to the exercise

41. You may well have found this exercise quite difficult at this stage. If you did, try not to worry. Practice makes perfect. However, trace all the figures in the balance sheet or trading profit and loss account, either to the information given at the beginning of the exercise, or to the workings shown above.

Summary of the chapter

42. In this chapter and the previous chapter, a number of accounting problems and techniques for calculating profit (and the values of assets and liabilities for the balance sheet) have been introduced.

- Trade discounts received are deducted from the cost of purchases. Trade discounts allowed are deducted from the value of sales. Cash and settlement discounts received are included as 'other income' of the period in the profit and loss account. Similarly, cash and settlement discounts allowed are shown as expenses in the profit and loss account.

- Bad debts written off are an expense in the profit and loss account.

- An increase in the provision for doubtful debts is an expense in the profit and loss account whereas a decrease in the provision for doubtful debts is shown as 'other income' in the P & L account.

- Debtors are valued in the balance sheet after deducting any provision for doubtful debts.

Definitions

43.
- Trade discount is a reduction in the catalogue price of an article, given by a wholesaler or manufacturer to a retailer. It is often given in return for bulk purchase orders.

- Cash discount is a reduction in the amount payable for the purchase of goods or services in return for payment in cash rather than taking credit.

- Settlement discount is a reduction in the amount payable for the purchase of goods or services in return for prompt payment within an agreed credit period.

- Bad debts are specific debts owed to a business which it decides are never going to be paid.

- Doubtful debts are debts which might become bad in the future, but are not yet bad.

- A *provision* is an amount written off to provide for depreciation or the fall in value of an asset, or to provide for any known liability of uncertain value. The amount is written off by:

  (a) charging the amount of the extra provision as an expense in the P & L account, and also;

  (b) reducing the value of the asset in the balance sheet by the amount of the provision.

TEST YOUR KNOWLEDGE

Numbers in brackets refer to paragraphs of this chapter

1. Distinguish between trade discount, cash discount and settlement discount. (5-7)

2. How is cash discount treated for accounting purposes? (13)

3. How are bad debts treated for accounting purposes? (24)

4. A decrease in the provision for doubtful debts is recorded as an expense in the profit and loss account. True or false? (32)

5. How is a provision for doubtful debts disclosed in the balance sheet? (34)

Chapter 7

FIXED ASSETS: DEPRECIATION, REVALUATION AND DISPOSAL

The purpose of this chapter is:

- to define and explain the process of depreciation

- to illustrate two different methods of calculating depreciation (the straight line method and the reducing balance method)

- to explain the accounting treatment of revaluations and disposals of fixed assets

---

Introduction

1. A fixed asset is acquired for use within a business with a view to earning profits. Its life extends over more than one accounting period, and so it earns profits over more than one period.

2. With the exception of land held on freehold or very long leasehold, every fixed asset eventually wears out over time. Machines, cars and other vehicles, fixtures and fittings, and even buildings do not last for ever. When a business acquires a fixed asset, it will have some idea about how long its useful life will be, and it might be decided either:

    (a) to keep on using the fixed asset until it becomes completely worn out, useless, and worthless; or
    (b) to sell off the fixed asset at the end of its useful life, either by selling it as a second-hand item or as scrap.

3. Since a fixed asset has a cost, and a limited useful life, and its value eventually declines, it follows that a charge should be made in the trading, profit and loss account to reflect the use that is made of the asset by the business. This charge is called depreciation.

Definition of depreciation

4. Suppose that a business buys a machine for £40,000. Its expected life is four years, and at the end of that time it is expected to be worthless.

5. Since the fixed asset is used to make profits for four years, it would be reasonable to charge the cost of the asset over those four years (perhaps by charging £10,000 per annum) so that at the end of the four years the total cost of £40,000 would have been charged against profits.

6. Indeed, one way of defining depreciation is to describe it as a means of spreading the cost of a fixed asset over its useful life, and so matching the cost against the full period during which it earns profits for the business. Depreciation charges are an example of the application of the accruals concept to calculate profits.

7. A better definition of depreciation is given by statement of standard accounting practice 12 (SSAP 12) *Accounting for depreciation.*

   'Depreciation is the measure of the wearing out, consumption or other reduction in the useful economic life of a fixed asset, whether arising from use, (passage of) time or obsolesence through technological or market changes. Depreciation should be allocated so as to charge a fair proportion of cost or valuation of the asset to each accounting period expected to benefit from its use.'

   (*Note:* as mentioned in an earlier chapter, statements of standard accounting practice are issued by the professional accounting bodies to standardise accounting practice in areas where various procedures would be theoretically possible. They do not have the force of law but members of the professional bodies are expected to comply with their requirements when preparing accounts.)

8. This definition makes two important points:

   (a) depreciation is a measure of the wearing out of a fixed asset through use, time or obsolescence;
   (b) depreciation charges should be spread fairly over a fixed asset's life, and so allocated to the accounting periods which are expected to benefit (ie make profits) from the asset's use.

   (*Note:* 'amortisation' means writing off and is therefore another term which represents depreciation. A 'wasting asset' is a fixed asset which wastes away through use, and the term is applied to mines, which are depleted both physically and in value as their resources are dug out and taken away.)

The total charge for depreciation

9. The total amount to be charged against profits over the life of a fixed asset (*the depreciable amount*) is usually its cost less any expected *residual* sales value or disposal value at the end of the asset's life.

   (a) A fixed asset costing £20,000 which has an expected life of five years and an expected residual value of nil should be depreciated by £20,000 in total over the five year period.

   (b) A fixed asset costing £20,000 which has an expected life of five years and an expected residual value of £3,000 should be depreciated by £17,000 in total over the five year period.

Depreciation in the accounts of a business

10. When a fixed asset is depreciated, two things must be accounted for.

   (a) The charge for depreciation is a cost or expense of the accounting period. For the time being, we shall charge depreciation as an expense in the profit and loss account.

   (b) At the same time, the cost of the asset is being written off, and so the value of the fixed asset in the balance sheet must be reduced by the amount of depreciation charged. The balance sheet value of the fixed asset will be its *net book value* which is the value net of depreciation in the books of account of the business.

11. The amount of depreciation deducted from the cost of a fixed asset to arrive at its net book value will build up (or 'accumulate') over time, as more depreciation is charged in each successive accounting period. This accumulated depreciation is a 'provision' because it provides for the fall in value of the fixed asset. The term 'provision for depreciation' refers to the 'accumulated depreciation' of a fixed asset.

12. For example, if a fixed asset costing £40,000 has an expected life of four years and an estimated residual value of nil, it might be depreciated by £10,000 per annum.

	Depreciation charge for the year (P & L a/c) (A) £	Accumulated depreciation at end of year (B) £	Cost of the asset (C) £	Net book value at end of year (C-B) £
At beginning of its life	–	–	40,000	40,000
Year 1	10,000	10,000	40,000	30,000
Year 2	10,000	20,000	40,000	20,000
Year 3	10,000	30,000	40,000	10,000
Year 4	10,000	40,000	40,000	0
	40,000			

At the end of year 4, the full £40,000 of depreciation charges have been made in the profit and loss accounts of the four years. The net book value of the fixed asset is now nil. In theory (although perhaps not in practice) the business will no longer use the fixed asset, which would now need replacing.

Methods of depreciation

13. There are several different depreciation methods. Of these, the most commonly used are:

   (a) the straight line method;
   (b) the reducing balance method;
   (c) the machine hour method;
   (d) the sum of the digits method.

The straight line method

14. This is the most commonly used method of all. The total depreciable amount is charged in equal instalments to each accounting period over the expected useful life of the asset. (In this way, the net book value of the fixed asset declines at a steady rate, or in a 'straight line' over time.)

15.

> The annual straight line depreciation charge is calculated as:
>
> $$\frac{\text{Cost of asset minus residual value}}{\text{Expected useful life of the asset}}$$

Example: straight line depreciation

16. (a) A fixed asset costing £20,000 with an estimated life of 10 years and no residual value would be depreciated at the rate of:

$$\frac{£20,000}{10 \text{ years}} = £2,000 \text{ per annum}$$

(b) A fixed asset costing £60,000 has an estimated life of 5 years and a residual value of £7,000. The annual depreciation charge using the straight line method would be:

$$\frac{£(60,000 - 7,000)}{5 \text{ years}} = £10,600 \text{ per annum}$$

The net book value of the fixed asset would be:

	After 1 year £	After 2 years £	After 3 years £	After 4 years £	After 5 years £
Cost of the asset	60,000	60,000	60,000	60,000	60,000
Accumulated depreciation	10,600	21,200	31,800	42,400	53,000
Net book value	49,400	38,800	28,200	17,600	7,000 *

* ie its estimated residual value.

17. Since the depreciation charge per annum is the same amount every year with the straight line method, it is often convenient to state that depreciation is charged at the rate of x per cent per annum on the cost of the asset. In the example in paragraph 16(a) above, the depreciation charge per annum is 10% of cost (ie 10% of £20,000 = £2,000).

Examination questions often describe straight line depreciation in this way.

18. The straight line method of depreciation is a fair allocation of the total depreciable amount between the different accounting periods, provided that it is reasonable to assume that the business enjoys equal benefits from the use of the asset in every period throughout its life.

Assets acquired in the middle of an accounting period

19. A business will purchase new fixed assets at any time during the course of an accounting period, and so it might seem fair to charge an amount for depreciation in the period when the purchase occurs which reflects the limited amount of use the business has had from the asset in that period.

Example

20. Suppose that a business which has an accounting year which runs from 1 January to 31 December purchases a new fixed asset on 1 April 19X1, at a cost of £24,000. The expected life of the asset is 4 years, and its residual value is nil.

What should be the depreciation charge for 19X1?

Solution

21. The annual depreciation charge will be $\dfrac{24,000}{4 \text{ years}}$ = £6,000 per annum

However, since the asset was acquired on 1 April 19X1, the business has only benefited from the use of the asset for 9 months instead of a full 12 months. It would therefore seem fair to charge depreciation in 19X1 of only

$$\tfrac{9}{12} \times £6,000 = £4,500$$

22. If an examination question gives you the purchase date of a fixed asset, which is in the middle of an accounting period, you should generally assume that depreciation should be calculated in this way, as a 'part-year' amount. However:

(a) you will only be given such a problem when the straight line method of depreciation is used; and

(b) in practice, many businesses ignore the niceties of part-year depreciation, and charge a full year's depreciation on fixed assets in the year of their purchase, regardless of the time of year they were acquired.

The reducing balance method

23.
> The reducing balance method of depreciation calculates the annual depreciation charge as a fixed percentage of the net book value of the asset, as at the end of the previous accounting period.

24. For example, suppose that a business purchases a fixed asset at a cost of £10,000. Its expected useful life is 3 years and its estimated residual value is £2,160. The business wishes to use the reducing balance method to depreciate the asset, and calculates that the rate of depreciation should be 40% of the reducing (net book) value of the asset. (The method of deciding that 40% is a suitable annual percentage is a problem of mathematics, not financial accounting, and is not described here.)

The total depreciable amount is £(10,000 - 2,160) = £7,840.

The depreciation charge per annum and the net book value of the asset as at the end of each year will be as follows:

	£		Accumulated depreciation £
Asset at cost	10,000		
Depreciation in year 1 (40%)	4,000	4,000	
Net book value at end of year 1	6,000		
Depreciation in year 2			
(40% of reducing balance)	2,400	6,400	(4,000 + 2,400)
Net book value at end of year 2	3,600		
Depreciation in year 3 (40%)	1,440	7,840	(6,400 + 1,440)
Net book value at end of year 3	2,160		

25. You should note that with the reducing balance method, the annual charge for depreciation is higher in the earlier years of the asset's life, and lower in the later years. In the example above, the annual charges for years 1,2 and 3 are £4,000, £2,400 and £1,440 respectively.

26. The reducing balance method might therefore be used when it is considered fair to allocate a greater proportion of the total depreciable amount to the earlier years and a lower proportion to later years, on the assumption that the benefits obtained by the business from using the asset decline over time.

The machine hour method of depreciation

27. As the name of this method implies, it is a method of depreciation which might be considered suitable for plant and machinery, where it is assumed that the fixed asset wears out through use rather than over time. Instead of calculating a depreciation charge relating to a period of time, depreciation is calculated according to the number of hours of use made of the machine by the business during the course of the period.

28. The life of the asset is estimated in hours (or miles or other conventional units) and each unit is given a money value for depreciation purposes. The rate of depreciation is calculated as:

$$\frac{\text{Cost of the asset minus estimated residual value}}{\text{Estimated useful life of the asset in hours of used time}}$$

Example: the machine hour method

29. A business purchases a machine at a cost of £45,000. Its estimated useful life is 8,000 hours of running time, and its estimated residual value is £5,000.

The rate of depreciation by the machine hour method will be:

$$\frac{£(45,000 - 5,000)}{8,000 \text{ hours}} = £5 \text{ per machine hour}$$

30. Suppose that the actual use of the machine each year is:

	Hours
Year 1	3,000
Year 2	1,500
Year 3	2,500
Year 4	1,000
	8,000

We can calculate the annual depreciation charge and net book value of the machine as at the end of each year as follows:

Year	*Depreciation charge in the P & L account of the year*	*Accumulated depreciation as at end of the year*	*Fixed asset at cost*	*Net book value as at end of the year*
	£	£	£	£
Start of life			45,000	45,000
Year 1 (3,000 x £5)	15,000	15,000	45,000	30,000
Year 2 (1,500 x £5)	7,500	22,500	45,000	22,500
Year 3 (2,500 x £5)	12,500	35,000	45,000	10,000
Year 4 (1,000 x £5)	5,000	40,000	45,000	5,000
	40,000			

Sum-of-the-digits method

31. This method of depreciation is similar to the reducing balance method, in the sense that it is considered fair to charge higher amounts of depreciation in the earlier years of an asset's life, and lesser amounts in later years. It differs from the reducing balance because the mathematics for working out the appropriate depreciation charge each year are more simple. The method is perhaps best explained using an example.

32. A business purchases a delivery van at a cost of £8,000. The van has an expected useful life of four years, after which it will be sold off for an estimated £1,500. The fixed asset should be depreciated using the sum-of-the-digits method. The 'digits' are 1,2,3 and 4 because the asset has a four year life. The highest digit refers to year 1, the next highest to year 2 etc and the lowest digit (which is always 1) relates to the final year of the asset's life.

Year	*Digits*
1	4
2	3
3	2
4	1
Sum of the digits	10

33. The sum of the digits is used to calculate a 'weighted' depreciation charge each year, as follows:

$$\frac{\text{Cost of the asset minus estimated residual value}}{\text{Sum of the digits}}$$

34. In this example, we have $\dfrac{£(8,000 - 1,500)}{10} = £650$ per digit

    The depreciation charge for each year is calculated by multiplying the number of digits for that year by the depreciation charge per digit.

Year	Digits		Depreciation charge
1	4	(x £650)	2,600
2	3	(x £650)	1,950
3	2	(x £650)	1,300
4	1	(x £650)	650
Accumulated depreciation over 4 years			6,500

Which method of depreciation should be used?

35. A business is faced with a choice between the various methods of depreciation for its different types of fixed assets. (A different method can be used for each type of asset, such as buildings, machinery, motor vehicles etc.) The method chosen, however, must be fair in allocating the charges between different accounting periods.

36. The following guidelines should be used in selecting the most suitable method.

    (a) A fair charge to each accounting period will be one which allocates costs in proportion to the amount of benefits, profits or revenues earned during each accounting period by the asset. These 'profits' almost certainly cannot be calculated exactly, but the business should be able to decide whether:

       (i) the asset provides great benefits in the earlier years of its life (in which case the reducing balance method might be suitable); or

       (ii) the asset provides equal benefits to each period throughout its life (in which case the straight line method would be suitable).

    (b) The costs of using an asset include both depreciation and also repairs and maintenance. If an asset provides equal benefits to each accounting period throughout its life, but has significantly increasing repairs and maintenance costs as it gets older, it might be appropriate to use the reducing balance method of depreciation, in order to even out the combined costs per annum of depreciation, repairs and maintenance.

       For example, the reducing balance method might be used for company cars, since car repairs increase as cars get older. In the illustration below depreciation is charged as one third of the reducing balance.

       All the figures below are for illustrative purposes only.

Cost of asset	£8,100
Estimated life	3 years

	Depreciation (A)	Net book value at end of year	Repair costs (B)	Sum of depreciation and repairs (A+B)
	£	£	£	£
Year 1 ($\frac{1}{3}$ of £8,100)	2,700	5,400	100	2,800
Year 2 ($\frac{1}{3}$ of £5,400)	1,800	3,600	800	2,600
Year 3 ($\frac{1}{3}$ of £3,600)	1,200	2,400	1,500	2,700

In this hypothetical example, use of the reducing balance method succeeds in arriving at a roughly equal annual cost for depreciation and repairs combined.

(c) The method of depreciation used by a business for any fixed asset should be the same as the method used for similar assets.

(d) The method of depreciation used should be one which is easy to apply in practice. There is no point in creating unnecessary complexities.

37. The straight line method, as mentioned earlier, is by far the most common method used in practice. It is easy to use, and it is generally fair to assume that all periods benefit more or less equally from the use of a fixed asset throughout its useful life.

A fall in the value of a fixed asset

38.
> When the 'market' value of a fixed asset falls so that it is worth less than the amount of its net book value, the asset should be written down to its new low market value. The charge in the profit and loss account for the diminution in the value of an asset during the accounting period should then be:
>
> Net book value at the beginning of the period
> Less: new reduced value
> Equals: the charge for the diminution in the asset's value in the period.
>
> This is an example of the prudence concept: the loss suffered by the business is recognised in the accounts as soon as it is foreseen.

Example: fall in asset value

39. A business purchased a leasehold property on 1 January 19X1 at a cost of £100,000. The lease has a 20 year life. After 5 years' use, on 31 December 19X5, the business decides that since property prices have fallen sharply, the leasehold is now worth only £60,000, and that the value of the asset should be reduced in the accounts of the business.

The leasehold was being amortised at the rate of 5% per annum on cost.

40. Before the asset is reduced in value, the annual depreciation charge is:

$\frac{£100,000}{20 \text{ years}}$ = £5,000 per annum (= 5% of £100,000)

After 5 years, the accumulated depreciation would be £25,000, and the net book value of the leasehold £75,000, which is £15,000 more than the new asset value. This £15,000 should be written off as a charge for depreciation or fall in the asset's value in year 5, so that the total charge in year 5 is:

Net book value of the leasehold after 4 years (£100,000 - 20,000)	80,000
Revised asset value at end of year 5	60,000
Charge against profit in year 5	20,000

An alternative method of calculation is:

	£
'Normal' depreciation charge per annum	5,000
Further fall in value, from net book value at end of year 5 to revised value	15,000
Charge against profit in year 5	20,000

41. The leasehold has a further 15 years to run, and its value is now £60,000. From year 6 to year 20, the annual charge for depreciation will be:

$$\frac{£60,000}{15 \text{ years}} = £4,000 \text{ per annum}$$

The revaluation of fixed assets

42. Because of inflation, it is now quite common for the market value of certain fixed assets to go up, in spite of getting older. The most obvious example of rising market values is land and buildings (both freehold and leasehold).

A business which owns fixed assets which are rising in value is not obliged to revalue those assets in its balance sheet. However, in order to give a more 'true and fair view' of the position of the business, it might be decided that some fixed assets should be revalued upwards; otherwise the total value of the assets of the business might seem unrealistically low. When this is done, the resulting accounts are referred to as modified historical cost accounts. The use of modified historical cost accounts was mentioned in an earlier chapter as one method of dealing with the accounting problems posed by inflation.

43. | When fixed assets are revalued, depreciation should be charged on the revalued amount.

Example: the revaluation of fixed assets

44. When Ira Vann commenced trading as a car hire dealer on 1 January 19X1, he purchased business premises freehold at a cost of £50,000.

For the purpose of accounting for depreciation, he decided that:

(a) the freehold land part of the business premises was worth £20,000 and would not be depreciated;

(b) the building part of the business premises was worth the remaining £30,000 and would be depreciated by the straight-line method to a nil residual value over 30 years.

After five years of trading on 1 January 19X6, Ira decides that his business premises are now worth £150,000, divided into:

	£
Land	75,000
Building	75,000
	150,000

He estimates that the building still has a further 25 years of useful life remaining.

Required: calculate the annual charge for depreciation in each of the 30 years of its life, and the balance sheet value of the land and building as at the end of each year.

Solution

45. Before the revaluation, the annual depreciation charge is £1,000 per annum on the building. This charge is made in each of the first five years of the asset's life.

The net book value of the asset will decline by £1,000 per annum, to:

(a) £49,000 as at 31.12.X1;
(b) £48,000 as at 31.12.X2;
(c) £47,000 as at 31.12.X3;
(d) £46,000 as at 31.12.X4;
(e) £45,000 as at 31.12.X5.

46. When the revaluation takes place, the amount of the revaluation is:

	£
New asset value	150,000
Net book value as at end of 19X5	45,000
Amount of revaluation	105,000

The asset will be revalued by £105,000 to £150,000. If you remember the accounting equation, that the total value of assets must be equalled by the total value of capital and liabilities, you should recognise that if assets go up in value by £105,000, capital or liabilities must also go up by the same amount. Since the increased value benefits the owners of the business, the amount of the revaluation is added to capital.

In the accounts of limited companies, the amount of the revaluation is added to a 'revaluation reserve' which is a part of the shareholders' capital but identified separately in the balance sheet of the company.

47. After the revaluation, depreciation will be charged on the building at a new rate of:

$$\frac{£75,000}{25 \text{ years}} = £3,000 \text{ per annum}$$

The net book value of the property will then fall by £3,000 per annum over 25 years, from £150,000 as at 1 January 19X6 to only £75,000 at the end of the 25 years - ie the building part of the property value will have been fully depreciated.

48. The revaluation of fixed assets is more likely to be made in the accounts of a limited company

than a sole trader because a company's management might need to inform its shareholders what the assets of the business are worth, whereas a sole trader should be aware of this information without the need to amend his balance sheet.

A change in the remaining expected life of an asset

49. The depreciation charge on a fixed asset depends not only on the cost (or value) of the asset and its estimated residual value, but also on its estimated useful life.

50. Suppose, however, that a business purchased a fixed asset costing £12,000 with an estimated life of four years and no residual value. If it used the straight line method of depreciation, it would make an annual provision of 25% of £12,000 = £3,000.

    Now what would happen if the business decided after two years that the useful life of the asset has been underestimated, and it still had five more years in use to come (making its total life seven years)?

    For the first two years, the asset would have been depreciated by £3,000 per annum, so that its net book value after two years would be £(12,000 - 6,000) = £6,000. If the remaining life of the asset is now revised to five more years, the remaining amount to be depreciated (here £6,000) should be spread over the remaining life, giving an annual depreciation charge for the final five years of:

$$\frac{\text{Net book value at time of life readjustment, minus residual value}}{\text{New estimate of remaining useful life}}$$

$$= \frac{£6,000}{5 \text{ years}} = £1,200 \text{ per annum}$$

Depreciation is not a cash expense

51. Depreciation spreads the cost of a fixed asset (less its estimated residual value) over the asset's life. The *cash* payment for the fixed asset will be made when, or soon after, the asset is purchased. Annual depreciation of the asset in subsequent years is not a cash expense – rather it allocates costs to those later years for a cash payment that has occurred previously.

52. It is sometimes (incorrectly) suggested that since depreciation reduces profit, but does not take cash out of the business, it is a way of keeping cash inside the business to provide for the eventual replacement of the asset at the end of its life.

53. If you are confused by this idea, a numerical example might help to explain it.

    Edward Rochester purchased some shop fittings for his antique goods store, 'Chain Hairlooms'. They cost £6,000 and had an expected life of three years with no residual value. He earned a net profit before depreciation of £20,000 per annum for each of these years, and it was his policy to take out all his net profit each year in drawings. He uses the straight line method of depreciation.

For the three years of the life of the shop fittings, the situation was as follows:

	Profit before depreciation	Depreciation	Net profit	Drawings	Retained profit
	£	£	£	£	£
Year 1	20,000	2,000	18,000	18,000	0
Year 2	20,000	2,000	18,000	18,000	0
Year 3	20,000	2,000	18,000	18,000	0
	60,000	6,000	54,000	54,000	0

54. If depreciation were not charged at all, net profit over the three year period would have totalled £60,000. Instead, the provision for depreciation reduced profit by £6,000, the cost of the asset, and so net profit and drawings were only £54,000. Since depreciation is not a cash expense, the effect of the provision has been to keep £6,000 of funds inside the business. Hence the suggestion that depreciation sets aside cash or funds for replacement of the asset (in this example £6,000) at the end of its life.

55. The suggestion is incorrect (and it is usually only ever made to provoke accountancy students into thinking harder about what depreciation is). It is a false suggestion for two reasons.

(a) A business will charge depreciation on fixed assets, but it will not set aside the same amount of cash in a bank account to provide for the replacement of the asset. Depreciation is not a way of saving for replacement assets.

(b) Depreciation allocates the purchase cost of a fixed asset over its life. At the end of its life, the asset might cost more to replace (because of inflation) or it might not be replaced at all, because a similar new asset might not be worth having. Even when a fixed asset will not be replaced, its purchase cost should still be charged as depreciation to accounting periods over its life.

Net book values are not a market valuation of the fixed asset

56. It is also tempting to suppose that the value of a fixed asset in the balance sheet of a business, at

(a) cost less accumulated depreciation; or at
(b) revalued amount less accumulated depreciation

should represent its current 'market value'.

Sometimes, fixed assets are valued at or close to their market price, especially in the case of land and buildings which, as we have seen already, are sometimes revalued (especially in the accounts of limited companies).

57. However, the general rule is that the net book value of a fixed asset is not necessarily remotely similar to the amount for which the business could sell off the fixed asset to a would-be purchaser. For example, if a printing business buys a new printing machine for £40,000, and expects it to have a five year life and no residual value, it might depreciate the machine by (20% of £40,000) £8,000 per annum. After one year, the net book value of the machine would be

£32,000 (£40,000 - £8,000). However, its sale value on the second-hand market after one year might be, say, £38,000. This does not matter. A net book value of £32,000, even when its market value is £38,000 is perfectly all right. After all, by the end of its life the full £40,000 of the asset's cost will have been charged against profit as depreciation, as intended. *It is not the purpose of depreciation to reduce the balance sheet net book value of an asset to its potential sell-off price.*

58. The importance of this point cannot be overstated. What it means is that if you were to look at the balance sheet of a business, the value given for its assets might bear no resemblance whatsoever to their market worth, neither individually as separate assets, nor collectively as a functioning business unit. This point was touched on in our discussion of the *going concern concept* in chapter 2.

59. However, when a net book value is significantly higher than its current 'market' value or 'realisable amount' the asset should be written down to this lower value at once, because it is prudent not to over-value fixed assets in the accounts. This procedure was described earlier in the chapter.

SSAP12 'Accounting for depreciation'

60. Statement of standard accounting practice 12 *Accounting for depreciation* has been mentioned already. It gives some guidelines on how to account for depreciation. The points of particular interest to you at this stage in your studies are as follows.

(a) A provision for depreciation should be made for fixed assets with a finite useful life, by allocating the cost (or revalued amount) less estimated residual values as fairly as possible to the periods expected to benefit from the use of the assets.

(b) When there is a revision of the estimated useful life of the asset, the remaining undepreciated amount should be charged over the revised remaining useful life.

(c) It is not appropriate to omit charging for depreciation when the market value of a fixed asset exceeds its current net book value. Instead, if required, the asset should be revalued and depreciation charged on the revalued amount.

(d) If at any time the net book value of a fixed asset exceeds the asset's estimated 'recoverable amount' it should be written down in value to this recoverable amount. Depreciation should subsequently be based on this revised value, over the remaining life of the asset.

(e) Freehold land does not have to be depreciated, but buildings should be. When an organisation has a freehold property, it should depreciate the building part of the property value, but not the land part. When property is revalued in the accounts, depreciation should be based on the revised value of the building. This means that an estimate must be made of the land element and building element in freehold property values.

7: FIXED ASSETS: DEPRECIATION, REVALUATION AND DISPOSAL

The disposal of fixed assets

61. Fixed assets are not purchased by a business with the intention of reselling them in the normal course of trade. However, they might be sold off at some stage during their life, either when their useful life is over, or before then. A business might decide to sell off a fixed asset long before its useful life has ended.

62. Whenever a business sells something, it will make a profit or a loss. When fixed assets are disposed of, there will be a profit or loss on disposal. Because it is a capital item being sold, the profit or loss will be a capital gain or a capital loss. These gains or losses are reported in the profit and loss account of the business (and not as a trading profit in the trading account). They are commonly referred to as 'profit on disposal of fixed asset' or 'loss on disposal'.

63. Examination questions on the disposal of fixed assets often ask for ledger accounts to be prepared, showing the entries in the accounts to record the disposal. Ledger accounts are described in the following chapters, and only the principles behind calculating the profit or loss on disposal of fixed assets are described here.

The principles behind calculating the profit or loss on disposal

64.
> The profit or loss on the disposal of a fixed asset is the difference between:
>
> (a) the net book value of the asset at the time of its sale; and
> (b) its net sale price, which is the price minus any costs of making the sale.
>
> A profit is made when the sale price exceeds the net book value, and a loss is made when the sale price is less than the net book value.

Example: disposal of a fixed asset

65. A business purchased a fixed asset on 1 January 19X1 for £25,000. It had an estimated life of six years and an estimated residual value of £7,000. The asset was eventually sold after three years on 1 January 19X4 to another trader who paid £17,500 for it.

   What was the profit or loss on disposal, assuming that the business uses the straight line method for depreciation?

Solution

66. Annual depreciation: $= \dfrac{£(25,000 - 7,000)}{6 \text{ years}}$

   $= £3,000 \text{ per annum}$

	£
Cost of the asset	25,000
Less accumulated depreciation (three years)	9,000
Net book value at date of disposal	16,000
Sale price	17,500
Profit on disposal	1,500

This profit will be shown in the profit and loss account of the business, where it will be an item of other income added to the gross profit brought down from the trading account.

Summary of the chapter

67.

- The cost of a fixed asset, less its estimated residual value, is allocated fairly between accounting periods by means of *depreciation*. The provision for depreciation is both:

  (a) charged against profit; and
  (b) deducted from the value of the fixed asset in the balance sheet.

- There are several different methods of depreciation, but the *straight line* method and the *reducing balance method* are most commonly used in practice. Every method described in this chapter allocates the total depreciable amount between accounting periods, although in different ways.

- When a fixed asset is *revalued*, depreciation is charged on the revalued amount.

- When a fixed asset is sold, there is likely to be a *profit or loss on disposal*. This is the difference between the net sale price of the asset and its net book value at the time of disposal.

Definition

Net book value means the cost or revalued amount of the asset, less accumulated depreciation.

TEST YOUR KNOWLEDGE

Numbers in brackets refer to paragraphs of this chapter

1. Define depreciation. (7)

2. What is the 'depreciable amount' of a fixed asset? (9)

3. Describe the method of calculating a depreciation charge under:
   (a) the straight line method. (15)
   (b) the reducing balance method. (24)

4. In the later years of an asset's life, depreciation charges are higher if the straight line method is used than if the reducing balance method is used. True or false? (25)

5. What effect does a change in an asset's estimated useful life have on the depreciation charge? (42)

6. The net book value of a fixed asset is intended to be an approximation of its market value. True or false? (49)

7. How is the profit or loss on disposal of a fixed asset calculated? (56)

Now try questions 1-3 at the end of this section

Chapter 8

THE PRINCIPLES
OF LEDGER ACCOUNTING

The purpose of this chapter is:

● to introduce the basic rules of double entry bookkeeping

● to illustrate the process of extracting a trial balance and preparing final accounts

Introduction

1. In the previous chapters we have looked at the theory of preparing accounts for the proprietor(s) of a business, by presenting a profit and loss account for a given period of time and a balance sheet as at the end of that period. We have also seen, by means of the accounting equation and the business equation, that it would be possible to prepare a statement of the affairs of a business at any time we like, and that a profit and loss account and a balance sheet could be drawn up on any date, relating to any period of time. To do so, however, would be a time-consuming and cumbersome administrative task. A business is continually making transactions, buying and selling etc, and we would not want to prepare a profit and loss account and a balance sheet on completion of every individual transaction.

2. It is common sense that a business should keep a record of the transactions that it makes, the assets it acquires and liabilities it incurs, and when the time comes to prepare a profit and loss account and a balance sheet, the relevant information can be taken from those records.

3. The records of transactions, assets and liabilities should be kept:

    (a) in a chronological order, and dated. This means that transactions can be related to a particular period of time; and

    (b) built up in cumulative totals. For example, a business should build up the total of its sales:

        (i)   day by day (eg total sales on Monday, total sales on Tuesday);
        (ii)   week by week;
        (iii) month by month;
        (iv)   year by year.

Although only (iv) will usually be relevant to preparing (end-of-year) accounts for the proprietor(s), (i),(ii) and (iii) will provide valuable information to managers, who are responsible for the day-to-day, week-to-week and month-to-month affairs of the business.

4.   The task of keeping the records of transactions, assets and liabilities is the job of accountants. The records are kept in accounts and the process of keeping the records is *book-keeping*, ie keeping the books of account in order.

Bookkeeping

5.   Bookkeeping is the 'art of recording commercial transactions'. The books which are kept will be described in this and the following chapters. In this chapter, we shall concentrate on ledger accounts. It might help, however, to mention at once that accounting terminology is rather Victorian and antiquated, so that when we refer to the 'books' of a large business, we might well be referring to records on a computer file.

The nominal ledger

6.   The nominal ledger is an accounting record which summarises the financial affairs of a business. It contains details of assets, liabilities and capital, income and expenditure, and so profit and loss. It consists of a large number of different accounts, each account having its own purpose or 'name' and an identity or code.

The nominal ledger is often called the 'general ledger'.

7.   Examples of accounts in the nominal ledger include:

- plant and machinery at cost (fixed asset)
- motor vehicles at cost (fixed asset)
- plant and machinery, provision for depreciation (liability)
- motor vehicles, provision for depreciation (liability)
- proprietor's capital (liability)
- stocks - raw materials (current assets)
- stocks - finished goods (current assets)
- total debtors (current assets)
- total creditors (current liability)
- wages and salaries (expense item)
- rent and rates (expense item)
- advertising expenses (expense item)
- bank charges (expense item)
- motor expenses (expense item)
- telephone expenses (expense item)
- sales (income)
- total cash or bank overdraft (current asset or liability).

Impersonal accounts and personal accounts: the sales ledger and purchase ledger

8.   The accounts in the nominal ledger relate to types of expense - rent, rates, insurance, electricity, telephone, postage etc - rather than the person to whom the money is paid. Because they are more concerned with the reason for payment than the person to be paid, they are impersonal accounts.

9. Impersonal accounts are distinct from personal accounts. Personal accounts are kept for each of the credit customers or suppliers of a business. Thehat the purchases or sales recorded in a personal account are between the business and another specified business, other organisation or individual. 'Personal' does not imply transactions that are between two individual people.

10. Personal accounts are kept in personal ledgers. There are two of these.

   (a) The sales ledger includes the personal accounts of credit customers (debtors).
   (b) The bought ledger or purchase ledger includes the personal accounts of suppliers (creditors).

11. Although personal accounts are recorded in the sales ledger and purchase ledger, a total of the transactions between debtors and creditors, and a total of the outstanding debtors and creditors at any time, is kept in the nominal ledger. The sales ledger and purchase ledger will be described further in a later chapter.

The format of a ledger account

12. If a ledger account were to be kept in an actual book rather than as a computer record, its format might be as follows:

ADVERTISING EXPENSES				ACCOUNT CODE N71			
Date	*Narrative*	*Folio*	£	*Date*	*Narrative*	*Folio*	£
19X6							
15 April	JFK Agency, for quarter to 31 March	PL34	82,500				

The folio number is a cross-referencing identity, whose purpose will become apparent later. Only one entry in the account is shown here, because the example is introduced here simply to illustrate the general format of a ledger account.

13. There are two sides to each account, and an account heading on top, and so it is convenient to think in terms of 'T' accounts. On top of the account is its name; there is a left hand side, or debit side, and there is a right hand side, or credit side.

NAME OF ACCOUNT

DEBIT SIDE	CREDIT SIDE

Double entry bookkeeping

14. As we have seen, since the total of liabilities plus capital is always equal to total assets, any transaction which changes the amount of total assets must also change the total liabilities plus capital, and vice versa. Alternatively, a transaction might use up assets of a certain value to obtain other assets of the same value. For example, if a business pays £50 in cash for some goods, its total assets will be unchanged, but as the amount of cash falls by £50, the value of goods in stock rises by the same amount.

15. Ledger accounts, with their debit and credit side, are kept in a way which allows the two-sided nature of business transactions to be recorded. This system of accounting was first expounded in Venice in 1494AD, by Luca Pacioli, in his *Summa de Arithmetica* and it is known as the 'double entry' system of bookkeeping, so called because every transaction is recorded twice in the accounts.

A word of caution

16. Double entry bookkeeping is not entirely standardised, and there are some variations found in practice in the way that business transactions are recorded. One example is that in some accounting systems, personal accounts are made a part of the double entry bookkeeping system, whereas in this study text personal accounts are outside the double entry system and are *memorandum* accounts only. In this text, double entry bookkeeping will be explained according to a given set of well practised 'rules'. Variations in these rules that are made in accounting systems of some businesses might be mentioned from time to time; however, if you learn the system as described here, you should be able to adapt your knowledge to any (minor) differences which either might appear in an examination question, or you might come across in your practical experience.

The rules of double entry bookkeeping

17. The rules of double entry bookkeeping can be related to what you have learned already about the balance sheet. However, it is probably easier to begin double entry bookkeeping by learning the basic rules, rather than by trying to relate the procedures to the fundamental principles of accounting.

18.
> The basic rule which must always be observed is that *every* transaction gives rise to two accounting entries, one a debit and the other a credit. The total debit entries in the nominal ledger are therefore always equal at any time to the total credit entries.

Which account receives the credit entry and which receives the debit depends on the nature of the transaction. Students coming to the subject for the first time often have difficulty in knowing where to begin. A good starting point is the cash account, ie the nominal ledger account in which receipts and payments of cash are recorded.

19. The rule to remember about the cash account is as follows:

(a) A cash *payment* is a *credit* entry in the cash account. Cash may be paid out, for example, to pay an expense (such as rates) or to purchase an asset (such as a machine). The debit entry is therefore made in the appropriate expense account or asset account.

(b) A cash *receipt* is a *debit* entry in the cash account. Cash might be received, for example, by a retailer who makes a cash sale. The credit entry would then be made in the sales account.

Example

20. Show the ledger account entries necessary to record the following transactions.

   (a)   A retail confectioner makes a cash sale for £2.
   (b)   A business pays a rent bill of £150.
   (c)   A business buys some goods for cash costing £100.
   (d)   A business buys some shelves for cash costing £200.

Solution

21. (a)   The two sides of the transaction are:

   (i)   cash is received (debit entry in the cash account);
   (ii)   sales increase by £2 (credit entry in the sale account).

CASH ACCOUNT

	£		£
Sales a/c	2		

SALES ACCOUNT

	£		£
		Cash a/c	2

(*Note* how the entry in the cash account is cross-referenced to the sales account and vice versa. This enables a person looking at one of the accounts to trace where the other half of the double entry can be found).

   (b)   The two sides of the transaction are:

   (i)   cash is paid (credit entry in the cash account);
   (ii)   rent expense increases by £150 (debit entry in the rent account).

CASH ACCOUNT

	£		£
		Rent a/c	150

RENT ACCOUNT

	£		£
Cash a/c	150		

   (c)   The two sides of the transaction are:

   (i)   cash is paid (credit entry in the cash account);
   (ii)   purchases increase by £100 (debit entry in the purchases account).

CASH ACCOUNT

	£		£
		Purchases a/c	100

PURCHASES ACCOUNT

	£		£
Cash a/c	100		

(d) The two sides of the transaction are:

(i)   cash is paid (credit entry in the cash account);
(ii) the asset 'shelves' increases by £200 (debit entry in the shelves account).

CASH ACCOUNT

	£		£
		Shelves a/c	200

SHELVES ACCOUNT

	£		£
Cash a/c	200		

22. If all four of these transactions related to the same business, the cash account of that business would end up looking as follows:

CASH ACCOUNT

	£		£
Sales a/c	2	Rent a/c	150
		Purchases a/c	100
		Shelves a/c	200

Credit transactions

23. As we have already seen, not all transactions are settled immediately in cash. A business might purchase goods or fixed assets from its suppliers on credit terms, so that the suppliers would be creditors of the business until settlement was made in cash. Equally, the business might grant credit terms to its customers who would then be debtors of the business. Clearly no entries in the cash book can be made when a credit transaction is entered into, because at that stage no cash has been received or paid. The solution to this problem is to use a debtors account and a creditors account.

24.

> When a business acquires goods or services on credit, the credit entry is made in an account designated 'creditors' instead of in the cash account. The debit entry is made in the appropriate expense or asset account, exactly as in the case of cash transactions. Similarly, when a sale is made to a credit customer the entries made are a debit to debtors account (instead of cash account) and a credit to sales account.

Example

25. Show the ledger account entries necessary to record the following transactions:

    (a)   a business sells goods on credit to a customer Mr A for £2,000;

    (b)   a business buys goods on credit from a supplier B Limited for £100.

Solution

26. (a)

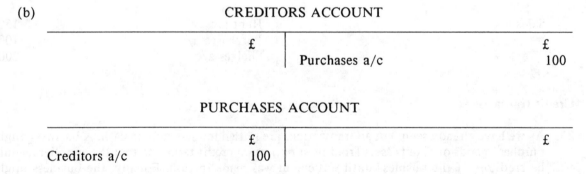

	£		£
DEBTORS ACCOUNT			
Sales a/c	2,000		
SALES ACCOUNT			
	£	Debtors a/c (Mr A)	£ 2,000

Compare this with the entries in paragraph 21(a) above.

    (b)

	£		£
CREDITORS ACCOUNT			
	£	Purchases a/c	£ 100
PURCHASES ACCOUNT			
Creditors a/c	100		£

Compare this with the entries in paragraph 21(c) above.

27. The entry of £2,000 in the debtors account indicates that the business is owed £2,000 by a customer. In practice, as already mentioned, the business would wish to maintain a memorandum record in addition to the debtors account so that the amounts owed by particular debtors, such as Mr A, could be separately identified when credit transactions became frequent.

28. What happens when a credit transaction is eventually settled in cash? Suppose that, in the example of paragraph 25(b) above, the business pays £100 to B Limited one month after the goods were acquired. The two sides of this new transaction are:

(a) cash is paid (credit entry in the cash account);
(b) the amount owing to creditors is reduced (debit entry in the creditors account).

CASH ACCOUNT

	£		£
		Creditors a/c	100
		(B Ltd)	

CREDITORS ACCOUNT

	£		£
Cash a/c	100		

29. If we now bring together the two parts of this example, the original purchase of goods on credit and the eventual settlement in cash, we find that the accounts appear as follows:

CASH ACCOUNT

	£		£
		Creditors a/c	100

PURCHASES ACCOUNT

	£		£
Creditors a/c	100		

CREDITORS ACCOUNT

	£		£
Cash account	100	Purchases a/c	100

30. The two entries in the creditors account cancel each other out, indicating that no money is owing to creditors any more. We are left with a credit entry of £100 in the cash account and a debit entry of £100 in the purchases account. These are exactly the entries which would have been made to record a *cash* purchase of £100 (compare para 21(c) above). This is what we would expect: after the business has paid off its creditors it is in exactly the position of a business which has made cash purchases of £100, and the accounting records reflect this similarity.

31. Similar reasoning applies when a credit customer settles his debt. When Mr A (para 25(a) above) pays his debt of £2,000 the two sides of the transaction are:

(a) cash is received (debit entry in the cash account);
(b) the amount owed by debtors is reduced (credit entry in the debtors account).

CASH ACCOUNT

	£		£
Debtors a/c	2,000		

DEBTORS ACCOUNT

	£		£
		Cash a/c	2,000

The accounts recording this sale to, and payment by, Mr A now appear as follows:

CASH ACCOUNT

	£		£
Debtors a/c	2,000		

SALES ACCOUNT

	£		£
		Debtors a/c	2,000

DEBTORS ACCOUNT

	£		£
Sales a/c	2,000	Cash a/c	2,000

The two entries in the debtors account cancel each other out; while the entries in the cash account and sales account reflect the same position as if the sale had been made for cash (see paragraph 21(a) above).

First exercise

32. See if you can identify the debit and credit entries in the following transactions:

   (a) bought a machine on credit from A, cost £8,000;

   (b) bought goods on credit from B, cost £500;

   (c) sold goods on credit to C, value £1,200;

   (d) paid D (a creditor) £300;

   (e) collected £180 from E, a debtor;

   (f) paid wages £4,000;

   (g) received rent bill of £700 from landlord G;

   (h) paid rent of £700 to landlord G;

   (i) paid insurance premium £90.

Solution

33.	(a)	*Debit*	Machine account (fixed asset)	£8,000
		Credit	Creditors (A)	£8,000
	(b)	*Debit*	Purchases account	£500
		Credit	Creditors (B)	£500
	(c)	*Debit*	Debtors (C)	£1,200
		Credit	Sales	£1,200
	(d)	*Debit*	Creditors (D)	£300
		Credit	Cash	£300
	(e)	*Debit*	Cash	£180
		Credit	Debtors (E)	£180
	(f)	*Debit*	Wages account	£4,000
		Credit	Cash	£4,000
	(g)	*Debit*	Rent account	£700
		Credit	Creditors (G)	£700
	(h)	*Debit*	Creditors (G)	£700
		Credit	Cash	£700
	(i)	*Debit*	Insurance costs	£90
		Credit	Cash	£90

Second exercise

34. See now whether you can record the ledger entries for the following transactions.
    Reg Knuckle set up a business selling keep fit equipment, trading under the name of Buy Your Biceps Shop. He put £7,000 of his own money into a business bank account (transaction A) and in his first period of trading, the following transactions occurred:

		£
Transaction		
B	Paid rent of shop for the period	3,500
C	Purchased equipment (stocks) on credit	5,000
D	Raised loan from bank	1,000
E	Purchase of shop fittings (for cash)	2,000
F	Sales of equipment: cash	10,000
G	Sales of equipment: on credit	2,500
H	Payments to trade creditors	5,000
I	Payments from debtors	2,500
J	Interest on loan (paid)	100
K	Other expenses (all paid in cash)	1,900
L	Drawings	1,500

All equipment purchased during the period was sold, and so there were no closing stocks of equipment.

Try to do as much of this exercise as you can by yourself before reading the solution.

Solution

35. Perhaps you are wondering what accounts there should be. Clearly, there should be an account for cash, debtors, creditors, purchases, a shop fittings account, sales, a loan account and a proprietor's capital account. It is also useful to keep a separate drawings account until the end of each accounting period. Other accounts should be set up as required and in this exercise, accounts for rent, bank interest and other expenses would seem appropriate.

It has been suggested to you that the cash account is a good place to start, if possible. You should notice that cash transactions include the initial input of capital by Ron Knuckle, subsequent drawings, the payment of rent, the loan from the bank, the interest, some cash sales and cash purchases, and payments to creditors, and by debtors. (The transactions are identified below by their label, to help you to find them.)

CASH

	£		£
Capital - Ron Knuckle (A)	7,000	Rent (B)	3,500
Bank loan (D)	1,000	Shop fittings (E)	2,000
Sales (F)	10,000	Trade creditors (H)	5,000
Debtors (I)	2,500	Bank loan interest (J)	100
		Incidental expenses (K)	1,900
		Drawings (L)	1,500
			14,000
		Balancing figure - the amount of cash left over after payments have been made	6,500
	20,500		20,500

CAPITAL (RON KNUCKLE)

	£		£
		Cash (A)	7,000

BANK LOAN

	£		£
		Cash (D)	1,000

PURCHASES

	£		£
Trade creditors (C)	5,000		

TRADE CREDITORS

	£		£
Cash (H)	5,000	Purchases (C)	5,000

RENT

	£		£
Cash (B)	3,500		

SHOP FITTINGS

	£		£
Cash (E)	2,000		

SALES

	£		£
		Cash	10,000
		Debtors	2,500
			12,500

DEBTORS

	£		£
Sales (G)	2,500	Cash (I)	2,500

BANK LOAN INTEREST

	£		£
Cash (J)	100		

OTHER EXPENSES

	£		£
Cash (K)	1,900		

DRAWINGS ACCOUNT

	£		£
Cash (L)	1,500		

Balancing ledger accounts

36. At the end of an accounting period a balance is struck on each account in turn. This means that all the debits on the account are totalled and so are all the credits. If the total debits exceed the total credits there is said to be a debit balance on the account; if the credits exceed the debits the account has a credit balance. If the basic principle of double entry has been correctly applied throughout the period it will be found that the credit balances equal the debit balances in total.

This can be illustrated by collecting together the balances on Ron Knuckle's accounts. This is called a *trial balance* and is referred to again later in this chapter.

RON KNUCKLE: TRIAL BALANCE AS AT . . . .

	Debit £	Credit £
Cash	6,500	
Capital		7,000
Bank loan		1,000
Purchases	5,000	
Trade creditors *	-	-
Rent	3,500	
Shop fittings	2,000	
Sales		12,500
Debtors *	-	-
Bank loan interest	100	
Other expenses	1,900	
Drawings	1,500	
	20,500	20,500

* On each of these accounts, the total debit entries equal the total credit entries and the account balance is therefore nil.

37. Once the balances have been established it is possible to summarise the trading results for the period by gathering together all the balances relating to income and expenses into a single ledger account, called the trading, profit and loss account. This account is part of the double entry system and of course the basic rule of double entry still applies: every debit entry must have an equal and opposite credit entry.

38. In the case of Ron Knuckle, the income and expense accounts consist of purchases, rent, sales, bank loan interest and other expenses. The balances on these accounts are transferred to the trading and profit and loss account as follows:

PURCHASES

	£		£
Trade creditors (C)	5,000	Trading, P & L a/c	5,000

RENT

	£		£
Cash (B)	3,500	Trading, P & L a/c	3,500

SALES

	£		£
Trading, P & L a/c	12,500	Cash (F)	10,000
		Debtors(G)	2,500
	12,500		12,500

BANK LOAN INTEREST

	£		£
Cash (J)	100	Trading, P & L a/c	100

OTHER EXPENSES

	£		£
Cash (K)	1,900	Trading, P & L a/c	1,900

TRADING PROFIT AND LOSS ACCOUNT

	£		£
Purchases	5,000	Sales	12,500
Rent	3,500		
Bank loan interest	100		
Other expenses	1,900		

39. Notice how the original debit balance of £5,000 on the purchases account has been eliminated by the insertion of a credit entry of £5,000. The corresponding debit entry appears in the trading, profit and loss account. The same procedure is applied to the rent, sales, bank loan interest and other expenses accounts. If we were now to compile a list of balances like the one in paragraph 36 we would find that all these accounts now have nil balances and have been replaced by a single new account, the trading, profit and loss account. This account has a credit balance of £2,000 (£12,500 - £5,000 - £3,500 - £100 - £1,900).

40. The remaining accounts must also be balanced and ruled off, but since these accounts represent assets and liabilities of the business (not income and expenses) their balances are not transferred to the trading profit and loss account. Instead they are *carried down* in the books of the business. This means that they become the opening balances for the next accounting period and indicate the value of the assets and liabilities at the end of one period and the beginning of the next.

41. The conventional method of ruling off a ledger account at the end of an accounting period is illustrated by the bank loan account in Ron Knuckle's books:

BANK LOAN ACCOUNT

	£		£
Balance carried down (c/d)	1,000	Cash (D)	1,000
		Balance brought down b/d	1,000

Ron Knuckle therefore begins the new accounting period with a credit balance of £1,000 on this account. A credit balance brought down denotes a liability; an asset would be represented by a debit balance brought down.

42. One further point is worth noting before we move on to complete this example. You will remember that a proprietor's capital comprises any cash introduced by him, plus any profits made by the business, less any drawings made by him. At the stage we have now reached these three elements are contained in different ledger accounts: cash introduced of £7,000 appears in the capital account; drawings of £1,500 appear in the drawings account; and the profit made by the business is represented by the £2,000 credit balance on the trading profit and loss account. It is convenient to gather together all these amounts into one capital account, in the same way as we earlier gathered together income and expense accounts into one trading and profit and loss account.

43. Ron Knuckle's remaining ledger accounts can then be balanced and ruled off:

CAPITAL

	£		£
Drawings	1,500	Cash (A)	7,000
Balance c/d	7,500	Trading, P & L a/c	2,000
	9,000		9,000
		Balance b/d	7,500

BANK LOAN

	£		£
Balance c/d	1,000	Cash (D)	1,000
		Balance b/d	1,000

SHOP FITTINGS

	£		£
Cash (E)	2,000	Balance c/d	2,000
Balance b/d	2,000		

TRADING, PROFIT AND LOSS ACCOUNT

	£		£
Purchases	5,000	Sales	12,500
Rent	3,500		
Bank loan interest	100		
Other expenses	1,900		
Capital a/c	2,000		
	12,500		12,500

DRAWINGS

	£		£
Cash (L)	1,500	Capital a/c	1,500

Balance sheet and trading, profit and loss account

44. You may have wondered whether the trading, profit and loss ledger account which we have just compiled for Ron Knuckle bears any relationship to the trading, profit and loss accounts prepared in an earlier chapter. The answer is that the ledger account contains all the figures needed for the kind of trading, profit and loss account you have already been preparing, but their arrangement may be haphazard. With a little rearrangement they could be presented as follows.

RON KNUCKLE: TRADING, PROFIT AND LOSS ACCOUNT

	£	£
Sales		12,500
Cost of sales (= purchases in this case as there is no stock)		(5,000)
Gross profit		7,500
Expenses:		
Rent	3,500	
Bank loan interest	100	
Other expenses	1,900	
		(5,500)
Net profit		2,000

45. You may also remember that in the earlier chapter it was stated that a balance sheet was a list of the outstanding balances on the ledger accounts of a business. Referring back to the balances brought down on Ron Knuckle's ledger accounts in paragraph 43 above (and including the cash account balance from paragraph 35) you should be able to see how the following balance sheet is constructed:

RON KNUCKLE: BALANCE SHEET AT END OF FIRST TRADING PERIOD

	£
Fixed assets	
Shop fittings	2,000
Current assets	
Cash	6,500
Total assets	8,500
Liabilities	
Bank loan	(1,000)
Net assets	7,500
Proprietor's capital	7,500

46. This exercise had the purpose of introducing you to double entry bookkeeping and also of indicating how ledger accounts may be used as the source for preparing a trading profit and loss account and a balance sheet. Remember that the trading profit and loss account is itself a ledger account within the double entry system; while a balance sheet is a list of the balances remaining on ledger accounts after income and expenses balances have been cleared to the trading profit and loss account.

Stocks: opening and closing balances

47. A slightly more complex problem is the treatment of opening and closing balances of goods in stock. As we have seen in an earlier chapter, we must match sales with the cost of those sales, and so if a business purchases more goods than it sells, or sells more than it purchases in a period, its goods in stock will rise or fall in value. You should remember, in fact, that a trading account (debit side) includes:

	£
Opening stock	X
Plus purchases	X
Less closing stock	(X)
Equals cost of goods sold	X

48. It has already been shown that purchases are introduced to the trading account by means of the double entry:

		£
Credit	Purchases account	X
Debit	Trading account	X

But what about opening and closing stocks?

49. The answer is that a stock account must be kept. This stock account is only ever used at the end of an accounting period, when the business counts up and values the stock in hand at the end of a period, in a stock-take.

    (a) When a stock-take is made, the business will have a value for its closing stock, and the double entry is:

Debit	Stock account (closing stock value)	X
Credit	Trading account	X

    However, rather than show the closing stock as a 'plus' value on the credit side of the trading account, it is often shown instead as a 'minus' value on the debit side – which comes to the same thing.

    (b) Closing stock at the end of one period becomes opening stock at the start of the next period. The account remains unchanged until the end of the next period, when the value of opening stock is then taken to the trading account:

		£
Debit	Trading account	X
Credit	Stock account (value of opening stock)	X

    These stock transactions will be illustrated in the following example.

Example: balancing accounts

50. A business is established with capital of £2,000, and this amount is paid into a business bank account by the proprietor. During the first year's trading, the following transactions occurred.

	£
Purchases of goods for resale, on credit	4,300
Payments to trade creditors	3,600
Sales, all on credit	4,000
Payments by debtors	3,200
Fixed assets purchased for cash	1,500
Other expenses, all paid in cash	900

- The bank has provided an overdraft facility of up to £3,000.
- All 'other expenses' relate to the current year.
- Closing stocks of goods are valued at £1,800.
- Ignore depreciation and drawings.

Required:

Prepare the ledger accounts, a trading, profit and loss account for the year and a balance sheet as at the end of the year.

Solution

51.

CASH

	£		£
Capital	2,000	Trade creditors	3,600
Debtors	3,200	Fixed assets	1,500
Balance c/d	800	Other expenses	900
	6,000		6,000
		Balance b/d	*800

CAPITAL

	£		£
Balance c/d	2,600	Cash	2,000
		P & L a/c	600
	2,600		2,600
		Balance b/d	2,600

* A credit balance b/d means that this cash item is a liability, not an asset. This indicates a bank overdraft of £800, with cash income of £5,200 falling short of payments of £6,000 by this amount.

TRADE CREDITORS

	£		£
Cash	3,600	Stores	
Balance c/d	700	(purchases)	4,300
	4,300		4,300
		Balance b/d	700

PURCHASES ACCOUNT

	£		£
Trade creditors	4,300	Trading a/c	4,300
	4,300		4,300

FIXED ASSETS

	£		£
Cash	1,500	Balance c/d	1,500
Balance b/d	1,500		

SALES

	£		£
Trading a/c	4,000	Debtors	4,000

DEBTORS

	£		£
Sales	4,000	Cash	3,200
		Balance c/d	800
	4,000		4,000
Balance b/d	800		

OTHER EXPENSES

	£		£
Cash	900	P & L a/c	900

TRADING, PROFIT AND LOSS ACCOUNT

	£		£
Purchases account	4,300	Sales	4,000
Gross profit c/d	1,500	Closing stock	1,800
	5,800		5,800
Other expenses	900	Gross profit /d	1,500
Net profit (transferred to			
capital account)	600		
	1,500		1,500

Alternatively, closing stock could be shown as a minus value on the debit side of the trading account, instead of a credit entry, giving purchases £4,300 less closing stock £1,800 equals cost of goods sold £2,500.

STOCK ACCOUNT

	£		£
Closing stock	1,800		

BALANCE SHEET AS AT THE END OF THE PERIOD

	£	£
Fixed assets		1,500
Current assets		
Goods in stock	1,800	
Debtors	800	
	2,600	
Current liabilities		
Bank overdraft	800	
Trade creditors	700	
	1,500	
Net current assets		1,100
		2,600
Capital		
At start of period		2,000
Net profit for period, all retained		600
		2,600

Trial balance

52. Before transferring the relevant balances at the year end to the profit and loss account and putting closing balances carried forward into the balance sheet, it is usual to test the accuracy of the double entry bookkeeping records by preparing a trial balance. This is done by taking all the balances on every account. Because of the self-balancing nature of the system of double entry the total of the debit balances will be exactly equal to the total of the credit balances (see paragraph 36 above).

53. If they are not equal, there must be an error in recording the transactions in the accounts. A trial balance, however, will not disclose the following types of errors:

    (a) the complete omission of a transaction, because neither a debit nor a credit is made;

    (b) the posting of a debit or credit to the correct side of the ledger, but to a wrong account;

    (c) compensating errors (eg omitting both a debit and a credit of £100);

    (d) errors of principle, eg cash received from debtors being debited to the debtors account and credited to cash instead of the other way round.

Example: trial balance

54. The trial balance in the example in paragraphs 50-51, as at the end of the year, would be prepared as follows. (The order of items in the list is unimportant.)

TRIAL BALANCE AS AT......

	Debits (Dr) £	Credits (Cr) £
Cash (bank overdraft)		800
Capital (note 1)		2,000
Trade creditors		700
Purchases	4,300	
Fixed assets	1,500	
Sales (note 2)		4,000
Debtors	800	
Other expenses	900	
	7,500	7,500

Notes:

1. The capital account balance is the amount before the P & L account is prepared: in other words, the retained net profit for the year shown in the account in paragraph 51 does not arise until after the trial balance has been prepared.

2. The sales of £4,000 are taken to the trading account, but the trial balance is drawn up before the trading, P & L account is prepared. This means that there is a balance of £4,000 for sales to appear in the trial balance. Similarly, there is a balance of £4,300 on the purchases account to appear in the trial balance, though later it would be transferred to the trading account.

3. The value for closing stock emerges in the trading account (ie so after the trial balance is drawn up) and so there is no entry in the trial balance for closing stock. However, if there had been any opening stock at the start of the period, this balance would have existed prior to the preparation of the trading account, and so opening stock values do appear in the trial balance.

Summary of the chapter

55.
- The *nominal ledger* is a collection of ledger accounts in which the assets, liabilities, income and expenditure of a business are summarised.

- The *basic principle of double entry bookkeeping* is that every business transaction gives rise to two entries in the nominal ledger, one a debit and the other a credit.

- A *trial balance* is a list of debit and credit items in the nominal ledger accounts, before the trading, P & L account or balance sheet is prepared. It mixes up P & L items with balance sheet items, but its purpose is to ensure that total debits and total credits are equal, so that there is no obvious error in the double entry records.

- An *examination question* might ask you to prepare a trading, profit and loss account and a balance sheet from trial balance data, and to make the exercise more difficult it might fail to distinguish debit balances and credit balances, merely listing all the figures in a single column, as was done in the previous chapter. You would then be expected to recognise the debit and credit balances yourself.

TEST YOUR KNOWLEDGE

Numbers in brackets refer to paragraphs of this chapter

1. What is the distinction between personal accounts and impersonal accounts? (8, 9)

2. A debit entry in the cash account signifies a receipt of cash. True or false? (19)

3. What are the ledger entries necessary to record:

   (a) payment of a rent bill? (21(b))
   (b) purchase of goods on credit? (26(b))

4. List three types of error which would *not* be disclosed by a trial balance. (53)

Chapter 9

LEDGER ACCOUNTING: FURTHER ASPECTS

The purpose of this chapter is:

● to explain the ledger accounting entries in respect of accruals and prepayments

● to explain the ledger accounting entries in respect of bad and doubtful debts

● to explain the ledger accounting entries in respect of depreciation and disposal of fixed assets

---

Introduction

1. Earlier chapters described how to account for accruals, prepayments, provisions etc, in terms of the trading, P & L account and the balance sheet and so the logic behind these items should now be familiar to you. In this chapter, we shall look at how they are recorded in ledger accounts.

Accruals

2. Accruals are expenses which relate to a current period's P & L account, but which have not yet become payable (nor an 'official' debt, since no invoice has yet been received from the supplier of the goods or services).

3. Suppose that Willie Woggle opens a shop on 1 May 19X6 to sell hiking and camping equipment. The rent of the shop is £12,000 per annum, payable quarterly in arrears (with the first payment on 31 July 19X6). Willie decides that his accounting period should end on 31 December each year.

4. The rent account as at 31 December 19X6 will record only two rental payments (on 31 July and 31 October) and there will be two months' accrued rental expenses (£2,000) since the next rental payment is not due until 31 January 19X7.

    The charge to the P & L account for the period to 31 December 19X6 will be for 8 months' trading (May-December inclusive) and so it follows that the total rental cost should be £8,000.

5. It is therefore necessary to make an entry in the rent account for the accrued rent; and it is done by using the balance carried down/brought down technique to preserve the double entry system of bookkeeping as follows.

Debit Rent account with accrued rental expenses
as a balance carried down   £2,000

Credit Rent account with the same accrued expenses
as a balance brought down   £2,000

The expenses in the rent account to 31 December 19X6 should then be taken to the P & L account. The balance on the account will appear in the balance sheet as at 31 December 19X6 as a liability (accrued rent).

RENT ACCOUNT

Date		£	*Date*		£
19X6			19X6		
31 July	Cash *	3,000			
31 Oct	Cash *	3,000			
31 Dec	Balance c/d (accrual)	2,000	31 Dec	P & L account	8,000
		8,000			8,000
			19X7		
			1 Jan	Balance b/d	2,000

* Or creditors, depending on whether the rent is paid with or without the need for an invoice. It is assumed here that rent is paid by standing order, and so the corresponding double entry is to cash.

6.   The rent account for the next year to 31 December 19X7, assuming no increase in rent in that year, would be as follows:

RENT ACCOUNT

Date		£	*Date*		£
19X7			19X7		
31 Jan	Cash	3,000	1 Jan	Balance b/d	2,000
30 Apr	Cash	3,000			
31 Jul	Cash	3,000			
31 Oct	Cash	3,000			
31 Dec	Balance c/d (accrual)	2,000	31 Dec	P & L account	12,000
		14,000			14,000
			19X8		
			1 Jan	Balance b/d	2,000

Prepayments

7.   Prepayments are expenses which have been paid (or for which an invoice demanding payment has been received) but which relate to a future accounting period, and so should be an expense in the P & L account of that future period.

8.   Suppose that Terry Trunk commences business as a landscape gardener on 1 September 19X5. He immediately decides to join his local trade association, the Confederation of Luton Gardeners for which the annual membership subscription is £180, payable annually in advance. He paid this amount on 1 September. Terry decides that his account period should end on 30 June each year.

In the first period to 30 June 19X6 (10 months), a full year's membership will have been paid, but only ten-twelfths of the subscription should be charged to the period (ie $\frac{10}{12}$ x £180 = £150). There is a prepayment of two months of membership subscription - ie $\frac{2}{12}$ x £180 = £30.

9.   It is therefore necessary to recognise the prepayment in the ledger account for subscriptions. This is done in much the same way as accounting for accruals, by using the balance carried down/brought down technique.

Credit	Subscriptions account with prepayment as a balance c/d	£30
Debit	Subscriptions account with the same balance b/d	£30

The remaining expenses in the subscriptions account should then be taken to the P & L account. The balance on the account will appear as a current asset (prepaid subscriptions) in the balance sheet as at 30 June 19X6.

SUBSCRIPTIONS ACCOUNT

Date		£	*Date*		£
19X5			19X6		
1 Sep	Cash	180	30 June	P & L account	150
			30 June	Balance c/d (prepayment)	30
		180			180
19X6					
1 July	Balance b/d	30			

10.   The subscription account for the next year, assuming no increase in the annual charge and that Terry Trunk remains a member of the association, will be:

SUBSCRIPTIONS ACCOUNT

Date		£	*Date*		£
19X6			19X7		
1 July	Balance b/d	30	30 Jun	P & L account	180
1 Sep	Cash	180	30 Jun	Balance c/d (prepayment)	30
		210			210
19X7					
1 July	Balance b/d	30			

Bad debts written off

11.   For bad debts written off, there is a bad debts account. The double-entry bookkeeping logic is fairly straightforward, but there are two separate transactions to record.

(a)   When it is decided that a particular debt will not be paid, the customer is taken out of the file of outstanding debtors, and becomes a bad debt.
We therefore:

Debit	Bad debts account
Credit	Debtors account

(b) At the end of the accounting period, accumulated bad debts are written off to the P & L account:

Debit   P & L account
Credit   Bad debts account

Example: bad debts written off

12. At 1 October 19X5, a business had total outstanding debts of £8,600. During the year to 30 September 19X6:

(a) credit sales amounted to £44,000;
(b) payments from various debtors amounted to £49,000;
(c) two debts, for £180 and £420, were declared bad. These are to be written off.

Required:

Prepare the debtors account and the bad debts account for the year.

Solution

13.
	DEBTORS		
	£		£
Opening balance b/f	8,600	Cash	49,000
Sales	44,000	Bad debt	180
		Bad debt	420
		Closing balance c/d	3,000
	52,600		52,600
Opening balance b/d	3,000		

	BAD DEBTS		
	£		£
Debtors	180	P & L account bad debts	600
Debtors	420		
	600		600

Provision for doubtful debts

14. A provision for doubtful debts is rather different. A business might know from past experience that, say, 2% of debtors' balances are unlikely to be collected. It would then be considered prudent to make a general provision of 2%. It may be that no particular balances are regarded as suspect and so it is not possible to write off any balances as bad debts. The procedure is then to leave the total debtors' balances completely untouched, but to open up a provision account by the following entries:

Debit   P & L account
Credit   Provision for doubtful debts

15. When preparing a balance sheet, the credit balance on the provision account is deducted from the total debit balances in the debtors' ledger.

16. In later years adjustments may be needed to the amount of the provision. The procedure to be followed then is:

   (a) calculate the provision required now;
   (b) compare it with the existing balance on the provision account;
   (c) credit the provision account to increase the existing balance if a higher provision is required; or debit the provision account if a lower provision is now required. In either case, complete the double entry by a debit or credit to the P & L account.

Example

17. Alex Gullible has total debtors' balances outstanding at 31 December 19X2 of £28,000. He believes that about 1% of these balances will not be collected and wishes to make an appropriate provision.

   On 31 December 19X3 his debtors balances amount to £40,000. His experience during the year has convinced him that a provision of 5% should be made.

   What accounting entries should Alex make on 31 December 19X2 and 31 December 19X3, and what figures for debtors will appear in his balance sheets as at those dates?

Solution

18. *At 31 December 19X2*
   Provision required   =   1% x £28,000
                        =   £280
   Alex will make the following entries

		£	£
Debit	P & L account (doubtful debts)	280	
Credit	Provision for doubtful debts		280

   In the balance sheet debtors will appear as follows under current assets:

	£
Sales ledger balances	28,000
Less provision for doubtful debts	280
	27,720

   At 31 December 19X3
   Following the procedure of paragraph 16, Alex will calculate as follows:

	£
Provision required now (5% x £40,000)	2,000
Existing provision	(280)
∴ Additional provision required	1,720

   He will make the following entries:

		£	£
Debit	P & L account (doubtful debts)	1,720	
Credit	Provision for doubtful debts		1,720

The provision account will by now appear as follows:

PROVISION FOR DOUBTFUL DEBTS

19X2		£	19X2		£
31 Dec	Balance c/d	<u>280</u>	31 Dec	P & L account	<u>280</u>
19X3			19X3		
			1 Jan	Balance b/d	280
31 Dec	Balance c/d	2,000	31 Dec	P & L account	1,720
		<u>2,000</u>			<u>2,000</u>
			19X4		
			1 Jan	Balance b/d	2,000

In the balance sheet debtors will appear as follows under current assets:

	£	£
Sales ledger balances	40,000	
Less provision for doubtful debts	<u>2,000</u>	
		<u>38,000</u>

19. In practice, it is unnecessary to show the total debtors balances and the provision as separate items. A balance sheet would normally show only the net figure (£27,720 in 19X2, £38,000 in 19X3).

Example: provision for doubtful debts

20. Horace Goodrunning fears that his business will suffer an increase in defaulting debtors in the future and so he decides to make a provision for doubtful debts of 2% of outstanding debtors at the balance sheet date from 28 February 19X6. On 28 February 19X8, Horace decides that the provision has been overestimated, and he reduces it to 1% of outstanding debtors. Outstanding debtors balances at the various balance sheet dates are as follows:

28.2.19X6	£15,200
28.2.19X7	£17,100
28.2.19X8	£21,400

You are required to show extracts from the following accounts for each of the three years above:

(a) debtors;

(b) provision for doubtful debts;

(c) profit and loss.

Show how debtors would appear in the balance sheet at the end of each year.

Solution

21. The entries for the three years are denoted by (a), (b) and (c) in each account.

DEBTORS (EXTRACT)

			£
(a)	28.2.19X6	Balance	15,200
(b)	28.2.19X7	Balance	17,100
(c)	28.2.19X8	Balance	21,400

PROVISION FOR DOUBTFUL DEBTS

			£				£
(a)	28.2.19X6	Balance c/d (2% of 15,200)	304	28.2.19X6	Profit & loss		304
			304				304
(b)	28.2.19X7	Balance c/d (2% of 17,100)	342	1.3.19X6	Balance b/d		304
				28.2.19X7	Profit & loss (note 1)		38
			342				342

			£				£
(c)	28.2.19X8	Profit & loss (note 2)	128	1.3.19X7	Balance b/d		342
	28.2.19X8	Balance c/d (1% of 21,400)	214				
			342				342
				1.3.19X8	Balance b/d		214

PROFIT AND LOSS (EXTRACT)

		£			£
28.2.19X6	Provision for doubtful debts	304			
28.2.19X7	Provision for doubtful debts	38			
			28.2.19X8	Provision for doubtful debts	128

Notes:

(1) The increase in the provision is £(342 − 304) = £38
(2) The decrease in the provision is £(342 − 214) = £128
(3) We disclose the provision for doubtful debts in the balance sheet as follows:

	19X6		*19X7*		*19X8*	
	£	£	£	£	£	£
Current assets						
Debtors	15,200		17,100		21,400	
Less provision for doubtful debts	304		342		214	
		14,896		16,758		21,186

Provision for depreciation

22. Fixed asset depreciation has been described and discussed at some length in an earlier chapter, and the only concern here is with the ledger accounts entries. There are two basic aspects of the provision for depreciation to remember:

    (a) a depreciation charge (provision) is made in the profit and loss account in each accounting period for every depreciable fixed asset;

    (b) the total accumulated depreciation on a fixed asset builds up as the asset gets older. Unlike a provision for doubtful debts, therefore, the total provision for depreciation is always getting larger, until the fixed asset is fully depreciated.

    If you understand these points, the similarity in the accounting treatment of the provision for doubtful debts and the provision for depreciation may become apparent to you.

23. The ledger accounting entries for the provision for depreciation are as follows.

    (a) There is a provision for depreciation account for each separate category of fixed assets.

    (b) The depreciation charge for an accounting period is an increase in the provision for depreciation and is accounted for as follows:

    Debit   P & L account
    Credit Provision for depreciation account

    with the depreciation charge for the period.

    (c) The balance on the provision for depreciation account is the total accumulated depreciation. This is always a credit balance brought forward in the ledger account for depreciation.

    (d) The fixed asset accounts are unaffected by depreciation. Fixed assets are recorded in these accounts at cost (or, if they are revalued, at their revalued amount).

    (e) In the balance sheet of the business, the total balance on the provision for depreciation account (ie accumulated depreciation) is set against the value of fixed asset accounts (ie fixed assets at cost or revalued amount) to derive the net book value of the fixed assets.

Example: provision for depreciation

24. Brian Box set up his own computer software business on 1 March 19X6. He purchased a computer system on credit from a manufacturer, at a cost of £16,000. The system has an expected life of three years and a residual value of £2,500. Using the straight line method of depreciation, the fixed asset account, provision for depreciation account and P & L account (extract) and balance sheet (extract) would be as follows, for each of the next three years, 28 February 19X7, 19X8 and 19X9.

FIXED ASSET - COMPUTER EQUIPMENT

Date		£	Date		£
(a) 1 March 19X6	Creditor	16,000	28 Feb 19X7	Balance c/d	16,000
(b) 1 March 19X7	Balance b/d	16,000	28 Feb 19X8	Balance c/d	16,000
(c) 1 March 19X8	Balance b/d	16,000	28 Feb 19X9	Balance c/d	16,000
(d) 1 March 19X9	Balance b/d	16,000			

In theory, the fixed asset has now lasted out its expected useful life. However, until it is sold off or scrapped, the asset will still appear in the balance sheet at cost (less accumulated depreciation) and it should remain in the ledger account for computer equipment until it is eventually disposed of.

PROVISION FOR DEPRECIATION

Date		£	Date		£
(a) 28 Feb 19X7	Balance c/d	4,500	28 Feb 19X7	P & L account	4,500
(b) 28 Feb 19X8	Balance c/d	9,000	1 March 19X7	Balance b/d	4,500
			28 Feb 19X8	P & L account	4,500
		9,000			9,000
(c) 28 Feb 19X9	Balance c/d	13,500	1 March 19X8	Balance b/d	9,000
			28 Feb 19X9	P & L account	4,500
		13,500			13,500
			1 March 19X9	Balance b/d	13,500

The annual depreciation charge is $\dfrac{(£16,000 - 2,500)}{3 \text{ years}} = £4,500 \text{ pa}$

At the end of three years, the asset is fully depreciated down to its residual value. If it continues to be used by Brian Box, it will not be depreciated any further (unless its estimated value is reduced).

P & L ACCOUNT (EXTRACT)

Date	£
(a) 28 Feb 19X7 Charge for depreciation	4,500
(b) 28 Feb 19X8 Charge for depreciation	4,500
(c) 28 Feb 19X9 Charge for depreciation	4,500

BALANCE SHEET (EXTRACT) AS AT 28 FEBRUARY

	19X7	19X8	19X9
	£	£	£
Computer equipment at cost	16,000	16,000	16,000
Less accumulated depreciation	4,500	9,000	13,500
Net book value	11,500	7,000	2,500

Second example: provision for depreciation

25. Brian Box prospers in his computer software business, and before long he purchases a car for himself, and later for his chief assistant Bill Ockhead. Relevant data is as follows:

	Date of purchase	Cost	Estimated life	Estimated residual value
Brian Box car	1 June 19X6	£20,000	3 years	£2,000
Bill Ockhead car	1 June 19X7	£ 8,000	3 years	£2,000

The straight line method of depreciation is to be used.

Required: prepare the motor vehicles account and provision for depreciation of motor vehicle account for the years to 28 February 19X7 and 19X8. (You should allow for the part-year's use of a car in computing the annual charge for depreciation). Calculate the net book value of the motor vehicles as at 28 February 19X8.

Solution

26. (a) *Workings*

   (i)   Brian Box car   Annual depreciation $\dfrac{£(20,000-2,000)}{3 \text{ years}}$ = £6,000 pa

   Monthly depreciation   £500

   Depreciation   1 June-19X6 - 28 February 19X7 (9 months) £4,500
                       1 March 19X7 - 28 February 19X8   £6,000

   (ii) Bill Ockhead car   Annual depreciation $\dfrac{£(8,000 - 2,000)}{3 \text{ years}}$ = £2,000 pa

   Depreciation   1 June 19X7 - 28 February 19X8 (9 months) £1,500

(b)   MOTOR VEHICLES

Date		£	Date		£
1 Jun 19X6	Creditors (or cash) (car purchase)	20,000	28 Feb 19X7	Balance c/d	20,000
1 Mar 19X7	Balance b/d	20,000			
1 Jun 19X7	Creditors (or cash) (car purchase)	8,000	28 Feb 19X8	Balance c/d	28,000
		28,000			28,000
1 Mar 19X8	Balance b/d	28,000			

PROVISION FOR DEPRECIATION OF MOTOR VEHICLES

Date		£	Date		£
28 Feb 19X7	Balance c/d	4,500	28 Feb 19X7	P & L account	4,500
			1 Mar 19X7	Balance b/d	4,500
28 Feb 19X8	Balance c/d	12,000	28 Feb 19X8	P & L account	7,500
				(6,000+1,500)	
		12,000			12,000
			1 Mar 19X8	Balance b/d	12,000

BALANCE SHEET (WORKINGS) AS AT 28 FEBRUARY 19X8

	Brian Box car		Bill Ockhead car		Total	
	£	£	£	£	£	£
Asset at cost		20,000		8,000		28,000
Accumulated depreciation:						
Year to:						
28 Feb 19X7	4,500		-			
28 Feb 19X8	6,000		1,500			
		10,500		1,500		12,000
Net book value		9,500		6,500		16,000

The disposal of fixed assets

27. Eventually, most tangible fixed assets are disposed of. They might be disposed of as soon as their estimated useful life is finished, or they might be disposed of either before then or later.

The earlier chapter on fixed assets described how the profit or loss on disposal of a fixed asset should be computed. A profit on disposal is an item of 'other income' in the P & L account, and a loss on disposal is an item of expense in the P & L account.

28. It is customary in ledger accounting to record the disposal of fixed assets in a disposal of fixed assets account.

(a) The profit or loss on disposal is the difference between:

(i) the sale price of the asset (if any); and
(ii) the net book value of the asset at the time of sale.

(b) The relevant items which must appear in the disposal of fixed assets account are therefore:

(i) the value of the asset (at cost, or revalued amount*);
(ii) the accumulated depreciation up to the date of sale;
(iii) the sale price of the asset.

*To simplify the explanation of the rules, we will assume now that the fixed assets disposed of are valued at cost.

(c) The ledger accounting entries are:

(i) *Debit*   Disposal of fixed asset account
      Credit Fixed asset account
      with the cost of the asset disposed of;

(ii) *Debit*   Provision for depreciation account
      Credit Disposal of fixed asset account
      with the accumulated depreciation on the asset as at the date of sale.

(iii) *Debit*   Debtor account or cash book
      Credit Disposal of fixed asset account
      with the sale price of the asset. The sale is therefore not recorded in a sales account, but in the disposal of fixed asset account itself;

(iv) the balance on the disposal account is the profit or loss on disposal and the corresponding double entry is recorded in the P & L account itself.

Example: disposal of assets

29. A business has £110,000 worth of machinery at cost. Its policy is to make a provision for depreciation at 20% per annum straight line. The total provision now stands at £70,000. The business now sells for £19,000 a machine which it purchased exactly two years ago for £30,000.

Show the relevant ledger entries.

Solution

30.   PLANT AND MACHINERY ACCOUNT

	£		£
Balance b/d	110,000	Plant disposals account	30,000
		Balance c/d	80,000
	110,000		110,000
Balance b/d	80,000		

           PLANT AND MACHINERY DEPRECIATION PROVISION

	£		£
Plant disposals (20% of £30,000 for 2 years)	12,000	Balance b/d	70,000
Balance c/d	58,000		
	70,000		70,000
		Balance b/d	58,000

PLANT DISPOSALS

	£		£
Plant and machinery account	30,000	Depreciation provision	12,000
Profit and loss a/c (profit		Cash	19,000
on sale)	1,000		
	31,000		31,000

Check:

	£
Asset at cost	30,000
Accumulated depreciation at time of sale	12,000
Net book value at time of sale	18,000
Sale price	19,000
Profit on sale	1,000

Example continued

31. Taking the example in paragraph 29, assume that, instead of the machine being sold for £19,000, it was exchanged for a new machine costing £60,000, a credit of £19,000 being received upon exchange. In other words £19,000 is the trade-in price of the old machine.

Solution

32.

PLANT AND MACHINERY ACCOUNT

	£		£
Balance b/d	110,000	Plant disposal	30,000
Cash (60,000 − 19,000)	41,000	Balance c/d	140,000
Plant disposals	19,000		
	170,000		170,000
Balance b/d	140,000		

Note: the new asset is recorded in the fixed asset account at cost £(41,000 + 19,000) = £60,000.

PLANT AND MACHINERY DEPRECIATION PROVISION

	£		£
Plant disposals			
(20% of £30,000 for 2 years)	12,000	Balance b/d	70,000
Balance c/d	58,000		
	70,000		70,000
		Balance b/d	58,000

PLANT DISPOSALS

	£		£
Plant and machinery	30,000	Depreciation provision	12,000
Profit transferred to P & L	1,000	Plant and machinery	19,000
	31,000		31,000

Further example: disposal of fixed assets

33. A business purchased two widget-making machines on 1 January 19X5 at a cost of £15,000 each. Each had an estimated life of five years and a nil residual value. The straight line method of depreciation is used.

Owing to an unforeseen slump in market demand for widgets, the business decided to reduce its output of widgets, and switch to making other products instead. On 31 March 19X7, one widget-making machine was sold (on credit) to a buyer for £8,000.

Later in the year, however, it was decided to abandon production of widgets altogether, and the second machine was sold on 1 December 19X7 for £2,500 cash.

Required: prepare the machinery account, provision for depreciation of machinery account and disposal of machinery account for the accounting year to 31 December 19X7.

Solution

34. (a) *Workings*

(i) At 1 January 19X7, accumulated depreciation on the machines will be

2 machines x 2 years x $\frac{£15,000}{5}$ per machine pa = £12,000, or

£6,000 per machine

(ii) Monthly depreciation is $\frac{£3,000}{12}$ = £250 per machine per month

(iii) The machines are disposed of in 19X7.

1. On 31 March - after 3 months of the year.
   Depreciation for the year on the machine = 3 months x £250 = £750.

2. On 1 December - after 11 months of the year.
   Depreciation for the year on the machine = 11 months x £250 = £2,750

(b) MACHINERY ACCOUNT

Date		£	Date		£
19X7			19X7		
1 Jan	Balance b/f	30,000	31 Mar	Disposal of machinery account	15,000
			1 Dec	Disposal of machinery account	15,000
		30,000			30,000

PROVISION FOR DEPRECIATION OF MACHINERY

Date		£	Date		£
19X7			19X7		
31 Mar	Disposal of machinery account*	6,750	1 Jan	Balance b/f	12,000
1 Dec	Disposal of machinery account**	8,750	31 Dec	P & L account***	3,500
		15,500			15,500

*	Depreciation at date of disposal £6,000 + £750	
**	Depreciation at date of disposal £6,000 + £2,750	
***	Depreciation charge for the year = £750 + £2,750	

DISPOSAL OF MACHINERY

Date		£	Date		£
19X7			19X7		
31 Mar	Machinery account	15,000	31 Mar	Debtor account (sale price)	8,000
			31 Mar	Provision for depreciation	6,750
1 Dec	Machinery	15,000	1 Dec	Cash (sale price)	2,500
			1 Dec	Provision for depreciation	8,750
			31 Dec	P & L account (loss on disposal)	4,000
		30,000			30,000

You should be able to calculate that there was a loss on the first disposal of £250, and on the second disposal of £3,750, giving a total loss of £4,000.

Labour costs in the installation of fixed assets

35. When a business uses its own work force to install some fixed assets, the cost of the labour may be added to the cost of the fixed asset. The ledger accounting entries are therefore simply:

Debit	Fixed asset account
Credit	Wages/salaries account

with the labour cost of the installation.

Example

36. A business purchased a fixed asset on credit at a cost of £100,000. It used its own work force to install the asset, and the labour cost of this work was £18,000, of which £4,000 was paid to the Inland Revenue authorities as income tax (PAYE, or Pay As You Earn).

The ledger accounting entries would be:

FIXED ASSET

	£		£
Creditor	100,000		
Wages account	18,000		
	118,000		

WAGES ACCOUNT

	£		£
Cash	14,000	Fixed asset account	18,000
Income tax (PAYE) payable a/c	4,000		

Carriage inwards

37. Carriage inwards paid by a business may be treated as a part of the cost of purchases. If so, the ledger accounting entries for carriage inwards would be:

   (a) *Debit* Carriage inwards account
       Credit Creditor's account or cash

   with the cost of the carriage inwards.

   (b) When the trading account is prepared:

   Debit Trading account
   Credit Carriage inwards

   This in effect adds the cost of carriage to purchases.

38. If carriage inwards is not added to the cost of purchases but is treated as a separate expense, it is simply accounted for by:

   Debit P & L account
   Credit Carriage inwards

Carriage outwards

39. For carriage outwards paid by a business, there is a carriage outwards (expense) account, and the accounting entries are:

   (a) *Debit* Carriage outwards
       Credit Creditor's account or cash

   (b) and later, of course:

   Debit P & L account
   Credit Carriage outwards

Goods returned

40. Sometimes goods which are purchased from suppliers are returned, perhaps because they are unsatisfactory, or perhaps they have been bought on a 'sale or return' basis, whereby the supplier agrees to take back the goods if they cannot be sold. Similarly, goods which are sold to customers are sometimes returned by them.

   (a) Goods returned to suppliers are called 'purchase returns' or 'returns outwards'.
   (b) Goods returned from customers are 'sales returns' or 'returns inwards'.

41. Obviously when customers return goods, the total value of sales falls. One way of accounting for sales returns is:

   Debit   Sales account
   Credit   Debtors accounts, or cash account (depending on whether the customer gets a cash refund, a reduction in what he owes, or a 'credit note').

42. Another way of accounting for sales returns is to have a separate sales returns account.

   Debit   Sales returns
   Credit   Debtors account or cash account

   When the trading account is prepared, the sales returns account is closed off:

   Debit   Trading account
   Credit   Sales returns

   (However, instead of showing sales returns as a 'plus' value on the debit side of the trading account, they can be shown instead as a 'minus' value on the credit side – ie total sales less returns equals net sales.)

43. The same principles and techniques are applied to purchase returns. These reduce the cost of purchases, and one way of accounting for the return is:

   Debit   Creditors account (or cash)
   Credit   Purchases

44. Alternatively, we can use a separate purchase returns account; and

   Debit   Creditors account (or cash)
   Credit   Purchase returns

   When the trading account is prepared:

   Debit   Purchase returns
   Credit   Trading account

   (Instead of showing purchase returns as a plus value on the credit side of the trading account, they can be shown as a minus value on the debit side – ie total purchases less returns equals net purchases.)

Example

45. Stanley runs a wholesale business, and for the year to 31 March 19X6, transactions were as follows:

	£
Stock in hand: 1 April 19X5	1,800
Purchases, all on credit	20,000
Purchase returns	700
Creditors at 1 April 19X5	2,400
Debtors at 1 April 19X5	6,000
Sales, all on credit	40,000
Sales returns	1,400
Payments to creditors	18,700
Payments from debtors	39,600
Fixed assets at cost	30,000
Provision for depreciation (as at 1 April 19X5)	9,000
Sundry expenses (paid in cash)	11,000

Depreciation is to be provided for at 10% of the cost of fixed assets.

Stock in hand at 31 March 19X6 was valued at £2,500.

All the sundry expenses relate to the current accounting year.

Required:
Prepare the ledger accounts of Stanley (as far as the information above permits) and his trading profit and loss account for the year to 31 March 19X6.

Work through the solution carefully.

Solution

46.

STOCK IN HAND

	£		£
Opening stock	<u>1,800</u>	Trading account	<u>1,800</u>
Trading a/c - closing stock	2,500		

PURCHASES

	£		£
Creditors	<u>20,000</u>	Trading account	<u>20,000</u>

CREDITORS

	£		£
Purchase returns	700	Balance b/f	2,400
Cash	18,700	Purchases	20,000
Balance c/d	<u>3,000</u>		
	<u>22,400</u>		<u>22,400</u>
		Balance b/d	3,000

PURCHASE RETURNS

	£		£
Trading account	700	Creditors	700

SALES

	£		£
Trading account	40,000	Debtors	40,000

DEBTORS

	£		£
Balance b/f	6,000	Sales returns	1,400
Sales	40,000	Cash	39,600
		Balance c/d	5,000
	46,000		46,000
Balance b/d	5,000		

SALES RETURNS

	£		£
Debtors	1,400	Trading account	1,400

CASH (EXTRACT)

	£		£
Balance b/f (not given)	?	Creditors	18,700
Debtors	39,600	Sundry expenses	11,000

SUNDRY EXPENSES

	£		£
Cash	11,000	P & L account	11,000

FIXED ASSETS

	£		£
Balance b/f	30,000		

CAPITAL (EXTRACT)

	£		£
		Balance b/f (not given)	?
		P & L account	6,000

PROVISION FOR DEPRECIATION

	£		£
		Balance b/f	9,000
Balance c/d	12,000	P & L account	3,000
	12,000		12,000
		Balance b/d	12,000

STANLEY
TRADING, PROFIT AND LOSS ACCOUNT FOR THE YEAR TO 31 MARCH 19X6

	£	£	£
Sales		40,000	
Less returns		(1,400)	
			38,600
Opening stock		1,800	
Purchases	20,000		
Less returns	700		
		19,300	
		21,100	
Closing stock		(2,500)	
Cost of goods sold			18,600
Gross profit			20,000
Expenses:			
Depreciation		3,000	
Sundry expenses		11,000	
			14,000
Net profit			6,000

Summary

47. This chapter has explained the double entry necessary to deal with:

   - accruals
   - prepayments
   - bad debts
   - provision for doubtful debts
   - provision for depreciation
   - the disposal of fixed assets
   - labour costs in the installation of fixed assets
   - carriage inwards
   - carriage outwards
   - goods returned

TEST YOUR KNOWLEDGE
Numbers in brackets refer to paragraphs of this chapter

1. Describe the double entry in respect of:

   (a) an accrued rental payment.   (5)
   (b) a prepaid subscription charge.   (9)

2. If a higher provision is required for doubtful debts, the provision account should be debited with the amount of the increase. True or false?   (16)

3. How is accumulated depreciation disclosed in the balance sheet?   (23)

4. Describe the ledger accounting entries in respect of the disposal of a fixed asset. (28)

Now try questions 4-9 at the end of this section

Chapter 10

BOOKS OF PRIME ENTRY

The purpose of this chapter is:

● to describe the principal books of prime entry

● to explain the postings made from books of prime entry to ledger accounts

● to describe the nature and function of the sales and purchase ledgers

---

Introduction

1. The previous chapter on ledger accounting should by now have made it clear to you that a vital principle in bookkeeping is the double entry aspect to every transaction: for every debit there must be an equal credit and vice versa.

2. In practice, however, we do not make the double entry for a transaction in the ledger accounts ('T' accounts) every time there is a sale, a purchase, or a payment etc. Instead, it may be convenient to allow a time lag.

3. A record needs to be kept of every transaction, so that it does not get 'lost'. On the other hand, since there are so many transactions to record, it would be too cumbersome a process to make a double entry for every transaction as it occurs. This might suggest to you the need for books of account in which transactions can be recorded and built up, and which can then be used later to make the appropriate double entry in the ledger accounts.

4. Several such subsidiary books of account are kept, to record the 'build-up' of like transactions. Because they are the books in which a transaction is first recorded in the accounts, they are called books of prime entry.

    At regular intervals the records in the books of prime entry are subsequently entered ('posted') in the ledger accounts.

5. The books of prime entry include:

    (a) cash book;
    (b) petty cash book;
    (c) sales day book;
    (d) purchase day book;

(e) sales returns day book;
(f) purchases returns day book;
(g) journal.

A day book is a book in which a daily record of transactions is entered as soon as the transactions occur. A sales day book keeps a cumulative daily record of credit sales as they occur, a purchase day book keeps a daily record of the receipt of suppliers' invoices to be paid, etc.

Cash book

6. The cash book is the day book which is used to keep a cumulative record of money received and money paid out by the business from the business bank account.

7. Some cash, in notes and coins, is usually kept on the business premises in order to make occasional payments for odd items of expense. This cash is accounted for separately not in the cash book, but in a *petty cash book* which is identical in layout with a cash book.

8. The cash book, like a ledger account, has a 'debit side' and a 'credit side', but it is also written up with an analysis of the receipts and expenditures, in analysis columns.

9. An example might help to illustrate this.

On 1 September 19X7, Robin Plenty had the following receipts and payments:

(a) cash sale - receipts of £80;
(b) cheque payment from credit customer Hay £400 less discount allowed £20;
(c) cheque payment from credit customer Been £720;
(d) cheque payment from credit customer Seed £150 less discount allowed £10;
(e) cheque received for cash to provide a short-term loan from Len Dinger £1,800;
(f) second cash sale - receipts of £150;
(g) cash received for sale of fixed asset £200;
(h) cheque payment to supplier Kew £120;
(i) cheque payment to supplier Hare £130;
(j) cheque payment of telephone bill £400;
(k) cheque payment of gas bill £280;
(l) £100 in cash withdrawn from bank for petty cash;
(m) cheque payment of £1,500 to Hess for new plant and machinery.

At the beginning of 1 September, Robin Plenty had £900 in the bank.

10. The debit side of the cash book records receipts of cash, and might be analysed as follows:

CASH BOOK (DEBIT SIDE)

Date	Narrative	Folio	Total	Discounts allowed*	Sales ledger** (debtors)	Cash sales	Sundry items
19X7			£	£	£	£	£
1 Sept	Balance b/d		900				900
	Cash sale		80			80	
	Debtor – Hay		380	20	380		
	Debtor – Been		720		720		
	Debtor – Seed		140	10	140		
	Loan – Len Dinger		1,800				1,800
	Cash sale		150			150	
	Sale of fixed asset		200				200
			4,370	30	1,240	230	2,900
2 Sept	Balance b/d ***		1,660				
					(credit)	(credit)	(credit)

* This column is used purely as a memorandum. As cash is received from debtors, a note is made of any discount which they have taken advantage of. The column total is then used to make the following entries in the nominal ledger:

Debit	Discounts allowed	£30
Credit	Debtors	£30

** The sales ledger will be described later. However, it might help you to note here that this column represents receipts of money owed by debtors.

*** See the credit side of the cash book, below.

The extract above shows that £4,370 was received on 1 September. The column headings indicate the double entry necessary.

11. The credit side of the cash book records payments of cash and might be analysed as follows:

CASH BOOK (CREDIT SIDE)

Date	Narrative	Folio	Total	Disc'nts received*	Purchase ledger**	Petty cash	Wages	Sundry items
19X7			£	£	£	£	£	£
1 Sept	Creditor-Kew		120		120			
	Creditor-Hare		310		310			
	Telephone		400					400
	Gas bill		280					280
	Petty cash		100			100		
	Machinery purchase		1,500					1,500
	Balance c/d		1,660					1,660
			4,370	0	430	100	0	3,840
					(debit)	(debit)	(debit)	(debit)

157

* Again. this is a memorandum column only.
** The purchase ledger will be described later. However, it represents payment of money owed to suppliers for purchases.

The total cash account (nominal ledger)

12. The cash book is sometimes used, not only as a book of prime entry, but also as a ledger account, with the total columns on the debit side and the credit side providing the T account for the cash ledger account.

Alternatively, and perhaps more simply, the cash book is simply a book of prime entry, from which a total cash account in the nominal ledger can be prepared. In the illustrative example above, the cash book would be used to make the following entries in the total cash account in the nominal ledger.

(TOTAL) CASH ACCOUNT

	£		£
1 September 19X7		1 September 19X7	
Balance b/f	900	Creditors	430
Debtors	1,240	Petty cash a/c	100
Sales (cash sales)	230	Fixed asset a/c	1,500
Loan a/c	1,800	Gas	280
Disposal of fixed asset a/c	200	Telephone expenses	400
		Balance c/f	1,660
	4,370		4,370
2 September 19X7			
Balance b/f	1,660		

Note: the items in the sundry income and sundry expenses analysis columns must be debited or credited to the appropriate account - eg loan account, fixed asset account, telephone expenses account etc.

Bank reconciliation

13. Every so often, a business will receive a bank statement. Bank statements should then be used to check that the amount shown as a balance in the cash book reconciles with the amount on the bank statement, and that no cash has 'gone missing'. The reconciliation of the cash book with a statement is the subject of a separate chapter later on.

Petty cash book

14. The petty cash account is used to:

   (a) make occasional small payments in cash - eg to pay the milkman, to buy a few postage stamps, to pay the office cleaner, to pay for some bus or taxi fares etc;
   (b) collect occasional small receipts, such as cash paid by a visitor to make a phone call, or take some photocopies etc.

Most cash transactions are payments, and petty cash must be 'topped up' from time to time with cash from the business bank account.

15. Under the imprest system, the amount of money in petty cash is kept at an agreed sum or 'float' (say £100). Expense items are recorded on vouchers as they occur, so that at any time:

	£
Cash still held in petty cash	X
Plus voucher payments	X
Must equal the agreed sum or float	X

The total float is made up regularly (to £100, or whatever the agreed sum is) say once a week, by means of a cash payment from the bank account and into petty cash. The amount of the 'top-up' into petty cash will be the total of the voucher payments since the previous top-up.

16. The format of a petty cash book is much the same as for the cash book, with analysis columns (chiefly for expenditure items, such as travel, postage, cleaning etc, on the credit side of the account).

Sales day book

17. The sales day book is used to keep a chronological list of all invoices sent out to credit customers. It is not a ledger account.

The sales day book can also be analysed into different types of credit sales being made. For example, a publisher of text books might wish to distinguish between sales of accountancy texts and sales of law texts.

A simple example of a sales day book is shown below.

SALES DAY BOOK

Page SDB 48

Date	Invoice number	Customer	Sales ledger folio *	Total amount invoiced	Accountancy sales	Law sales
19X0				£	£	£
Jan 10	247	Jones & Co	SL14	105.00	105.00	
	248	Smith Ltd	SL 8	86.40		86.40
	249	Alex & Co	SL 6	31.80		31.80
	250	Enor College	SL 9	1,264.60	721.00	543.60
				1,487.80	826.00	661.80
				NL 7	NL51	NL52
				(debit)	(credit)	(credit)

* The sales ledger folio references are explained in paragraphs 19-23 below.

18. The extract above shows that four sales invoices (numbers 247 to 250) were raised on 10 January 19X0. The coding at the foot of the extract shows the double entry necessary to enter these sales, in total, in the nominal ledger.

Debit	Debtors (account number 7 in the nominal ledger)	£1,487.80
Credit	Accountancy sales (account number 51 in the nominal ledger)	£ 826.00
Credit	Law sales (account number 52 in the nominal ledger)	£ 661.80

In this example we are assuming that posting to the nominal ledger takes place at the end of each day. It would be equally possible to make the double entry at longer intervals. For example, a business might accumulate sales invoices in its sales day book for a week or a month before posting totals to the nominal ledger.

The sales ledger

19. The sales day book provides a chronological record of invoices sent out by a business to credit customers. For many businesses, this might involve very large numbers of invoices per day or per week, and a single customer, making several credit purchases over a period of time, will appear several times in different parts of the sales day book.

In addition to keeping a chronological record of invoices, a business should also keep a record of how much money each individual credit customer owes, and what this total debt consists of. The need for a 'personal account' for each customer is a practical one.

(a) A customer might telephone, and ask how much he currently owes. The business needs to be able to tell him.

(b) It is a common practice to send out statements to credit customers at the end of each month, showing how much they still owe, and itemising new invoices sent out and payments received during the month.

(c) The business will want to keep a check on the credit position of an individual customer, and to ensure that no customer is exceeding his credit limit by purchasing more goods.

(d) Most important is the need to match payments received against debts owed. If a customer makes a payment, the business must be able to set off the payment against the customer's debt and establish how much he still owes on balance.

20. Personal accounts for each individual credit customer are therefore kept, and these make up the sales ledger.

The invoices sent out and money received, which are recorded in a customer's personal account can be represented by a T account, as follows:

On the debit side	*On the credit side*
Invoices sent out	Payments received
	Sales returns
	Discounts allowed

When entries in the sales day book (invoices sent out) or cash book (payments received) are recorded in the personal accounts of customers, we say that the transactions are posted to the sales ledger.

21. But although the T account format is a convenient one for recording transactions with individual debtors you should not be misled into thinking that these personal accounts in the sales ledger form part of the double entry accounting system. As explained in paragraph 18 above, sales invoices recorded in the sales day book are debited in total to the debtors account in the nominal ledger, and credited in total to the sales account(s) in the nominal ledger. This

completes the double entry. The subsequent entry of each invoice separately in sales ledger personal accounts is merely a memorandum undertaken for the administrative reasons listed in paragraph 19 above.

22. Returning to the example in paragraph 17, each invoice would be posted separately to the relevant personal account in the sales ledger. For example, if Enor College already owed £250 before 10 January 19X0 the personal account might appear as follows:

ENOR COLLEGE

A/c no: SL9

	£		£
Balance b/f	250.00		
10.1.X0 Sales - SDB 48			
(invoice no 150)	1,264.60	Balance c/d	1,514.60
	1,514.60		1,514.60
11.1.X0 Balance b/d	1,514.60		

Purchase day book

23. The purchase day book is used to keep a list of all the invoices received from suppliers. Like the sales day book, it is not a ledger account. Also like the sales day book, it may have analysis columns for the different types of purchases made.

An example of a purchase day book is as follows:

PURCHASE DAY BOOK

Page PDB 37

Date	Supplier	Purchase ledger folio	Total amount invoiced	Purchases	Electricity etc...
19X8			£	£	£
March 15	Cook & Co	PL31	315.00	315.00	
	W Butler	PL46	29.40	29.40	
	EEB	PL42	116.80		116.80
	Show Fair Limited	PL12	100.00	100.00	
			561.20	444.40	116.80
			NL 12 (credit)	NL 70 (debit)	NL 77 (debit)

24. The extract above shows that four suppliers' invoices were received on 15 March 19X8. Three of them related to goods purchased for resale, while the fourth was an electricity bill. A typical PDB includes many columns in which invoices can be analysed under suitable expense headings.

The coding at the foot of the extract shows the double entry necessary to enter these invoices, in total, in the nominal ledger.

Credit	Creditors (account number 12 in the nominal ledger)	£561.20
Debit	Purchases (account number 70 in the nominal ledger)	£444.40
Debit	Electricity (account number 77 in the nominal ledger)	£116.80

The purchase ledger (bought ledger)

25. The purchase ledger, like the sales ledger, consists of a number of personal accounts. These are separate accounts for each individual supplier, and they enable a business to keep a continuous record of how much it owes each supplier at any time.

    The purchase ledger, and the personal accounts of suppliers in it, are not a part of the double entry bookkeeping system, although transactions can be shown in a T account format, as follows:

On the debit side	On the credit side
Payments made	Invoices received
Purchases returns	
Discounts received	

26. Returning to the example in paragraph 23, the four transactions are posted to the four different personal accounts of suppliers in the purchase ledger. For example, suppose that at the beginning of 15 March, the business owed Cook & Co £200.

COOK & CO

A/c no: PL 31

	£		£
		Balance b/f	200.00
		15 March 19X8	
		Invoice received	315.00
Balance c/d	515.00	PDB 37	
	515.00		515.00
		16 March 19X8	
		Balance b/d	£515.00

Summary

27. The roles of the sales day book and purchases day book are therefore very similar, with one book dealing with invoices sent out and the other with invoices received. The sales ledger and purchases ledger also serve similar purposes, with one consisting of personal accounts for credit customers and the other consisting of personal accounts for creditors.

Sales returns day book

28. When customers return goods, the returns are recorded in the sales returns day book. The customers will either:

    (a) be refunded in cash (or by cheque) or

    (b) be issued with a credit note, which is a note to indicate to the customer that his total debt has been reduced by the amount indicated on the note (and that the customer can set off the amount on the credit note against future debts incurred).

    Of course, if goods are returned before payment has been made by the customer, then a credit note would be issued purely for the sake of good form.

29. The sales returns day book is then used:

    (a) to post sales returns to the personal accounts of the individual customers in the sales ledger. (The postings will be credit entries, reducing the customers' debts). This is not a part of the double entry system;

    (b) to debit the total sales returns in the sales returns account in the nominal ledger, as the debit 'half' of the transactions in the double entry bookkeeping system;

    (c) to credit total debtors in the nominal ledger, as the credit 'half' of the same transactions.

Sales returns day book: example

30. In April 19X6, a business made sales totalling £60,000. Total debtors as at 30 April 19X6 were £5,600. One particular customer, Owen Plenty, owed £850.

    At the last moment two further transactions on 30 April 19X6 needed to be accounted for:

    (a) Owen Plenty bought more goods on credit, at a sales value of £240;
    (b) Owen Plenty also returned goods valued at £170.

    Owen Plenty's account reference number in the sales ledger of the business is SL123.

31. The transactions would be recorded in:

    (a) the sales day book for the credit sale:

SALES DAY BOOK (EXTRACT)
                                        Total
                                        £
30 April 19X6 Owen Plenty (SL 123)   240.00

SALES RETURNS DAY BOOK (EXTRACT)
                                        Total
30 April 19X6 Owen Plenty (SL 123)   170.00

SALES (NOMINAL LEDGER) - EXTRACT

	£		£
30 April 19X6 Trading a/c	60,240	Balance b/f	60,000
		Debtors	240
	60,240		60,240

SALES RETURNS (NOMINAL LEDGER) - EXTRACT

30 April 19X6 Debtors	170	Trading account	170

TOTAL DEBTORS (NOMINAL LEDGER) - EXTRACT

		£		£
30 April 19X6	Balance b/d	5,600	Sales returns	170
	Sales	240	Balance c/d	5,670
		5,840		5,840
1 May 19X7	Balance b/d	5,670		

TRADING ACCOUNT (NOMINAL LEDGER)
EXTRACT FOR APRIL 19X6

	£	£	£
Sales		60,240	
Less returns		170	
			60,070

The sales returns could be shown as a debit entry in the trading account. More often, however, they are shown as a 'minus' entry on the credit side, which is the same thing.

SALES LEDGER FOLIO SL123 - OWEN PLENTY

	£		£
30 April 19X6			
Balance b/f	850	Sales returns day book	
Sales day book (folio ref -)	240	(folio ref -)	170
		Balance c/f	920
	1,090		1,090
1 May 19X6			
Balance b/f	920		

(Remember: the sales ledger personal account for Owen Plenty is not a part of the double entry bookkeeping system)

Purchase returns day book

32. In the same way, the purchase returns day book keeps a list of all items returned to suppliers. The business might expect a cash refund or a credit note from the supplier. In the meantime, however, it might choose to issue a debit note to the supplier, indicating the amount by which the business expects its total debt to the supplier to be reduced.

33. The purchase returns day book is used:

   (a) to post purchase returns to the personal accounts of individual creditors in the purchase ledger;

   (b) to credit the purchase returns account in the nominal ledger with the total value of purchase returns, as the credit 'half' of the transactions in the double entry bookkeeping system;

   (c) to debit total creditors in the nominal ledger with the total value of purchase returns, as the debit 'half' of the transactions in the double entry bookkeeping system.

The journal

34. The term 'journal' means 'day-book' (or 'diary') but it is now used to describe a book of prime entry which is used less frequently. It is used to provide a permanent record, with narrative, of unusual movements between accounts. Although it is a book of prime entry, and it is not a part of the double entry bookkeeping system itself, the journal:

   (a) indicates both the debit entry and the credit entry in the ledger accounts;
   (b) is subsequently used to post the transactions to the ledger accounts as a debit and also a credit entry.

35. The types of transactions recorded in the journal are:

    (a) the correction of errors. For example, if an incorrect posting has been made in the accounts, the correction of the error will be noted in the journal, from which the ledger accounts will subsequently be corrected;

    (b) to transfer an amount from one account in the nominal ledger to the profit and loss account. When the trading, P & L account of a business is prepared, the transfers from various ledger accounts to the P & L account (itself ultimately a ledger account) is first of all noted in the journal;

    (c) to transfer amounts from a ledger account which has been used as a 'collecting station' for a certain item - eg drawings, which are subsequently transferred to the capital account.

The format of journal entries

36. Whatever type of transaction is being recorded, the format of a journal entry is:

Date	Folio	Debit £	Credit £
Account to be debited		X	
Account to be credited			X
(Narrative to explain the transaction)			

(Remember: in due course, the ledger accounts will be written up to include the transactions listed in the journal.)

A narrative explanation must accompany each journal entry. It is required for audit and control, to indicate the purpose and authority of every transaction which is not first recorded in a book of prime entry.

37. An example might help to illustrate the format.

A business ends its accounting year on 30 June. In the year to 30 June 19X6, the total expenditure in the wages and salaries account is £120,000 and there are no accrued or prepaid wages and salaries.

To prepare the P & L account for the year, an entry will be made in the journal to close off the wages and salaries account.

	Folio	Debit £	Credit £
P & L account		120,000	
Wages and salaries			120,000

Wages and salaries for the year to 30.6.X6.

Further example: journal entries

38. An examination question might ask you to 'journalise' transactions which would not in practice be recorded in the journal at all. If you are faced with such a problem, you should simply record the debit and credit entries for every transaction you can recognise, giving some supporting narrative to each transaction.

39. The following is a summary of the transactions of Yve's hairdressing business of which Paul Brown is the sole proprietor.

1 January	Put in cash of £2,000 as capital
	Purchased brushes and combs for cash £50
	Purchased hair driers from Z Limited on credit £150
30 January	Paid three months rent to 31 March £300
	Collected and paid in takings £600
31 January	Sent Mrs X her January account for £80.

(a) Show the transactions by means of journal entries.
(b) Ignoring depreciation, prepare the balance sheet as at 31 January.

Solution

40. (a)

JOURNAL

			Debit £	Credit £
1 January	Cash		2,000	
	Paul Brown - capital account			2,000
	Initial capital introduced			
1 January	Brushes and combs account		50	
	Cash			50
	The purchase for cash of brushes and combs as fixed assets			
1 January	Hair dryer account		150	
	Sundry creditors account*			150
	The purchase on credit of hair driers as fixed assets			
30 January	Cash		600	
	Sales			600
	Cash takings			
30 January	Rent account		300	
	Cash			300
	The payment of rent to 31 March			
31 January	Debtors account		80	
	Sales account			80
	Credit account customer's sales			

31 January	P & L account	100	
	Rent account		100
	The transfer of one month's rent to the		
	P & L account		

31 January	Sales account	680	
	P & L account		680
	The transfer of one month's sales to the		
	P & L account		

31 January	P & L account	580	
	Capital account		580
	The profit for the month (January)		

Note: creditors who have supplied fixed assets are included amongst sundry creditors, as distinct from creditors who have supplied raw materials or goods for resale, who are trade creditors.

(b)

BALANCE SHEET AS AT 31 JANUARY

	£	£
Fixed assets		
Brushes and combs at cost	50	
Hair dryer at cost	150	
		200
Current assets		
Debtors	80	
Rent paid in advance	200	
Cash at bank and in hand	2,250	
	2,530	
Creditor: Z Limited	(150)	
		2,380
		2,580
Proprietor's capital		
Capital introduced		2,000
Profit		580
		2,580

Note: Cash at bank and in hand is:

	£	£
Capital introduced		2,000
Cash takings		600
		2,600
Less payments:		
Brushes and combs	50	
Rent	300	
		350
Cash in hand at 31 January		2,250

WHY NOT HAIR DRYER.

The correction of errors

41. Errors corrected by the journal must be capable of correction by means of a double entry in the ledger accounts. (When errors are made which break the rule of double entry, that debits and credits must be equal, the initial step in identifying and correcting the error is to open up a *suspense account*, to restore equality between total debits and total credits. Errors leading to the creation of a suspense account are corrected initially by making a record in the journal. However, suspense accounts are the subject of a separate chapter in this text).

42. There are several common types of error.

    (a) *Errors of transposition.* For example, suppose that a sale is recorded in the sales account as £6,843 instead of £6,483, but it has been correctly recorded in the total debtors account as £6,483. The error is the transposition of the 4 and the 8. The consequence is that total debits will not be equal to total credits, and the imbalance will first of all lead to the creation of a suspense account. A useful clue to a transposition error is that the imbalance will always be divisible by 9 (eg the above imbalance is £360).

    (b) *Errors of omission.* Omission means failing to record a transaction at all, or making a debit or credit entry, but not the corresponding double entry.

        (i) If a business receives an invoice from a supplier for, say, £250, the transaction might be omitted from the books entirely. When the omission is eventually discovered, it will be logged in the journal.

	Debit £	Credit £
Purchases	250	
Creditors		250

A transaction previously omitted.

        (ii) If a business receives an invoice from a supplier for, say, £300, the creditor's account might be credited, but the debit entry in the purchases account might be omitted. In this case, since total debits and total credits would not be equal as a result of the omission, the first step in the correction procedure would be to open up a suspense account (to take the omitted debit entry of £300).

    (c) *Errors of principle.* An error of principle involves making a double entry in the belief that the transaction is being entered in the correct accounts, but subsequently finding out that the accounting entry breaks the 'rules' of an accounting principle. A typical example of such an error is to treat certain revenue expenditure incorrectly as capital expenditure.

        (i) For example, repairs to a machine costing £150 should be treated as revenue expenditure, and debited to a repairs account. If, instead, the repair costs are added to the cost of the fixed asset (capital expenditure) an error of principle would have occurred. The correction should be logged in the journal. In our example, the correction would be:

	Debit £	Credit £
Repairs account	150	
Fixed asset (machinery) a/c		150

The correction of an error of principle. Repair costs incorrectly added to fixed asset costs.

(ii) Similarly, suppose that the proprietor of the business sometimes takes cash out of the till for his personal use and during a certain year these takings amount to £280. The bookkeeper states that he has reduced cash sales by £280 so that the cash book could be made to balance. This would be an error of principle, to be corrected in the journal by:

	Debit £	Credit £
Drawings account	280	
Sales		280

An error of principle, in which sales were reduced to compensate for cash drawings not accounted for.

(d) *Errors of commission.* These are errors whereby the book-keeper makes a mistake in carrying out his or her task of recording transactions in the accounts. These errors include:

(i) putting a debit entry or a credit entry in the wrong account. For example, if telephone expenses of £540 are debited to the electricity expenses account, an error of commission would have occurred. The correction should be journalised, in this example as follows:

	Debit £	Credit £
Telephone expenses	540	
Electricity expenses		540

Correction of an error. Telephone expenses wrongly charged to the electricity account.

(ii) errors of adding up (*casting*) in the sales day book or purchase day book. Suppose for example that the total daily credit sales in the sales day book of a business should add up to £28,425, but are incorrectly added up as £28,825. The total sales in the sales day book are then used to credit total sales and debit total debtors in the ledger accounts, so that total debits and total credits are still equal, although incorrect. The error, once identified, would be corrected after being logged in the journal.

	Debit £	Credit £
Sales	400	
Debtors		400

The correction of a casting error in the sales day book.

Why is it necessary to journalise errors?

43. Errors which are corrected are logged in the journal because the journal provides a lasting diary or record of such mistakes, which might be of some value as information to management, and help in the prevention of fraud.

Journal vouchers

44. Journal entries might be logged, not in a single 'book' or journal, but on a separate slip of paper, called a journal voucher. A journal voucher is used to record the equivalent of one entry in the journal. Its fairly widespread use is perhaps explained by:

(a) the repetitive nature of certain journal entries. Vouchers can be pre-printed, to standardise the narrative of such entries, and to save time in writing them out;

(b) a voucher is able to hold more information than a conventional journal record.

Contra entries

45. Sometimes, a business might both purchase goods from and sell goods to the same person on credit. If it does so:

(a) purchases will be recorded in the purchase day book when invoices are received, and an entry subsequently posted to the supplier's individual account in the purchase ledger;

(b) credit sales will be recorded in the sales day book when invoices are sent out, and an entry subsequently posted to the customer's individual account in the sales ledger.

46. Even though the supplier and the customer are one and the same person, he will have a separate account in each ledger. For example, if A owes B £200 for purchases and B owes A £350 for credit sales, the net effect is that B owes A £150. However, in the books of A:

(a) there would be a creditor in the purchase ledger - B - for £200; and
(b) there would be a debtor in the sales ledger - B - for £350.

Now, if A and B decide to settle their accounts by netting off their respective debts (and getting B to write a single cheque for the balance) settlement would be made *in contra*.

The contra entries in the accounts of A would be to set off the smaller amount (£200 owed to B) against the larger amount (£350 owed by B).

(a)		(b)	
In the sales ledger and purchase ledger	and	In the nominal ledger	
Debit Creditors account (B) £200		*Debit* Total creditors	£200
Credit Debtor's account (B) £200		*Credit* Total debtors	£200

This would 'wipe out' the debt to B, and reduce the debt of B by £200, leaving B as a debtor for £150. The contra entries must be made in both the personal accounts of B and also in the total creditors and debtors accounts in the nominal ledger.

Summary of the chapter

47.
> - Business transactions are not recorded directly as double entries in the ledger accounting system. Instead, books of prime entry are used as staging posts, to record transactions in chronological sequence, and from which postings to other accounts are subsequently made.
>
> - Personal accounts in the sales ledger and purchase ledger stand outside the double entry bookkeeping system, and are memorandum accounts.
>
> - However, debit and credit entries are made in these accounts to record the amounts still owed by individual customers or to individual suppliers.

TEST YOUR KNOWLEDGE

Numbers in brackets refer to paragraphs of this chapter

1. List the seven books of prime entry discussed in this chapter. (5)

2. What is meant by an 'imprest system'? (15)

3. Why is it necessary for businesses to maintain a sales ledger? (19)

4. What types of transaction are recorded in the journal? (35)

5. List four types of error which may occur in maintaining a bookkeeping system. (42)

Now try questions 10 to 12 at the end of this section

Chapter 11

BILLS OF EXCHANGE

The purpose of this chapter is:

●   to explain the function of bills of exchange

●   to illustrate the accounting entries relating to bills of exchange

---

What is a bill of exchange?

1.   A bill of exchange is 'an unconditional order in writing, addressed by one person to another, signed by the person giving it, requiring the person to whom it is addressed to pay on demand or at a fixed or determinable future time a sum certain in money to or to the order of a specified person or bearer'. (Bills of Exchange Act 1882).

2.   This legal definition of a bill of exchange might seem a little complex, and so it will be useful to look at several parts of the definition in turn.

    (a)   A bill of exchange is the legal recognition of a debt. It is not so much an IOU as a 'You owe me' because it is issued (drawn up) by the person to whom the money is owed. This person is called the *drawer* of the bill.

    (b)   The drawer of a bill of exchange specifies on the bill:

        (i)   how much is to be paid, and in what currency (many bills of exchange are 'foreign' bills, specifying a foreign currency as the amount owed);
        (ii)   when the money is to be paid. This might be immediately or 'at sight' of the bill, in which case the bill is a sight bill. However, the bill might well allow a specified period of credit - say, 60 days or 90 days from the date of the bill;
        (iii)   to whom the money is to be paid (the *payee*). This is usually the drawer himself;
        (iv)   who should pay the money.

    (c)   The bill is then sent to the person who should pay the bill. This person is called the *drawee*, because the bill has been drawn on him requesting him to pay the money on the agreed date.

    (d)   The drawee then signs the bill, or accepts it. When a bill has been accepted, it is no longer so much a 'You owe me' issued by the drawer as a legally-enforceable 'I agree to pay' signed by the drawee.

(e)   In the case of a sight bill, the money owed must be paid at once. In the case of a bill which allows the drawee some period of credit, the drawee returns the bill of exchange to the drawer or payee. The drawer would now hold a bill of exchange, accepted by the drawee, which can be presented for payment when payment becomes due.

3.   A bill of exchange is a negotiable instrument, a legal term which means that it can be transferred from one person to another by endorsement. If a drawer A holds a bill of exchange accepted by the drawee B, whereby B has agreed to pay £1,000 to A after 90 days (say on 1 April 19X5), then A can either:

(a)   hold on to the bill until 1 April 19X5, and then obtain payment from B;

(b)   transfer the bill to someone else, usually by selling it at a discount. A's bank will probably be willing to buy the bill for less than £1,000 (ie to *discount* the bill) - say for £980. A would then have £980 in cash now, and the bank would wait until 1 April 19X5 to claim the £1,000 in full from B. (In fact, the bank might discount the bill in turn to another bank. In the UK there are several discount houses which specialise in trade in bills of exchange, on the discount market, one of the money markets in the City of London.)

Accounting for bills of exchange

4.   If a business either draws or accepts bills of exchange in the course of its trading operations, the bills which allow some period of credit, being a special type of debt, must be accounted for.

5.   We must first of all make a distinction between:

(a)   bills of exchange accepted by the business - ie where the business is the drawee. These are called *bills payable*, because they are sums of money that the business has agreed to pay at a specified future date; and

(b)   bills of exchange drawn on someone else by the business, and accepted by that drawee, ie where the business, as the drawer, is owed money. These are called *bills receivable*.

Bills payable

6.   When a business accepts a bill of exchange and returns it to the drawer, the drawer is no longer a specific creditor of the business. Instead, the drawer holds a bill of exchange, which is a sort of 'delayed-action' cheque.

7.   The acceptance of a bill of exchange, which is now a 'bill payable', is accounted for by:

(a)   debiting the creditor's account; and
(b)   crediting the bills payable account.

8.   Eventually, the bill will be paid on the due date, and the cash payment will be accounted for in the ledger accounts as:

Debit   Bills payable account
Credit   Cash account

Example: bills payable

9. Tuff Traders purchases goods from Swift Sellers on 1 April 19X5 at a price of £4,000. The purchase is on credit, but Tuff Traders agrees to accept a bill of exchange for £4,000, payable on 1 July 19X5, drawn by Swift Sellers. Tuff Traders accepts the bill on 9 April. On 1 July, Tuff Traders honours the bill by paying the £4,000 when the bill is presented for payment. The accounting entries would be, in the books of Tuff Traders:

PURCHASES

	£		£
1 April 19X5 Creditors (Swift Sellers)	4,000		

CREDITORS (SWIFT SELLERS)

	£		£
9 April 19X5 Bills payable	4,000	1 April 19X5 Purchases	4,000

BILLS PAYABLE

	£		£
1 July 19X5 Cash	4,000	9 April 19X5 Creditors (Swift Sellers)	4,000

CASH

	£		£
		1 July 19X5 Bills payable	4,000

10. At the end of an accounting period, the business will prepare a balance sheet. Any bills payable which have not yet reached their due date for payment must be shown as current liabilities.

Bills receivable

11. When a business draws a bill of exchange on a debtor, who then accepts the bill and returns it to the drawer, the business will possess a 'bill receivable' and the drawee will cease to be a specific debtor. The business has been given a 'delayed-action' cheque, and the accounting entries to record this transaction would be:

Debit   Bills receivable account
Credit Debtors account

12. When the bill becomes due for payment, it will be presented, and the cash paid. The accounting entries to record the cash receipt would be:

Debit   Cash account
Credit Bills receivable account

11: BILLS OF EXCHANGE

Example: bills receivable

13. Taking the example in paragraph 9, but looking now at the books of the drawer of the bill, Swift Sellers, the accounting entries would be:

SALES

	£		£
		1 April 19X5 Debtors (Tuff Traders)	4,000

DEBTORS (TUFF TRADERS)

	£		£
1 April 19X5 Sales	4,000	9 April 19X5 Bills receivable	4,000

BILLS RECEIVABLE

	£		£
9 April 19X5 Debtors (Tuff Traders)	4,000	1 July 19X5 Cash	4,000

CASH

	£		£
1 July 19X5 Bills receivable	4,000		

14. At the end of an accounting period, any bills of exchange receivable held by a business, which are not yet due for payment, will be shown as current assets in the balance sheet.

Dishonoured bills

15. A bill receivable might be *dishonoured* when it is presented for payment, which means that the drawee, for one reason or another, fails to pay the money due. When this occurs, the drawee becomes either:

    (a) a debtor again; or
    (b) a bad debt to be written off.

    Option (b) might become necessary eventually, but option (a) is more likely to be the immediate course of action.

Example: dishonoured bills

16. Good Faith Traders sold goods to Rogue Merchants on 1 March 19X5 for £3,000. On 15 March, Rogue Merchants accepted a bill of exchange drawn by Good Faith Traders, promising to pay the £3,000 on 1 June 19X5.

    On 1 June when the bill is presented for payment, Good Faith Traders are informed that the bill cannot be paid, because Rogue Merchants have gone into liquidation.

11: BILLS OF EXCHANGE

On 18 August 19X5, the receiver dealing with the liquidation of Rogue Merchants pays a 'final dividend' of 50 pence in £1 to creditors of the business, which means that businesses owed money by Rogue Merchants are paid half of what they are owed.

The accounting entries would be:

SALES

	£
1 March 19X5 Debtors	3,000

DEBTORS (ROGUE MERCHANTS)

	£		£
1 March 19X5 Sales	3,000	15 March 19X5 Bills receivable	3,000
1 June 19X5 Bills receivable	3,000	18 August 19X5 Cash	1,500
(bill dishonoured		18 August 19X5 Bad debts	1,500
	6,000		6,000

BILLS RECEIVABLE

	£		£
15 March 19X5 Debtors	3,000	1 June 19X5 Debtors (Rogue Merchants – bill dishonoured)	3,000

CASH

	£		£
18 August 19X5 Debtors	1,500		

BAD DEBTS

	£		£
18 August 19X5 Debtors	1,500		

Discounted bills

17. It was mentioned earlier that the holder of a bill receivable might decide to sell the bill at a discount, usually to a bank. For example, a bill for £5,000 might be discounted by a bank, which will pay, say, £4,750 for it. If this were to happen, the accounting entries would then be:

		£	£
Debit	Cash	4,750	
Debit	Bank charges	250	
Credit	Bills receivable		5,000

18. If the bill is subsequently dishonoured by the drawee, however, the bank would have a right of *recourse* against the drawer of the bill (or any subsequent endorser which sold it the bill).

176

19. In the example above of the bill for £5,000, if the bank later comes back and states that the bill was dishonoured, it could claim the full £5,000 from the drawer instead - not just its 'money back' (£4,750). The drawer, if obliged to pay the money instead of the drawee, would account for the transaction by reinstating the drawee as a debtor; ie

		£
Debit	Debtors (the account of the drawee who dishonoured the bill)	5,000
Credit	Cash (money paid to the bank)	5,000

Conclusion

20. Bills of exchange might appear in an examination question, in which case you should be able to recognise what they are, and what the necessary ledger accounting entries should be. Basically, however, they are similar to debtors and creditors, so unless they are dishonoured bills (bad debts) or discounted bills, bills of exchange are more relevant to the preparation of a balance sheet rather than to the profit and loss account.

TEST YOUR KNOWLEDGE

Numbers in brackets refer to paragraphs of this chapter

1. Define a bill of exchange. (1)

2. Explain the process of 'discounting' a bill of exchange. (3)

3. 'Bills receivable' in the books of a business record amounts of money owing to the business. True or false? (5)

4. What are the accounting entries when a bill with a face value of £5,000 is discounted for £4,750? (17)

Now try question 13 at the end of this section

Chapter 12

CONTROL ACCOUNTS

The purpose of this chapter is:

- to explain the nature and function of control accounts

- to illustrate typical entries in a control account

- to illustrate the reconciliation of control accounts with sales ledger and purchase ledger listings

---

Introduction

1. In an earlier chapter we saw how sales invoices and purchase invoices were logged in day books. Each invoice is posted singly to an appropriate personal account in the sales ledger or purchase ledger. But these personal accounts are for memorandum purposes only and form no part of the double entry system.

2. To record these transactions in the double entry system we do not deal with each invoice singly. Instead, the day books are totalled at convenient intervals (eg daily, weekly or monthly) and these total amounts are recorded in the nominal ledger as follows:
    For sales invoices:

Debit	Debtors (control) account
Credit	Sales account(s)

    For purchase invoices:

Debit	Expenses accounts (purchases etc)
Credit	Creditors (control) account

Control accounts

3. A control account is an account in which a record is kept of the total value of a number of similar but individual items. Control accounts are used chiefly for debtors and creditors.

    (a) A debtors control account is an account in which records are kept of transactions involving all debtors in total. The balance on the debtors control account at any time will be the total amount due to the business at that time from its debtors.

(b)   A creditors control account is an account in which records are kept of transactions involving all creditors in total, and the balance on this account at any time will be the total amount owed by the business at that time to its creditors.

4.   Although control accounts are used mainly in accounting for debtors and creditors, they can also be kept for other items, such as stocks of goods, wages and salaries. The first important idea to remember, however, is that a control account is an account which keeps a total record for a collective item (eg debtors) which in reality consists of many individual items (eg individual debtors).

5.   A control account is an (impersonal) ledger account which will appear in the nominal ledger.

Control accounts and personal accounts

6.   The personal accounts of individual debtors are kept in the sales ledger, and the amount owed by each debtor will be a balance on his personal account. The amount owed by all the debtors together will be a balance on the debtors control account.

At any time the balance on the debtors control account should be equal to the sum of the individual balances on the personal accounts in the sales ledger.

7.   For example, if a business has three debtors, A Arnold who owes £80, B Bagshaw who owes £310 and C Cloning who owes £200, the balances on the various accounts would be:

Sales ledger (personal accounts)

	£
A Arnold	80
B Bagshaw	310
C Cloning	200

Nominal ledger - debtors control account	590

All these balances would be debit balances. Now, if you think about this carefully, you might appreciate that the debit balances are accounted for in duplicate, once in the sales ledger (individual personal accounts) and once collectively in the nominal ledger. It therefore follows that accounting entries for debtors must be made twice, once in the sales ledger and once in the nominal ledger. It was explained in the previous chapter that this does not break the normal rule of double entry accounting, because the entries in the personal accounts are for memorandum purposes only.

Example: accounting for debtors

8.   You might still be uncertain why we need to have control accounts at all. Before turning our attention to this question, it will be useful first of all to see how transactions involving debtors are accounted for by means of an illustrative example. Folio numbers are shown in the accounts to illustrate the cross-referencing that is needed, and in the example folio numbers beginning:

(a)   SDB, refer to a page in the sales day book;
(b)   SL, refer to a particular account in the sales ledger;

(c) NL, refer to a particular account in the nominal ledger;
(d) CB, refer to a page in the cash book.

9. At 1 July 19X2, the Outer Business Company had no debtors at all. During July, the following transactions affecting credit sales and customers occurred.

(a) July 3: invoiced A Arnold for the sale on credit of hardware goods: £100;
(b) July 11: invoiced B Bagshaw for the sale on credit of electrical goods: £150;
(c) July 15: invoiced C Cloning for the sale on credit of hardware goods: £250;
(d) July 10: received payment from A Arnold of £90, in settlement of his debt in full, having taken a permitted discount of £10 for payment within seven days;
(e) July 18: received a payment of £72 from B Bagshaw in part settlement of £80 of his debt. A discount of £8 was allowed for payment within seven days of invoice;
(f) July 28: received a payment of £120 from C Cloning, who was unable to claim any discount.

Account numbers are as follows:

SL4   Personal account A Arnold
SL9   Personal account B Bagshaw
SL13   Personal account C Cloning
NL6   Debtors control account
NL7   Discount allowed
NL21   Sales - hardware
NL22   Sales - electrical
NL1   Cash control account

10. The accounting entries, suitably dated, would be as follows:

SALES DAY BOOK   SDB 35

Date 19X2	Name	Folio	Total £	Hardware £	Electrical £
July 3	A Arnold	SL 4 Dr	100.00	100.00	
11	B Bagshaw	SL 9 Dr	150.00		150.00
15	C Cloning	SL13 Dr	250.00	250.00	
			500.00	350.00	150.00
			NL 6 Dr	NL 21 Cr	NL 22 Cr

Note:
The personal accounts in the sales ledger are debited on the day the invoices are sent out. The double entry in the ledger accounts might be made at the end of each day, week or month; here it is made at the end of the month, by posting from the sales day book as follows:

		Debit £	Credit £
NL 6	Debtors control account	500	
NL21	Sales - hardware		350
NL22	Sales - electrical		150

CASH BOOK EXTRACT
RECEIPTS CASH BOOK – JULY 19X2 CB 23

Date	Narrative	Folio	Total	Discount allowed	Debtors control
19X2			£	£	£
July 10	A Arnold	SL 4 Cr	90.00	10.00	90.00
18	B Bagshaw	SL 9 Cr	72.00	8.00	72.00
28	C Cloning	SL13 Cr	120.00	–	120.00
			282.00	18.00	282.00
			NL 6 Cr	NL 7 Cr	NL 1 Dr

Notes:
The discount allowed column in the cash book is purely memorandum and does not form part of the double entry. The column total will be used to make the following nominal ledger entries:

Debit	NL 7 Discount allowed
Credit	NL 6 Debtors control account

However, a cross reference to the page in the cash book (CB23) will appear as the folio reference in the discount allowed account, and similarly CB23 will be the folio reference in the debtors control account for both the cash received and the discount allowed.

The personal accounts in the sales ledger are memorandum accounts, because they are not a part of the double entry system:

MEMORANDUM SALES LEDGER
ARNOLD A/c no: SL4

Date	Narrative	Folio	£	Date	Narrative	Folio	£
19X2				19X2			
July 3	Sales	SDB 35	100.00	July 10	Cash	CB 23	90.00
					Discount	CB 23	10.00
			100.00				100.00

B BAGSHAW A/c no: SL9

Date	Narrative	Folio	£	Date	Narrative	Folio	£
19X2				19X2			
July 11	Sales	SDB 35	150.00	July 18	Cash	CB 23	72.00
					Discount	CB 23	8.00
				July 31	Balance c/d		70.00
			150.00				150.00
Aug 1	Balance b/d		70.00				

C CLONING
A/c no: SL13

Date	Narrative	Folio	£	Date	Narrative	Folio	£
19X2				19X2			
July 15	Sales	SDB 35	250.00	July 28	Cash	CB 23	120.00
				July 31	Balance c/d		130.00
			250.00				250.00
Aug 1	Balance b/d		130.00				

In the nominal ledger, the accounting entries can be made from the books of prime entry to the ledger accounts, in this example at the end of the month.

NOMINAL LEDGER (EXTRACT)
TOTAL DEBTORS (SALES LEDGER CONTROL ACCOUNT)
A/c no: NL6

Date	Narrative	Folio	£	Date	Narrative	Folio	£
19X2				19X2			
July 31	Sales	SDB 35	500.00	July 31	Cash	CB23	282.00
					Discount allowed	CB23	18.00
				July 31	Balance c/d		200.00
			500.00				500.00
Aug 1	Balance b/d		200.00				

Note: at 31 July the closing balance on the debtors control account (£200) is the same as the total of the individual balances on the personal accounts in the sales ledger (£0 + £70 + £130).

DISCOUNT ALLOWED
A/c no: NL7

Date	Narrative	Folio	£	Date	Narrative	Folio	£
19X2							
July 31	Debtors	CB 23	18.00				

CASH CONTROL ACCOUNT
A/c no: NL1

Date	Narrative	Folio	£	Date	Narrative	Folio	£
19X2							
July 31	Cash received	CB 23	282.00				

SALES - HARDWARE
A/c no: NL21

Date	Narrative	Folio	£	Date	Narrative	Folio	£
				19X2			
				July 31	Debtors	SDB 35	350.00

SALES - ELECTRICAL   A/c no: NL22

Date	Narrative	Folio	£	Date 19X2	Narrative	Folio	£
				July 31	Debtors	SDB35	150.00

11. If we took the balance on the accounts shown in this example as at 31 July 19X2 the 'trial balance' (insofar as it is appropriate to call these limited extracts by this name) would be:

TRIAL BALANCE

	Debit £	Credit £
Cash (all receipts)	282	
Debtors	200	
Discount allowed	18	
Sales - hardware		350
Sales - electrical		150
	500	500

The trial balance is shown here to emphasise the point that a trial balance includes the balances on control accounts, but excludes the balances on the personal accounts in the sales ledger and purchase ledger.

12. If you were able to follow the example in paragraphs 9-10 dealing with the debtors control account, you should have no difficulty in dealing with similar examples relating to purchases/creditors. If necessary refer back to the previous chapter to revise the entries made in the purchase day book and purchase ledger personal accounts.

Entries in control accounts

13. Typical entries in the control accounts are listed below. Folio reference Jnl indicates that the transaction is first lodged in the journal before posting to the control account and other accounts indicated. References SRDB and PRDB are to sales returns and purchase returns day books.

SALES LEDGER (DEBTORS) CONTROL

	Folio	£		Folio	£
Opening debit balances	b/d	7,000	Opening credit balances	b/d	200
Sales	SDB	52,390	(if any)		
Dishonoured bills or			Cash received	CB	52,250
cheques	Jnl	1,000	Discounts allowed	CB	1,250
Cash paid to clear			Returns inwards from		
credit balances	CB	110	debtors	SRDB	800
Closing credit balances	c/d	120	Bad debts	Jnl	300
			Closing debit balances	c/d	5,820
		60,620			60,620
Debit balances b/d		5,820	Credit balances b/d		120

Note: opening credit balances are unusual in the debtors control account. They represent debtors to whom the business owes money, probably as a result of the over payment of debts or for advance payments of debts for which no invoices have yet been sent.

BOUGHT LEDGER (CREDITORS) CONTROL

	Folio	£		Folio	£
Opening debit balances (if any)	b/d	70	Opening credit balances	b/d	8,300
Cash paid	CB	29,840	Purchases and other expenses	PDB	31,000
Discounts received	CB	30	Cash received clearing debit balances	CB	20
Returns outwards to suppliers	PRDB	60	Closing debit balances (if any)	c/d	80
Closing credit balances	c/d	9,400			
		39,400			39,400
Debit balances	b/d	80	Credit balances	b/d	9,400

Note: opening debit balances in the creditors control account would represent suppliers who owe the business money, perhaps because debts have been overpaid or because debts have been prepaid before the supplier has sent an invoice.

14. Posting from the journal to the memorandum sales or bought ledgers and to the nominal ledger may be effected as in the following example, where C Cloning has returned goods with a sales value of £50.

Journal entry	Folio	Dr £	Cr
Sales	NL 21	50	
To debtors' control	NL 6		50
To C Cloning (memorandum)	SL 13	-	50

Return of electrical goods inwards.

Exercise

15. See now whether you can do the following exercise yourself.

On examining the books of Exports Limited, you ascertain that on 1 October 19X8 the debtors' ledger balances were £8,024 debit and £57 credit, and the creditors' ledger balances on the same date £6,235 credit and £105 debit.

For the year ended 30 September 19X9 the following particulars are available:

	£
Sales	63,728
Purchases	39,974
Cash received from debtors	55,212
Cash paid to creditors	37,307
Discount received	1,475
Discount allowed	2,328
Returns inwards	1,002
Returns outwards	535
Bad debts written off	326
Cash received in respect of debit balances in creditors' ledger	105
Amount due from customer as shown by debtors' ledger, offset against amount due to the same firm as shown by creditors' ledger (settlement by contra)	434
Cash received in respect of debt previously written off as bad	94
Allowances to customers on goods damaged in transit	212

On 30 September 19X9 there were no credit balances in the debtors' ledger except those outstanding on 1 October 19X9, and no debit balances in the creditors' ledger.

You are required to write up the following accounts recording the above transactions bringing down the balances as on 30 September 19X9:

(a) debtors control account; and
(b) creditors control account.

Solution

16. (a)   DEBTORS CONTROL (OR TOTAL) ACCOUNT

19X8		£	19X8		£
Oct 1	Balances b/f	8,024	Oct 1	Balances b/f	57
19X9			19X9		
Sept 30	Sales	63,728	Sept 30	Cash received from	
	Bad debts account	94		debtors	55,212
	Balances c/f	57		Discount allowed	2,328
				Returns	1,002
				Bad debts written off	326
				Transfer creditors	
				control account	434
				Cash - bad debt	
				recovered	94
				Allowances on goods	
				damaged	212
				Balances c/f	12,238
		71,903			71,903

(b)   CREDITORS CONTROL (OR TOTAL) ACCOUNT

19X8		£	19X8		£
Oct 1	Balances b/f	105	Oct 1	Balances b/f	6,235
19X9			19X9		
Sept 30	Cash paid to creditors	37,307	Sept 30	Purchases	39,974
	Discount received	1,475		Cash	105
	Returns outwards	535			
	Transfer debtors				
	control account	434			
	Balances c/f	6,458			
		46,314			46,314

The reason for having control accounts

17. The examples given in this chapter on the debtors control account and the creditors control account do not really explain why we need to have control accounts at all. After all, in theory at least, the personal accounts in the sales ledger for debtors and purchase ledger for creditors could be used as part of the double entry system. There is no obvious reason why they should be memorandum accounts.

18. The reasons for having control accounts are as follows.

   (a) They provide a check on the accuracy of entries made in the personal accounts in the sales ledger and purchase ledger. It is very easy to make a mistake in posting entries, because there might be hundreds of entries to make. Figures might get transposed. Some entries might be omitted altogether, so that an invoice or a payment transaction does not appear in a personal account as it should. By comparing:

      (i) the total balance on the debtors control account with the total of individual balances on the personal accounts in the sales ledger; and

      (ii) the total balance on the creditors control account with the total of individual balances on the personal accounts in the purchase ledger;

      it is possible to identify the fact that errors have been made.

   (b) The control accounts could also assist in the location of errors, where postings to the control accounts are made daily or weekly, or even monthly. If a clerk fails to record an invoice or a payment in a personal account, or makes a transposition error, it would be a formidable task to locate the error or errors at the end of a year, say, given the hundreds or thousands of transactions during the year. By using the control account, a comparison with the individual balances in the sales or purchase ledger can be made for every week or day of the month, and the error found much more quickly than if control accounts did not exist.

   (c) Where there is a separation of clerical (bookkeeping) duties, the control account provides an internal check. The person posting entries to the control accounts will act as a check on a different person whose job it is to post entries to the sales and purchase ledger accounts.

   (d) To provide a debtors and a creditors balance more quickly for producing a trial balance or balance sheet. A single balance on a control account is obviously extracted more simply and quickly than many individual balances in the sales or purchase ledger. This means also that the number of accounts in the double entry bookkeeping system can be kept down to a manageable size, since the personal accounts are memorandum accounts only and the control accounts instead provide the accounts required for a double entry system.

Balancing and agreeing control accounts with sales and bought ledgers

19. The control accounts should be balanced regularly (at least monthly), and the balance on the account agreed with the sum of the individual debtors' or creditors' balances extracted from the sales or bought ledgers respectively. It is one of the sad facts of an accountant's life that more often than not the balance on the control account does not agree with the sum of balances extracted, for one or more of the following reasons:

   (a) an incorrect amount has been posted to the control account because of a miscast of the total in the book of prime entry (ie adding up incorrectly the total value of invoices or payments). The nominal ledger debit and credit postings will balance, but the control account balance will not agree with the sum of individual balances extracted from the (memorandum) sales ledger or purchase ledger. A journal entry must then be made in the nominal ledger to correct the control account and the corresponding sales or expense account;

(b) a transposition error has occurred in posting an individual's balance from the book of prime entry to the memorandum ledger, eg the sale to C Cloning of £250 might be posted to his account as £520. This means that the sum of balances extracted from the memorandum ledger must be corrected. No accounting entry would be required to do this, except to alter the figure in C Cloning's account;

(c) a transaction is recorded in the control account and not in the memorandum ledger, or vice versa. This requires an entry in the ledger that has been missed out which means a double posting if the control account has to be corrected, and a single posting if it is the individual's balance in the memorandum ledger that is at fault;

(d) the sum of balances extracted from the memorandum ledger is incorrectly extracted or miscast. This would involve simply correcting the total of the balances.

Agreeing control account balances with the sales and bought ledgers: example

20. Reconciling the control account balance with the sum of the balances extracted from the (memorandum) sales ledger or bought ledger should be done in two stages.

(a) Correct the total of the balances extracted from the memorandum ledger. (The errors must be located first of course.)

	£	£
Sales ledger total		
Original total extracted		15,320
Add difference arising from transposition error		
(£95 written as £59)		36
		15,356
Less:		
Credit balance of £60 extracted as a debit balance		
(£60 x 2)	120	
Overcast of list of balances	90	
		210
		15,146

(b) Bring down the balance before adjustments on the control account, and adjust or post the account with correcting entries: eg

DEBTORS CONTROL

	£		£
Balance before adjustments	15,091	Petty cash - posting omitted	10
		Returns inwards - individual posting omitted from control account	35
Undercast of total invoices issued in sales day book	100	Balance c/d (now in agreement with the corrected total of individual balances in (a))	15,146
	15,191		15,191
Balance b/d	15,146		

Summary of the chapter

21.

> The two most important control accounts are those for debtors and creditors. They are part of the double entry system.
>
> - Cash books and day books are totalled periodically (say once a month) and the appropriate totals are posted to the control accounts.
>
> - Meanwhile, the individual entries in cash and day books will have been entered one by one in the appropriate personal accounts contained in the sales ledger and purchase ledger.
>
> - These personal accounts are *not* part of the double entry system: they are memorandum only.
>
> - At suitable intervals the balances on personal accounts are extracted from the ledgers, listed and totalled. The total of the outstanding balances can then be reconciled to the balance on the appropriate control account and any errors located and corrected.

TEST YOUR KNOWLEDGE

Numbers in brackets refer to paragraphs of this chapter

1. What is a control account?   (4)

2. What ledger entries are made from the discounts allowed column in the cash book?   (10)

3. Give three examples of typical entries on the credit side of a debtors control account.   (13)

4. List three reasons why control accounts should be maintained.   (18)

Now try questions 14-16 at the end of this section

Chapter 13

ACCOUNTING FOR WAGES
AND SALARIES

The purpose of this chapter is:

● to explain the concept of gross pay

● to describe the principal deductions that may be made from gross pay

● to illustrate the ledger accounting entries in respect of payroll costs

---

Introduction

1. The employees of a business are rewarded for their services by wages or salary payments. Such payments are commonly expressed in terms of a gross amount. For example:

    (a) an hourly-paid employee might have a wage rate of £5 per hour gross;
    (b) a weekly-paid employee might have a wage rate of £150 per week gross, with additional payments for any overtime worked;
    (c) a monthly-paid employee might have an annual salary of £6,000 gross. His gross monthly salary payment would be calculated as £6,000 ÷ 12 = £500.

2. A distinction is often made between wages staff and salaried staff. Wages staff are usually paid by reference to a weekly or hourly wage rate and receive their pay weekly. Salaried staff are usually paid by reference to an annual salary and receive their pay monthly. Traditionally, wages staff have tended to be paid in cash at the end of each week, while salaried staff have been paid monthly by automatic transfer from the business bank account to the employee's bank account. The distinction is now being eroded as more and more employees are paid by bank transfer.

3. For accounting purposes, there is no essential difference between wages procedures and salary procedures.

Deductions from gross pay

4. Although an employee's pay may be expressed as a gross amount, the amount of pay he actually receives will invariably be reduced by certain deductions. The most important of these are for income tax and National Insurance contributions.

5. The government requires that all employees (except those with very low incomes) should pay tax on their earnings. Employees are also required to contribute to the cost of the welfare state by making contributions to a National Insurance fund.

6. You might think that these obligations of the employee are no concern of his employer. It can be argued that the employer should pay the agreed gross wage and leave the employee to settle his own liability with the Inland Revenue.

7. In practice, this is not the system that applies. The government requires that businesses should act as collecting agents on behalf of the Inland Revenue. When a business makes a wages or salary payment to an employee, it must calculate the amount of tax and National Insurance due from the employee. These amounts must be deducted from the employee's gross remuneration and paid by the business to the Inland Revenue. The employee receives only the net amount remaining after these deductions.

8. Because an employee effectively pays off his income tax liability in instalments, each time he receives a wages payment, this system of income tax collection is referred to as PAYE or pay-as-you-earn.

9. Apart from these obligatory deductions which all businesses are required to operate, there may be other, voluntary, deductions from an employee's pay. For example:

(a) some businesses run savings schemes. An employee may agree to save £5 a week with the intention of withdrawing his savings at Christmas time. Each week the £5 would be deducted from his gross pay and held for him by his employer until such time as he decides to withdraw it;

(b) some businesses encourage contributions to charity. An employee might agree to a weekly deduction of 50p from his wages as a contribution to Oxfam. The employer would deduct the agreed amount each week and at suitable intervals hand over the money collected to the charity;

(c) some businesses run pension schemes to which employees contribute.

Example

10. Suppose that Mr Little's gross pay for the week ending 31.10.19X6 is £140. His employer, Mr Big, calculates that income tax of £20 and National Insurance of £13 are due on that level of earnings. In addition, Little received a loan from the business in June 19X6 which he is repaying by means of weekly deductions of £5; he also voluntarily contributes 20p per week to a local charity, again by deduction from his gross wages.

How should these amounts be accounted for?

Solution

11. The cost to Mr Big is the gross pay of £140 and this is the amount to be charged in his profit and loss account. The amount actually paid to Little is only £101.80 (£140 − £20 − £13 − £5 − 20p).

The deductions should be accounted for as follows.

(a) PAYE of £20 and National Insurance contribution of £13 must be handed over by Mr Big to the Inland Revenue. In practice, this payment would not be made every week. Mr Big would accumulate the amounts due in respect of all his employees and would make a single payment to Inland Revenue once a month.

(b) The £5 deduction is applied to reduce the amount of the loan outstanding from Little.

(c) The 20p deduction must be handed over by Mr Big to the local charity. Again, it would probably be convenient to accumulate these amounts for a number of weeks before making a payment.

Employer's National Insurance contributions

12. We have already seen that employees are normally obliged to pay National Insurance contributions which are deducted from their gross pay and paid over by their employer on their behalf. But employers also have to make a contribution themselves in respect of each of their employees. This is not a deduction from the employee's gross pay; it is an *extra* cost, borne by the employer. The employer's profit and loss account must show the total cost of employing staff and this includes not only the gross pay of each employee, but also the employer's National Insurance contributions.

13. When an employer is making his monthly payment to the Inland Revenue the amount paid must therefore include:

(a) PAYE income tax for each employee. This is deducted from the employees' gross pay;
(b) employees' National Insurance contributions, also deducted from the employees' gross pay;
(c) employer's National Insurance contributions, paid from the employer's own funds.

Calculating PAYE taxation and National Insurance contributions

14. Calculating National Insurance contributions is easy. An employee must pay a fixed percentage of his gross income and this amount is deducted from his pay. The percentage to apply depends on the level of the employee's income. For the employer's contribution, again a fixed percentage is applied to the employee's gross pay, but the percentage may differ from that used in calculating the employee's contribution.

15. Currently, employees' NI contributions are subject to a maximum amount. There is no limit on the amount of an employer's contributions.

16. The government publishes tables detailing the amount of NI contributions payable at all levels of income. This means that employers never need to understand how NI is calculated: they simply extract the amounts from the tables.

17. PAYE contributions are more complicated, but again the use of Inland Revenue tables simplifies matters in practice. Briefly, it is necessary to do the calculations on a cumulative basis, rather than looking at each salary/wages payment in isolation.

18. First add up the amount of the employee's gross pay, up to and including his gross pay for the current week, to arrive at his gross pay for the tax year to date. (Tax years run from 6 April to 5 April). Next calculate the amount of tax due for the year to date. This will depend on the employee's tax code, which reflects the value of tax allowances to which his personal circumstances entitle him.

19. The tax due for the year to date is then compared with the tax actually paid by the employee up to and including the previous week/month. The difference is the amount of tax due from the employee in the current week/month. This is the amount to be deducted from his gross wages.

20. It may sometimes be found that the tax due for the year to date is *less* than the tax already paid by the employee. In that case the employee will be entitled to a tax refund as an *addition* to his gross pay.

Accounting for wages and salaries: control accounts

21. It is now necessary to look at the double entry involved in accounting for wages and salaries. There are various ways of doing this but the method below involves the use of three control accounts:

    Wages control account
    PAYE control account
    NIC control account

22. The first step is to calculate the total costs of employment to be borne by the business. These consist of employees' gross pay plus employer's National Insurance contributions. The double entry is then:

Debit	P & L account - wages/salaries
Credit	Wages control account (gross pay)
Credit	NIC control account (employer's NIC)

23. The amount of deductions must be calculated for PAYE and employee's NIC. These amounts are debited to wages control account and credited to PAYE control account and NIC control account respectively.

24. The remaining credit balance on wages control account is then eliminated by paying employees their net pay: credit cash, debit wages control.

25. In due course, the credit balances on PAYE control and NIC control are eliminated by making payments to Inland Revenue.

26. Any voluntary deductions permitted by employees must be debited to wages control account and credited to a liability account until they are eventually paid over by the employer as appropriate.

13: ACCOUNTING FOR WAGES AND SALARIES

Example

27. At 1 October 19X5 Netpay Ltd had the following credit balances on ledger accounts:

	£
PAYE control account	4,782
NIC control account	2,594
Employee savings account	1,373

The company's wages records for the month of November 19X5 showed the following:

	£
Total gross pay	27,294
PAYE	6,101
Employer's NIC	2,612
Employees' NIC	2,240
Employees' savings deductions	875
Net amounts paid to employees	18,078

The company paid £9,340 to Inland Revenue during the month, being £4,750 PAYE and £4,590 NIC.

You are required to show the ledger accounts recording these transactions.

Solution

28.

WAGES CONTROL ACCOUNT

	£		£
PAYE control	6,101	Wages expense a/c - gross pay	27,294
NIC control - employees' contributions	2,240		
Employee savings a/c	875		
Bank - net pay	18,078		
	27,294		27,294

PAYE CONTROL ACCOUNT

	£		£
Bank	4,750	Balance b/f	4,782
Balance c/d	6,133	Wages control	6,101
	10,883		10,883
		Balance b/d	6,133

NIC CONTROL ACCOUNT

	£		£
Bank	4,590	Balance b/f	2,594
Balance c/d	2,856	Wages control - employees' NIC	2,240
		Wages expense a/c - employer's NIC	2,612
	7,446		7,446
		Balance b/d	2,856

EMPLOYEE SAVINGS ACCOUNT

	£		£
Balance c/d	2,248	Balance b/f	1,373
		Wages control	875
	2,248		2,248
		Balance b/d	2,248

(NB. This account shows the company's liability to employees, who may wish to withdraw their savings at any time.)

Summary of the chapter

29. The cost of employing staff must be shown in a business's profit and loss account. It comprises the gross pay earned by employees, plus employer's NIC.

A business must deduct PAYE income tax and employees' NIC from employees' gross pay. Only the net amount is then paid to employees. The amounts deducted are paid over every month by the employer to the Inland Revenue.

TEST YOUR KNOWLEDGE

Numbers in brackets refer to paragraphs of this chapter

1. What do the initials PAYE stand for? (8)

2. List three voluntary deductions that an employee might permit from his gross pay. (9)

3. What is the total cost of employing staff shown in an employer's profit and loss account? (12)

4. Briefly summarise the principles of calculating PAYE income tax. (17–19)

5. What ledger accounting entries are necessary once the total payroll costs have been calculated? (22)

6. What ledger accounting entries are made in respect of voluntary deductions permitted by employees? (26)

Now try question 17 at the end of this section

Chapter 14

BANK RECONCILIATIONS

The purpose of this chapter is:

- to explain the reasons why bank statement balances do not coincide with cash book balances

- to illustrate the procedures for reconciling bank statements with the cash book

---

Introduction

1.   The cash book of a business is the record of how much cash the business believes that it has in the bank. In the same way, you yourself might keep a private record of how much money you think you have in your own personal account at your bank, perhaps by making a note in your cheque book of income received and the cheques you write. If you do keep such a record you will probably agree that when your bank sends you a bank statement from time to time the amount it shows as being the balance in your account is rarely exactly the amount that you have calculated for yourself as being your current balance.

2.   Why might your own estimate of your bank balance be different from the amount shown on your bank statement? The possible explanations are:

   (a)   *error*. Errors in calculation, or recording income and payments, are more likely to have been made by yourself than by the bank, but it is conceivable that the bank has made a mistake too;

   (b)   *bank charges or bank interest*. The bank might deduct charges for interest on an overdraft or for its services, which you are not informed about until you receive the bank statement;

   (c)   *time differences*. When a bank prepares your bank statement:

      (i)   there might be some cheques that you have received and paid into the bank, but which have not yet been 'cleared' and added to your account. So although your own records show that some cash has been added to your account, it has not yet been acknowledged by the bank - although it will be in a very short time when the cheque is eventually cleared;

      (ii)   similarly, you might have made some payments by cheque, and reduced the balance in your account accordingly in the record that you keep, but the person who receives the cheque might not bank it for a while. Even when it is banked, it takes a day or two for the banks to process it and for the money to be deducted from your account.

3.   If you do keep a personal record of your cash position at the bank, and if you do check your periodic bank statements against what you think you should have in your account, you will be doing exactly the same thing that the bookkeepers of a business do when they make a bank reconciliation. A bank reconciliation is a comparison of a bank statement (probably sent monthly by the bank) with the cash book. Differences between the balance on the bank statement and the balance in the cash book will be errors or timing differences, and they should be identified and satisfactorily explained.

The bank statement

4.   It is a common practice for a business to issue a monthly statement to each credit customer, itemising:

(a)   the balance he owed on his account at the beginning of the month;
(b)   new debts incurred by the customer during the month;
(c)   payments made by him during the month;
(d)   the balance he owes on his account at the end of the month.

In the same way, a bank statement is sent by a bank to its short-term debtors and creditors - ie customers with bank overdrafts and customers with money in their account - itemising the balance on the account at the beginning of the period, receipts into the account and payments from the account during the period, and the balance at the end of the period.

5.   It is necessary to remember, however, that if a customer has money in his account, the bank owes him that money, and the customer is therefore a creditor of the bank (hence the phrase 'to be in credit' means to have money in your account). This means that if a business has £8,000 cash in the bank, it will have a debit balance in its own cash book, but the bank statement, if it reconciles exactly with the cash book, will state that there is a credit balance of £8,000. (The bank's records are a 'mirror image' of the customer's own records, with debits and credits reversed).

Why is a bank reconciliation necessary?

6.   A bank reconciliation is needed to identify errors, either in the cash book of the business or errors made by the bank itself.

(a)   *Errors*, once identified, must be corrected. Most errors are likely to be made by the business itself rather than the bank and they should be corrected in the cash book.

(b)   *Bank charges* should be credited in the cash book of the business, and debited to the account for bank charges in the nominal ledger.

(c)   *Time differences* should be listed and these ought to reconcile the balance on the bank statement with the balance on the corrected cash book.

What to look for when doing a bank reconciliation

7.   The cash book and bank statement will rarely agree at a given date. If you are doing a bank reconciliation, you may have to look for the following items:

(a) corrections and adjustments to the cash book; for

    (i) payments made into the account or from the account by way of standing order, direct debit etc, which have not yet been entered in the cash book;

    (ii) dividends received (on investments held by the business), paid direct into the bank account but not yet entered in the cash book;

    (iii) bank interest and bank charges, not yet entered in the cash book;

(b) items reconciling the correct cash book balance to the bank statement, namely:

    (i) cheques drawn (ie paid) by the business and credited in the cash book, which have not yet been presented to the bank, or 'cleared' and so do not yet appear on the bank statement;

    (ii) cheques received by the business, paid into the bank and debited in the cash book, but which have not yet been cleared and entered in the account by the bank, and so do not yet appear on the bank statement.

Simple example

8. At 30 September 19X6, the balance in the cash book of Wordsworth Limited was £805.15. A bank statement on 30 September 19X6 showed Wordsworth Limited to be in credit by £1,112.30.

On investigation of the difference between the two sums, it was established that:

(a) the cash book had been undercast by £90.00 on the debit side;
(b) cheques paid in not yet credited by the bank amounted to £208.20;
(c) cheques drawn not yet presented to the bank amounted to £425.35.

Required: show

(a) the correction to the cash book; and
(b) a statement reconciling the balance per bank statement to the balance per cash book.

Solution

9. (a)

	£	£
Cash book balance brought forward		805.15
Add:		
Correction of undercast		90.00
Corrected balance		895.15

(b)

	£	£
Balance per bank statement		1,112.30
Add:		
Cheques paid in, recorded in the cash book, but not yet credited to the account by the bank	208.20	
Less:		
Cheques paid by the company but not yet presented to the company's bank for settlement	425.35	
		(217.15)
Balance per cash book		895.15

Another example

10. On 30 June 19X0, Cook's cash book showed that he had an overdraft of £300 on his current account at the bank. A bank statement as at the end of June 19X0 showed that Cook was in credit with the bank by £65.

On checking the cash book with the bank statement you find the following:

(a) cheques drawn, amounting to £500, had been entered in the cash book but had not been presented;

(b) cheques received, amounting to £400, had been entered in the cash book, but had not been credited by the bank;

(c) on instructions from Cook the bank had transferred interest of £60 from his deposit account to his current account, recording the transfer on 5 July 19X0. This amount had, however, been credited in the cash book as on 30 June 19X0;

(d) bank charges of £35 shown in the bank statement had not been entered in the cash book;

(e) the payments side of the cash book had been undercast by £10;

(f) dividends received amounting to £200 had been paid direct to the bank and not entered in the cash book;

(g) a cheque for £50 drawn on deposit account had been shown in the cash book as drawn on current account;

(h) a cheque issued to Jones for £25 was replaced when out of date. It was entered again in the cash book, no other entry being made. Both cheques were included in the total of unpresented cheques shown above.

You are required:

(a) to indicate the appropriate adjustments in the cash book; and

(b) to prepare a statement reconciling the amended balance with that shown in the bank statement.

Solution

11. (a) The errors to correct are given in notes (c) (e) (f) (g) and (h) of the problem. Bank charges (note (d)) also call for an adjustment.

		Adjustments in cash book	
		Debit	*Credit*
		(ie add to cash balance)	*(ie deduct from cash balance)*
		£	£
Item			
(c)	Cash book incorrectly credited with interest on 30 June. It should have been debited with the receipt.	60	
(c)	Debit cash book (current a/c) with transfer of interest from deposit a/c (note 1)	60	
(d)	Bank charges		35
(e)	Undercast on payments (credit) side of cash book		10
(f)	Dividends received should be debited in the cash book	200	
	c/f	320	45

		Debit £	Credit £
	b/f	320	45
(g)	Cheque drawn on deposit account, not current account. Add cash back to current account	50	
(h)	Cheque paid to Jones is out of date and so cancelled. Cash book should not be debited, since previous credit entry is no longer valid (note 2)	25	
		395	45

Cash book : balance on current account as at 30 June 19X0		(300)
Adjustments and corrections:		
Debit entries (adding to cash)	395	
Credit entries (reducing cash balance)	(45)	
Net adjustments		350
Corrected balance in the cash book		50

Notes:

1. Item (c) is rather complicated. The transfer of interest from the deposit to the current account was presumably given as an instruction to the bank on or before 30 June 19X0. Since the correct entry is to debit the current account (and credit the deposit account) the correction in the cash book should be to debit the current account with 2 x £60 = £120 - ie to cancel out the incorrect credit entry in the cash book and then to make the correct debit entry. However, the bank does not record the transfer until 5 July, and so it will not appear in the bank statement.

2. Item (h). Two cheques have been paid to Jones, but one is now cancelled. Since the cash book is credited whenever a cheque is paid, it should be debited whenever a cheque is cancelled. The amount of cheques paid but not yet presented should be reduced by the amount of the cancelled cheque.

(b)   BANK RECONCILIATION STATEMENT AT 30 JUNE 19X0

	£	£
Balance per bank statement		65
Add: outstanding lodgements		
(ie cheques paid in but not yet credited)	400	
deposit interest not yet credited	60	
		460
		525
Less: unpresented cheques	500	
cheque to Jones cancelled	25	
		475
Balance per corrected cash book		50

12. Notice that in preparing a bank reconciliation it is good practice to begin with the balance shown by the bank statement and end with the balance shown by the cash book. It is this corrected cash book balance which will appear in the balance sheet as 'cash at bank'. But examination questions sometimes ask for the reverse order: as always, read the question carefully.

13. You might be interested to see the adjustments to the cash book in part (a) of the problem presented in the 'debit and credit' account format, as follows:

CASH BOOK

		£			£
19X0			19X0		
June 30	Bank interest: reversal of incorrect entry	60	June 30	Balance brought down	300
				Bank charges	35
	Dividends paid direct to bank	200		Correction of under-cast	10
	Cheque drawn on deposit account written back	50		Balance carried down	50
	Cheque issued to Jones cancelled	25			
		395			395

Summary of the chapter

14. • A bank reconciliation is a comparison between the bank balance recorded in the books of a business and the balance appearing on the bank statement.

   • The comparison may reveal errors or omissions in the records of the business, which should be corrected by appropriate adjustments in the cash book (or in the nominal ledger cash account).

   • Once the cash book has been corrected it should be possible to reconcile its balance with the bank statement balance by taking account of timing differences, ie payments made and cheques received which are recorded in the cash book but have not yet cleared to the bank statement.

TEST YOUR KNOWLEDGE

Numbers in brackets refer to paragraphs of this chapter

1. What are the possible explanations for differences between the balance shown on a bank statement and the balance shown by a cash book? (2)

2. Describe the procedure for performing a bank reconciliation. (7)

Now try questions 18 and 19 at the end of this section

Chapter 15

SUSPENSE ACCOUNTS

The purpose of this chapter is:

- to describe the reasons why suspense accounts are established

- to illustrate the kind of entries required to eliminate suspense account balances

---

Introduction

1. A suspense account is a temporary account. It is used to 'collect' a debit or credit entry when the bookkeeper doesn't know what else to do. There are two situations where a suspense account might be needed.

   (a) The bookkeeper knows in which account to make the debit entry for a transaction but does not know where to make the corresponding credit entry. Until the mystery is sorted out, the credit entry can be recorded in a suspense account. A typical example is when the business receives cash through the post from a source which cannot be determined. The double entry in the accounts would be a debit in the cash book, and a credit to a suspense account.

   Similarly, when the bookkeeper knows in which account to make a credit entry, but for some reason does not know where to make the corresponding debit, the debit can be posted to a suspense account.

   (b) A bookkeeping error might have occurred, resulting in the failure of the total debits and total credits in the ledger accounts to be equal. To restore equality between debits and credits, the balancing figure can be posted to a suspense account. Errors in book-keeping were described in the chapter on the books of prime entry, in the paragraphs dealing with the journal, and suspense accounts were referred to then in the context of errors of omission, and errors of transposition.

2. Before we look at some examples to see how suspense accounts are operated, you should be aware that a suspense account can only be temporary. Postings to a suspense account are only made when the bookkeeper doesn't know yet what to do, or when an error has occurred. Mysteries must be solved, and errors must be corrected. Under no circumstances should there be a suspense account when it comes to preparing the balance sheet of a business.

15: SUSPENSE ACCOUNTS

Example: not knowing where to post a transaction

3. Windfall Garments received a cheque through the post for £620. The name on the cheque is R J Beaseley Esq, but Windfall Garments have no idea who this person is, nor why he should be sending £620. The bookkeeper decides to open a suspense account, so that the double entry for the transaction is:

Debit	Cash	£620
Credit	Suspense account	£620

    Eventually, it transpires that the cheque was in payment for a debt owed by the Haute Couture Corner Shop, and paid out of the proprietor's personal bank account. The suspense account can now be cleared, as follows:

Debit	Suspense account	£620
Credit	Debtors	£620

Example: transposition error

4. The bookkeeper of Mixem Gladly Limited made a transposition error when entering an amount for sales in the sales account. Instead of entering the correct amount, £37,453.60, he entered £37,543.60, transposing the 4 and 5. The debtors were posted correctly, and so when total debits and credits on the ledger accounts were compared, it was found that credits exceeded debits by £(37,543.60 - 37,453.60) = £90.

    The initial step is to equalise the total debits and credits by posting a debit of £90 to a suspense account.

    When the cause of the error is discovered, the double entry to correct it (logged in the journal first of all) should be:

Debit	Sales	£90
Credit	Suspense account	£90

Example: error of omission

5. When Guttersnipe Builders paid the monthly salary cheques to its office staff, the payment of £5,250 was correctly entered in the cash account, but the bookkeeper omitted to debit the office salaries account.

    As a consequence, the total debit and credit balances on the ledger accounts were not equal, and credits exceeded debits by £5,250.

    The initial step in correcting the situation is to debit £5,250 to a suspense account, to equalise the total debits and total credits.

    When the cause of the error is discovered, the ledger entries to correct the error (logged in the journal first of all) should be:

Debit	Office salaries account	£5,250
Credit	Suspense account	£5,250

15: SUSPENSE ACCOUNTS

Example: error of commission

6. A bookkeeper might make a mistake by entering what should be a debit entry as a credit, or vice versa. For example, suppose that a credit customer pays £460 of the £660 he owes to Ashdown Tree Felling Contractors, but Ashdown's bookkeeper has debited £460 on the debtors account by mistake.

    The total debit balances in Ashdown's ledger accounts would now exceed the total credits by 2 x £460 = £920. The initial step in correcting the error would be to make a credit entry of £920 in a suspense account. When the cause of the error is discovered, it should be corrected as follows:

Debit	Suspense account	£920
Credit	Debtors	£920

    In the personal account of the customer in the sales ledger, the correction would appear as follows:

    #### DEBTORS ACCOUNT

	£		£
Balance b/f	660	Suspense account:	920
Payment incorrectly debited	460	error corrected	
		Balance c/f	200
	1,120		1,120

Suspense accounts might contain several items

7. If more than one error or unidentifiable posting to a ledger account arises during an accounting period, they will all be merged together in the same suspense account. Indeed, until the causes of the errors are discovered, the bookkeepers are unlikely to know exactly how many errors there are. An examination question might give you a balance on a suspense account, together with enough information to make the necessary corrections, leaving a nil balance on the suspense account and correct balances on various other accounts.

    Study the following example, and if you think you understand the correcting entries, attempt the further example which follows.

Example

8. You are the accountant of Mini Moguls Limited. When you come to prepare the accounts for the year ended 31 December 19X5, you find that the bookkeeper has raised a suspense account with a credit balance of £80,530. On further investigation you ascertain that this balance is made up of the following items:

    (a) proceeds from an issue of shares (at nominal value) during the year amounting to £50,000;

    (b) proceeds from the sale of land, shown in the books at a cost of £20,000, amounting to £30,000;

    (c) an excess of the total of the debit side over the credit side of the trial balance due to:

    > (i) salaries of £690 being incorrectly entered as £960;
    > (ii) cash received from a debtor, B Snow, amounting to £130 which was incorrectly debited to his account.

Your job is to clear the suspense account, showing the transfers to the relevant accounts.

Solution

9.
SUSPENSE

		£			£
31.12.19X5	Share capital	50,000	31.12.19X5	Balance b/f	80,530
	Disposal of land	30,000			
	Salaries (over-statement)	270			
	Debtors(130+130)	260			
		80,530			80,530

SHARE CAPITAL

		£			£
			1.1.19X5	Balance	X
			31.12.19X5	Suspense	50,000

LAND (AT COST)

		£			£
1.1.19X5	Balance	20,000	31.12.19X5	Disposal of land	20,000

DISPOSAL OF LAND

		£			£
31.12.19X5	Land	20,000	31.12.19X5	Suspense	30,000
	Profit on sale	10,000			
		30,000			30,000

SALARIES

		£			£
31.12.19X5	Balance	X	31.12.19X5		270

DEBTOR - B SNOW

		£			£
1.1.19X5	Balance	130	31.12.19X5	Suspense	260
	Cash (incorrect)	130			
		260			260

Notes:

(a) Share capital is the proprietor's capital in a limited company. A new share issue raises cash of £50,000 and adds £50,000 to capital. Presumably in this example, the cash account has been debited correctly, but the share capital account has not yet been credited.

(b) The £30,000 received from the sale of the land in the suspense account indicates that the disposal has not been recorded in the accounts at all. Not only should the disposal of land account be credited with £30,000, but also the fixed asset account should be credited and the disposal account debited with the cost of the land, to complete the ledger entries.

(c) The error of transposition in (c) (i) and error of commission in (c) (ii) are corrected in the ways described earlier.

Now try question 20 at the end of this section

Chapter 16

ACCOUNTING FOR STOCKS

The purpose of this chapter is:

- to explain how quantities of stock are established

- to describe the principles of stock valuation

- to illustrate the methods by which costs may be attributed to units of stock

- to illustrate the effect of stock valuation on profitability

---

Introduction

1. Business trading is a continuous activity, but accounting statements must be drawn up as at a particular date. In preparing a balance sheet it is necessary to 'freeze' the activity of a business so as to determine its assets and liabilities at a given moment. This can create problems with the asset of stocks.

2. A business buys stocks continually during its trading operations and either sells the goods onwards to customers or incorporates them as raw materials in manufactured products. This constant movement of stocks makes it difficult to establish the value of stock held at a precise moment.

3. There are two aspects to consider:

    (a) the quantity of stock units held at the balance sheet date;
    (b) the monetary amount to be attributed to each stock unit.

4. The managers of a business often establish detailed cost accounting systems so that they can ascertain the quantities and values of stock held at any moment. Such systems fall within the scope of cost accounting practice, which goes beyond the present syllabus. But the disclosure of stocks in financial accounts will be discussed briefly in this chapter.

Establishing quantities of stocks on hand

5. In simple cases, quantities of stocks on hand at the balance sheet date can be determined by physically counting them in a stocktake. While counting the stocks, staff will look out for any damaged or obsolete items which need to be discarded or repaired.

6.   The continuous nature of trading activity may cause a problem in that stock movements will not necessarily cease during the time that the physical stocktake is in progress. Two possible solutions are:

(a) to close down the business while the count takes place; or
(b) to keep detailed records of stock movements during the course of the stocktake.

7.   An alternative approach to establishing stock quantities is to maintain continuous stock records. Even with continuous records, though, there will be a need for periodic stocktakes. This is because stocks can disappear (eg by being stolen) without being recorded; or stocks can deteriorate while in store.

8.   There are two particular points worth mentioning in connection with stocktaking.

(a)   A company may receive free samples from potential suppliers. These should not be regarded as trading stocks. They should be excluded from the stock count and from the stock valuation.

(b)   A company may send 'sale or return' goods to customers. The customers have the option to return the goods if they are unable to sell them on. Until the customer confirms that he has been able to sell the goods, the company cannot take credit for any sale. Indeed, no sales invoice should be raised when goods are sent out on a sale or return basis. But because the company has not 'sold' the goods, it follows that they still form part of the company's stock, even though they are not on the company's own premises.

Establishing the value of stocks: the basic rule

9.   The need to value closing stocks arises from the accruals concept. Revenues should be matched with the costs incurred in earning them. When a company has stocks on hand at the end of an accounting period, those stocks will be used to make sales and earn revenue in the following period. It is therefore appropriate that the cost of such stocks should be carried forward rather than written off in the period when the stocks were acquired.

10.   There are several amounts which, in theory, might be used in the valuation of stock items. For example:

(a)   stocks might be valued at their expected selling price. This might be described as their gross realisable value;

(b)   stocks might be valued at their expected selling price, less any costs still to be incurred in getting them ready for sale and then selling them. This amount is referred to as the *net realisable value* (NRV) of stocks;

(c)   stocks might be valued at their historical cost;

(d)   stocks might be valued at the amount it would cost to replace them once they are sold. This amount is referred to as the current replacement cost of stocks.

11. Current replacement costs are used widely in accounts prepared under the current cost convention. They are not used in historical cost accounts.

12. The use of selling prices in stock valuation is ruled out by the prudence concept. If a business purchases a stock item for £30 and values it in the balance sheet at its expected selling price of £45, the business is claiming to have made a £15 profit at a time when the item has not yet been sold. This conflicts with the prudence concept, which requires that profits should only be recognised when they are realised: they should not be anticipated.

13. The same objection usually applies to the use of NRV in stock valuation. Say that the item purchased for £30 requires £5 of further expenditure in getting it ready for sale and then selling it (eg £5 of processing costs and distribution costs). If its expected selling price is £45, its NRV is £(45-5) = £40. To value it at £40 in the balance sheet would still be to anticipate a £10 profit.

14. We are left with historical cost as the normal basis of stock valuation. The only time when historical cost is not used is in the exceptional cases where the prudence concept requires a lower value to be used.

15. Staying with the example in paragraph 13, suppose that the market in this kind of product suddenly slumps and the item's expected selling price is only £28. The item's NRV is then £(28-5) = £23 and the business has in effect made a loss of £7 (£30 - £23). The prudence concept requires that losses should be recognised as soon as they are foreseen. This can be achieved by valuing the stock item in the balance sheet at its NRV of £23.

16. The argument developed in paragraphs 12-15 suggests that the rule to follow is that stocks should be valued at cost or, if lower, net realisable value. The accounting treatment of stock is governed by an accounting standard, SSAP9 *Stocks and long-term contracts*. SSAP9 states that stock should be valued at the lower of cost and net realisable value. This is an important rule and one which you should learn by heart.

Applying the basic valuation rule

17. If a business has many stock items on hand the comparison of cost and NRV should theoretically be carried out for each item separately. It is not sufficient to compare the total cost of all stock items with their total NRV. An example will show why.

18. Suppose a company has four items of stock on hand at the end of its accounting period. Their costs and NRVs are as follows:

Stock item	Cost	NRV	Lower of cost/NRV
	£	£	£
1	27	32	27
2	14	8	8
3	43	55	43
4	29	40	29
	113	135	107

19. It would be incorrect to compare total costs (£113) with total NRV (£135) and to state stocks at £113 in the balance sheet. The company can foresee a loss of £6 on item 2 and this should be recognised. If the four items are taken together in total the loss on item 2 is masked by the anticipated profits on the other items. By performing the cost/NRV comparison for each item separately the prudent valuation of £107 can be derived. This is the value which should appear in the balance sheet.The procedure whereby a separate cost/NRV comparison is carried out for each stock item is an application of the separate valuation principle described in chapter 2.

20. For a company with large amounts of stock this procedure may be impracticable. In this case it is acceptable to group similar items into categories and perform the comparison of cost and NRV category by category, rather than item by item.

21. There are many practical difficulties in establishing the cost of stock items, especially when a company makes frequent stock purchases at varying prices. These difficulties will be covered later in this chapter. For the moment it is enough to know that the basic rule is to value stocks at the lower of cost and NRV.

Accounting for stock in hand in the trading account and balance sheet

22. After the stock in hand has been counted in the end-of-year stocktaking, and then valued, the value of the stock will be used to prepare the trading account and the balance sheet of the business. Although accounting for stock has already been explained in an earlier chapter, it might be useful to go over the procedures again here.

23. There is a stock account in the nominal ledger. This is used to keep a record of the value of the stock which is counted and valued at the end of the accounting year. At the beginning of a year, the opening balance brought forward on the stock account (a debit entry, since stocks are an asset of the business) will be the value of closing stocks at the end of the previous year, which is of course the same as opening stocks at the beginning of the current year.

24. There is a purchases account in the nominal ledger. This keeps a record of stock purchases throughout the year. At the end of the year, the balance on the purchases account is transferred to the trading account in full.

Also at the end of the year, the balance on the stock account is transferred to the trading account.

25. The trading account therefore has two debit entries:

(a) opening stock brought forward;
(b) purchases during the year.

26. The value of closing stock is then taken into account:

Debit   Stock account
Credit   Trading account

By convention, the credit entry in the trading account is often shown as a minus value on the debit side rather than as a plus value on the credit side (but either way, it comes to the same thing).

The value of closing stock will also be a current asset in the end-of-year balance sheet.

Example: accounting for stock

27. Newbegin Tools has an accounting year which ends on 28 February. At 28 February 19X6, the business had stocks valued at £545.

    During the year to 28 February 19X7, the business purchased stocks costing £5,130. Sales amounted to £10,000. When the annual stock count was made at the end of the day on 28 February 19X7, the value placed on closing stock was £1,095.

    Required: show the ledger entries for the year ended 28 February 19X7 in the purchases account, stock account and trading account.

Solution

28.

PURCHASES

		£			£
Year to					
28.2.X7	Cash/creditors	5,130	28.2.X7	Trading account (a)	5,130

STOCK ACCOUNT

		£			£
1.3.X6	Balance b/f	545	28.2.X7	Trading account (b)	545
28.2.X7	Trading account (c) (closing stock)	1,095	28.2.X7	Balance c/d	1,095
1.3.X7	Balance b/d	1,095			

NEWBEGIN TOOLS
TRADING ACCOUNT FOR THE YEAR ENDED 28 FEBRUARY 19X7

	£	£
Sales		10,000
Opening stock (b)	545	
Purchases (a)	5,130	
	5,675	
Less closing stock (c)	1,095	
Cost of sales		4,580
Gross profit		5,420

28. Closing stock appears in the balance sheet as follows:

NEWBEGIN TOOLS
BALANCE SHEET EXTRACT AS AT 28 FEBRUARY 19X7

	£
Current assets	
Stock on hand	1,095

Stock losses

29. Any trading concern will expect to have loss of stock from wastage, damage and petty theft, and as it is a concomitant part of business, such losses are treated as normal. In such cases no accounting entries are required since the value of the stock taken at the financial year end will be less than the value of the stock had no losses occurred. This means that deducting a reduced amount of closing stock from the total of opening stock and purchases will give us an increased cost of sales which in turn gives a decreased gross profit.

30. Abnormal losses, such as loss of stock in a fire, or through a burglary, are a different matter. An abnormal loss occurs as a single event, and is characterised by the significance of the amount lost. If no separate account of abnormal losses is taken when they occur, then the gross profit for that financial year, and more particularly the gross profit percentage which is:

$$\frac{\text{Gross profit}}{\text{Sales}} \times 100\%$$ will compare extremely unfavourably with the results of other accounting

periods. This is because the abnormal loss would be a cost in the trading account, reducing the gross profit.

31. Of course the abnormal loss will have occurred, and unless the business is fully insured against the loss it must suffer a reduction in its profit. The point at issue, however, is that although the net profit must be reduced, it would distort the gross profit and the ratio of gross profit as a percentage of sales, if the gross profit were reduced too. This might seem to be a quibble about something which does not matter at the end of the day: it is the net profit that really matters. Nevertheless, abnormal losses are accounted for in such a way that the gross profit is calculated excluding the cost of such losses, which are then charged as an expense in the profit and loss account.

32. This is done by means of the double entry:

    Credit   Trading account (cost of abnormal loss)
    Debit   Profit and loss account

For example, if a business incurs an abnormal stock loss of £11,100.

TRADING ACCOUNT

	£		£
		Profit and loss - abnormal	
		stock loss	11,100

PROFIT AND LOSS
£

Trading account - abnormal
stock loss   11,100

However, the abnormal stock loss would normally be deducted from the debit side of the trading account rather than being shown on the credit side.

Example: stock losses

33.   The following information relates to A Limited. Prepare a trading and profit and loss account for the year ended 31 December 19X6, treating the stock loss as:

(a)   normal;
(b)   abnormal.

	£
Sales for year to 31.12.19X6	80,000
Opening stock at 1.1.19X6	26,000
Purchases for year to 31.12.19X6	66,000
Closing stock at 31.12.19X6 - valued as per stock count	18,000
Value of stock lost in burglary at cost	10,000

The company normally achieves a gross profit percentage of 20%.

Solution

34.   (a)   If the stock loss is treated as a normal loss:

A LIMITED
TRADING AND PROFIT AND LOSS ACCOUNT
FOR THE YEAR ENDED 31 DECEMBER 19X6

	£	£
Sales		80,000
Cost of sales:		
Opening stock	26,000	
Purchases	66,000	
	92,000	
Less closing stock	18,000	
		74,000
Gross profit		6,000

The gross profit percentage is only 6,000/80,000 x 100% = 7.5%. This would suggest that the company has traded much less efficiently than usual.

(b) If the stock loss is treated as an abnormal loss:

	£	£	£
Sales			80,000
Cost of sales:			
Opening stock		26,000	
Purchases		66,000	
		92,000	
Closing stock	18,000		
Stock loss	10,000		
		28,000	
			64,000
Gross profit			16,000
Expenses:			
Stock lost in burglary			(10,000)

The gross profit percentage is 16,000/80,000 x 100% = 20%. By presenting the stock loss in this way we can see that the company has traded as efficiently as usual, but has suffered from an abnormal loss.

The cost of items of stock

35. Earlier in this chapter we stated the rule that in financial accounts stocks should be stated at the lower of their cost and their net realisable value. This rule sounds simple enough but in fact there are two significant difficulties in deciding what the 'cost' of a stock item is.

36. The first problem is to decide what specific expenses should be regarded as making up the cost of a stock item. SSAP9 says that cost comprises 'all expenditure which has been incurred in the normal course of business in bringing the product or service to its present location and condition'. For an item of raw material this may mean simply the cost of purchasing the item from a supplier. But for items of work in progress or finished goods we have to take account of conversion costs, ie any costs (such as direct labour) incurred in working on the raw materials.

37. The second problem is to determine the purchase cost of a stock item. A business may be continually purchasing consignments of a particular component, say. As each consignment is received from suppliers they are stored in the appropriate bin, where they will be mingled with previous consignments. When the storekeeper issues components to production he will simply pull out from the bin the nearest components to hand, which may have arrived in the latest consignment or in an earlier consignment or in several different consignments.

38. This would not cause a problem if all consignments were purchased at the same unit price. But in practice prices change because of inflation or because advantage may sometimes be taken of bulk discounts or for other reasons. Some procedure must be devised to attribute a cost both to items issued to production and to items remaining in stock at the balance sheet date.

39. In the rest of this chapter we will look at each of these problems in turn and finally examine the importance of stock valuations in computing profit.

What does the cost of a unit of stock comprise?

40. The cost of *raw materials* comprises the purchase price charged by the supplier. As mentioned above, this purchase price is not necessarily easy to determine and we will look later at the various methods which have been devised to do so. It is important to establish the cost of raw materials issued to production, because the cost of production eventually becomes part of the cost of sales and directly affects both gross profit and net profit.

41. The cost of *work in progress* obviously includes the purchase price of any raw materials used in creating partly-finished goods. But even this might be difficult to establish. For example, in a continuous process industry (such as much food and drinks manufacture) there will be a continuous flow of input raw materials and output finished goods. It might be impossible to determine how much raw material is comprised in a given batch of work in progress and management would have to make an educated guess by assessing the degree of completion of the batch.

42. In addition to raw material costs, the work in progress valuation will include costs of conversion. These will comprise the direct wages of employees whose work can be specifically attributed to the creation of the partly-finished goods, plus any other direct expenses incurred, plus (sometimes) an appropriate proportion of production overheads. It will be necessary to keep records of time spent by employees on particular jobs and also of any other direct or indirect production expenses.

43. The cost of *finished goods* similarly comprises raw materials costs plus conversion costs.

Determining the purchase cost of raw materials

44. This is the second problem referred to in paragraph 35. In paragraph 37 above we referred to a storekeeper who pulls out a group of components from a stores bin to issue them to production. As accountants, we are not concerned with identifying by physical means which consignment(s) those components originally formed part of. Our concern is to devise a pricing technique, a rule of thumb which we can use to attribute a cost to each of the components issued from stores.

45. There are several techniques which are used in practice. The ones we will discuss here are:

   (a) FIFO (first in, first out). Using this technique, we assume that components are used in the order in which they are received from suppliers. The components issued to production are deemed to have formed part of the oldest consignment still unused and are costed accordingly;

   (b) LIFO (last in, first out). This involves the opposite assumption, that components issued to production originally formed part of the most recent delivery, while older consignments lie in the bin undisturbed;

   (c) average cost. As purchase prices change with each new consignment, the average price of components in the bin is constantly changed. Each component in the bin at any moment is assumed to have been purchased at the average price of all components in the bin at that moment;

(d) standard cost. A pre-determined standard cost is applied to all stock items. If this standard price differs from prices actually paid during the period it will be necessary to write off the difference as a variance in the profit and loss account;

(e) replacement cost. The arbitrary assumption is made that the cost at which a stock unit was purchased is the amount it would cost to replace it. This is often (but not necessarily) the unit cost of stocks purchased in the next consignment *following* the issue of the component to production. For this reason, a method which produces similar results to replacement costs is called NIFO (next in, first out).

46. Any or all of these methods might provide suitable cost accounting information for management. But it is worth mentioning here that if you are preparing *financial* accounts you would normally expect to use FIFO for the balance sheet valuation of stock. SSAP 9 specifically discourages the use of LIFO and replacement costs.

47. To illustrate the various pricing methods, the following transactions will be used in each case:

TRANSACTIONS DURING MAY 19X3

	Quantity (units)	Unit cost £	Total cost £	Market value per unit on date of transactions £
Opening balance 1 May	100	2.00	200	
Receipts 3 May	400	2.10	840	2.11
Issues 4 May	200			2.11
Receipts 9 May	300	2.12	636	2.15
Issues 11 May	400			2.20
Receipts 18 May	100	2.40	240	2.35
Issues 20 May	100			2.35
Closing balance 31 May	200		1,916	2.38

The problem is to put a valuation on:

(a) the issues of materials;
(b) the closing stock.

FIFO (first in, first out)

48. FIFO assumes that materials are issued out of stock in the order in which they were delivered into stock, ie issues are priced at the cost of the earliest delivery remaining in stock.

The cost of issues and closing stock value in the example, using FIFO would be as follows:

Date of issue	Quantity issued units	Value	£	Cost of issues £
4 May	200	100 o/s at £2	200	
		100 at £2.10	210	
				410
11 May	400	300 at £2.10	630	
		100 at £2.12	212	
				842
20 May	100	100 at £2.12		212
				1,464
Closing stock value	200	100 at £2.12	212	
		100 at £2.40	240	
				452
				1,916

Notes:

(a) The cost of materials issued plus the value of closing stock equals the cost of purchases plus the value of opening stock (£1,916).

(b) The market price of purchased materials is rising. In a period of inflation, there is a tendency for:

(i) materials to be issued at a cost lower than the current market value;
(ii) but closing stocks tend to be valued at a cost appoximating to current market value.

LIFO (last in, first out)

49. LIFO assumes that materials are issued out of stock in the reverse order to which they were delivered, ie most recent deliveries are issued before earlier ones, and are priced accordingly.

50. The following table shows a method of calculating the cost of issues and the closing stock value under the LIFO method.

	Opening stock in units	Purchases in units 3 May	9 May	18 May
Issues	100	400	300	100
4 May		(200)		
11 May		(100)	(300)	
20 May				(100)
Closing stock	100	100	-	-

			£	£
Issues:	4 May	200 @ £2.10		420
	11 May	100 @ £2.10	210	
		300 @ £2.12	636	
				846
	20 May	100 @ £2.40		240
Cost of materials issued				1,506
Closing stock valuation:		100 @ £2.00	200	
		100 @ £2.10	210	
				410
				1,916

Notes:

(a) The cost of materials issued plus the value of closing stock equals the cost of purchases plus the value of opening stock (£1,916).

(b) In a period of inflation, there is a tendency with LIFO for:

(i) materials to be issued at a price which approximates to current market value;
(ii) closing stocks to become undervalued when compared to market value.

Average cost

51. There are various ways in which average costs may be used in pricing stock issues. The most common (cumulative weighted average pricing) is illustrated below.

52. The cumulative weighted average pricing method calculates a weighted average price for all units in stock. Issues are priced at this average cost, and the balance of stock remaining would have the same unit valuation.

53. A new weighted average price is calculated whenever a new delivery of materials into store is received. This is the key feature of cumulative weighted average pricing.

53. In our example, issue costs and closing stock values would be:

Date	Received units	Issued units	Balance units	Total stock value	Unit cost	Price of issue
				£	£	£
Opening stock			100	200	2.00	
3 May	400			840	2.10	
			500	1,040	2.08 *	
4 May		200		(416)	2.08	416
			300	624	2.08	
9 May	300			636	2.12	
			600	1,260	2.10 *	
11 May	400			(840)	2.10	840
			200	420	2.10	
18 May	100			240	2.40	
			300	660	2.20 *	
20 May		100		(220)	2.20	220
						1,476
Closing stock value			200	440	2.20	440
						1,916

* A new unit cost of stock is calculated whenever a new receipt of materials occurs.

Notes:

(a) The cost of materials issued plus the value of closing stock equals the cost of purchases plus the value of opening stock (£1,916).

(b) In a period of inflation, using the cumulative weighted average pricing system, the value of material issues will rise gradually but will tend to lag a little behind the current market value at the date of issue. Closing stock values will also be a little below current market value.

Standard cost pricing

54. Under the standard costing method, all issues are at pre-determined standard price.

55. Let us assume in our example that the standard price applied is £2 per unit:

(a)

Date of issue	Quantity issued units	Valuation £
4 May	200 x £2	400
11 May	400 x £2	800
20 May	100 x £2	200
		1,400
Closing stock	200 x £2	400
		1,800

(b) There is a materials price variance:

Date of purchase	Quantity received (Units)	Expected cost £	Actual cost £	Price variance £
3 May	400	800	840	40 (adverse)
9 May	300	600	636	36 (adverse)
18 May	100	200	240	40 (adverse)
	800	1,600	1,716	116 (adverse)

Notes:

(i) The cost of the materials issued plus the value of closing stock (£1,800) differs from the combined value of opening stock plus purchases (£1,916) by the amount of the materials price variance (£116). At the end of an accounting period this variance will be taken as an adjustment to the profit and loss account to reconcile actual costs paid.

(ii) In a period of inflation, the standard cost will generally be above or below the market price, so that price variances will occur when materials are bought and the cost of materials issued will not be at current market value.

(iii) Although the problems of inflation are difficult to manage with standard costs, standard costing is nevertheless widely used because:

1 it is easy to use and administratively convenient;
2 it is used to set standards of performance which can be used for management control reporting.

Replacement costing

56. In the preceding description of different methods for pricing materials, the problems of inflation have been repeatedly stressed. There is a strong body of accountancy opinion which argues that:

(a) when materials are issued out of stores, they will be replaced with a new delivery. The cost of issues should therefore be priced at the current cost to the business of replacing them in stores;

(b) closing stocks should be valued at current replacement cost in the balance sheet to show the true value of the assets of the business.

57. In our example, the cost of issues and the value of closing stock would be as follows:

Date of issue	Quantity issued units	Replacement cost £ per unit	Valuation £
4 May	200	2.11	422
11 May	400	2.20	880
20 May	100	2.35	235
Closing stock	200	2.38	476
			2,013
Value of opening stock plus purchases			1,916
Difference			97

Notes:

(a) In a period of inflation, replacement costing will give a high (current) valuation to materials, thereby reducing 'true profit' in the profit and loss account, so as to preserve the assets of the business intact - ie allow for replacement of the materials used.

(b) As with standard costing, there will be a difference between the cost of opening stock plus purchases and the value of materials issued plus closing stock (in this case £97). Unlike materials price variance, however, this difference is not taken to the profit and loss account at the end of a period. It is a difference which must be kept away from the profit figure in order that a 'true profit' from operations may be calculated, and it is written instead to a 'stock revaluation reserve' which will appear in the balance sheet.

58. Replacement costing is recommended as a method of accounting for price changes. Unfortunately, in many instances, it may be difficult or impossible to maintain a record of material replacement market values, and replacement costing may therefore be impracticable.

59. It is worth noting that use of the LIFO method often produces a profit figure similar to that obtained under replacement costing. This is because materials issued to production are charged out at the cost of the most recent acquisition, ie at up-to-date prices. The disadvantage is that the balance sheet valuation of closing stock is based on prices which may be many months out of date. In the context of *financial* accounts this disadvantage is regarded as so important that use of the LIFO method for stock valuation is not countenanced by SSAP 9. But in cost accounts the use of LIFO can provide management with useful information.

Stock valuations and profitability

60. In the previous descriptions of FIFO, LIFO, average costing etc, the example used raw materials as an illustration. Each method of valuation produced different costs of both closing stocks and also of material issues. Since raw material costs affect the cost of production, and the cost of production works through eventually into the cost of sales, it follows that different methods of stock valuation will provide different profit figures. An example may help to illustrate this point.

Example: stock valuations and profitability

61. On 1 November 19X2 a company held 300 units of finished goods item No 9639 in stock. These were valued at £12 each. During November 19X2 three batches of finished goods were received into store from the production department, as follows:

Date	Units received	Production cost per unit
10 November	400	£12.50
20 November	400	£14
25 November	400	£15

Goods sold out of stock during November were as follows:

Date	Units sold	Sale price per unit
14 November	500	£20
21 November	500	£20
28 November	100	£20

Required:

What was the profit from selling stock item 9639 in November 19X2, applying the following principles of stock valuation:

(a) FIFO;
(b) LIFO
(c) cumulative weighted average costing?

Ignore administration, sales and distribution costs.

Solution

62. (a) FIFO:

		Issue cost Total £	Closing stock £
Date:	Issue costs		
14 November	300 units x £12 plus		
	200 units x £12.5	6,100	
21 November	200 units x £12.5 plus		
	300 units x £14	6,700	
28 November	100 units x £14	1,400	
Closing stock	400 units x £15		6,000
		14,200	6,000
(b) LIFO:			
14 November	400 units x £12.5 plus		
	100 units x £12	6,200	
21 November	400 units x £14 plus		
	100 units x £12	6,800	
28 November	100 units x £15	1,500	
Closing stock	300 units x £15 plus		
	100 units x £12		5,700
		14,500	5,700

(c) Cumulative weighted average costs:

		Unit cost	Balance in stock £	Total cost of issues £	Closing stock £
1 November Opening stock	300	12.000	3,600		
10 November	400	12.500	5,000		
	700	12.286	8,600		
14 November	500	12.286	6,143	6,143	
	200	12.286	2,457		
20 November	400	14.000	5,600		
	600	13.428	8,057		
21 November	500	13.428	6,714	6,714	
	100	13.428	1,343		
25 November	400	15.000	6,000		
	500	14.686	7,343		
28 November	100	14.686	1,469	1,469	
30 November	400	14.686	5,874	14,326	5,874

(d)

	FIFO £	LIFO £	Weighted average £
Profitability			
Opening stock	3,600	3,600	3,600
Cost of production	16,600	16,600	16,600
	20,200	20,200	20,200
Closing stock	6,000	5,700	5,874
Cost of sales	14,200	14,500	14,326
Sales (1,100 x £20)	22,000	22,000	22,000
Profit	7,800	7,500	7,674

63. Different stock valuations have produced different costs of sale, and therefore different profits. In our example opening stock values are the same, therefore the difference in the amount of profit under each method is the same as the difference in the valuations of closing stock.

64. The profit differences are only temporary. In our example, the opening stock in December 19X2 will be £6,000, £5,700 or £5,874, depending on the stock valuation used. Different opening stock values will affect the cost of sales and profits in December, so that in the long run inequalities in costs of sales each month will even themselves out.

65. As a final note on this example, it is significant that in a period of rising prices, LIFO gives the highest cost of sales and lowest profit in the month, and FIFO gives the lowest cost of sales and highest profit. Average costs come in between. The value of closing stocks, in contrast, is highest with FIFO and lowest (ie most out of date) with LIFO.

Summary of the chapter

66.
- The quantity of stocks held at the year end is established by means of a physical count of stock in an annual stocktaking exercise.

- The value of these stocks is then calculated, taking the lower of cost and net realisable value for each separate item or group of stock items.

- The value of closing stocks is accounted for by debiting a stock account and crediting the trading account.

- Opening stocks brought forward in the stock account are transferred to the trading account, and so at the end of the accounting year, the balance on the stock account ceases to be the opening stock value b/f, and becomes instead the closing stock value c/f.

- There are two problems in determining the cost of stock items:

   (a) What expenditure should be included in cost?
   (b) How should purchase cost be determined when identical items are being purchased or produced continually?

- Point (a) involves consideration of the conversion costs to be included in the calculation of work in progress and finished goods.

- For point (b), some rule of thumb must be adopted. The possibilities include FIFO, LIFO, average costs, standard costs, replacement costs and NIFO. Remember that in *financial* accounts FIFO should normally be used.

Definitions

67.
- *Net realisable value* is the amount that would be realised from the disposal of stock as at the balance sheet date, after allowing for all expenditure that would be incurred on or before disposal. If there is no such expenditure, NRV is the selling price of the stock.

- *Stocks* and *work in progress* consist of:

   (a) trading goods for resale;
   (b) consumable stores;
   (c) raw materials and components purchased for incorporation into manufactured products for resale;
   (d) products and services still in the process of manufacture or completion;
   (e) finished goods.

TEST YOUR KNOWLEDGE

Numbers in brackets refer to paragraphs of this chapter

1. Describe the accounting treatment of free samples received from suppliers and 'sale or return' goods held by customers. (8)

2. Define 'net realisable value'. (10)

3. What is the basic rule regulating the value at which stocks should be stated in the balance sheet? (16)

4. Explain how the separate valuation principle is relevant in stock valuation. (19)

5. What is the double entry in respect of closing stock? (26)

6. What elements of expenditure are included in the 'cost' of work in progress? (41)

7. Explain how the following three pricing techniques work:

   (a) FIFO;
   (b) LIFO;
   (c) average cost. (45)

8. Which of the above three pricing techniques is likely to produce a profit figure similar to that obtained under replacement costing? (60)

Now try questions 21 and 22 at the end of this section

Chapter 17

INTANGIBLE FIXED ASSETS

The purpose of this chapter is:

● to explain the nature of business goodwill and its accounting treatment

● to explain the accounting treatment of amounts spent on research and development activities

---

Introduction

1. Intangible fixed assets are fixed assets which have a value to the business because they have been paid for, but which do not have any physical substance. The most significant of such intangible assets are goodwill and deferred development costs.

The concept of goodwill

2. The concept of goodwill might be familiar to you already, from common everyday knowledge. Goodwill is created by good relationships between a business and its customers, for example:

    (a) by building up a reputation (by word of mouth perhaps) for high quality products or high standards of service;
    (b) by responding promptly and helpfully to queries and complaints from customers;
    (c) through the personality of the staff and their attitudes to customers.

3. The value of goodwill to a business might be extremely significant. However, goodwill is not usually valued in the accounts of a business at all, and we should not normally expect to find an amount for goodwill in its balance sheet. For example, the welcoming smile of the bar staff may contribute more to a pub's profits than the fact that a new electronic cash register has recently been acquired; even so, whereas the cash register will be recorded in the accounts as a fixed asset, the staff would be ignored (for accounting purposes).

4. On reflection, this omission of goodwill from the accounts of a business might be easy to understand.

    (a) The goodwill is inherent in the business but it has not been paid for, and it does not have an 'objective' value. We can guess at what such goodwill is worth, but such guesswork would be a matter of individual opinion, and not based on hard facts.

(b) Goodwill changes from day to day. One act of bad customer relations might damage goodwill and one act of good relations might improve it. Staff with a favourable personality might retire or leave to find another job, to be replaced by staff who need time to find their feet in the job, etc. Since goodwill is continually changing in value, it cannot realistically be recorded in the accounts of the business.

Purchased goodwill

5. There is one exception to the general rule that goodwill has no objective valuation. This is when a business is sold. People wishing to set up in business have a choice of how to do it - they can either buy their own fixed assets and stock and set up their business from scratch, or they can buy up an existing business from a proprietor willing to sell it. When a buyer purchases an existing business, he will have to purchase not only its fixed assets and stocks (and perhaps take over its creditors and debtors too) but also the goodwill of the business.

6. For example, suppose that Tony Tycoon agrees to purchase the business of Clive Dunwell for £30,000. Clive's business has net fixed assets valued at £14,000 and net current assets of £11,000, all of which are taken over by Tony. Tony will be paying more for the business than its tangible assets are worth, because he is purchasing the goodwill of the business too. The balance sheet of Tony's business when it begins operations (assuming that he does not change the value of the tangible fixed and current assets) will be:

TONY TYCOON
BALANCE SHEET AS AT THE START OF BUSINESS

	£
Intangible fixed asset: goodwill	5,000
Tangible fixed assets - net book value	14,000
Net current assets	11,000
	30,000
Capital	30,000

7. Purchased goodwill can be shown in the balance sheet because it has been paid for. It has no tangible substance, and so it is an intangible fixed asset.

Purchased goodwill has been defined as 'the excess of the price paid for a business over the fair market value of the individual assets and liabilities acquired'.

Exercise

8. To make sure that you understand goodwill, try a solution to the following quick exercise.

Toad goes into business with £10,000 capital and agrees to buy Thrush's shoe-repair shop in the centre of a busy town for £6,500. Thrush's recent accounts show net assets of £3,500, which Toad values at £4,000.

Required: prepare the balance sheet of Toad's business

(a) before he purchases Thrush's business; and
(b) after the purchase.

Solution

9. (a) Toad's balance sheet before the purchase is:

Cash   10,000

Proprietor's interest   10,000

(b) Thrush's valuation of the assets to be acquired is irrelevant to Toad who sees the situation thus:

	£
Consideration (cash to be paid)	6,500
Less net assets acquired (at Toad's valuation)	4,000
Difference (= goodwill)	2,500

Toad must credit his cash book with the £6,500 paid. He can only debit sundry assets with £4,000. A further debit of £2,500 is thus an accounting necessity and he must open up a goodwill account.

Toad's balance sheet immediately after the transfer would therefore be:

	£
Goodwill	2,500
Sundry assets	4,000
Cash (£10,000 – £6,500)	3,500
	10,000

Proprietor's interest   10,000

(Normally one would have more detail as to the breakdown of the sundry assets into fixed assets, current assets etc, but this is not relevant to the illustration. The main point is that the sundry assets acquired are tangible whereas the goodwill is not.)

This exercise highlights the difference between 'internally generated' goodwill, which (as in Thrush's case above) is not shown in the books and 'purchased' goodwill, which is. The purchased goodwill in this case is simply Thrush's internally generated goodwill, which has changed hands, bought by Toad at a price shown in Toad's accounts.

The accounting treatment of purchased goodwill

10. Once purchased goodwill appears in the accounts of a business, we must decide what to do with it. Purchased goodwill is basically a premium paid for the acquisition of a business as a going concern: indeed, it is often referred to as a 'premium on acquisition'. When a purchaser agrees to pay such a premium for goodwill, he does so because he believes that the true value of the business is worth more to him than the value of its tangible assets. One major reason why he might think so is that the business will earn good profits over the next few years, and so he will pay a premium now to get the business, in the expectation of getting his money back later. However, he pays for the goodwill at the time of purchase, and the value of the goodwill will eventually wear off. Goodwill, it was suggested earlier, is a continually changing thing. A business cannot last forever on its past reputation; it must create new goodwill as time goes on. Even goodwill created by a favourable location might suddenly disappear - for example, a newsagent's shop by a bus stop will lose its location value if the bus route is axed by the local transport authorities.

11. Since goodwill wears off, and is basically unstable anyway, it would be inadvisable to keep purchased goodwill indefinitely in the accounts of a business. The treatment of goodwill is the subject of an accounting standard, SSAP 22 *Accounting for goodwill*. SSAP 22 permits two alternative accounting treatments for purchased goodwill:

    (a) write off goodwill immediately by treating it as a reduction in the retained profits of the business acquiring the goodwill;

    (b) treat goodwill as an intangible fixed asset which, like all fixed assets, must be depreciated or amortised over its expected 'economic' life.

12. The advantage of immediately writing off goodwill is that it is prudent and it avoids goodwill ever appearing on the balance sheet. The disadvantage is that it ignores the fact that goodwill does have some longer-term value when first acquired (however difficult to quantify).

13. If goodwill is to be written off over a period of years it is shown in the balance sheet as an intangible fixed asset. The gradual 'write-off' approach is based on the idea that goodwill has a limited life and is a cost to be offset against future profits. The advantage of this approach is that it is probably a better representation of its gradual loss of value to the purchaser, as old goodwill is replaced by new goodwill. It is however less prudent than the immediate write-off and poses the problem of determining the estimated useful life of the goodwill, which tends to be subjective. An arbitrary figure such as five years is often used.

How is the value of purchased goodwill decided?

14. When a business is sold, there is likely to be some purchased goodwill in the selling price. But how is the amount of this purchased goodwill decided?

    This is not really a problem for accountants, who must simply record the goodwill in the accounts of the new business. The value of the goodwill is a matter for the purchaser and seller to agree upon in fixing the purchase/sale price. However, two methods of valuation are worth mentioning here:

    (a) The seller and buyer agree on a price without specifically quantifying the goodwill. The purchased goodwill will then be the difference between the price agreed and the value of the tangible assets in the books of the new business.

    (b) However, the calculation of goodwill often precedes the fixing of the purchase price and becomes a central element of negotiation. There are many ways of arriving at a value for goodwill and most of them are related to the profit record of the business in question. Some of these ways are illustrated below.

15. For an illustration of a few possible methods, let us suppose that a business being sold on 31.12.X3 has recently generated profits as follows:

Year ending 31.12.X1 - £4,000
Year ending 31.12.X2 - £5,000
Year ending 31.12.X3 - £7,000
Capital employed £20,000

Goodwill might be valued at:

(a) twice the final year's profit - ie 2 x £7,000 =   £14,000

or

(b) twice the average profit for the past three years

ie 2 x $\frac{£4,000 + £5,000 + £7,000}{3}$ £10,667

or perhaps

(c) three times the average profit for the past two years

ie 3 x $\frac{£5,000 + £7,000}{2}$ =   £18,000

(d) Alternatively the 'super profits' approach could be used. This relates the profit to the capital employed in one of a number of ways. Let us assume that in this particular business a reasonable return on capital employed would be 10% and that a reasonable salary for the proprietor would be £4,000. For the year 19X3 the return on the proprietor's funds, in excess of the salary that he could earn elsewhere, is therefore £3,000.

We could say:

(i) the £3,000 represents a 10% return on the assets of the business; the assets must therefore be:

$\frac{100}{10}$ x £3,000 ie   £30,000

Of the £30,000 we know that £20,000 exists in tangible form (net assets employed). Therefore the remaining £10,000 must be intangible, ie goodwill is   £10,000

In other words as well as our 10% return on tangible assets (£20,000 x 10% = £2,000) our intangible asset, goodwill, earns us a further £1,000 (£10,000 x 10%) which is the 'super profit'.

(ii) we could regard the intangible asset as having limited life and purchase, say seven years 'super profits'

Goodwill would therefore be 7 x £1,000 =   £7,000

Many other variations are possible. A formula may be agreed between vendor and purchaser in advance or there may be much haggling to reach agreement. The goodwill element of the purchase price is of course additional to the value of tangible assets acquired.

16. Any attempt to quantify goodwill in financial terms is purely arbitrary. Using the above methods we have calculated goodwill as high as £18,000 and as low as £7,000. Neither of these figures is the 'correct' figure because there is no correct figure; once a basis for the calculation has been agreed (eg two years purchase of average profits for the past three years) then a figure can be arrived at, but selection of the basis is entirely subjective. In practice, examination questions will always tell you the basis on which goodwill is to be calculated, and it will usually be some version of methods (a) to (c) above. The 'super profits' concept is generally considered rather old-fashioned, but it is mentioned for completeness.

17. No matter how goodwill is calculated within the total agreed purchase price, the goodwill shown by the purchaser in his accounts will be the difference between the purchase consideration and his own valuation of the tangible net assets acquired. If A values his tangible net assets at £40,000, goodwill is agreed at £21,000 and B agrees to pay £61,000 for the business but values the tangible net assets at only £38,000, then the goodwill in B's books will be £61,000 – £38,000 = £23,000.

Deferred development costs

18. This is the other intangible fixed asset you should know about. Large companies may spend significant amounts of money on research and development (R & D) activities. Obviously, any amounts so expended must be credited to cash and debited to an account for research and development expenditure. The accounting problem is how to treat the debit balance on R & D account at the balance sheet date.

19. There are two possibilities:

    (a) The debit balance may be classified as an expense and transferred to the profit and loss account. This is referred to as 'writing off' the expenditure.

    (b) The debit balance may be classified as an asset and included in the balance sheet. This is referred to as 'capitalising' or 'carrying forward' or 'deferring' the expenditure.

20. The argument for writing off R & D expenditure is that it is an expense just like rates or wages and its accounting treatment should be the same.

    The argument for carrying forward R & D expenditure is based on the accruals concept. If R & D activity eventually leads to new or improved products which generate revenue, the costs should be carried forward to be matched against that revenue in future accounting periods.

21. Like goodwill, R & D expenditure is the subject of an accounting standard, SSAP 13 *Accounting for research and development*. SSAP 13 (and the Companies Act 1985) requires that *research* expenditure should always be written off in the period in which it is incurred. This is because the advantages derived from general research activities are too remote to justify carrying the expenditure forward.

22. Development expenditure is different. It usually relates to a specific project (eg the development of a new product) which can be profitably exploited in the foreseeable future. Provided the viability of the project has been carefully assessed, there is a strong argument for capitalising the development costs associated with it.

23. SSAP 13 allows companies to capitalise development expenditure in their accounts, provided that certain criteria are satisfied. Broadly, it is permissible to carry forward such expenditure in the circumstances described in paragraph 22 above. Even so, a company is never *obliged* to do so; it is always open to a company to take the most prudent view and write off development expenditure in the same way as research expenditure.

24. If a company capitalises development expenditure, it will appear in the balance sheet as an intangible asset. Like capitalised goodwill, it must be depreciated (amortised). The process of amortisation should begin when the development project is brought into commercial production.

25. An example will illustrate the accounting entries required in respect of goodwill and development expenditure.

Example

26. The accounts of Intangible Ltd at 1 January 19X6 include deferred development costs of £26,500. During the year ended 31 December 19X6 Intangible Ltd purchased a new business. The consideration paid to the proprietor included £4,800 in respect of goodwill. The company also spent £7,900 on research and £3,500 on development activities.

    The directors of Intangible Ltd intend to write off goodwill evenly over its estimated economic life of four years. They believe that £22,600 of development costs should be carried forward at 31 December 19X6.

    Show the ledger accounts for goodwill and research and development in the books of Intangible Ltd.

Solution

27. The important point is to distinguish between the amounts actually spent during the year and the amounts charged to profit and loss account.

PURCHASED GOODWILL

	£		£
Cash	4,800	P & L a/c – amortisation	1,200
		Balance c/d	3,600
	4,800		4,800
Balance b/d	3,600		

RESEARCH AND DEVELOPMENT EXPENDITURE

	£		£
Balance b/f	26,500	∴ P & L a/c *	15,300
Cash: research	7,900	Development expenditure c/d	22,600
development	3,500		
	37,900		37,900
Balance b/d	22,600		

* The P & L charge includes the £7,900 spent on research. The balance (£15,300 – £7,900) = £7,400 consists of amortisation of development expenditure.

Summary of the chapter

28.

- Intangible fixed assets are those which have a value to the business but which do not have any physical substance. The most significant intangible assets are goodwill and deferred development expenditure.

- If a business has goodwill, it means that the value of the business as a going concern is greater than the value of its separate tangible assets. The valuation of goodwill is extremely subjective and fluctuates constantly. For this reason, goodwill is not normally shown as an asset in the balance sheet.

- The exception to this rule is when someone purchases a business as a going concern. In this case the purchaser and vendor will fix an agreed price which includes an element in respect of goodwill. The way in which goodwill is then valued is not an accounting problem, but a matter of agreement between the two parties.

- Purchased goodwill may then either be immediately written off as an expense in the profit and loss account, or be retained in the balance sheet as an intangible asset. If it is retained in the balance sheet, it must be amortised over its estimated useful economic life.

- Expenditure on research activities must always be written off in the period in which it is incurred.

- Expenditure on development activities may also be written off in the same way. But if the criteria laid down by SSAP 13 are satisfied, such expenditure *may* be capitalised as an intangible asset. It must then be amortised, beginning from the time when the development project is brought into commercial production.

TEST YOUR KNOWLEDGE

Numbers in brackets refer to paragraphs of this chapter

1. List three factors which might help to create goodwill in a business. (2)

2. Why is it unusual to record goodwill as an asset in the accounts? (4)

3. What is purchased goodwill? (5, 7)

4. What two methods of accounting for purchased goodwill are permitted by SSAP22? (11)

5. How is the amount of purchased goodwill calculated? (17)

6. What is the required accounting treatment for expenditure on research? (21)

7. In what circumstances may development expenditure be capitalised? (22, 23)

Chapter 18

ACCOUNTING FOR VALUE ADDED TAX

The purpose of this chapter is:

- to explain the nature of VAT and the way it is collected

- to describe the accounting entries in respect of VAT

Introduction

1. VAT is an indirect tax, levied on the sale of goods and services. It is administered by Customs and Excise, rather than the Inland Revenue; however, most of the work of collecting the tax falls on VAT-registered businesses, which hand the tax they collect over to the authorities.

2. Before we look at how to account for VAT, it is first of all necessary to understand how VAT works.

    Firstly, it is a cumulative tax, which might be collected at various stages of a product's life. In the illustrative example below, a manufacturer of a television buys materials and components to make the machine from suppliers, and then sells the television to a wholesaler, who in turn sells it to a retailer, who then sells it to a customer. It is assumed that the rate for VAT is 15% on all items. All the other figures given are hypothetical, for illustration only.

			Price net of VAT £	VAT 15% £	Total price £
(a)	(i)	Manufacturer purchases raw materials and components	40	6	46
	(ii)	Manufacturer sells the completed television to a wholesaler for, say	200	30	230
		The manufacturer hands over to Customs and Excise, in VAT		24	
(b)	(i)	Wholesaler purchases television for	200	30	230
	(ii)	Wholesaler sells television to a retailer for, say	300	45	345
		Wholesaler hands over to Customs and Excise in VAT		15	

(c)		Price net of VAT	VAT 15%	Total price
(i)	Retailer purchases television for	300	45	345
(ii)	Retailer sells television for, say	460	69	529
	Retailer hands over to Customs and Excise in VAT		24	
(d)	Customer purchases television for	460	69	529

3. The total tax is borne by the ultimate consumer – in the example above £69. However, the tax is handed over to the authorities in stages. If we assume in the example that the VAT of £6 on the initial supplies to the manufacturer is paid by the supplier, Customs and Excise would get its VAT money as follows:

	£
Supplier of materials and components	6
Manufacturer	24
Wholesaler	15
Retailer	24
Total VAT paid	69

Input and output VAT

4. The example in paragraphs 2 and 3 assumes that the supplier, manufacturer, wholesaler and retailer are all VAT-registered traders.

A VAT-registered trader
(a) charges VAT on the goods and services it sells, at the rate prescribed by the government;
(b) collects the VAT from its customers;
(c) pays VAT on goods or services it purchases from other businesses;
(d) pays to Customs and Excise in VAT the difference between the VAT collected on its sales and the VAT paid to its suppliers for purchases. (Payments are made at quarterly intervals.)

5. VAT charged on goods and services sold by a business (or 'output' by a business) is referred to as output VAT; VAT paid on goods and services 'bought in' by a business is referred to as input VAT.

(a) If output VAT exceeds input VAT, the business pays the difference in tax to the authorities.

(b) If output VAT is less than input VAT in a period, Customs and Excise will refund the difference to the business.

In other words, a VAT-registered trader must pay to Customs and Excise any VAT he has charged on his own outputs and collected from his customers. But he can normally reclaim any VAT paid to his suppliers for his inputs.

Irrecoverable VAT

6. There are some circumstances in which traders are *not* allowed to reclaim VAT paid on their inputs. In these cases the trader must bear the cost of VAT himself and account for it accordingly. Three such cases need to be considered:

    (a) non-registered persons;
    (b) registered persons carrying on exempted activities;
    (c) non-deductible inputs.

7. Traders whose sales (outputs) are below a certain minimum level need not register for VAT. Non-registered persons will pay VAT on their inputs and, because they are not registered, they cannot reclaim it. The VAT paid will effectively increase the cost of their P & L expenses and the cost of any fixed assets they may purchase. Non-registered persons do not charge VAT on their outputs.

8. All outputs of registered traders are either taxable or exempt. Taxable outputs are charged to VAT either at zero per cent (zero-rated items) or at 15% (standard rated items).

9. Traders carrying on exempt activities (such as banks) cannot reclaim VAT paid on their inputs, even though they may be VAT-registered. But some traders and companies carry on a mixture of taxable and exempt activities. Such traders need to apportion the VAT paid on inputs; only VAT relating to *taxable* outputs may be reclaimed.

10. Finally, some inputs are described as non-deductible. In the case of non-deductible inputs, VAT paid may *never* be recovered by traders, even if they are registered and carrying on taxable activities.

    The most common non-deductible inputs are:

    (a) all entertainment expenses;and

    (b) the cost of cars, unless they are cars bought for resale by a person trading in cars. For example, the cost of cars bought by a company for its sales reps would include VAT, but the VAT would not be recoverable. The case is different for vans, lorries, etc; input tax paid on vans and lorries *is* recoverable.

11. Where VAT is not recoverable, for any of the reasons described above, it must be regarded as an inherent part of the cost of the items purchased and included in the P & L charge or in the balance sheet as appropriate.

Other aspects of VAT

12. VAT is charged on the price net of any discount and this general principle is carried to the extent that where a cash discount is offered, VAT is charged on the net amount even where the discount is not taken up by the customer.

13. Where a bad debt is incurred, the full amount of the bad debt including VAT is borne by the business.

Accounting for VAT

14. If you think you understand the general principles of VAT, you might find it easier to follow the method of accounting for VAT.

Profit and loss account

15. A business does not make any profit out of the VAT it charges. It therefore follows that its sales should not include VAT. For example, if a business sells goods for £500 + VAT £75, ie for £575 total price, the sales account should only record the £500 excluding VAT. The accounting entries to record the sale would be:

Debit	Cash or debtors	£575	
Credit	Sales		£500
Credit	VAT creditor (output VAT)		£75

(The VAT creditor is the Customs and Excise authorities.)

16. The cost of purchases in the profit and loss account may or may not include the 'input' VAT paid, depending on whether or not the input VAT is recoverable - ie depending on whether or not the input VAT can be set against output VAT in deciding how much tax to hand over to Customs and Excise.

(a) If input VAT is recoverable, the cost of purchases should exclude the VAT and be recorded net of tax. For example, if a business purchases goods on credit for £400, on which VAT of £60 is charged, the transaction would be recorded as follows:

Debit	Purchases	£400	
Debit	VAT creditor (input VAT recoverable)	£60	
Credit	Trade creditors		£460

(b) If the input VAT is not recoverable, the cost of purchases must include the tax, because it is the business itself which is at the 'end of the line' and which must bear the cost of the tax itself.

VAT in the cash book, sales day book and purchase day book

17. When a business makes a credit sale, the total amount invoiced, including VAT, will be recorded in the sales day book. The analysis columns will then separate the VAT from the sales income of the business; eg

Date	*Total*	*Sales income*	*VAT*
	£	£	£
A Detter and Sons	115	100	15

18. When a business is invoiced by a supplier, the total amount payable, including VAT, will be recorded in the purchase day book. The analysis columns will then separate the recoverable input VAT from the net purchase cost to the business; eg

Date	Total	Purchase cost	VAT
	£	£	£
A Splier (Merchants)	161	140	21

19. When debtors pay what they owe, or creditors are paid, there is no need to show the VAT in an analysis column of the cash book, because input and output VAT, for tax purposes, arise when the sale is made, not when the debt is settled.

20. However, VAT charged on cash sales or VAT paid on cash purchases will be analysed in a separate column of the cash book. This is because output VAT having just arisen from the cash sale, must now be credited to the VAT creditor in the ledger accounts, and similarly input VAT paid on cash purchases, having just arisen, must be debited to the VAT creditor.

21. For example, the receipts side of a cash book might be written up as follows:

Date	Narrative	Folio	Total	Sales ledger (debtors)	Cash sales	Output VAT on cash sales
				Analysis columns		
			£	£	£	£
	A Detter & Sons		115	115		
	Owen Limited		660	660		
	Cash sales		230		200	30
	Newgate Merchants		184	184		
	Cash sales		92		80	12
			1,281	959	280	42

The payments side of a cash book might be written up as follows:

Date	Narrative	Folio	Total	Purchase ledger (creditors)	Cash purchases and sundry items	Input VAT on cash purchases
				Analysis columns		
			£	£	£	£
	A Splier (Merchants)		161	161		
	Telephone bill paid		253		220	33
	Cash purchase of calculator		23		20	3
	VAT paid to Customs and Excise		1,400		1,400	
			1,837	161	1,640	36

22. The VAT paid to the authorities each quarter is the difference between recoverable input VAT on purchases and output VAT on sales. For example, if a business is invoiced for input VAT of £8,000 and charges VAT of £15,000 on its credit sales and VAT of £2,000 on its cash sales, the VAT creditor account would be as follows:

VAT CREDITOR

	£		£
Creditors (input VAT)	8,000	Debtors (output VAT invoiced)	15,000
Cash (payment to authorities)	9,000	Cash (output VAT on cash sales)	2,000
	17,000		17,000

Creditor for VAT in the balance sheet

23. Payments to the authorities do not coincide with the end of the accounting period of a business, and so at the balance sheet date there will be a balance on the VAT creditor account. If this balance is for an amount payable to the authorities, the outstanding creditor for VAT will appear as a current liability in the balance sheet. (Occasionally, a business will be owed money back by the authorities, and in such a situation, the VAT refund owed by the authorities would be a current asset in the balance sheet.)

Bad debts and VAT

24. When a business writes off a debt as bad, it must suffer the loss of VAT itself unless the customer has become formally insolvent. For example, if a business sells goods on credit to a customer on 1 March 19X5 for £240 + VAT £36 and the debt is later written off as bad on 1 November 19X5, the relevant ledger accounting entries would be:

DEBTORS

	£		£
1 March Sales/VAT creditor	276	1 November Bad debts	276

VAT CREDITOR

	£		£
		1 March Debtors	36

SALES

	£		£
		1 March Debtors	240

BAD DEBTS

	£		£
1 November Debtors	276		

Longer example: accounting for VAT

25. You are required to prepare the ledger account entries you consider necessary to give effect to the transactions listed below. Assume that discounts receivable and allowable were taken into account when VAT was charged.

PESWICK LIMITED
EXTRACT OF BALANCES

	At 1 June 19X6 £	At 31 Dec 19X6 £
Sundry debtors	40,000	43,000
Sundry creditors	22,000	23,000
Creditors for VAT	4,100	4,400

The following extract relates to certain transactions during the year to 31 December 19X6:

	£
Invoiced sales less returns, including VAT	396,000
Discount received	5,000
Discount allowed	9,100
VAT on invoiced sales less returns	36,000

Bank payments	£
Creditors, including VAT	203,000
Purchase of plant, excluding VAT	30,000
Purchase of plant VAT	3,000
Creditor for VAT (ie payment of tax to the authorities)	14,000

Bank receipts	£
Sale of machinery (excluding VAT charged)	3,000
VAT on sale of machinery	300

You are also informed that:

(a) the rate of VAT during the year was 10% and applied to all relevant transactions without exception;
(b) bad debts amounting to £7,900 were written off sundry debtors;
(c) VAT charged on materials purchased, less returns, for stock amounted to £19,000.

You might like to attempt a solution yourself first; however, check the solution carefully.

Solution

26.

SUNDRY DEBTORS

	£		£
Balance b/f	40,000	Discount allowed	9,100
Sales and VAT creditor	396,000	Bad debts	7,900
		∴ Bank (balancing figure)	376,000
		Balance c/f	43,000
	436,000		436,000

239

SUNDRY CREDITORS

	£		£
Discount received	5,000	Balance b/f	22,000
Bank	203,000	Purchases and VAT creditor	
Balance c/f	23,000	(£19,000 x $\frac{110}{10}$)	209,000
	231,000		231,000

VAT CREDITOR

	£		£
Bank – VAT on purchase		Balance b/f	4,100
of plant	3,000	Debtors (£396,000 x $\frac{10}{110}$)	36,000
Bank	14,000		
Creditors – VAT on purchases	19,000	Bank – VAT on sale of machinery	300
Balance c/f	4,400		
	40,400		40,400

SALES

	£		£
		Debtors (£396,000 x $\frac{100}{110}$)	360,000

PURCHASES

	£		£
Creditors (£19,000 x $\frac{100}{10}$)	190,000		

FIXED ASSETS

	£		£
Bank – purchase of plant	30,000 *		

(*Note that purchase costs exclude the recoverable VAT)

FIXED ASSET DISPOSAL

	£		£
		Bank	3,000

BANK

	£		£
Fixed asset disposal and		Creditors	203,000
VAT creditor	3,300	Fixed assets and VAT creditor	33,000
Debtors	376,000	VAT creditor	14,000

Note: the discounts received and allowed are included in the example merely to show that there is no subsequent adjustment to input or output VAT when the discount is taken - see paragraph 7.

Other aspects of VAT

28. Some goods and services are zero-rated for VAT. (At the time of writing, an example is printing: however, it is likely that some zero-rated items will eventually be given a non-zero VAT rate as the government puts more emphasis on to indirect taxation in its fiscal policies.) No output VAT is charged on zero-rated items. However, a business which sells zero-rated items can still claim the repayment of input VAT. Its balance sheet will therefore regularly include a current asset for amounts of refundable input VAT owing from the authorities.

29. As explained earlier some traders are exempt from VAT, which means that they do not charge output VAT on their goods and services, but nor can they reclaim any input VAT at all. The purchases made by these businesses will therefore always include the VAT charged by their suppliers.

TEST YOUR KNOWLEDGE

Numbers in brackets refer to paragraphs of this chapter

1. If output VAT exceeds input VAT, the difference can be reclaimed from Customs and Excise. True or false? (5)

2. What are the two rates of VAT which may be applicable to taxable outputs? (8)

3. Give two examples of expenditure on which input VAT is not recoverable. (11)

4. A business purchases goods valued at £400. VAT is charged at 15%. What is the double entry to record the purchase? (16)

Now try question 23 at the end of this section

1. A COMPANY'S PLANT AND MACHINERY

A company's plant and machinery account at 31 December 19Y6 and the corresponding depreciation provision account broken down into years of purchase, are as follows:

Year of purchase £	Plant and machinery at cost £	Depreciation provision
19X0	20,000	20,000
19X6	30,000	30,000
19X7	100,000	95,000
19X8	70,000	59,500
19Y5	50,000	7,500
19Y6	30,000	1,500
	300,000	213,500

Depreciation is at the rate of 10% per annum on cost. It is the company's policy to assume that all purchases, sales or disposals of plant occurred on 30 June in the relevant year for the purposes of calculating depreciation, irrespective of the precise date on which these events occurred.

During 19Y7 the following transactions took place:

1. Purchase of plant and machinery amounted to £150,000.
2. Plant that had been bought in 19X6 for £17,000 was scrapped.
3. Plant that had been bought in 19X7 for £9,000 was sold for £500.
4. Plant that had been bought in 19X8 for £24,000 was sold for £1,500.

You are required to:

(a) Calculate the provision for depreciation of plant and machinery for the year ended 31 December 19Y7. In calculating this provision you should bear in mind that it is the company's policy to show any profit or loss on the sale or disposal of plant as a completely separate item in the profit and loss account.

(b) Show the following as at 31 December 19Y6 and 31 December 19Y7:

(i) plant and machinery, at cost;
(ii) depreciation provision (ie accumulated depreciation);
(iii) the net book value of plant and machinery;
(iv) the profit or loss on sales or disposals of plant and machinery.

Tutorial note: it would help you to reconcile the figures as at 31 December 19Y6 with the figures as at 31 December 19Y7 for items (i) and (ii) by calculating the 1 January figures, and then making adjustments for disposals and additional purchases during 19Y7 in order to arrive at the figures for 31 December 19Y7.

2. ASHTON

Mr K Ashton started a manufacturing business on 1 January 19X2. He had not kept a ledger but wished to have accounts prepared for the year 19X6. A preliminary statement of assets and liabilities was drawn up as at 31 December 19X5 and 31 December 19X6, as follows:

	31.12.X5 £	31.12.X6 £
Bank overdraft	5,040	3,270
Trade creditors	4,450	4,820
Accrued expenses	570	370
Prepayments	1,250	1,500
Trade debtors	12,300	14,600
Stocks:		
Finished goods	7,900	10,050
Work in progress	5,300	4,600
Raw materials	6,900	7,790
Loan from Mrs K Ashton	–	500

Mr Ashton had started with a capital of £50,000 in 19X2 and had introduced a further £10,000 in 19X6. The machinery he bought for £20,000 on 1 January 19X2 had been depreciated at the rate of 10% per annum on the straight line method. A machine which had then cost £1,500 had been sold on 1 January 19X6 for its written down value of £900. Ashton carried on his business in premises which he owned and for which he had paid £25,000. His drawings for the year 19X6 were £12,000.

Required:

(a) Prepare a statement of affairs as at 31 December 19X5 and 31 December 19X6 respectively, in columnar form.

(b) Prepare a statement of profit for the year 19X6 after charging depreciation for that year.

(c) Prepare a statement showing the written down value at 31.12.X6 of plant and machinery purchased for £20,000 on 1 January 19X2.

Tutorial note: a statement of affairs is a statement which lists all the assets and liabilities of a business so as to arrive at a figure for proprietor's capital. The statement prepared in the suggested solution is very similar in format to a normal balance sheet.

SECTION 2: ILLUSTRATIVE QUESTIONS

3. S TRADER

S Trader carries on a merchanting business. The following balances have been extracted from his books on 30 September 19X1:

	£
Capital - S Trader at 1 October 19X0	24,239
Office furniture and equipment	1,440
Cash drawings - S Trader	4,888
Stock on hand - 1 October 19X0	14,972
Purchases	167,760
Sales	203,845
Rent	1,350
Lighting and heating	475
Insurance	304
Salaries	6,352
Stationery and printing	737
Telephone and postage	517
General expenses	2,044
Travellers' commission and expenses	9,925
Discounts allowed	517
Discounts received	955
Bad debts written off	331
Debtors	19,100
Creditors	8,162
Balance at bank to S Trader's credit	6,603
Petty cash in hand	29
Provision for doubtful debts	143

The following further information is to be taken into account:

(a) Stock on hand on 30 September 19X1 was valued at £12,972.
(b) Provision is to be made for the following liabilities and accrued expenses as at 30 September 19X1: rent £450; lighting and heating £136; travellers' commission and expenses £806; accountancy charges £252.
(c) Provision for doubtful debts is to be raised to 3% of the closing debtor balances.
(d) Office furniture and equipment is to be depreciated by 10% on book value.
(e) Mr Trader had removed stock costing £112 for his own use during the year.

You are required to:

(a) prepare trading and profit and loss accounts for the year ended 30 September 19X1 grouping the various expenses under suitable headings; and
(b) prepare a balance sheet as at that date.

4. JAMES

James opened a shop on 1 July 19X2 and during his first month in business, the following transactions occurred:

19X2
1 July	James contributes £20,000 in cash to the business out of his private bank account.
2 July	He opens a business bank account by transferring £18,000 of his cash in hand.
5 July	Some premises are rented, the rent being £500 per quarter payable in advance in cash.
6 July	James buys some second-hand shop equipment for £300 paying by cheque.

9 July	He purchases some goods for resale for £1,000 paying for them in cash.
10 July	Seddon supplies him with £2,000 of goods on credit
20 July	James returns £200 of the goods to Seddon.
23 July	Cash sales for the week amount to £1,500.
26 July	James sells goods on credit for £1,000 to Frodsham.
28 July	Frodsham returns £500 of the goods to James.
31 July	James settles his account with Seddon by cheque, and is able to claim a cash discount of 10%.
31 July	Frodsham sends James a cheque for £450 in settlement of his account, any balance remaining on his account being treated as a cash discount.
31 July	During his initial trading, James has discovered that some of his shop equipment is not suitable, but he is fortunate in being able to dispose of it for £50 in cash. There was no profit or loss on disposal.
31 July	He withdraws £150 in cash as part payment towards a holiday for his wife.

You are required to:

(a)   enter the above transactions in James' ledger accounts, balance off the accounts and bring down the balances as at 1 August 19X2; and

(b)   extract a trial balance as at 31 July 19X2

5.   HACKER

Hacker commenced business as a retail butcher on 1 January 19X0. The following is a summary of the transactions which took place during the first three months of trading:

(a)   Cash sales amounted to £3,000, including £500 of sales on Access and Barclaycard.

(b)   Credit sales totalled £1,600 and of this £300 was outstanding at the end of the period.

(c)   On the commencement of business Hacker had paid £4,000 into the business, and a full year's rent of £600 had been paid immediately.

(d)   A delivery van was purchased on 1 January at a cost of £900. It was agreed that this should be depreciated at the rate of 20% per annum.

(e)   During the period suppliers had been paid £1,600 for meat and invoices totalling £400 remained unpaid at 31 March.

(f)   The stock of meat at the close of business on 31 March was valued at cost at £360.

(g)   Sundry expenses (all paid during the period and relating to it) amounted to £400, and during March Hacker drew £200 from the business.

From this information you are required:

(a)   to write up the ledger accounts and cash book of Hacker;

(b)   to extract a trial balance;

(c)   to prepare a trading and profit and loss account for the three months ending 31 March 19X0, and balance sheet at that date.

Note: keep firmly in your mind the fact that you are preparing quarterly accounts, whereas some expenses above are given as an annual amount.

You might also be interested in the new idea given in (a), that sales on Access and Barclaycard can be treated in the same way as sales paid by cheque - ie as cash sales.

6. SPARK

Spark has been trading for a number of years as an electrical appliance retailer and repairer in premises which he rents at an annual rate of £1,500 payable in arrears. Balances appearing in his books at 1 January 19X1 were as follows:

	£	£
Capital account		1,808
Motor van		1,200
Fixtures and fittings		806
Provision for depreciation on motor van		720
Provisions for depreciation on fixtures and fittings		250
Stock at cost		366
Debtors for credit sales:		
Brown	160	
Blue	40	
Stripe	20	
		220
Cash at bank		672
Cash in hand		5
Loan from Flex		250
Creditors for supplies:		
Live	143	
Negative	80	
Earth	73	
		296
Amount owing for electricity		45
Rates paid in advance		100

Although Sparks has three credit customers the majority of his sales and services are for cash, out of which he pays various expenses before banking the balance.

The following transactions took place during the first four months of 19X1:

	January £	February £	March £	April £
Suppliers' invoices:				
Live	468	570	390	602
Negative	-	87	103	64
Earth	692	-	187	-
Capital introduced		500		
Bankings of cash (from cash sales)	908	940	766	1,031
Expenditure out of cash sales before banking:				
Drawings	130	120	160	150
Stationery	12	14	26	21
Travelling	6	10	11	13
Petrol and van repairs	19	22	37	26
Sundry expenses	5	4	7	3
Postage	12	10	15	19
Cleaner's wages	60	60	65	75
Goods invoiced to credit customers:				
Brown	66	22	10	12
Blue	120	140	130	180
Stripe	44	38	20	48
Cheque payments (other than those to suppliers):				
Telephone	40	49	59	66
Electricity	62	47	20	106
Rates	-	-	220	-
Motor van (1.2.X1)	-	800	-	-
Unbanked at the end of April	-	-	-	12

Spark pays for goods by cheque one month after receipt of invoice, and receives a settlement discount of 15% from each supplier.

Credit customers also pay by cheque one month after receipt of invoice, and are given a settlement discount of 10% of the invoice price.

You are required:

(a) to write up the ledger accounts of Spark for the four months to 30 April 19X1, and extract a trial balance after balancing off the accounts;

(b) to prepare:

(i) trading and profit and loss accounts for the four months; and
(ii) a balance sheet on 30 April 19X1;

after dealing with the following matters:

(i) the payment of £800 for a new motor van represents the balance paid to the garage after being granted a part-exchange value of £500 on the old van;

(ii) depreciation is provided at the rate of 20% per annum on the cost of motor vans and at the rate of 10% on the cost of fixtures and fittings. No depreciation is to be provided in the period of disposal;

(iii) interest on the loan from Flex is to be accrued at 10% per annum and credited to his account;

    (iv)   amounts owing at 30 April 19X1 were electricity £22, and telephone £15. The payment for rates was for six months in advance from 1 March;

    (v)   included in the payments for telephone was one of Spark's private bills of £37 which is to be charged to him;

    (vi) stock at cost on 30 April 19X1 amounted to £390.

Calculations are to be made to the nearest £.

7. ASPLEY

The following information has been extracted from the machine register of R Aspley as at 31 October 19X6:

Machine number	Date of purchase	Original cost £	Depreciation %
10	1.11.X2	1,000	10
12	1. 4.X4	6,000	15
14	31.10.X5	5,000	5
16	1. 8.X6	10,000	20

Notes:

(1) The company operates a straight line method of depreciation based on the original cost of each machine. It is assumed that at the end of its life each machine will have a scrap value equivalent to 10% of its original cost.

(2) A full year's depreciation is charged in the year of acquisition (irrespective of the date of purchase), but no depreciation is charged in the year of disposal.

(3) Separate ledger accounts are not kept for each machine.

(4) During the year to 31 October 19X7 the following transactions occurred:

    (a)   On 1 April 19X7 machine number 10 was sold for £600 in cash.

    (b)   On 1 June 19X7 machine number 17 was purchased for £15,000 in part exchange for machine number 14. It was agreed that machine number 14 had a part exchange value of £4,600, the balance of £10,400 being paid in cash. Machine number 17's depreciation is to be 10%.

    (c)   On 1 August 19X7 machine number 18 was purchased for £7,000 and was paid for in cash; its depreciation rate is to be 20%.

You are required to:

(a) write up the following accounts for the year to 31 October 19X7:

    (i)   machines account;

    (ii)   accumulated depreciation on machines account; and

    (iii) disposal of machines account: and

(b) show how the machines account and the accumulated depreciation on machines account would appear in Aspley's balance sheet at 31 October 19X7.

8. **GEORGE**

George is a wholesaler and the following information relates to his accounting year ending 30 September 19X2:

(1) Goods are sold on credit terms, but some cash sales are also transacted.
(2) At 1 October 19X1 George's trade debtors amounted to £30,000 against which he had set aside a provision for doubtful debts of 5%.
(3) On 15 January 19X2 George was informed that Fall Limited had gone into liquidation, owing him £2,000. This debt was outstanding from the previous year.
(4) Cash sales during the year totalled £46,800, whilst credit sales amounted to £187,800.
(5) £182,500 was received from trade debtors.
(6) Settlement discounts allowed to credit customers were £5,300.
(7) Apart from Fall Limited's bad debt, other certain bad debts amounted to £3,500.
(8) George intends to retain the provision for doubtful debts account at 5% of outstanding trade debtors as at the end of the year, and the necessary entry is to be made.

You are required to enter the above transactions in George's ledger accounts and (apart from the cash and bank and profit and loss accounts) balance off the accounts and bring down the balances as at 1 October 19X2.

9. **STATIONERY AND TELEPHONE**

You are required, using the information given below, to compile a company's stationery and telephone account for the year ended 31 January 19X4 showing clearly the charge to profit and loss account.

The value of the company's stock of stationery on 31 January 19X3 was £241. At that date the prepaid telephone rental amounted to £20, there was an accrued liability of £137 for telephone calls during December 19X2 and January 19X3 and an accrued liability of £25 for stationery.

During the year ended 31 January 19X4, the following transactions occurred:

19X3		£	£
February 20	Purchase of stationery for		103
March 19	Payment of telephone account of consisting of:		262
	rent for quarter ended 31 May 19X3	60	
	calls for December 19X2	79	
	January 19X3	58	
	February 19X3	65	
June 28	Payment of telephone account of consisting of:		281
	rent for quarter ended 31 August 19X3	60	
	calls for March, April and May 19X3	221	
August 12	Purchase of stationery for		156
September 15	Payment of telephone account of consisting of:		305
	rent for quarter ended 30 November 19X3	75	
	calls for June, July and August 19X3	230	
November 13	Purchase of stationery for		74

		£	£
December 20	Payment of telephone account of consisting of:		282
	rent for quarter ended 29 February 19X4	75	
	calls for September, October and November 19X3	207	

At 31 January 19X4 the stock of stationery was valued at £199 and there was an accrued liability for stationery of £13. On March 23 19X4 a telephone account of £298 was paid consisting of:

	£
rent for the quarter ended 31 May 19X4	75
calls for December 19X3	86
January 19X4	63
February 19X4	74

(*Tutorial note:* opening and closing stocks of stationery should be included in the account.)

10. MILLER

Before preparing his firm's trading and profit and loss account for the year ended 31 March 19X3, A Miller needs to make the following adjustments:

1 Depreciate plant and machinery by £12,000
2 A Miller has drawn out goods for his own use amounting to £220 of which there is no record in the books.
3 Rent accrued amounts to £400.
4 The account of carriage inwards includes £160 paid on the purchase of new machinery.
5 The provision for bad debts is to be increased by £3,500.

Required:

Prepare the journal entries necessary to implement the above adjustments.

11. BIFFINS BISCUIT COMPANY

At 1 July 19X5 the balances on certain ledger accounts of Biffin's Biscuit Company were as follows:

	£
Rent and rates payable:	
- prepayments	1,720
- accruals	640
Motor vehicles - at cost	58,000
Provision for depreciation on motor vehicles	31,400
Telephone expenses - prepayment	380

Transactions for the year to 30 June 19X6 were as follows:

	£
paid by cheque: rent	5,800
rates	4,700
telephone bills	3,600
disposal of motor vehicle: original cost	7,800
accumulated depreciation	5,900
purchase of new vehicle: total price	11,600
paid for by trade-in allowance on disposal of vehicle	2,500
balance paid by cheque	9,100

At 30 June 19X6, the balances on the ledger accounts were as follows:

	£
Rent and rates payable	
- prepayments	1,470
- accruals	780
Vehicles at cost	(not given here)
Provision for depreciation on motor vehicles	39,200
Telephone expenses - accrued	650

Required: for the year ended 30 June 19X6 journalise the transactions indicated above, including transfer entries to the P & L account where applicable.

12. STAN DOFFISH

In preparing the final accounts of Stan Doffish for the year to 31 December 19X6, the following items need to be taken into account at the year end.

(a) The amount of accrued wages and salaries, payable on 3 January 19X7, is:

	£
Wages	834.60
Salaries	993.70

(b) There was a general increase in wages and salaries in September 19X6, backdated to the beginning of April. Several employees had resigned or retired between April and September, but although most of these had been given the back-pay owing to them, some have not been traced, and so £528.30 is still owing in back pay. It has now been decided that the notes and coins currently held in wage packets should be paid back into the business bank account, until the ex-employees can be traced and paid.

(c) The provision for doubtful debts is to be raised from £860 to £1,150.

(d)   The provision for discounts allowed to debtors is to be reduced from £350 to £180.

(e)   Bad debts worth £769.10 are to be written off.

(f)   A debt of £210.50, written off as bad in the previous year, has been recovered in full. However, the cheque in payment has only just been received, and has not yet been banked or posted to the accounts.

(g)   Owing to a mistake, a credit customer was allowed a discount of 5% instead of 8% on a sale with a gross value of £700. The customer has taken the 5% discount offered, but has already indicated that he should be entitled to a further 3%.

(h)   In December 19X6, Stan Doffish sold goods to Cool Cats Garments worth £370.40 and had bought overalls from the same company, on credit, worth £156.60. The sums have been correctly posted to their respective accounts in the sales ledger and purchase ledger. However, the accounts are to be settled in contra at 31 December 19X6 with the remaining balance to be settled by cheque on 3 January 19X7.

(i)   There is prepaid rent of £840.30 and accrued heating expenses of £415.

(j)   In the middle of 19X6, repairs and redecorations to the business premises by a firm of local builders amounted to £2,800. These costs were incorrectly debited to the Buildings account. The company makes a provision for depreciation on its buildings of 2¼% per annum, using the straight line method and assuming nil residual value.

Required:

Prepare suitable journal entries for Stan Doffish to record each of the items listed above, at 31 December 19X6. (Your entries should also include items affecting the cash and bank account.)

13. SST LIMITED (10 marks)

You are required to journalise the following transactions in the books of SST Limited:

January

27   Sold goods on credit to RBB Limited for £10,000.

February

2   Purchased goods on credit from ACD Limited for £5,000.

5   RBB Limited accepted a three months' bill of exchange for £10,000 drawn on it by SST Limited.

16   SST Limited accepted a three months' bill of exchange drawn by ACD Limited for £5,000.

March

5   Discounted the £10,000 bill of exchange from RBB Limited with the bank for £9,750.

16   ACD Limited discounted the £5,000 bill of exchange from SST Limited with the bank for £4,875.

May

10   The bank informed SST Limited that RBB Limited had dishonoured its acceptance for £10,000 and that accordingly the current account of SST Limited had been debited with this amount.

16   Paid the bill originally drawn on SST Limited by ACD Limited.

December

9   The liquidator of RBB Limited paid a final dividend of 30 pence in the £1 to all creditors of that company.

14. ALEX AUTOS

The following information has been extracted from the incomplete records of Alex Autos for the year to 31 October 19X4:

	£
Provision for doubtful debts (at 1 November 19X3)	6,300
Cash paid to trade creditors	274,000
Cash received from trade debtors	663,000
Credit purchases	310,000
Credit sales	690,000
Discounts allowed	14,000
Discounts received	15,000
Purchases returned (all credit)	10,000
Sales returned (all credit)	8,000
Trade creditors (at 1 November 19X3)	43,000
Trade debtors (at 1 November 19X3)	63,000

The following additional information for the year to 31 October 19X4 is to be taken into account:

1   The provision for doubtful debts should be made equal to 10% of the outstanding trade debtors as at 31 October 19X4.
2   One of Alex Autos customers went into liquidation on 1 August 19X4 owing the company £7,000. It is most unlikely that this debt will ever be recovered.
3   A cheque for £3,000 received from a trade debtor was returned by the bank marked 'account unknown'.
4   Alex Autos owed a customer £4,000 and it was agreed that this amount should be offset against an amount owing to Alex Autos by the same customer.

You are required to write up the following accounts for the year to 31 October 19X4:

(a)   provision for doubtful debts;
(b)   trade creditors' control account;
(c)   trade debtors' control account.

15. APRIL SHOWERS

April Showers sells goods on credit to most of its customers. In order to control its debtor collection system, the company maintains a sales ledger control account. In preparing the accounts for the year to 30 October 19X3 the accountant discovers that the total of all the personal accounts in the sales ledger amounts to £12,802, whereas the balance on the sales ledger control account is £12,550.

Upon investigating the matter, the following errors were discovered:

1   Sales for the week ending 27 March 19X3 amounting to £850 had been omitted from the control account.
2   A debtor's account balance of £300 had not been included in the list of balances.
3   Cash received of £750 had been entered in a personal account as £570.
4   Discounts allowed totalling £100 had not been entered in the control account.
5   A personal account balance had been undercast by £200.
6   A contra item of £400 with the purchase ledger had not been entered in the control account.
7   A bad debt of £500 had not been entered in the control account.

8   Cash received of £250 had been debited to a personal account.
9   Discounts received of £50 had been debited to Bell's sales ledger account.
10   Returns inwards valued at £200 had not been included in the control account.
11   Cash received of £80 had been credited to a personal account as £8.
12   A cheque for £300 received from a customer had been dishonoured by the bank, but no adjustment had been made in the control account.

You are required to:

(a) prepare a corrected sales ledger control account, bringing down the amended balance as at 1 November 19X3;

(b) prepare a statement showing the adjustments that are necessary to the list of personal account balances so that it reconciles with the amended sales ledger control account balance.

16. FRONTLOADER

Frontloader Limited is a business which acts as a distributor of washing machines entirely on credit terms to a wide range of customers. The following balances were extracted from its ledgers at 30 June 19X5:

	£	£
Sales		723,869
Creditors - balance at 30 June 19X4		49,781
Debtors - balance at 30 June 19X4	84,611	
Purchases of washing machines	342,916	
Discounts allowed	8,214	
Discounts received		6,978
Cash received from debtors	699,267	
Cash paid to creditors		321,853
Returns inwards	36,925	
Carriage outwards	5,264	
Overdraft interest	12,748	
Provision for doubtful debts as at 30 June 19X4		4,813

Subsequent enquiries reveal the following:
A cheque for £1,246 from A Brown, a customer, has been returned by the bank marked 'refer to drawer'. Bad debts totalling £6,854 are to be written off, and the provision for doubtful debts is to be raised to 8% of the debtor balances at 30 June 19X5.

On the last day of the year a cheque is received for £1,000 from the liquidator of J Smith Limited. This customer had owed Frontloader £7,500 when it ceased to trade in March 19X2, and the debt had been written off as a bad debt in the year ended 30 June 19X2. No entry in respect of this cheque has yet been made in the books.

You are required to prepare for the year ended 30 June 19X5:

(a) the debtors ledger control account;
(b) the bad and doubtful debts account; and
(c) the balance sheet entry for debtors.

17. PAYROLL LIMITED

As at 1 November 19X3, the following balances existed in the ledger of Payroll Limited:

	£'000
Creditors	800
Bad debts provision	450
Wages control	38
PAYE income tax deductions	35
National Insurance contributions liability	44

During the year ended 31 October 19X4 the following transactions occurred:

	£'000
Gross wages earned	2,000
Cash paid to suppliers	5,400
Discounts received	100
Debtors and creditors accounts set off against each other and settled by contra	700
Sales on credit	12,000
Purchases on credit	6,000
Cash received from customers	11,800
Discounts allowed	300
Bad debts written off against the provision	200
Bad debts previously written off now recovered in cash	50
Increase in the bad debts provision charged to profit and loss account	100
Net wages paid in cash	1,330
PAYE income tax deducted from employees' wages	407
National Insurance contributions deducted from employees' wages	260
National Insurance contributions, employer's contribution	290
Cash paid to Inland Revenue for:	
PAYE income tax deductions	400
Employer's and employees' National Insurance contributions	546

Debtors at 31 October 19X4 amounted to £1,000.

There were no cash sales or cash purchases during the year.

You are required to write up the following accounts in the company's ledger for the year ended 31 October 19X4:

    Creditors
    Debtors
    Provision for doubtful debts
    Wages control
    PAYE income tax deductions
    National Insurance contributions liability.

18. CAMFORD

The Treasurer of the Camford School Fund is attempting to reconcile the balance shown in the cash book with that appearing on the bank pass sheets. According to the cash book, the balance at the bank as at 31 May 19X2 was £1,900, whilst the bank pass sheets disclosed an overdrawn amount of £470. Upon investigation, the treasurer identified the following discrepancies:

(1) A cheque paid to Summer Limited for £340 had been entered in the cash book as £430.
(2) Cash paid into the bank for £100 had been entered in the cash book as £90.
(3) A transfer of £1,500 to the Midlands Savings Bank had not been entered in the cash book.
(4) A receipt of £10 shown on the bank statement had not been entered in the cash book.
(5) Cheques drawn amounting to £40 had not been paid into the bank.
(6) The cash book balance had been incorrectly brought down at 1 June 19X1 as a debit balance of £1,200 instead of a debit balance of £1,100.
(7) Bank charges of £20 do not appear in the cash book.
(8) Receipts of £900 paid into the bank on 31 May 19X2 do not appear on the bank pass sheets until 1 June 19X2.
(9) A standing order payment of £30 had not been entered in the cash book.
(10) A cheque for £50 previously received and paid into the bank had been returned by the subscriber's bank marked 'account closed'.
(11) The bank received a direct debit of £100 from an anonymous subscriber.
(12) Cheques paid into the bank had been incorrectly totalled. The total amount should have been £170 instead of £150.

You are required to draw up a bank reconciliation statement as at 31 May 19X2.

19. RECTIFY

A summary of the cash book of Rectify Limited for the year to 31 May 19X5 is as follows:

CASH BOOK

	£		£
Opening balance b/f	805	Payments	146,203
Receipts	145,720	Closing balance c/f	322
	146,525		146,525

After some investigation of the cash book and vouchers you discover that:

(a) bank charges of £143 shown on the bank statement have not yet been entered in the cash book;
(b) a cheque drawn for £98 has been entered in the cash book as £89, and another drawn at £230 has been entered as a receipt;
(c) a cheque received from a customer for £180 has been returned by the bank marked 'refer to drawer', but it has not yet been written back in the cash book;
(d) an error of transposition has occurred in that the opening balance of the cash book should have been brought down as £850;
(e) cheques paid to suppliers totalling £630 have not yet been presented at the bank, whilst payments in to the bank of £580 on 31 May 19X5 have not yet been credited to the company's account;
(f) a cheque for £82 has been debited to the company's account in error by the bank;
(g) the company owes £430 to the electricity board;

(h) standing orders appearing on the bank statement have not yet been entered in the cash book:

(i) interest for the half year to 31 March on a loan of £20,000 at 11% pa;
(ii) hire purchase repayments on the managing director's car - 12 months at £55 per month;
(iii) dividend received on a trade investment - £1,147;

(i) a page of the receipts side of the cash book has been undercast by £200;
(j) the bank statement shows a balance overdrawn of £870.

You are required to produce well presented statements to:

(a) adjust the cash book in the light of the above discoveries;
(b) reconcile the bank statement balance to the cash book balance.

20. CHI KNITWEAR LIMITED

Chi Knitwear Limited is an old fashioned firm with a hand-written set of books. A trial balance is extracted at the end of each month, and a profit and loss account and balance sheet are computed. This month however the trial balance will not balance, the credits exceeding debits by £1,536.

You are asked to help and after inspection of the ledgers discover the following errors.

(1) A balance of £87 on a debtors account has been omitted from the schedule of debtors, the total of which was entered as debtors in the trial balance.

(2) A small piece of machinery purchased for £1,200 had been written off to repairs.

(3) The receipts side of the cash book had been undercast by £720.

(4) The total of one page of the sales day book had been carried forward as £8,154, whereas the correct amount was £8,514.

(5) A credit note for £179 received from a supplier had been posted to the wrong side of his account.

(6) An electricity bill in the sum of £152, not yet accrued for, is discovered in a filing tray.

(7) Mr Smith whose past debts to the company had been the subject of a provision, at last paid £731 to clear his account. His personal account has been credited but the cheque has not yet been entered in the the cash book.

You are required to:

(a) write up the suspense account to clear the trial balance difference; and
(b) state the effect on the accounts of correcting each error.

21. AFTER THE STOCK COUNT

After its end of year physical stock count and valuation, the accounts staff of Caveat Emptor Limited have reached a valuation of £153,699 at cost for total stocks held as at the year end.

However, on checking the figures, the chief bookkeeper has come across the following additional facts:

(a) On one of the stock sheets, a sub-total value of £6,275 had been carried forward on to the next sheet as £6,725.

(b) 260 units of stock number 73113X which cost £0.60 each have been extended into the total value column at £6.00 each.

(c) The purchasing department has informed the accounts department that it is in possession of a number of free samples given to them by potential suppliers. Their estimated value, at purchase cost, would be £1,750. They were not included in the stock referred to above.

(d) The stock count includes £4,658 of goods bought on credit and still not paid for as at the year end.

(e) The stock count includes damaged goods which originally cost £2,885. These could be repaired at a cost of £921 and sold for £3,600.

(f) The stock count excludes 300 units of stock item 730052 which were sold to a customer Seesafe Limited on a sale or return basis, at a price of £8 each. The original cost of the units was £5 each. Seesafe Limited has not yet indicated to Caveat Emptor Limited whether these goods have been accepted, or whether they will eventually be returned.

(g) The stock count includes 648 units of stock item 702422. These cost £7.30 each originally but because of dumping on the market by overseas suppliers, a price war has flared up and the unit price of the item has fallen to £6.50. The price reduction is expected to be temporary, lasting less than a year or so, although some observers of the market predicted that the change might be permanent. Caveat Emptor Limited has already decided that if the price reduction lasts longer than six months, it will reduce its resale price of the item from £10.90 to about £10.

Required:

Calculate the closing stock figure for inclusion in the annual accounts of Caveat Emptor Limited, making whatever adjustments you consider necessary in view of items (a) - (g). Explain your treatment of each item.

SECTION 2: ILLUSTRATIVE QUESTIONS

22. BIG AND SMALL

Big and Small keep a detailed stock record of all material purchases and of all issues of materials to production. The following information relates to the purchase and issue to production of Material MF for the month of October 19X4.

| Date | RECEIPTS | | | ISSUES | | | BALANCE | |
	Quantity Kilograms	Price £	Value £	Quantity Kilograms	Price £	Value £	Quantity Kilograms	Value £
1.10.X4							200	200
1.10.X4				100				
5.10.X4	700	3.00	2,100					
8.10.X4				300				
12.10.X4	400	5.00	2,000					
15.10.X4				200				
19.10.X4	800	2.00	1,600					
22.10.X4				600				
26.10.X4	1,100	4.00	4,400					
29.10.X4				1,500				

Required:

(a) Calculate the total charge to production of material MF during October 19X4 using the first-in, first-out (FIFO) method of pricing the issue of goods to production;

(b) calculate the closing stock value of material MF as at 31 October 19X4 using the last-in, first-out (LIFO) method of pricing the issue of goods to production;

(c) calculate the issue price per kilogram of material MF on 29 October 19X4 using the continuous weighted average method of pricing the issue of goods to production; and

(d) calculate the issue price per kilogram of material MF during the month of October 19X4 using the periodic weighted average method of pricing the issue of goods to production.

(AAT December 1984)

23. VAT

The transactions below relate to Vatco Limited's accounting year ended 30 September 19X4. All amounts are stated inclusive of any VAT which may be applicable.

	£
Debtors and sales	
Balance on debtors' control account at 1 October 19X3	2,415
Zero-rated sales	4,000
Standard-rated sales	24,150
Discounts allowed to customers (all in respect of standard-rated sales)	1,035
Cash received from customers	27,600
Creditors and purchases	
Balance on creditors' control account at 1 October 19X3	1,955
Standard-rated purchases	18,400
Discounts received from suppliers	575
Cash paid to suppliers	17,480

At 1 October 19X3 there was a balance of VAT owing to Customs and Excise of £760. During the year ended 30 September 19X4 payments to Customs and Excise totalled £1,040.

The standard rate of VAT is 15%.

You are required to prepare the following ledger accounts:

(a) debtors' control account;
(b) creditors' control account;
(c) VAT control account.

1. A COMPANY'S PLANT AND MACHINERY

Tutorial notes

(a) (i) Fixed assets purchased in 19X0 and 19X6 cannot be depreciated further, because they are already fully depreciated.

(ii) Fixed assets purchased in mid-19X7 had been depreciated by 95% ($\frac{1}{2}$ years) by 31 December 19Y6. All these assets will be fully depreciated by mid-19Y7, when some of them are sold for £500.

(iii) Fixed assets purchased in 19X8 and sold in 19Y6 would be 90% depreciated at the time of sale. Fixed assets purchased in 19X8 and not sold would be 95% depreciated by the end of the year.

(b) In answering this question you must make a clear distinction in your mind between:

(i) depreciation charged in the P & L account for 19Y7. Assets sold during the year would still incur a depreciation charge for the six months they are in use; and

(ii) accumulated depreciation on assets owned by the business as at the end of the year.

Solution

(a)

Year of purchase	Plant and machinery at cost £	Depreciation charge as a % of cost		Depreciation charge – P & L account £
19X0	20,000	(fully depreciated)–	0%	0
19X6	30,000	(fully depreciated)–	0%	0
19X7	100,000	(note (ii) above)	5%	5,000

Year of purchase		At cost £	Depreciation	%	P & L a/c Depreciation £
19X7			(as above)		5,000
19X8	Assets sold in 19Y7	24,000	(sold in mid-year)	5%	1,200
	Assets not sold in 19Y7	46,000		10%	4,600
19Y5		50,000		10%	5,000
19Y6		30,000		10%	3,000
19Y7		150,000	(bought in mid-year)	5%	7,500

Total provision for depreciation for the year   26,300

(b) (i)   Plant and machinery

Year of purchase	At cost, as at 31 Dec 19Y6 £	Disposals during 19Y7 £	Additions during 19Y7 £	At cost, as at 31 Dec 19Y7 £
19X0	20,000			20,000
19X6	30,000	(17,000)		13,000
19X7	100,000	(9,000)		91,000
19X8	70,000	(24,000)		46,000
19Y5	50,000			50,000
19Y6	30,000			30,000
19Y7	-		150,000	150,000
Total	300,000	(50,000)	150,000	400,000

(ii) Provision for depreciation

Year of purchase	Accumulated depreciation as at 31 Dec 19Y6 £	Accumulated depreciation on items disposed of in 19Y7 £	Provision for depreciation 19Y7 £	Accumulated depreciation as at 31 Dec 19Y7 £
19X0	20,000	-	-	20,000
19X6	30,000	(17,000)	-	13,000
19X7	95,000	(9,000)	5,000	91,000
19X8	59,500	(21,600) *	5,800	43,700 **
19Y5	7,500	-	5,000	12,500
19Y6	1,500	-	3,000	4,500
19Y7	-	-	7,500	7,500
Total	213,500	(47,600)	26,300	192,200

* 90% depreciated at time of sale, 90% x £24,000 = £21,600.
** 95% depreciated 95% x £46,000 = £43,700.

(iii)

	31 Dec 19Y6 £	31 Dec 19Y7 £
Fixed assets		
Plant and machinery at cost	300,000	400,000
Provision for depreciation	213,500	192,200
Net book value	86,500	207,800

(iv)

| | Disposal of item of plant purchased in | | |
	19X6 £	19X7 £	19X8 £
Cost of plant disposed of	17,000	9,000	24,000
Accumulated depreciation on plant disposed of (see (ii))	17,000	9,000	21,600
Net book value of plant at date of disposal	0	0	2,400
Net sale price	0	500	1,500
Profit/(loss) on disposal	0	500	(900)

There is a total loss of £400 on sale/disposal of the three items.

2. ASHTON

(a) STATEMENT OF AFFAIRS AS AT 31 DECEMBER 19X5 AND 19X6

	19X5 £	19X5 £	19X6 £	19X6 £
Fixed assets				
Premises (note 1)		25,000		25,000
Machinery (see (c) below)		12,000		9,250
		37,000		34,250
Current assets				
Stocks (total)	20,100		22,440	
Trade debtors	12,300		14,600	
Prepayments	1,250		1,500	
		33,650		38,540
Total assets		70,650		72,790
Current liabilities				
Bank overdraft	5,040		3,270	
Trade creditors	4,450		4,820	
Accrued expenses	570		370	
	10,060		8,460	
Long-term liability				
Loan (Mrs Ashton)	–		500	
Total liabilities		(10,060)		(8,960)
Capital (= total assets less total liabilities)		60,590		63,830

(b) The business equation is:

$$P = I + D - C_i$$
$$= £(63,830 - 60,590) + £12,000 - £10,000$$
$$= £5,240$$

(c) PLANT AND MACHINERY

	Cost £	Dep'n £	Net £
Purchase price 1 January 19X2	20,000		20,000
Depreciation in 19X2 (10% x £20,000)		2,000	(2,000)
Depreciation in 19X3		2,000	(2,000)
Depreciation in 19X4		2,000	(2,000)
Depreciation in 19X5		2,000	(2,000)
As at 31 December 19X5	20,000	8,000	12,000
Disposal on 1 January 19X6*	(1,500)	(600)	(900)
	18,500	7,400	11,100
Depreciation in 19X6 (10% x £18,500)		1,850	(1,850)
As at 31 December 19X6	18,500	9,250	9,250

* When the machine is disposed of, its cost is removed from the pool of machinery. Similarly, the accumulated depreciation provided on it is removed from the depreciation pool.

Notes:

1. We are given no information about depreciation of Mr Ashton's premises, which are therefore assumed to be valued at cost.

2. In part (b), the only capital introduced in the year by the proprietor, Mr Ashton, is the sum of £10,000. The £500 loan contributed by Mrs Ashton is strictly an amount owed by the business to an outsider, and is not part of the proprietor's capital.

3. S TRADER

Introductory notes
There are one or two items in this problem which might have caused you some difficulty.

(a) Stock taken for own use. The stocks are drawings. The cost of goods sold must therefore exclude the £112 of stock purchased but taken as drawings. Drawings will include the £112 of stock.

(b) Provision for doubtful debts and bad debts written off:

	£
New provision (3% of £19,100)	573
Previous provision	143
Increase in the provision (a charge to P & L)	430

The value of debtors in the balance sheet will be reduced by the provision for doubtful debts of £573.

The bad debts written off (£331) are also a charge in the P & L account.

You might wonder why the value of debtors is not reduced by the £331 of bad debts written off. The answer is that when bad debts are written off, the total debtors are immediately reduced in value, so that the £19,100 of debtors in the question are after deduction of the bad debts. In contrast, a general provision for bad debts indicates that no specific bad debts have been written off, and so the total value of debtors in the 'books' of the business - ie the total amount invoiced and owed - will be the total before deducting any provision for bad debts.

(c) Accrued expenses are unpaid liabilities in the balance sheet. They should be added to the expenditures incurred and paid for, to arrive at the total expenditure for the P & L account.

(d) The order of items in the profit and loss account. The expenditure items in the solution below are grouped into establishment expenses, administration expenses and selling expenses. You will possibly have grouped the expenses under two headings (administration and selling and possibly finance). There is no hard-and-fast rule about groupings, but you should have made a conscious effort at making appropriate groupings of your own.

S TRADER
TRADING AND PROFIT AND LOSS ACCOUNT
FOR THE YEAR ENDED 30 SEPTEMBER 19X1

	£	£
Sales		203,845
Stock on hand, 1 October 19X0	14,972	
Purchases £(167,760 – 112)	167,648	
	182,620	
Less stock on hand 30 September 19X1	12,972	
Cost of sales		(169,648)
Gross profit		34,197
Add discount received		955
		35,152
Establishment expenses:		
Rent £(1,350 + 450)	1,800	
Lighting and heating £(475 + 136)	611	
Insurance	304	
Depreciation of office furniture	144	
	2,859	
Administration expenses:		
Salaries	6,352	
General expenses	2,044	
Telephone	517	
Stationery	737	
Accountancy charges	252	
	9,902	
Selling expenses:		
Travellers' commission and expenses £(9,925 + 806)	10,731	
Discount allowed	517	
Increase in provision for doubtful debts	430	
Bad debts written off	331	
	12,009	
		(24,770)
Net profit		10,382

S TRADER
BALANCE SHEET AS AT 30 SEPTEMBER 19X1

	£	£	£
Fixed assets			
Office furniture and equipment			1,440
Less accumulated depreciation			144
			1,296
Current assets			
Stock		12,972	
Debtors	19,100		
Less provision for doubtful debts	573		
		18,527	
Balance at bank		6,603	
Petty cash in hand		29	
		38,131	
Current liabilities			
Trade creditors	8,162		
Accruals £(450 + 136 + 806 + 252)	1,644		
		9,806	
Net current assets			28,325
			29,621
Capital			
Balance at 1 October 19X0			24,239
Net profit for the year			10,382
			34,621
Less drawings £(4,888 + 112)			5,000
Balance at 30 September 19X1			29,621

4. **JAMES**

Tutorial note: this question introduces a distinction between the cash account (representing cash in hand) and the bank account (representing cash at bank). When cash in hand is paid into the bank the transaction is accounted for as a payment from the cash account and a receipt of cash by the bank account.

(a)

CASH ACCOUNT

		£			£
1.7.X2	Capital	20,000	2.7.X2	Bank	18,000
23.7.X2	Sales	1,500	5.7.X2	Rent	500
31.7.X2	Equipment	50	9.7.X2	Purchases	1,000
			31.7.X2	Drawings	150
				Balance c/d	1,900
		21,550			21,550
1.8.X2	Balance b/d	1,900			

CAPITAL ACCOUNT

		£			£
31.7.X2	Balance c/d	20,000	1.7.X2	Cash	20,000
			1.8.X2	Balance b/d	20,000

BANK ACCOUNT

		£			£
2.7.X2	Cash	18,000	6.7.X2	Equipment	300
31.7.X2	Debtors	450	31.7.X2	Creditors	1,620
				Balance c/d	16,530
		18,450			18,450
1.8.X2	Balance b/d	16,530			

RENT ACCOUNT

		£			£
5.7.X2	Cash	500	31.7.X2	Balance c/d	500
31.7.X2	Balance b/d	500			

EQUIPMENT ACCOUNT

		£			£
6.7.X2	Bank	300	31.7.X2	Cash	50
				Balance c/d	250
		300			300
1.8.X2	Balance b/d	250			

PURCHASES ACCOUNT

		£			£
9.7.X2	Cash	1,000	31.7.X2	Balance c/d	3,000
10.7.X2	Creditors (Seddon)	2,000			
		3,000			3,000
1.8.X2	Balance b/d	3,000			

CREDITORS ACCOUNT

		£			£
20.7.X2	Purchase returns	200	10.7.X2	Purchases	2,000
31.7.X2	Bank	1,620			
	Discounts received	180			
		2,000			2,000

PURCHASES RETURNS ACCOUNT

		£			£
31.7.X2	Balance c/d	200	20.7.X2	Creditors	200
			1.8.X2	Balance b/d	200

SALES ACCOUNT

		£			£
31.7.X2	Balance c/d	2,500	23.7.X2	Cash	1,500
			26.7.X2	Debtors (Frodsham)	1,000
		2,500			2,500
			1.8.X2	Balance b/d	2,500

DEBTORS ACCOUNT

	£			£
26.7.X2 Sales	1,000	28.7.X2	Sales returns	500
		31.7.X2	Bank	450
			Discounts allowed	50
	1,000			1,000

SALES RETURNS ACCOUNT

	£			£
28.7.X2 Debtors	500	31.7.X2	Balance c/d	500
1.8.X2 Balance b/d	500			

DISCOUNTS RECEIVED ACCOUNT

	£			£
31.7.X2 Balance c/d	180	31.7.X2	Creditors	180
		1.8.X2	Balance b/d	180

DISCOUNTS ALLOWED ACCOUNT

	£			£
31.7.X2 Debtors	50	31.7.X2	Balance c/d	50
1.8.X2 Balance b/d	50			

DRAWINGS ACCOUNT

	£			£
31.7.X2 Cash	150	31.7.X2	Balance c/d	150
1.8.X2 Balance b/d	150			

(b) ### TRIAL BALANCE AS AT 31 JULY 19X2

	Debit	Credit
	£	£
Cash	1,900	
Capital		20,000
Bank	16,530	
Rent	500	
Equipment	250	
Purchases	3,000	
Purchase returns		200
Sales		2,500
Sales returns	500	
Discounts received		180
Discounts allowed	50	
Drawings	150	
	22,880	22,880

SECTION 2: SUGGESTED SOLUTIONS

5.   HACKER

(a)

	CASH BOOK	
	£		£
Capital	4,000	Rent	600
Debtors - cash received	1,300	Delivery van	900
Cash sales	3,000	Creditors	1,600
		Sundry expenses	400
		Drawings	200
		Balance c/d	4,600
	8,300		8,300
Balance b/d	4,600		

	SALES	
	£		£
Trading a/c *	4,600	Cash book	3,000
		Debtors - credit sales	1,600
	4,600		4,600

	DEBTORS	
	£		£
Sales - on credit	1,600	Cash book	1,300
		Balance c/d	300
	1,600		1,600
Balance b/d	300		

	CAPITAL	
	£		£
Drawings *	200	Cash book	4,000
Balance c/d *	6,165	Profit and loss a/c *	2,365
	6,365		6,365
		Balance b/d	6,165

	RENT	
	£		£
Cash book	600	Profit and loss a/c *	150
		Prepayment c/d *	450
	600		600
Balance b/d	450		

	DELIVERY VAN	
	£		£
Cash book	900		

	CREDITORS	
	£		£
Cash book	1,600	∴ Purchases *	2,000
Balance c/d	400		
	2,000		2,000
		Balance b/d	400

269

PURCHASES

	£		£
Creditors	2,000	Trading a/c*	2,000

SUNDRY EXPENSES

	£		£
Cash book	400	Profit and loss a/c *	400

DRAWINGS

			£
Cash book	200	Capital a/c*	200

(b) ## TRIAL BALANCE

	Dr £	Cr £
Cash book	4,600	
Sales		4,600
Debtors	300	
Capital		4,000
Rent	600	
Delivery van	900	
Creditors		400
Purchases	2,000	
Sundry expenses	400	
Drawings	200	
	9,000	9,000

NB Please note that the asterisked entries will be made after the trial balance has been extracted.

(c) ## TRADING AND PROFIT AND LOSS ACCOUNT
FOR THE 3 MONTHS ENDING 31 MARCH

	£	£
Sales		4,600
Purchases	2,000	
Less closing stock	360	
Cost of sales		1,640
Gross profit		2,960
Rent	150	
Sundry expenses	400	
Depreciation on van ($\frac{3}{12}$ x 20% x £900)	45	
		595
Net profit (to capital account)		2,365

STOCK ON HAND AT END OF 3 MONTHS

	£	£
Trading a/c	360	

PROVISION FOR DEPRECIATION

	£	£
Profit and loss a/c		45

BALANCE SHEET AT 31 MARCH

	£	£
Fixed assets		
Van: cost	900	
less depreciation	45	
		855
Current assets		
Stock at cost	360	
Debtors	300	
Prepayments	450	
Cash	4,600	
	5,710	
Creditors	(400)	
		5,310
		6,165
Hacker's capital		
Original capital		4,000
Profit	2,365	
Less drawings	200	
Retained profit		2,165
		6,165

6. SPARK

(a) Check the balances on your ledger accounts with the trial balance shown below:

	Debit £	Credit £
Cash book:		
Bank (note below)	1,703	
Cash (unbanked at end of period)	12	
Nominal ledger:		
Drawings	560	
Postage and stationery	129	
Travelling expenses	40	
Motor expenses	104	
Cleaning expenses	260	
Sundry expenses	19	
Telephone	214	
Electricity	190	
Motor vans	2,000	
Rates	320	
Fixtures and fittings	806	
Capital		2,308
Purchases	3,163	
Discounts received		419
Credit sales		830
Cash sales		4,764
Discount allowed	81	
Provision for depreciation:		
Motor van		720
Fixtures and fittings		250
Stock at 1.1.X1	366	
Loan - Flex		250
Sales ledger:		
Brown	12	
Blue	180	
Stripe	48	
Purchase ledger:		
Live		602
Negative		64
Earth		-
	10,207	10,207

	£
Note on cash at bank:	
Opening balance	672
Bankings of cash (908+940+766+1031)	3,645
Capital introduced	500
Received from customers 90% x (160+66+22+10+40+120+140+130	
+20+44+38+20) = 90% of 810	729
	5,546
Less cheque payments (telephone, electricity, rates, van)	(1,469)
Payments to suppliers 85% x (143+468+570+390+80+87+103+73	
+692+187) = 85% x 2,793	(2,374)
Closing balance	1,703

272

(b) (i)   SPARK- TRADING AND PROFIT AND LOSS ACCOUNT
FOR THE FOUR MONTHS ENDED
30 APRIL 19X1

	£	£
Sales		5,594
Opening stock	366	
Purchases	3,163	
	3,529	
Closing stock	390	
		3,139
Gross profit		2,455
Discount received		419
Profit on sale of motor van		20
		2,894
Rent *(Working 1)*	500	
Rates *(Working 2)*	174	
Electricity	212	
Telephone *(Working 3)*	192	
Motor expenses	104	
Travelling	40	
Postage and stationery	129	
Cleaning	260	
Sundry expenses	19	
Depreciation *(Working 4)*		
Motor van	65	
Fixtures and fittings	27	
	92	
Discount allowed	81	
Loan interest *(Working 5)*	8	
		1,811
Net profit		1,083

Workings

1   Rent: 4/12 x £1,500 = £500; Accrual of £500 at 30 April

2   Rates: £100 + 2/6 x £220 = £174; Prepayment of £146 at 30 April

3   Telephone: £214 + £15 - £37 = £192

4   Depreciation: Motor van: 20% x £1,300 x 3/12 = £65
                 Fixtures: 10% x £806 x 4/12 = £27

5   Loan interest: 10% x £250 x 4/12 = £8

(b) (ii)   SPARK BALANCE SHEET ON 30 APRIL 19X2

	Cost £	Dep'n £	£
Fixed assets			
Motor van	1,300	65	1,235
Fixtures and fittings	806	277	529
	£2,106	£342	1,764
Current assets			
Stock at cost		390	
Debtors		240	
Payments in advance		146	
Cash at bank		1,703	
Cash in hand		12	
		2,491	
Current liabilities			
Trade creditors	666		
Accrued expenses	537		
		1,203	
			1,288
			3,052
Loan account - Flex			(258)
			2,794
Capital account			£
Balance at 1 January			1,808
Capital introduced			500
Profit for the four months			1,083
			3,391
Less drawings			597
			2,794

7. ASPLEY

Tutorial note: the comment in note 2 to the question is one which is frequently found in examination questions. It simplifies the problem by making it unnecessary to calculate depreciation on part years.

(a) (i)   MACHINES ACCOUNT

		£			£
1.11.X6	Balance b/f	22,000	1.4.X7	Disposal a/c - machine 10	1,000
1. 6.X7	Machine 17:		1.6.X7	Disposal a/c - machine 14	5,000
	Cash	10,400	31.10.X7	Balance c/d:	
	Disposals a/c	4,600		Machine 12	6,000
		15,000		Machine 16	10,000
1.8.X7	Cash-machine 18	7,000		Machine 17	15,000
				Machine 18	7,000
		44,000			44,000
1.11.X7	Balance b/d	38,000			

(ii) ACCUMULATED DEPRECIATION ON MACHINES ACCOUNT

		£				£
1.4.X7	Disposal a/c - machine 10	360	1.11.X6	Balance b/f (W)		5,040
1.6.X7	Disposal a/c - machine 14	450	31.10.X7	Profit and loss a/c:		
31.10.X7	Balance c/d (W)	9,450		12	810	
				16	1,800	
				17	1,350	
				18	1,260	
						5,220
		10,260				10,260
			1.11.X7	Balance b/d		9,450

DISPOSAL OF MACHINES ACCOUNT

		£			£
1.3.X7	Machines a/c-10	1,000	1.4.X7	Depreciation a/c-10	360
				Cash	600
1.6.X7	Machines a/c-14	5,000	1.6.X7	Depreciation a/c-14	450
30.10.X7	P & L a/c - profit on disposals	10		Machine a/c - part exchange proceeds	4,600
		6,010			6,010

(NB:				
	Profit on disposal of 14	- £(4,600 + 450 - 5,000)		50
	Less loss on disposal of 10 - £(600 + 360 - 1,000)			40
	Net profit on disposals			10

(b)
BALANCE SHEET (EXTRACT)
AS AT 31 OCTOBER 19X7

	£
Fixed assets	
Machines at cost	38,000
Less accumulated depreciation	9,450
Net book value	28,550

Working

Depreciation on machines

Machine No	10	12	14	16	17	18
Year ending 31 October	£	£	£	£	£	£
19X3	90					
19X4	90	810				
19X5	90	810	225			
19X6	90	810	225	1,800		
Accumulated at 31.10.X6	360	2,430	450	1,800		
19X7						
Disposals	(360)		(450)			
Charge for year		810		1,800	1,350	1,260
Accumulated at 31.10.X7	-	3,240	-	3,600	1,350	1,260

In each case the annual depreciation is calculated by taking original cost, less estimated residual value (10% of cost) and applying the appropriate annual depreciation rate. Thus for machine 10:

	£
Cost	1,000
Less residual value (10% x £1,000)	100
Amount to be depreciated	900

At annual rate of 10% = 90

Note that a year's depreciation is calculated on machine 14 in 19X5, even though the machine was acquired on the last day of that year.

8.   GEORGE

DEBTORS ACCOUNT

		£			£
1.10.X1	Balance b/f (2)	30,000	15.1.X2	Bad debts-Fall Ltd (3)	2,000
30.9.X2	Sales (4)	187,800	30.9.X2	Cash (5)	182,500
				Discounts allowed (6)	5,300
				Bad debts (7)	3,500
				Balance c/d	24,500
		217,800			217,800
1.10.X2	Balance b/d	24,500			

SALES ACCOUNT

		£			£
30.9.X2	Trading P & L a/c	234,600	30.9.X2	Cash (4)	46,800
				Debtors (4)	187,800
		234,600			234,600

BAD DEBTS ACCOUNT

		£			£
15.1.X2	Debtors-Fall Ltd (3)	2,000	30.9.X2	Trading P & L a/c	5,500
30.9.X2	Debtors (7)	3,500			
		5,500			5,500

PROVISION FOR DOUBTFUL DEBTS ACCOUNT

		£			£
30.9.X2	Balance c/d (8) 5% x £24,500	1,225	1.10.X1	Balance b/f (2) 5% x £30,000	1,500
	Trading P & L a/c - reduction in provision	275			
		1,500			1,500
			1.10.X2	Balance b/d	1,225

DISCOUNTS ALLOWED ACCOUNT

		£			£
30.9.X2	Debtors	5,300	30.9.X2	Trading P & L a/c	5,300

CASH ACCOUNT (EXTRACT)

		£
30.9.X2	Debtors	182,500
	Sales	46,800

TRADING PROFIT AND LOSS ACCOUNT (EXTRACT)

		£			£
30.9.X2	Bad debts	5,500	30.9.X2	Sales	234,600
	Discounts allowed	5,300		Provision for doubtful debts	275

9. STATIONERY AND TELEPHONE

STATIONERY AND TELEPHONE ACCOUNT

19X3		£	19X3		£
1 Jan	Stocks (stationery) brought forward *	241	1 Jan	Accrued stationery b/f	25
1 Jan	Prepaid telephone rent b/f	20	1 Jan	Accrued telephone calls b/f	137
20 Feb	Creditors - stationery purchase	103			
19 Mar	Cash - telephone	262	19X4		
28 Jun	Cash - telephone	281	31 Jan	Profit and loss a/c	
12 Aug	Creditors - stationery purchase	156		- Stationery	363
				- Telephone	1,137
15 Sept	Cash - telephone	305	31 Jan	Stocks - stationery a/c c/f	199
13 Nov	Creditors - stationery purchase	74	31 Jan	Prepaid telephone rent c/f	25
20 Dec	Cash - telephone	282			
19X4					
31 Jan	Stocks of stationery b/f	13			
31 Jan	Accrued telephone calls c/f	149			
		1,886			1,886

*Not trading stock and so shown in the stationery and telephone account.

SECTION 2: SUGGESTED SOLUTIONS

Workings

			£	£
(a)	P & L a/c stationery	opening stock		241
		purchases £(103+156+74)		333
				574
		closing stock		199
				375
		Accrued stationery		
		brought forward	(25)	
		carried forward	13	
				(12)
				363

(b) Telephones: accrued calls (for Dec & Jan) £86 + £63 (March bill) = £149

(c) Telephones: prepaid rent (Dec bill) One month at £75 per quarter = £25

			£	£
(d)	Telephones:	P & L account		
		Prepaid rent b/f		20
		Accrued calls c/f		149
		Payments in year £(262+281+305+282)		1,130
				1,299
		Less accrued calls b/f	137	
		Prepaid rent c/f	25	
				(162)
				1,137

10. MILLER

		Debit £	Credit £
1.	Depreciation expense (P & L account)	12,000	
	Accumulated depreciation (balance sheet)		12,000
	Being the year's charge for depreciation on plant and machinery		
2.	Drawings*	220	
	Purchases		220
	Being goods taken by proprietor for own use		
3.	Rent expense (P & L account)	400	
	Rent accrual (balance sheet)		400
	Being rent due but not paid at year end		
4.	Machinery	160	
	Carriage inwards		160
	Being correction of error. Carriage inwards now added to cost of machine		
5.	Bad and doubtful debts (P & L account)	3,500	
	Provision for doubtful debts (balance sheet)		3,500
	Being increase required in provision for doubtful debts		

*The goods were originally purchased for resale and would have been debited to the purchases account. In the event, they were withdrawn by the proprietor, just as he might withdraw cash. They should therefore not be included in purchases in the trading account, and instead are accounted for as drawings.

11. BIFFINS BISCUIT COMPANY

The question asks for journal entries, but not all of the transactions below would be journalised in practice:

	Debit £	Credit £
Rent and rates payable	5,800	
Cash		5,800
Being the payment by cheque for rent		
Rent and rates payable	4,700	
Cash		4,700
Being the payment by cheque for rates		
P & L account	10,890	
Rent and rates payable		10,890
Being the charge for rent and rates for the year *(see Working 1 below)*		
Telephone expenses	3,600	
Cash		3,600
Being the payment by cheque for telephone expenses		
P & L account	4,630	
Telephone expenses		4,630
Being the charge for telephone expenses for the year *(see Working 2)*		
Disposal of motor vehicle account	7,800	
Motor vehicles		7,800
Provision for depreciation on motor vehicles	5,900	
Disposal of motor vehicle account		5,900
Being the cost and accumulated depreciation of motor vehicle disposed of		
Motor vehicles	11,600	
Disposal of motor vehicle account		2,500
Cash		9,100
Being the purchase of a new motor vehicle, in part exchange for vehicle disposed of		
Disposal of motor vehicle account	600	
P & L account		600
Being the profit on the disposal of the vehicle *(see Working 3)*		

P & L account   13,700
Provision for depreciation on motor vehicle account   13,700
Being the charge for depreciation on motor vehicles for
the year (see Working 4)

Workings: the journalised entries might be easier to sort out by looking at the ledger accounts. Prepayments are current assets and so are debit entries brought forward. Accruals are liabilities and so are credit entries brought forward.

1.   RENT AND RATES PAYABLE
	£		£
Balance b/f (prepayments)	1,720	Balance b/f (accruals)	640
Cash (rent)	5,800	Balance c/f (prepayments)	1,470
Cash (rates)	4,700	P & L account (balancing	
Balance c/f (accruals)	780	item)	10,890
	13,000		13,000

2.   TELEPHONE EXPENSES
	£		£
Balance b/f (prepayment)	380	P & L account (balancing	
Cash	3,600	item)	4,630
Balance c/f (accrual)	650		
	4,630		4,630

3.   DISPOSAL OF MOTOR VEHICLE ACCOUNT
	£		£
Motor vehicle (disposal)	7,800	Accumulated depreciation	5,900
		Motor vehicle account	
P & L account (profit on		- (part exchange value of	
disposal)	600	old car for new car)	2,500
	8,400		8,400

4. The total depreciation charge for the year on cars can be calculated.

PROVISION FOR DEPRECIATION ON MOTOR VEHICLES
	£		£
Disposal of motor vehicle a/c	5,900	Balance b/f	31,400
Balance c/d	39,200	P & L account (balancing	
		item)-depreciation for	
		the year	13,700
	45,100		45,100
		Balance b/d	39,200

12. STAN DOFFISH

		Debit £	Credit £
(a)	P & L account: wages	834.60	
	P & L account : salaries	993.70	
	Creditors for wages and salaries		1,828.30
	Being accrued wages unpaid at the year end		
(b)	Bank	528.30	
	Creditors for unclaimed wages		528.30
	Being wages paid back into the business bank account from unclaimed wage packets		
(c)	P & L account	290.00	
	Provision for doubtful debts		290.00
	Being an increase in the provision for doubtful debts		
(d)	Provision for discounts allowed to debtors	170.00	
	P & L account		170.00
	Being a reduction in the provision for discounts allowed		
(e)	Bad debts	769.10	
	Debtors		769.10
	Being bad debts written off (see also (f) (ii) below)		
(f) (i)	Debtors	210.50	
	Bad debts		210.50
	Being the recovery of a debt previously written off as bad		
(ii)	P & L account	558.60	
	Bad debts		558.60
	Being the net amount of bad debts to be written off		
(g)	Discounts allowed	21.00	
	Debtors		21.00
	Being the correction of a discount allowed to a customer		
(h)	Creditors (Cool Cats Garments)	156.60	
	Debtors (Cool Cats Garments)		156.60
	Being settlement in contra		

(i) (*Note:* accruals and prepayments are accounted for by means of the double entry between the balance carried forward at the end of the period and the corresponding balance brought forward at the start of the next period. These entries are not journalised. However, it might be advisable to present the transactions in the solution to the question as follows.)

(i)	Rent (prepaid rent)	840.30	
	P & L account		840.30
(ii)	P & L account	415.00	
	Heating expenses (accrued heating)		415.00

Being adjustments for prepaid rent and accrued heating expenses

(j) (i)	Repairs and redecorations	2,800.00	
	Buildings account		2,800.00

Being the correction of an error whereby revenue expenditure was accounted for as capital expenditure

(ii)	P & L account	2,800.00	
	Repairs and redecorations		2,800.00

Being the charge in the P & L account for repairs and redecorations

(iii)	Provision for depreciation	35.00	
	P & L account (depreciation)		35.00

Being the correction of an over statement of depreciation in the P & L account (note, equal to 1½% of £2,800)

13. SST LIMITED

Date		Debit £	Credit £
27 January	Debtors (RBB Limited)	10,000	
	Sales		10,000
	Being the sale of goods on credit		
2 February	Purchases	5,000	
	Creditors (ACD Limited)		5,000
	Being the purchase of goods on credit		
5 February	Bills receivable	10,000	
	Debtors (RBB Limited)		10,000
	Being the acceptance of a bill of exchange drawn on RBB Limited		
16 February	Creditors (ACD Limited)	5,000	
	Bills payable		5,000
	Being the acceptance of a bill of exchange drawn by ACD Limited		
5 March	Cash	9,750	
	Bank charges	250	
	Bills receivable		10,000
	Being the cash received and discount costs incurred on discounting the bill of RBB Limited		

10 May	Debtors (RBB Limited)	10,000	
	Cash		10,000
	Being RBB's bill dishonoured		
16 May	Bills payable	5,000	
	Cash		5,000
	Being the payment of bill due		
9 December	Cash	3,000	
	Bad debts	7,000	
	Debtors (RBB Limited)		10,000
	Being the payment to creditors of RBB Limited		
	of 30 pence in £1, final dividend		

(*Note:* the transaction of 16 March is irrelevant to SST Limited. SST Limited will pay the £5,000 it owes on 16 May. The fact that ACD Limited discounts the bill for cash before then has no affect on the debt of SST Limited and is a transaction of ACD, not SST.)

14. ALEX AUTOS

PROVISION FOR DOUBTFUL DEBTS

	£		£
Balance c/d (10% x £60,000)	6,000	Balance b/f	6,300
Profit and loss account -			
provision no longer required	300		
	6,300		6,300
		Balance b/d	6,000

TRADE CREDITORS CONTROL ACCOUNT

	£		£
Cash	274,000	Balance b/f	43,000
Discounts received	15,000	Purchases	310,000
Purchase returns	10,000		
Trade debtors control	4,000		
Balance c/d	50,000		
	353,000		353,000
		Balance b/d	50,000

TRADE DEBTORS CONTROL ACCOUNT

	£		£
Balance b/f	63,000	Cash	663,000
Sales	690,000	Discounts allowed	14,000
Cash - cheque returned	3,000	Sales returns	8,000
		Bad debts	7,000
		Trade creditors control	4,000
		Balance c/d	60,000
	756,000		756,000
Balance b/d	60,000		

15. APRIL SHOWERS

Tutorial note: note that the question specifically requires the correction of the control account *before* the correction of the list of balances. You should of course follow the examiner's requirements, even though the opposite order was recommended in this chapter.

(a)

SALES LEDGER CONTROL ACCOUNT

	£		£
Uncorrected balance b/f	12,550	Discounts omitted (4)	100
Sales omitted (1)	850	Contra entry omitted (6)	400
Bank - cheque dishonoured		Bad debt omitted (7)	500
(12)	300	Returns inwards omitted (10)	200
		Amended balance c/d	12,500
	13,700		13,700
Balance b/d	12,500		

Note- items 2,3,5,8,9 and 11 are matters affecting the personal accounts of customers. They have no effect on the control account.

(b) STATEMENT OF ADJUSTMENTS TO LIST OF PERSONAL ACCOUNT BALANCES

	£	£
Original total of list of balances		12,802
Add: debit balance omitted (2)	300	
debit balance understated (5)	200	
		500
		13,302
Less: transposition error (3)-understatement of		
cash received	180	
cash debited instead of credited (2 x £250) (8)	500	
discounts received wrongly debited to Bell (9)	50	
understatement of cash received (11)	72	
		(802)
		12,500

16. FRONTLOADER

Tutorial note: one problem you must deal with in answering this question is identifying which items in the ledgers are relevant to the debtors ledger control account. Irrelevant items are creditors and purchases of washing machines (purchase ledger), discounts received, cash paid to creditors, carriage outwards (it is assumed that Frontloader Limited must bear these costs itself, and does not charge them to customers) and overdraft interest. The provision for doubtful debts, also, does not appear in the debtors ledger control account, although it is relevant to a solution to part (b) of the question.

Solution

Workings

	£
Sales	723,869
Less discounts allowed	8,214
	715,655
Less returns inwards	36,925
Net sales	678,730
Opening debtors	84,611
Opening debtors plus net sales	763,341
Cash received from debtors (excluding J Smith)	699,267
Closing debtors before adjustments for the subsequent entries	64,074
Subsequent entries:	
Bad debts written off	6,854
	57,220
A Brown's cheque dishonoured. A Brown becomes a debtor again	1,246
Closing debtors	58,466

A small problem arises in deciding how to record the payment of £1,000 by J Smith. J Smith's debt was written off in 19X2, and some money is finally received in 19X5. The revenue will be recorded in the debtors ledger by:

(a) adding £1,000 to debtors;
(b) recording the cash paid of £1,000.

These items are shown in the debtors ledger control account below.

(a)   DEBTORS LEDGER CONTROL ACCOUNT

	£		£
Opening balance	84,611	Cash received (debit bank a/c)	699,267
Sales on credit (credit sales a/c)	723,869	Discounts allowed	8,214
A Brown's dishonoured cheque (credit bank a/c)	1,246	Returns inwards (debit sales a/c)	36,925
J Smith: bad debt written back (credit bad debts a/c)	1,000	Bad debts written off (debit bad debts a/c)	6,854
		Cash received from J Smith (debit bank a/c)	1,000
		Closing balance c/d	58,466
	810,726		810,726
Opening balance b/d	58,466		

(b) The provision for doubtful debts as at 30 June 19X5 should be 8% of £58,466 = £4,677. The reduction in the provision for doubtful debts in the year is £(4,813 - 4,677) = £136.

BAD AND DOUBTFUL DEBTS

	£		£
Debtors a/c: bad debts		Provision for doubtful debts	
written off	6,854	b/d	4,813
Provision for doubtful debts :		Debtors a/c: bad debt of J	
closing balance c/d	4,677	Smith written back	1,000
		P & L account (balance)	5,718
	11,531		11,531
		Balance b/d	4,677

The amount written off to the P & L account consists of the net amount of bad debts written off (£5,854) less the reduction in the provision for doubtful debts (£136). These separate amounts could be itemised separately in the account.

(c)

	£
Debtors	58,466
Less provision for doubtful debt	4,677
	53,789

17. PAYROLL LIMITED

CREDITORS

	£		£
Cash	5,400	Balance b/f	800
Discounts received	100	Purchases	6,000
Debtors - contra	700		
Balance c/d	600		
	6,800		6,800
		Balance b/d	600

DEBTORS

	£		£
Balance b/d (bal. fig)	2,000	Creditors - contra	700
Sales	12,000	Cash	11,800
		Discounts allowed	300
		Bad debts	200
		Balance c/d	1,000
	14,000		14,000
Balance b/d	1,000		

PROVISION FOR DOUBTFUL DEBTS

	£		£
Debtors	200	Balance b/f	450
Balance c/d	400	Cash - bad debt recovered	50
		P&L a/c - increase in provision	100
	600		600
		Balance b/d	400

WAGES CONTROL

	£		£
Bank	1,330	Balance b/f	38
PAYE control	407	Wages expense a/c – gross wages	2,000
NIC control	260		
Balance c/d	41		
	2,038		2,038
		Balance b/d	41

PAYE CONTROL

	£		£
Cash	400	Balance b/f	35
Balance c/d	42	Wages control	407
	442		442
		Balance b/d	42

NIC CONTROL

	£		£
Cash	546	Balance b/f	44
Balance c/d	48	Wages control – employees	260
		Wages expense a/c – employer	290
	594		594
		Balance b/d	48

18. CAMFORD

The first step is to correct the errors in the cash book.

CASH BOOK

	£		£
Uncorrected balance b/f	1,900	Transfer to Midlands Savings	
Transposition error (1)	90	Bank – previously omitted (3)	1,500
Cash lodgement understated (2)	10	Error in bringing down	
Sundry receipt omitted (4)	10	balance at 1.6.X1 (6)	100
Subscription credited directly		Bank charges (7)	20
(11)	100	Standing order (9)	30
		Subscriptions – cheque returned	
		(10)	50
		Corrected balance c/d	410
	2,110		2,110
Corrected balance b/d	410		

BANK RECONCILIATION STATEMENT AS AT 31 MAY 19X2

	£	£	
Balance shown by bank statement		470	o/d
Unpresented cheques (5)		40	
		510	o/d
Outstanding lodgements (8)	900		
Error on bank statement (12)	20		
		920	
Balance shown in cash account		410	

19. RECTIFY

(a)

CASH BOOK

	£		£
Balance b/f	322	Bank charges	143
		Cheque drawn entered as £89	9
		Cheque drawn entered as receipt (2 x £230)	460
Error in opening balance	45	Cheque returned written back	180
Dividend received	1,147	Loan interest	1,100
Undercast	200	HP repayments	660
Balance c/f	838		
	2,552		2,552

(b)

BANK RECONCILIATION STATEMENT

	£	
Balance per bank statement (31.5.X5)	870	o/d
Cheque debited in error by bank	82	
Corrected balance per bank statement	788	o/d
Cheques not yet presented	630	
	1,418	o/d
Receipts not yet credited	580	
Balance per cash book (31.5.X5)	838	o/d

Note: item (g) in the question is irrelevant.

20. CHI KNITWEAR LIMITED

(a)

SUSPENSE ACCOUNT

	£		£
Opening balance	1,536	Debtors - balance omitted	87
Sales - under-recorded	360	Cash book - receipts undercast	720
		Creditors: credit note posted to wrong side	358
		Cash book: Mr Smith's debt paid but cash receipt not recorded	731
	1,896		1,896

Notes

1   Error number 2 is an error of principle, whereby a fixed asset item (capital expenditure) has been accounted for as revenue expenditure. The correction will be logged in the journal, but since the error did not result in an inequality between debits and credits, the suspense account would not have been used.

2   The electricity bill has been omitted from the accounts entirely. The error of omission means that both debits and credits will be logged in the journal, but the suspense account will not be involved, since there is equality between debits and credits in the error.

SECTION 2: SUGGESTED SOLUTIONS

(b) 1   The error means that debtors are understated. The correction of the error will increase the total amount for debtors to be shown in the balance sheet.

     2   The correction of this error will add £1,200 to fixed assets at cost (balance sheet item) and reduce repair costs by £1,200. The P & L account will therefore show an increased profit of £1,200, less any depreciation now charged on the fixed asset.

     3   The undercasting (ie under-adding) of £720 on the receipts side of the cash book means that debits of cash will be £720 less than they should have been. The correction of the error will add £720 to the cash balance in the balance sheet.

     4   This transposition error means that total sales would be under-recorded by £8,514 – £8,154 = £360 in the sales account. The correction of the error will add £360 to total sales, and thus add £360 to the profits in the P & L account.

     5   The credit note must have been issued for a purchase return to the supplier by the business. It should have been debited to the creditor's account, but instead has been credited. Assuming that the purchase returns account was credited correctly, the effect of the error has been to overstate total creditors by 2 x £179 = £358, and this amount should be credited from the suspense account and debited to the creditors account. The effect will be to reduce the total for creditors in the balance sheet by £358.

     6   The electricity bill, when entered in the accounts, will increase creditors by £152, and reduce profits (by adding to electricity expenses) by £152, assuming that none of this cost is a prepayment of electricity charges.

     7   Since the cheque has not yet been recorded in the cash book, the correction of the error will add £731 to the cash balance in the balance sheet. At the same time, the provision for doubtful debts can be reduced, which will increase the net amount for debtors in the balance sheet by £731 (ie debtors less provision for doubtful debts, although the reduction in gross debtors by £731 has already been accounted for, due to the cash received) and increase profits by £731.

21. AFTER THE STOCK COUNT

			Adjustment	
			Add to stock value	Subtract from stock value
Item	Explanation		£	£
(a)	The sub-total error has over-valued stocks by £(6,725 - 6,275)			450
(b)	This arithmetical error has over-valued the stock item by £(6 - 0.6) per unit for 260 units			1,404
(c)	Free samples received are not trading items and should be excluded from the valuation			
(d)	Goods in stock should be included in the valuation regardless of whether or not they have been paid for yet.			
(e)	Cost £2,885. Net realisable value £(3,600 - 921) = £2,679. The stock should be valued at the lower of cost and NRV. Since NRV is lower, the original valuation of stocks (at cost) will be reduced by £(2,885 - 2,679)			206
(f)	Stocks issued on sale or return and not yet accepted by the customer should be included in the stock valuation and valued at the lower of cost and NRV, here at £5 each (cost)		1,500	
(g)	The cost (£7.30) is below the current and fore-seeable selling price (£10 or more) which is assumed to be the NRV of the item. Since, the current valuation is at the lower of cost and NRV no change in valuation is necessary			
			1,500	2,060

	£	£
Original valuation of stocks, at cost		153,699
Adjustments and corrections:		
to increase valuation	1,500	
to decrease valuation	(2,060)	
		(560)
Valuation of stocks for the annual accounts		153,139

SECTION 2: SUGGESTED SOLUTIONS

22. BIG AND SMALL

(a) *FIFO method*

	RECEIPTS			ISSUES			BALANCE	
Date	Quantity (kg)	Price £	Value £	Quantity (kg)	Price £	Value £	Quantity (kg)	Value £
19X4								
1.10							200	200
1.10				100	1.00	100	100	100
5.10	700	3.00	2,100				800	2,200
8.10				300	100 @ 1.00	100		
					200 @ 3.00	600	500	1,500
12.10	400	5.00	2,000				900	3,500
15.10				200	3.00	600	700	2,900
19.10	800	2.00	1,600				1,500	4,500
22.10				600	300 @ 3.00	900		
					300 @ 5.00	1,500	900	2,100
26.10	1,100	4.00	4,400				2,000	6,500
29.10				1,500	100 @ 5.00	500		
					800 @ 2.00	1,600		
					600 @ 4.00	2,400	500	2,000
Total charge to production						£8,300		

(b) *LIFO method*

	RECEIPTS			ISSUES			BALANCE	
1.10							200	200
1.10				100	1.00	100	100	100
5.10	700	3.00	2,100				800	2,200
8.10				300	3.00	900	500	1,300
12.10	400	5.00	2,000				900	3,300
15.10				200	5.00	1,000	700	2,300
19.10	800	2.00	1,600				1,500	3,900
22.10				600	2.00	1,200	900	2,700
26.10	1,100	4.00	4,400				2,000	7,100
29.10				1,500	1,100 @ 4.00	4,400		
					200 @ 2.00	400		
					200 @ 5.00	1,000	500	1,300

Closing stock value = <u>£1,300</u>

(c) *Continuous weighted average method*

Date	RECEIPTS Quantity (kg)	Price £	Value £	ISSUES Quantity (kg)	Price £	Value £	BALANCE Quantity (kg)	Value £
19X4								
1.10							200	200
1.10				100	1.00	100	100	100
5.10	700	3.00	2,100				800	2,200
8.10				300	2.75	825	500	1,375
12.10	400	5.00	2,000				900	3,375
15.10				200	3.75	750	700	2,625
19.10	800	2.00	1,600				1,500	4,225
22.10				600	2.82	1,692	900	2,533
26.10	1,100	4.00	4,400				2,000	6,933
29.10				1,500	3.47	5,205	500	1,728

Issue price per kilogram on 29 October = £3.47

(d) *Periodic weighted average method*

$$\frac{\text{Total cost of purchases in October}}{\text{Quantity purchased in October}} = \frac{£10,100}{3,000}$$

$$= £3.37$$

∴ Issue price per kilogram during October = £3.37

23. VAT

(a)

DEBTORS' CONTROL ACCOUNT

	£		£
Balance b/f	2,415	Discounts allowed	1,035
Zero-rated sales	4,000	Cash received	27,600
Standard-rated sales	24,150	Balance c/d	1,930
	£30,565		£30,565
Balance b/d	1,930		

(b)

CREDITORS' CONTROL ACCOUNT

	£		£
Discounts received	575	Balance b/f	1,955
Cash paid	17,480	Purchases	18,400
Balance c/d	2,300		
	£20,355		£20,355
		Balance b/d	2,300

(c)

VAT CONTROL ACCOUNT

	£		£
Discounts allowed		Balance b/f	760
(15/115 x £1,035)	135	Standard-rated sales	
Purchased (15/115 x £18,400)	2,400	(15/115 x £24,150)	3,150
Cash paid	1,040	Discount received	
Balance c/d	410	(15/115 x £575)	75
	£3,985		£3,985
		Balance b/d	410

SECTION 3

FINAL ACCOUNTS

Chapter 19

INCOMPLETE RECORDS

The purpose of this chapter is:

● to explain the ways in which final accounts can be prepared from incomplete accounting records

● to illustrate an approach to dealing with incomplete records problems in the examination

---

Introduction

1. Incomplete records problems occur when a business does not have a full set of accounting records, either because:

   (a) the proprietor of the business does not keep a full set of accounts; or
   (b) some of the business accounts are accidentally lost or destroyed.

2. The problem for the accountant is to prepare a set of year-end accounts for the business; ie a trading, profit and loss account, and a balance sheet. Since the business does not have a full set of accounts, preparing the final accounts is not a simple matter of closing off accounts and transferring balances to the trading P&L account, or showing outstanding balances in the balance sheet. The task of preparing the final accounts involves:

   (a) establishing the cost of purchases and other expenses;
   (b) establishing the total amount of sales;
   (c) establishing the amount of creditors, accruals, debtors and prepayments at the end of the year.

3. Examination questions often take incomplete records problems a stage further, by introducing an 'incident' - such as fire or burglary- which leaves the owner of the business uncertain about how much stock has been destroyed or stolen.

4. The great merit of incomplete records problems is that they focus attention on the relationship between cash received and paid, sales and debtors, purchases and creditors, and stocks, as well as calling for the preparation of final accounts from basic principles.

5. To understand what incomplete records are about, it will obviously be useful now to look at what exactly might be incomplete. The items we shall consider in turn are:

(a) the opening balance sheet;

(b) credit sales and debtors;

(c) purchases and trade creditors;

(d) purchases, stocks and the cost of sales;

(e) stolen goods or goods destroyed;

(f) the cash book;

(g) accruals and prepayments;

(h) drawings.

The opening balance sheet

6. In practice there should not be any missing item in the opening balance sheet of the business, because it should be available from the preparation of the previous year's final accounts. However, an examination problem might provide information about the assets and liabilities of the business at the beginning of the period under review, but then leave the balancing figure - ie the proprietor's business capital - unspecified.

Example

7. Suppose a business has the following assets and liabilities as at 1 January 19X3:

	£
Fixtures and fittings at cost	7,000
Provision for depreciation, fixtures and fittings	4,000
Motor vehicles at cost	12,000
Provision for depreciation, motor vehicles	6,800
Stock in trade	4,500
Trade debtors	5,200
Cash at bank and in hand	1,230
Trade creditors	3,700
Prepayment	450
Accrued rent	2,000

You are required to prepare a balance sheet for the business, inserting a balancing figure for proprietor's capital.

Solution

8. Balance sheet as at 1 January 19X3

	£	£	£
Fixed assets			
Fixtures and fittings at cost		7,000	
Less accumulated depreciation		4,000	
			3,000
Motor vehicles at cost		12,000	
Less accumulated depreciation		6,800	
			5,200
			8,200
Current assets			
Stock in trade		4,500	
Trade debtors		5,200	
Prepayment		450	
Cash		1,230	
		11,380	
Current liabilities			
Trade creditors	3,700		
Accrual	2,000		
		5,700	
Net current assets			5,680
			13,880
Proprietor's capital as at 1 January 19X3 (balancing figure)			13,880

Credit sales and debtors

9. If a business does not keep a record of its sales on credit, the value of these sales can be derived from the opening balance of trade debtors, the closing balance of trade debtors, and the payments received from trade debtors during the period.

	£
Credit sales are:	
Payments received from trade debtors	X
Plus closing balance of trade debtors (since these represent sales in the current period for which cash payment has not yet been received)	X
Less opening balance of trade debtors (unless these become bad debts, they will pay what they owe in the current period for sales in a previous period)	(X)
	X

10. For example, suppose that a business had trade debtors of £1,750 on 1 April 19X4 and trade debtors of £3,140 on 31 March 19X5. If payments received from trade debtors during the year to 31 March 19X5 were £28,490, and if there are no bad debts, then credit sales for the period would be:

	£
Cash received from debtors	28,490
Plus closing debtors	3,140
Less opening debtors	(1,750)
Credit sales	29,880

If there are bad debts during the period, the value of sales will be increased by the amount of bad debts written off, no matter whether they relate to opening debtors or credit sales during the current period.

11. The same calculation could be made in a T account, with credit sales being the balancing figure to complete the account.

DEBTORS

	£		£
Opening balance b/f	1,750	Cash received	28,490
Credit sales (balancing fig)	29,880	Closing balance c/f	3,140
	31,630		31,630

12. The same interrelationship between credit sales, cash from debtors, and opening and closing debtors balances can be used to derive a missing figure for cash from debtors, or opening or closing debtors, given the values for the three other items. For example, if we know that opening debtors are £6,700, closing debtors are £3,200 and credit sales for the period are £69,400, then cash received from debtors during the period would be:

DEBTORS

	£		£
Opening balance	6,700	Cash received (balancing	
Sales (on credit)	69,400	figure)	72,900
		Closing balance c/f	3,200
	76,100		76,100

An alternative way of presenting the same calculation would be:

	£
Opening balance of debtors	6,700
Credit sales during the period	69,400
Total money owed to the business	76,100
Less closing balance of debtors	3,200
Equals cash received during the period	72,900

Purchases and trade creditors

13. A similar relationship exists between purchases of stock during a period, the opening and closing balances for trade creditors, and amounts paid to trade creditors during the period.

If we wish to calculate an unknown amount for purchases, the amount would be derived as follows:

	£
Payments to trade creditors during the period	X
Plus closing balance of trade creditors	X
(since these represent purchases in the current period for which payment has not yet been made)	
Less opening balance of trade creditors	(X)
(these debts, paid in the current period, relate to purchases in a previous period)	
Purchases during the period	X

14. For example, suppose that a business had trade creditors of £3,728 on 1 October 19X5 and trade creditors of £2,645 on 30 September 19X6. If payments to trade creditors during the year to 30 September 19X6 were £31,479, then purchases during the year would be:

	£
Payments to trade creditors	31,479
Plus closing balance of trade creditors	2,645
Less opening balance of trade creditors	(3,728)
Purchases	30,396

15. The same calculation could be made in a T account, with purchases being the balancing figure to complete the account.

CREDITORS

	£		£
Cash payments	31,479	Opening balance b/f	3,728
Closing balance c/f	2,645	Purchases (balancing figure)	30,396
	34,124		34,124

Purchases, stocks and the cost of sales

16. When the value of purchases is not known, a different approach might be required to find out what they were, depending on the nature of the information given to you.

17. One approach would be to use information about the cost of sales, and opening and closing stocks, in other words, to use the trading account rather than the trade creditors account to find the cost of purchases.

		£
Since	opening stocks	X
	plus purchases	X
	less closing stocks	(X)
	equals the cost of goods sold	X
then	the cost of goods sold	X
	plus closing stocks	X
	less opening stocks	(X)
	equals purchases	X

18. Suppose that the stock in trade of a business on 1 July 19X6 has a balance sheet value of £8,400, and a stock taking exercise at 30 June 19X7 showed stock to be valued at £9,350. Sales for the year to 30 June 19X7 are £80,000, and the business makes a gross profit of $33\frac{1}{3}$% on cost for all the items that it sells. What were the purchases during the year?

19. The cost of goods sold can be derived from the value of sales, as follows:

		£
Sales	$(133\frac{1}{3}$%)	80,000
Gross profit	$(33\frac{1}{3}$%)	20,000
Cost of goods sold	(100%)	60,000

The cost of goods sold is 75% of sales value.

	£
Cost of goods sold	60,000
Plus closing stock	9,350
Less opening stocks	(8,400)
Purchases	60,950

Stolen goods or goods destroyed

20. A similar type of calculation might be required to derive the value of goods stolen or destroyed. When an unknown quantity of goods is lost, whether they are stolen, destroyed in a fire, or lost in any other way such that the quantity lost cannot be counted, then the cost of the goods lost is the difference between

    (a) the cost of goods sold; and

    (b) opening stock of the goods (at cost) plus purchases less closing stock of the goods (at cost).

In theory (a) and (b) should be the same. However, if (b) is a larger amount than (a), it follows that the difference must be the cost of the goods purchased and neither sold nor remaining in stock - ie the cost of the goods lost.

First example: cost of goods destroyed

21. Orlean Flames is a shop which sells fashion clothes. On 1 January 19X5, it had stock in trade which cost £7,345. During the 9 months to 30 September 19X5, the business purchased goods from suppliers costing £106,420. Sales during the same period were £154,000. The shop makes a gross profit of 40% on cost for everything it sells. On 30 September 19X5, there was a fire in the shop which destroyed most of the stock in it. Only a small amount of stock, known to have cost £350, was undamaged and still fit for sale.

How much stock was lost in the fire?

Solution

		£
22. (a)	Sales (140%)	154,000
	Gross profit (40%)	44,000
	Cost of goods sold (100%)	110,000

		£
(b)	Opening stock, at cost	7,345
	Plus purchases	106,420
		113,765
	Less closing stock, at cost	350
	Equals cost of goods sold and goods lost	113,415

		£
(c)	Cost of goods sold and lost	113,415
	Cost of goods sold	110,000
	Cost of goods lost	3,415

Second example: cost of goods stolen

23. Beau Gullard runs a jewellery shop in the High Street. On 1 January 19X9, his stock in trade, at cost, amounted to £4,700 and his trade creditors were £3,950.

During the six months to 30 June 19X9, sales were £42,000. Beau Gullard makes a gross profit of $33\frac{1}{3}$% on the sales value of everything he sells.

On 30 June, there was a burglary at the shop, and all the stock was stolen.

In trying to establish how much stock had been taken, Beau Gullard was only able to say that

(a) he knew from his bank statements that he had paid £28,400 to creditors in the 6 month period to 30 June 19X9;

(b) he currently owed creditors £5,550.

Required:

(a) how much stock was stolen?
(b) a trading account for the 6 months to 30 June 19X9.

Solution

24. (a) The first 'unknown' is the amount of purchases during the period. This is established by the method previously described in this chapter.

CREDITORS

	£		£
Payments to creditors	28,400	Opening balance b/f	3,950
Closing balance c/f	5,550	Purchases (balancing figure)	30,000
	33,950		33,950

(b) The cost of goods sold is also unknown, but this can be established from the gross profit margin and the sales for the period.

		£
Sales	(100%)	42,000
Gross profit	($33\frac{1}{3}$%)	14,000
Cost of goods sold	($66\frac{2}{3}$%)	28,000

(c) The cost of the goods stolen is:

	£
Opening stock at cost	4,700
Purchases	30,000
	34,700
Less closing stock (after burglary)	0
Cost of goods sold and goods stolen	34,700
Cost of goods sold (see (b) above)	28,000
Cost of goods stolen	6,700

(d) The cost of the goods stolen will not be a charge in the trading account, and so the trading account for the period is as follows:

BEAU GULLARD
TRADING ACCOUNT FOR THE SIX MONTHS TO 30 JUNE 19X9

	£	£
Sales		42,000
Less cost of goods sold:		
Opening stock	4,700	
Purchases	30,000	
	34,700	
Less stock stolen	6,700	
		28,000
Gross profit		14,000

Accounting for stock destroyed, stolen or otherwise lost

25. When stock is stolen, destroyed or otherwise lost, the loss must be accounted for somehow. The procedure was described briefly in the earlier chapter on accounting for stocks. Since the loss is an extraordinary one, the cost of the goods lost is not included in the trading account, as the previous example showed. The accounting double entry is therefore

Debit   See below
Credit   Trading account (although instead of showing the cost of the loss as a credit, it is usually shown as a deduction on the debit side of the trading account, which is the same as a 'plus' on the credit side).

26. The account that is to be debited is one of two possibilities, depending on whether or not the lost goods were insured against the loss.

(a) If the lost goods were not insured, the business must bear the loss, and the loss is shown in the P & L account: ie

Debit Profit and loss
Credit Trading account

(b) If the lost goods were insured, the business will not suffer a loss, because the insurance will pay back the cost of the lost goods. This means that there is no charge at all in the P&L account, and the appropriate double entry is:

Debit Insurance claim account (debtor account)
Credit Trading account

with the cost of the loss. The insurance claim will then be a current asset, and shown in the balance sheet of the business as such. When the claim is paid, the account is then closed by

Debit Cash
Credit Insurance claim account

The cash book

27. The construction of a cash book, largely from bank statements showing receipts and payments of a business during a given period, is often an important feature of incomplete records problems. In an examination, the purpose of an incomplete records question is largely to test the understanding of candidates about how various items of receipts or payments relate to the preparation of a final set of accounts for a business.

28. We have already seen in this chapter that information about cash receipts or payments might be needed to establish:

    (a)   the amount of purchases during a period; or

    (b)   the amount of credit sales during a period.

    Other items of receipts or payments might be relevant to establishing:

    (a)   the amount of cash sales; or

    (b)   the amount of certain expenses in the P & L account; or

    (c)   the amount of drawings by the business proprietor.

29. It might therefore be helpful, if a business does not keep a cash book day-to-day, to construct a cash book at the end of an accounting period. A business which typically might not keep a day-to-day cash book is a shop, where:

    (a)   many sales, if not all sales, are cash sales (ie with payment by notes and coins, cheques, or credit cards at the time of sale);

    (b)   some payments are made in notes and coins out of the till rather than by payment out of the business bank account by cheque.

30. Where there appears to be a sizeable volume of receipts and payments in cash (ie notes and coins), then it is also helpful to construct a two column cash book. This is a cash book with one column for receipts and payments, and one column for money paid into and out of the business bank account.

    An example will illustrate the technique and the purpose of a two column cash book.

Example

31. Jonathan Slugg owns and runs a shop selling fishing tackle, making a gross profit of 25% on the cost of everything he sells. He does not keep a cash book.

On 1 January 19X7 the balance sheet of his business was:

	£	£
Net fixed assets		20,000
Stock	10,000	
Cash in the bank	3,000	
Cash in the till	200	
	13,200	
Trade creditors	1,200	
		12,000
		32,000
Proprietor's capital		32,000

In the year to 31 December 19X7:

(a)   there were no sales on credit;
(b)   £41,750 in receipts were banked;
(c)   the bank statements of the period show the payments

(i)	to trade creditors	£36,000
(ii)	sundry expenses	£5,600
(iii)	in drawings	£4,400

(d)   payments were also made in cash out of the till:

(i)	to trade creditors	£800
(ii)	sundry expenses	£1,500
(iii)	in drawings	£3,700

At 31 December 19X7, the business had cash in the till of £450 and trade creditors of £1,400. The cash balance in the bank was not known and the value of closing stock has not yet been calculated. There were no accruals or prepayments. No further fixed assets were purchased during the year. The depreciation charge for the year is £900.

Required:

(a)   a two column cash book for the period;
(b)   the trading, profit and loss account for the year to 31 December 19X7 and the balance sheet as at 31 December 19X7.

Discussion and solution

32. A two column cash book is completed as follows:

(a)   enter the opening cash balances;
(b)   enter the information given about cash payments (and any cash receipts, if there had been any such items given in the problem);
(c)   the cash receipts banked are a 'contra' entry, being both a debit (bank column) and a credit (cash in hand column) in the same account;

(d) enter the closing cash in hand (cash in the bank at the end of the period is not known).

CASH BOOK

	Cash in hand £	Bank £		Cash in hand £	Bank £
Balance b/f	200	3,000	Trade creditors	800	36,000
Cash receipts banked			Sundry expenses	1,500	5,600
(contra)		41,750	Drawings	3,700	4,400
Sales*	48,000				
Balance c/f		*1,250	Cash receipts banked		
			(contra)	41,750	
			Balance c/f	450	
	48,200	46,000		48,200	46,000

* Balancing figure

(e) The closing balance of money in the bank is a balancing figure.
(f) Since all sales are for cash, a balancing figure that can be entered in the cash book is sales, in the cash in hand (debit) column.

33. It is important to notice that since not all receipts from cash sales are banked, the value of cash sales during the period is:

	£
Receipts banked	41,750
Plus expenses and drawings paid out of the till in cash	6,000
£(800 + 1,500 + 3,700)	
Plus any cash stolen (here there is none)	0
Plus the closing balance of cash in hand	450
	48,200
Less the opening balance of cash in hand	(200)
Equals cash sales	48,000

34. The cash book constructed in this way has enabled us to establish both the closing balance for cash in the bank and also the volume of cash sales. The trading, profit and loss account and the balance sheet can also be prepared, once a value for purchases has been calculated.

CREDITORS

	£		£
Cash book:		Balance b/f	1,200
Payments from bank	36,000	Purchases (balancing figure)	37,000
Cash book:			
Payments in cash	800		
Balance c/f	1,400		
	38,200		38,200

The gross profit margin of 25% on cost indicates that the cost of the goods sold is £38,400, ie:

	£
Sales (125%)	48,000
Gross profit (25%)	9,600
Cost of goods sold (100%)	38,400

The closing stock amount is now a balancing figure in the trading account.

JONATHAN SLUGG -TRADING, PROFIT AND LOSS ACCOUNT
FOR THE YEAR ENDED 31 DECEMBER 19X7

	£	£
Sales		48,000
Less cost of goods sold:		
Opening stock	10,000	
Purchases	37,000	
	47,000	
Less closing stock (balancing figure)	8,600	
		38,400
Gross profit (25/125 x £48,000)		9,600
Expenses		
Sundry £(1,500 + 5,600)	7,100	
Depreciation	900	
		8,000
Net profit		1,600

JONATHAN SLUGG
BALANCE SHEET AS AT 31 DECEMBER 19X7

	£	£	£
Net fixed assets £(20,000 - 900)			19,100
Stock		8,600	
Cash in the till		450	
		9,050	
Bank overdraft	1,250		
Trade creditors	1,400		
		2,650	
Net current assets			6,400
			25,500
Proprietor's capital:			
Balance b/f			32,000
Net profit for the year			1,600
			33,600
Drawings £(3,700 + 4,400)			(8,100)
Balance c/f			25,500

Theft of cash from the till

35. When cash is stolen from the till, the amount stolen will be a credit entry in the cash book, and a debit in either the P&L account or insurance claim account, depending on whether the business is insured. The missing figure for cash sales, if this has to be calculated, must not ignore cash received but later stolen - see paragraph 33.

Accruals and prepayments

36. Where there is an accrued expense or a prepayment, the charge to be made in the P&L account for the item concerned should be found from the opening balance b/f, the closing balance c/f, and cash payments for the item during the period. The charge in the P&L account is perhaps most easily found as the balancing figure in a T account.

37. For example, suppose that on 1 April 19X6 a business had prepaid rent of £700 which relates to the next accounting period. During the year to 31 March 19X7 it pays £9,300 in rent, and at 31 March 19X7 the prepayment of rent is £1,000. The cost of rent in the P&L account for the year to 31 March 19X7 would be the balancing figure in the following T account. (Remember that a prepayment is a current asset, and so is a debit balance b/f.)

RENT

	£		£
Prepayment: balance b/f	700	P & L account (balancing figure)	9,000
Cash	9,300	Prepayment: balance c/f	1,000
	10,000		10,000
Balance b/f	1,000		

38. Similarly, if a business has accrued telephone expenses as at 1 July 19X6 of £850, pays £6,720 in telephone bills during the year to 30 June 19X7, and has accrued telephone expenses of £1,140 as at 30 June 19X7, then the telephone expense to be shown in the P&L account for the year to 30 June 19X7 is the balancing figure in the following T account. (Remember that an accrual is a current liability, and so is a credit balance b/f.)

TELEPHONE EXPENSES

	£		£
Cash	6,720	Balance b/f (accrual)	850
Balance c/f (accrual)	1,140	P&L a/c (balancing figure)	7,010
	7,860		7,860
		Balance b/f	1,140

Drawings

39. Drawings would normally represent no particular problem at all in preparing a set of final accounts from incomplete records, but it is not unusual for examination questions to introduce a situation in which:

    (a) the business owner pays income into his bank account which has nothing whatever to do with the business operations. For example, the owner might pay dividend income, or other income from investments into the bank, from stocks and shares which he owns personally, separate from the business itself. (In other words, there are no investments in the business balance sheet, and so income from investments cannot possibly be income of the business);

    (b) the business owner pays money out of the business bank account for items which are not business expenses, such as life insurance premiums or a payment for his family's holidays etc.

40. Where such personal items of receipts or payments are made:

    (a) receipts should be set off against drawings. For example, if a business owner receives £600 in dividend income and pays it into his business bank account, although the dividends are from investments not owned by the business, then the accounting entry is:

    Debit Cash
    Credit Drawings;

(b) payments should be charged to drawings; ie

> *Debit* Drawings
> *Credit* Cash

Drawings: beware of the wording in an examination question

41. You should note that:

(a) if a question states that a proprietor's drawings during a given year are 'approximately £40 per week' then you should assume that drawings for the year are £40 x 52 weeks = £2,080;

(b) however, if a question states that drawings in the year are 'between £35 and £45 per week', do not assume that the drawings average £40 per week and so amount to £2,080 for the year. You could not be certain that the actual drawings did average £40, and so you should treat the drawings figure as a missing item that needs to be calculated.

An approach to dealing with incomplete records problems

42. A suggested approach to dealing with incomplete records problems brings together the various points described so far in this chapter. The nature of the 'incompleteness' in the records will vary from problem to problem, but the approach, suitably applied, should be successful in arriving at the final accounts whatever the particular characteristics of the problem might be.

43. The approach is:

(a) *Step 1.* If possible, and if it is not already known, establish the opening balance sheet and the proprietor's interest.

(b) *Step 2.* Open up four accounts:

(i) trading account (if you wish, leave space underneath for entering the P&L account later);

(ii) a cash book, with two columns if cash sales are significant and there are payments in cash out of the till;

(iii) a debtors account

(iv) a creditors account

(c) *Step 3.* Enter the opening balances in these accounts.

(d) *Step 4.* Work through the information you are given line by line; and each item should be entered into the appropriate account if it is relevant to one or more of these four accounts.

You should also try to recognise each item as a 'P&L account income or expense item' or a 'closing balance sheet item'.

It may be necessary to calculate an amount for drawings and an amount for fixed asset depreciation.

(e) *Step 5*. Look for the balancing figures in your accounts. In particular you might be looking for a value for credit sales, cash sales, purchases, the cost of goods sold, the cost of goods stolen or destroyed, or the closing bank balance. Calculate these missing figures, and make any necessary double entry (eg to the trading account from the creditors account for purchases, to the trading account from the cash book for cash sales, and to the trading account from the debtors account for credit sales).

(f) *Step 6*. Now complete the P&L account and balance sheet. Working T accounts might be needed where there are accruals or prepayments.

44. An example will illustrate this approach.

Example: an incomplete records problem

45. John Snow is the sole distribution agent in the Branton area for Diamond floor tiles. Under an agreement with the manufacturers, John Snow purchases the Diamond floor tiles at a trade discount of 20% off list price and annually in May receives an agency commission of 1% of his purchases for the year ended on the previous 31 March.

For several years, John Snow has obtained a gross profit of 40% on all sales. In a burglary in January 19X1 John Snow lost stock costing £4,000 as well as many of his accounting records. However, after careful investigations, the following information has been obtained covering the year ended 31 March 19X1.

(i) Assets and liabilities at 31 March 19X0 were as follows:

	£
Buildings: at cost	10,000
provision for depreciation	6,000
Motor vehicles: at cost	5,000
provision for depreciation	2,000
Stock: at cost	3,200
Trade debtors (for sales)	6,300
Agency commission due	300
Prepayments (trade expenses)	120
Balance at bank	4,310
Trade creditors	4,200
Accrued vehicle expenses	230

(ii) John Snow has been notified that he will receive an agency commission of £440 on 1 May 19X1.

(iii) Stock, at cost, at 31 March 19X1 was valued at an amount £3,000 more than a year previously.

(iv) In October 19X0 stock costing £1,000 was damaged by dampness and had to be scrapped as worthless.

(v) Trade creditors at 31 March 19X1 related entirely to goods received whose list prices totalled £9,500.

(vi) Discounts allowed amounted to £1,620 whilst discounts received were £1,200.

(vii) Trade expenses prepaid at 31 March 19X1 totalled £80.

(viii) Vehicle expenses for the year ended 31 March 19X1 amounted to £7,020.

(ix) Trade debtors (for sales) at 31 March 19X1 were £6,700.

(x) All receipts are passed through the bank account.

(xi) Depreciation is provided annually at the following rates: buildings 5% on cost
                                             motor vehicles 20% on cost.

(xii)   Commissions received are paid directly to the bank account.

(xiii)   In addition to the payments for purchases, the bank payments were:

	£
Vehicle expenses	6,720
Drawings	4,300
Trade expenses	7,360

(xiv)   John Snow is not insured against loss of stock owing to burglary or damage to stock caused by dampness.

Required

John Snow's trading and profit and loss account for the year ended 31 March 19X1 and a balance sheet on that date.

Discussion and solution

46.   This is an incomplete records problem because we are told that John Snow has lost many of his accounting records. In particular we do not know sales for the year, purchases during the year, or all the cash receipts and payments.

47.   The first step is to find the opening balance sheet, if possible. In this case, it is. The proprietor's capital is the balancing figure.

JOHN SNOW
BALANCE SHEET AS AT 31 MARCH 19X0

	Cost £	Dep'n £	£
Fixed assets			
Buildings	10,000	6,000	4,000
Motor vehicles	5,000	2,000	3,000
	15,000	8,000	7,000
Current assets			
Stock		3,200	
Trade debtors		6,300	
Commission due		300	
Prepayments		120	
Balance at hand		4,310	
		14,230	
Current liabilities			
Trade creditors		4,200	
Accrued expenses		230	
		4,430	
			9,800
			16,800
Proprietor's capital as at 31 March 19X0			16,800

48.   The next step is to open up a trading account, cash book, debtors account and creditors account and to insert the opening balances, if known. Cash sales and payments in cash are not a feature of the problem, and so a single column cash book is sufficient.

49. The problem should then be read line by line, identifying any transactions affecting those accounts.

TRADING ACCOUNT

	£	£
Sales (note 6)		60,000
Opening stock	3,200	
Purchases (note 1)	44,000	
	47,200	
Less: damaged stock written off (note 3)	(1,000)	
stock stolen (note 5)	(4,000)	
	42,200	
Less closing stock (note 2)	6,200	
Cost of goods sold		36,000
Gross profit (note 6)		24,000

CASH BOOK

	£		£
Opening balance	4,310	Trade creditors	
Trade debtors (see below)	57,980	(see creditors a/c)	39,400
Agency commission (note 7)	300	Trade expenses	7,360
		Vehicle expenses	6,720
		Drawings	4,300
		Balance c/f	4,810
	62,590		62,590

TRADE DEBTORS

	£		£
Opening balance b/f	6,300	Discounts allowed (note 4)	1,620
Sales (note 6)	60,000	Cash received	
		(balancing figure)	57,980
		Closing balance c/f	6,700
	66,300		66,300

TRADE CREDITORS

	£		£
Discounts received (note 4)	1,200	Opening balance b/f	4,200
Cash paid (balancing figure)	39,400	Purchases (note 1)	44,000
Closing balance c/f	7,500		
	48,200		48,200

VEHICLE EXPENSES

	£		£
Cash	6,720	Accrual b/f	230
Accrual c/f (balancing figure)	530	P & L account	7,020
	7,250		7,250

50. The trading account is complete already, but now the P&L account and balance sheet can be prepared. Remember not to forget items such as the stock losses, commission earned on purchases, discounts allowed and discounts received.

JOHN SNOW – TRADING, PROFIT AND LOSS ACCOUNT
FOR THE YEAR ENDED 31 MARCH 19X1

	£	£
Sales (note 6)		60,000
Opening stock	3,200	
Purchases (note 1)	44,000	
	47,200	
Less: damaged stock written off (note 3)	(1,000)	
stock stolen	(4,000)	
	42,200	
Less closing stock (note 2)	6,200	
Cost of goods sold		36,000
Gross profit (note 6)		24,000
Add: commission on purchases		440
discounts received		1,200
		25,640
Expenses		
Trade expenses (note 8)	7,400	
Stock damaged	1,000	
Stock stolen	4,000	
Vehicle expenses	7,020	
Discounts allowed	1,620	
Depreciation:		
Buildings	500	
Motor vehicles	1,000	
		22,540
Net profit (to capital account)		3,100

JOHN SNOW
BALANCE SHEET AS AT 31 MARCH 19X1

	Cost £	Dep'n £	£
Fixed assets			
Buildings	10,000	6,500	3,500
Motor vehicles	5,000	3,000	2,000
	15,000	9,500	5,500
Current assets			
Stock		6,200	
Trade debtors		6,700	
Commission due		440	
Prepayments (trade expenses)		80	
Balance at bank		4,810	
		18,230	
Current liabilities			
Trade creditors	7,600		
Accrued expenses	530		
		8,130	
			10,100
			15,600

		£	£
Proprietor's capital			
As at 31 March 19X0			16,800
Net profit for year to 31 March 19X1		3,100	
Less drawings		(4,300)	
Retained deficit			(1,200)
As at 31 March 19X1			15,600

Notes

1. The agency commission due on 1 May 19X1 indicates that purchases for the year to 31 March 19X1 were

    100%/1% x £440 = £44,000

2. Closing stock at cost on 31 March 19X1 was £(3,200 + 3,000) = £6,200.

3. Stock scrapped (£1,000) is accounted for by
    Credit   Trading account
    Debit   P&L account

4. Discounts allowed are accounted for by
    Debit   Discounts allowed account
    Credit   Debtors

    Similarly, discounts received are
    Debit   Creditors
    Credit   Discounts received

    Note: discounts received represents *settlement* discounts, not *trade* discounts, which are not usually accounted for as they are given automatically at source.

5. Stocks lost in the burglary are accounted for by
    Credit   Trading account
    Debit   P&L account

6. The trade discount of 20% has already been deducted in arriving at the value of the purchases. The gross profit is 40% on sales, so with cost of sales = £36,000

		£
Cost	(60%)	36,000
Profit	(40%)	24,000
Sales	(100%)	60,000

    (It is assumed that trade expenses are not included in the trading account, and so should be ignored in this calculation.)

7. The agency commission of £300 due on 1 May 19X0 would have been paid to John Snow at that date.

8. The P&L account expenditure for trade expenses and closing balance on vehicle expenses account are as follows:

TRADE EXPENSES

	£		£
Prepayment	120	P&L account	
Cash	7,360	(balancing figure)	7,400
		Prepayment c/f	80
	7,480		7,480

Using a debtors account to calculate both cash sales and credit sales

51. A final point which needs to be considered is how a missing value can be found for cash sales and credit sales, when a business has both, but takings banked by the business are not divided between takings from cash sales and takings from credit sales.

Example

52. Suppose, for example, that a business had, on 1 January 19X8, trade debtors of £2,000, cash in the bank of £3,000, and cash in hand of £300.

During the year to 31 December 19X8 the business banked £95,000 in takings.

It also paid out the following expenses in cash from the till:

Drawings	£1,200
Sundry expenses	£800

On 29 August 19X8 a thief broke into the shop and stole £400 from the till.

At 31 December 19X8 trade debtors amounted to £3,500, cash in the bank £2,500 and cash in the till £150.

What was the value of sales during the year?

Solution

53. If we tried to prepare a debtors account and a two column cash book, we would have insufficient information, in particular about whether the takings which were banked related to cash sales or credit sales.

DEBTORS

	£		£
Balance b/f	2,000	Payments from debtors	
Credit sales	*Unknown*	(credit sales)	*Unknown*
		Balance c/f	3,500

CASH BOOK

	Cash £	Bank £		Cash £	Bank £
Balance b/f	300	3,000	Drawings	1,200	
			Sundry expenses	800	
Debtors-payments		Unknown	Cash stolen	400	
Cash sales		Unknown	Balance c/f	150	2,500

All we do know is that the combined sums from debtors and cash takings banked is £95,000.

The value of sales can be found instead by using the debtors account, which should be used to record cash takings banked as well as payments by debtors. The balancing figure in the debtors account will then be a combination of credit sales and some cash sales. The cash book only needs to be a single column.

DEBTORS

	£		£
Balance b/f	2,000	Cash banked	95,000
Sales-to trading account	96,500	Balance c/f	3,500
	98,500		98,500

CASH (EXTRACT)

	£		£
Balance in hand b/f	300	Payments in cash:	
Balance in bank c/f	3,000	Drawings	1,200
Debtors a/c	95,000	Expenses	800
		Other payments	?
		Cash stolen	400
		Balance in hand c/f	150
		Balance in bank c/f	2,500

The remaining 'undiscovered' amount of cash sales is now found as follows:

	£	£
Payments in cash out of the till		
Drawings	1,200	
Expenses	800	
		2,000
Cash stolen		400
Closing balance of cash in hand		150
		2,550
Less opening balance of cash in hand		(300)
Further cash sales		2,250

(This calculation is similar to the one described in paragraph 33.)

	£
Total sales for the year are:	
From debtors account	96,500
From cash book	2,250
Total sales	98,750

Summary of the chapter

54.
- Incomplete records questions may test your ability to prepare accounts in the following situations:

  (a) a trader does not maintain a ledger and therefore has no continuous double entry record of transactions;

  (b) accounting records are destroyed by accident, such as fire;

  (c) some essential figure is unknown and must be calculated as a balancing figure. This may occur as a result of stock being damaged or destroyed, or because of a defalcation.

- The approach to incomplete records questions is to build up the information given so as to complete the necessary double entry. This may involve reconstructing control accounts for:

  (a) cash and bank (often in columnar format)
  (b) debtors and creditors

- Where stock, sales or purchases is the unknown figure it will be necessary to use information on gross profit percentages so as to construct a trading account in which the unknown figure can be inserted as a balance.

TEST YOUR KNOWLEDGE

Numbers in brackets refer to paragraphs of this chapter

1. In the absence of a sales account or sales day book, how can a figure of sales for the year be computed? (9)

2. In the absence of a purchase account or purchases day book, how can a figure of purchases for the year be computed? (13)

3. What is the accounting double entry to record the loss of stock by fire or burglary? (25, 26)

4. If a business proprietor pays his personal income into the business bank account, what is the accounting double entry to record the transaction? (40)

Now try questions 1-2 at the end of this section

Chapter 20

INCOME AND EXPENDITURE ACCOUNTS

The purpose of this chapter is:

● to explain the differences between the accounts of non-trading organisations and those of businesses

● to illustrate the preparation of income and expenditure accounts for non-trading organisations

---

Introduction

1. An income and expenditure account is simply the name that is given to what is effectively the profit and loss account of a non-trading organisation, such as sports clubs, social clubs, societies and other associations, and charities etc. Since a non-trading organisation does not exist to make a profit, it is inappropriate to refer to its 'profit and loss' account. However, a non-trading organisation must be able to pay its way, and so it is still important to ensure that income covers expenses. For this reason, an 'income and expenditure' account, together with a balance sheet, is an important report for judging the financial affairs of the organisation. The principles of 'accruals' accounting (ie the matching concept) are applied to income and expenditure accounts in the same way as for profit and loss accounts.

What is different about the accounts of a non-trading organisation?

2. There are one or two differences between the final accounts of a non-trading organisation and those of a business.

   (a) Since non-trading organisations do not exist to make profits, the difference between income and matching expenditure in the income and expenditure account is referred to as a surplus or a deficit rather than a profit or loss.

   (b) The capital or proprietorship of the organisation is referred to as the accumulated fund, rather than the capital account. In addition, other separate funds might be kept by the organisation (see below, paragraph 6).

   (c) There is usually no separate trading account. Instead, it is usual to net off expenditure against income for like items. To explain this point further, it will be useful to consider the sources of income for a non-trading organisation in further detail.

Sources of income for non-trading organisations

3. Non-trading organisations differ in purpose and character, but we shall concentrate here on sports clubs, social clubs or societies. These will obtain their income from various sources, including:

    (a) membership subscriptions for annual membership of the club (and initial joining subscriptions for first year members);

    (b) payments for life membership;

    (c) 'profits' from bar sales;

    (d) 'profits' from the sale of food in the club restaurant or cafeteria;

    (e) 'profits' from social events, such as dinner-dances;

    (f) interest received on investments.

4. Netting off expenditure against income for like items means that where some sources of income have associated costs, the net surplus or deficit should be shown in the income and expenditure account, so that:

    (a) if a club holds an annual dinner-dance, the income and expenditure account will net off the costs of the event against the revenue to show the surplus or deficit;

    (b) similarly, if a club has a bar, the income and expenditure account will show the surplus or deficit on its trading. Although the organisation itself does not trade, the bar within the organisation does, and so it is in fact correct to refer to 'profits' from the bar.

5. Where there is trading activity within a non-trading organisation (eg bar sales, cafeteria sales etc) so that the organisation must hold stocks of drink or food etc it is usual to prepare a trading account for that particular activity, and then to record the surplus or deficit from trading in the income and expenditure account. An example is given here:

FOOLSMATE CHESS CLUB

BAR TRADING ACCOUNT FOR THE YEAR TO 31 DECEMBER 19X5

	£	£
Sales		18,000
Less cost of goods sold:		
Bar stocks 1 January 19X5	1,200	
Purchases	15,400	
	16,600	
Less bar stocks at 31 December 19X5	1,600	
		15,000
Surplus (taken to I & E account)		3,000

Funds of non-trading organisations

6. Although the capital of a non-trading organisation is generally accounted for as the accumulated fund, some separate funds might be set up for particular purposes.

    (a) A life membership fund is a fund for the money subscribed for life membership by various members of the organisation. The money paid for life membership is commonly invested outside the organisation (eg in a building society account). The investment then earns interest for the organisation.

(b) A building fund might be set up whereby the organisation sets aside money to save for the cost of a new building extension. The money put into the fund will be invested outside the organisation, earning interest, until it is eventually needed for the building work. It might take several years to create a fund large enough for the building work planned.

7. The basic principles of accounting for special funds are as follows:

(a) when money is put into the fund:
Debit   Cash
Credit   Special-purpose fund

(b) when the cash is invested:
Debit   Investments (eg building society account)
Credit   Cash

(c) when the investments earn interest:
Debit   Cash
Credit   Interest received account (and subsequently, the income and expenditure account, or possibly the fund account itself).

Preparing income and expenditure accounts

8. Many charities, clubs, etc have little if any accounting expertise, and keep records only of cash received and paid.

Examination questions often provide a *receipts and payments account* (ie a list of cash amounts received and paid by the organisation during the period), balances of assets and liabilities at the beginning of the period, and details of accruals and prepayments at the end of the period. You would be required typically to give:

(a) the balance on the accumulated fund at the beginning of the period;
(b) a trading account for a particular activity for the period;
(c) an income and expenditure account for the period;
(d) a balance sheet at the end of the period.

9. Before looking at an example of an income and expenditure account, however, we need to look at each of the following items in some detail:

(a) membership subscriptions;
(b) bar trading account;
(c) life membership.

These are items which we have not yet come across in previous chapters, because they are not found in the accounts of businesses. We must not forget, however, that in many respects the accounts of non-trading organisations are similar to those of businesses with fixed assets, a provision for depreciation, current assets and current liabilities, expense accounts (eg electricity, telephone, stationery etc) accruals and prepayments.

Membership subscriptions

10. Annual membership subscriptions of clubs and societies are usually payable one year in advance.

    A club or society therefore receives payments from members for benefits which the members have yet to enjoy, and so payments in advance by members, being receipts in advance to the club or society, will be shown in the balance sheet of the society as a current liability, to the extent that the year's membership has still to run as at the balance sheet date.

11. A numerical example might help to clarify this point:

    The Mudflannels Cricket Club charges an annual membership of £50 payable in advance on 1 October each year. All 40 members pay their subscriptions promptly on 1 October 19X4. If the club's accounting year ends on 31 December, of the total subscriptions of 40 x £50 = £2,000:

    (a) $40 \times \dfrac{9 \text{ months}}{12 \text{ months}} = \times £50 = £1,500$ will appear in the balance sheet of the club

    as at 31 December 19X4 as a current liability 'subscriptions in advance' (These subscriptions relate to the period 1 January – 30 September 19X5).

    (b) $40 \times \dfrac{3 \text{ months}}{12 \text{ months}} \times £50 = £500$ will appear as income in the income and expenditure

    account for the period 1 October to 31 December 19X4.

12. When members are in arrears with subscriptions and owe money to the club or society, they are 'debtors' of the organisation and so appear as current assets in the balance sheet 'subscriptions in arrears'.

    These should be shown as a separate item in the balance sheet, and should not be netted off against subscriptions in advance.

13. For example, suppose that the Bluespot Squash Club has 100 members, each of whom pays an annual membership of £60 on 1 November. Of those 100 members, 90 pay their subscriptions before 31 December 19X5 (for the 19X5/X6 year) but 10 have still not paid. If the club's accounting year ends on 31 December, then as at 31 December 19X5, the balance sheet of the club would include:

    (a) subscriptions in advance (current liability) are

    $90 \text{ members} \times \dfrac{10 \text{ months}}{12 \text{ months}} \times £60 = £4,500$

    (b) subscriptions in arrears (current asset) are

    $10 \text{ members} \times \dfrac{2 \text{ months}}{12 \text{ months}} \times £60 = £100$

    It is not uncommon, however, for clubs to take no credit for subscription income until the money is received. In such a case, any subscriptions in arrears are *not* credited to income and *not* shown as a current asset. It is essential to read the question carefully.

Membership subscriptions: another example

14. At 1 January 19X8, the Little Blithering Debating Society had membership subscriptions paid in advance of £1,600, and subscriptions in arrears of £250. During the year to 31 December 19X8 receipts of subscription payments amounted to £18,400. At 31 December 19X8 subscriptions in advance amounted to £1,750 and subscriptions in arrears to £240.

    What is the income from subscriptions to be shown in the income and expenditure account for the year to 31 December 19X8?

Solution

15. The question does not say that subscriptions are only accounted for when received. You may therefore assume that the society takes credit for subscriptions as they become due, whether or not they are received.

    The income for the income and expenditure account consists of:

	£	£
Payments received in the year		X
Add: subscriptions due but not yet received (ie subscriptions in arrears c/f)		X
subscriptions received last year relating to current year (ie subscriptions in advance b/f)		X
		X
Less: subscriptions received in current year relating to last year (ie subscriptions in arrears b/f)	X	
subscriptions received in current year relating to next year (ie subscriptions in advance c/f)	X	
		(X)
Income from subscriptions for the year		X

16. In this example:

	£	£
Payments received in the year		18,400
Add: subscriptions in arrears 31 Dec 19X8	240	
subscriptions in advance 1 Jan 19X8	1,600	
		1,840
		20,240
Less: subscriptions in arrears 1 Jan 19X8	250	
subscriptions in advance 31 Dec 19X8	1,750	
		2,000
Income from subscriptions for the year		18,240

17. You may find it simpler to do this calculation as a ledger account:

SUBSCRIPTIONS ACCOUNT

	£		£
Subscriptions in arrears b/f	250	Subscriptions in advance b/f	1,600
I & E a/c (balancing figure)	18,240	Cash	18,400
Subscriptions in advance c/d	1,750	Subscriptions in arrears c/d	240
	20,240		20,240
Subscriptions in arrears b/d	240	Subscriptions in advance b/d	1,750

Bar trading account

18. If a club has a bar or cafeteria a separate trading account will be prepared for its trading activities. A bar trading account will consist of:

   (a) bar takings;
   (b) opening stocks of goods, purchases and closing stocks of goods, to give the cost of bar sales;
   (c) a gross profit-item (a) minus item (b);
   (d) other expenses directly related to the running of the bar, if any;
   (e) a net profit-item (c) minus item (d).

The net bar profit is then included as income in the income and expenditure account. (A loss on the 'bar' would be an 'expenditure'. Since the bar or cafeteria sells goods it does make a 'profit' or 'loss' and it is appropriate to use these words, even within an income and expenditure account.)

Life membership

19. Some clubs offer membership for life in return for a given lump sum subscription. Life members, having paid this initial lump sum, do not have to pay any further annual subscriptions. In return the club receives a sum of money, which it can then invest, with the annual interest from these investments being accounted for as income in the income and expenditure account.

The 'once-and-for-all' payments from life members are not income relating to the year in which they are received by the club, because the payment is for the life of the members, which can of course be a very long time to come. Because they are long-term payments, they are recorded in the club accounts as an addition to a Life Membership Fund: ie

   Debit   Cash
   Credit   Life membership fund

20. The Life Membership Fund is shown in the balance sheet of the club or society immediately after the accumulated fund: ie

	£
Accumulated fund	
Balance at the beginning of the year	X
Add surplus or less deficit for the year	X
Balance at the end of year	X
Life membership fund	X

21. Life members enjoy the benefits of membership over their life, and so their payment to the club is 'rewarded' as time goes by. Accounting for life membership over time can be explained with an example.

    Suppose that Annette Cord pays a life membership fee of £300 to the Tumbledown Tennis Club. The £300 will initially be put into the club's life membership fund. We will suppose that this money is invested by the club, and earns interest of £30 per annum.

22. There are two ways of accounting for the life membership fee.

    (a) To keep the £300 in the life membership fund until Annette Cord dies. (Since the £300 earns interest of £30 pa this interest can be said to represent income for the club in lieu of an annual subscription.)

    When Annette eventually dies (in 5 years, or 50 years, or whenever) the £300 she contributed can then be transferred (on death of the life member) out of the life membership fund and directly into the accumulated fund.

    (b) To write off subscriptions to the life membership fund by transferring a 'fair' amount from the fund into the income and expenditure account. A 'fair' amount will represent the proportion of the total life membership payment which relates to the current year. We do not know how long any life member will live, but if an estimated average life from becoming a life member until death is, say, 20 years, it might seem reasonable to write off payments to the fund over a 20 year period. In each year, one-twentieth of life membership fees would then be:

    (i) deducted from the fund and;
    (ii) added as income in the income and expenditure account.

    In the case of Annette Cord, the annual transfer would be £15, and after 20 years, her contribution to the fund would have been written off in full from the fund and transferred to the income and expenditure accounts of those 20 years.

    (This transfer of £15 to the income and expenditure account will of course be supplementary to the interest of £30 pa earned by the club each year from investing the fee of £300.)

23. If method (b) is selected in preference to method (a), the life membership fund could be written down by either a straight line method or a reducing balance method, in much the same way as fixed assets are depreciated - with the exception that it is a capital fund being written off, and the amount of the annual write-off is income to the club, and not an expense like depreciation.

24. A further feature of method (b) is that there is no need to record the death of individual members (unlike method (a)). The annual write off is based on an average expected life of members, and it does not matter when any individual member dies. The same average write off each year will be used.

25. A possible reason for preferring method (b) to method (a) is that life membership subscriptions eventually pass through the income and expenditure account as income of the club, which is logically reasonable, since life members although they pay a long time in advance, do eventually enjoy the benefits of membership in return for their payment. Why therefore, should life

membership fees be essentially different from ordinary annual membership subscriptions? It is fair that in due course of time, life membership fees should be accounted for as income of the club, to boost the annual surpluses, or reduce the annual deficits.

26. In spite of the logical reasons why method (b) should perhaps be preferable, method (a) is still commonly used. In an examination question, unless you are told about a rate for 'writing off' the life membership fund annually, you should assume that method (a) should be used, where the question gives you information about the death of club life members.

Example: life membership fund

27. The Coxless Rowing Club has a scheme whereby as an alternative to paying annual subscriptions, members can at any time opt to pay a lump sum which gives them membership for life. Lump sum payments received for life membership are held in a life membership fund but then credited to the income and expenditure account in equal instalments over a 10-year period, beginning in the year when the lump sum payment is made and life membership is acquired.

The treasurer of the club, Beau Trace, establishes the following information:

(a) At 31 December 19X4, the balance on the life membership fund was £8,250.
(b) Of this opening balance, £1,200 should be credited as income for the year to 31 December 19X5.
(c) During the year to 31 December 19X5, new life members made lump sum payments totalling £1,500.

Required:

Show the movements in the life membership fund for the year to 31 December 19X5, and in doing so, calculate how much should be transferred as income from life membership fund to the income and expenditure account.

Solution

28.   LIFE MEMBERSHIP FUND

	£	£
As at 31 December 19X4		8,250
New life membership payments received in 19X5		1,500
		9,750
Less transfer to income and expenditure account:		
Out of balance as at 31 December 19X5	1,220	
Out of new payments in 19X5 (10% of £1,500)	150	
		1,370
Fund as at 31 December 19X5		8,380
The income and expenditure account for the year would show:		
Income from life membership		1,370

A building fund

29. Sometimes a club may wish to provide for future building work. The club could appropriate a proportion of its annual surplus to a building fund, the double entry being to debit income and expenditure account each year and to credit a building fund account. The accumulated balance on the fund account would represent a capital fund, shown in the balance sheet after the accumulated fund and the life membership fund.

30. This bookkeeping exercise, however, would not provide the actual cash required for the building work (just as the creation of an accumulated depreciation account by means of annual depreciation charges does not make cash available for asset replacement - see earlier chapter on depreciation).

31. If the club wishes to make cash available for the proposed building work then, in addition to the entries described above, cash must be transferred from the main bank account to a building fund bank account. The cash in the building fund bank account would increase by the annual transfer and by interest earned. Eventually, if the club has budgeted correctly, sufficient cash will have accumulated to pay for the building work by the time it commences.

Accounting for the sale of investments and fixed assets

32. In accounting for clubs and societies, the income and expenditure account is used to record the surplus or deficit in the transactions for the year. Occasionally a club or society might sell off some of its investments or fixed assets, and in doing so might make a profit or loss on the sale.

    (a) The profit/loss on the sale of an investment is simply the difference between the sale price and the balance sheet value (usually cost) of the investment.

    (b) The profit/loss on the sale of a fixed asset is the difference between the sale price and the net book value of the asset at the date of sale.

33. There is nothing different or unusual about the accounts of non-trading organisations in computing the amount of such profits or losses. What is different, however, is how the profit or losses should be recorded in the accounts.

    (a) The profit or loss on the sale of investments is not shown in the income and expenditure account. Instead, the profit is directly added to (or loss subtracted from) the accumulated fund.

    (b) The profit or loss on the sale of a fixed asset which is not subject to depreciation charges in the income and expenditure account, is also taken directly to the accumulated fund.

    (c) The profit or loss on the sale of fixed assets which have been subject to depreciation charges is recorded in the income and expenditure account.

34. The point of difference in (c) compared with (a) and (b) is that since depreciation on the asset has been charged in the income and expenditure account in the past, it is appropriate that a profit or loss on sale should also be reported through the account.

Income and expenditure accounts: an example

35. The preceding explanations might be sufficient to enable you to prepare an income and expenditure account yourself. A lengthy example is given below. If you think you understand the explanations given in it, you should go on to attempt the illustrative questions at the end of the chapter.

Example

36. The assets and liabilities of the Berley Sports Club at 31 December 19X4 were as follows:

	£
Pavilion at cost less depreciation	13,098
Bank and cash	1,067
Bar stock	291
Bar debtors	231
Rates prepaid	68
Contributions owing to sports club by users of sports club facilities	778
Bar creditors	427
Loans to sports club	1,080
Accruals: water	13
electricity	130
miscellaneous	75
loan interest	33
Contributions paid in advance to sports club by users of sports club facilities	398

A receipts and payments account for the year ended 31 December 19X5 was produced as follows:

	£		£
Opening balance	1,067	Bar purchases	2,937
Bar sales	4,030	Repayment of loan capital	170
Telephone	34	Rent of ground	79
Contributions from users of		Rates	320
club facilities	1,780	Water	38
Socials	177	Electricity	506
Miscellaneous	56	Insurance	221
		Repairs to equipment	326
		Expenses of socials	67
		Maintenance of ground	133
		Wages of groundsman	140
		Telephone	103
		Bar sundries	144
		Loan interest	97
		Miscellaneous	163
		Closing balance	1,700
	7,144		7,144

20: INCOME AND EXPENDITURE ACCOUNTS

The following information as at 31 December was also provided:

	£
Bar stock	394
Bar debtors	50
Bar creditors	901
Rent prepaid	16
Water charges owing	23
Electricity owing	35
Creditors for bar sundries	65
Contributions by users of sports club facilities:	
owing to sports club	425
paid in advance to sports club	657
Rates prepaid	76

Depreciation on the pavilion for the year was £498.

You are asked to prepare a statement showing the gross and net profits earned by the bar, an income and expenditure account for the year ended 31 December 19X5 and a balance sheet as at that date.

Approach to a solution

37. We are not given the size of the accumulated fund as at the beginning of the year, but it can be calculated as the balancing figure to make total liabilities plus capital equal to total assets (as at 31 December 19X4).

Calculation of accumulated fund at 1.1.19X5:

		£
Assets		
Pavilion at cost less depreciation		13,098
Bank and cash		1,067
Bar stock		291
Bar debtors		231
Rates prepaid		68
Contributions in arrears		778
		15,533
Liabilities		
Bar creditors	427	
Loans	1,080	
Accrued charges £(13 + 130 + 75 + 33)	251	
Contributions received in advance	398	
		(2,156)
∴ Accumulated fund at 1.1.19X5		13,377

38. The next step is to analyse the various items of income and expenditure.

(a) There is a bar, and so a bar trading account can be prepared.
(b) Income from the telephone (presumably from members paying the club for calls they make) can be netted off against telephone expenditure.
(c) The revenue from socials has associated expenses to net off against it.
(d) There is also miscellaneous income and contributions from club members.

329

39. The bar trading account can only be put together after we have calculated bar sales and purchases.

(a) We are given bar debtors as at 1 January 19X5 and 31 December 19X5 and also cash received from bar sales. The bar sales for the year are therefore:

BAR DEBTORS

		£			£
1.1.19X5	Balance b/f	231	31.12.19X5	Cash	4,030
31.12.19X5	∴ Bar sales	3,849	31.12.19X5	Balance c/f	50
		4,080			4,080

(b) Similarly, purchases for the bar are calculated from opening and closing amounts for bar creditors, and payments for bar purchases.

BAR CREDITORS

		£			£
31.12.19X5	Cash	2,937	1.1.19X5	Balance b/f	427
31.12.19X5	Balance c/f	901	31.12.19X5	∴ Bar purchases	3,411
		3,838			3,838

(c) Be clear in your own mind that cash receipts from bar sales and cash payments for bar supplies are not the bar sales and cost of bar sales that we want. Cash receipts and payments in the year are not for matching quantities of goods, nor do they relate to the actual goods sold in the year.

(d) Other bar trading expenses are bar sundries, at a cost for the year of:

	£
Cash payments for bar sundries	144
Add creditors for bar sundries as at 31.12.19X5	65
	209
Less creditors for bar sundries as at 1.1.19X5	0
Expenses for bar sundries for the year	209

40.
BAR TRADING ACCOUNT
FOR THE YEAR ENDED 31 DECEMBER 19X5

	£	£
Sales		3,849
Cost of sales:		
Opening stock	291	
Purchases	3,411	
	3,702	
Less closing stock	394	
		3,308
Gross profit		541
Sundry expenses		209
Net profit		332

41. Other workings:

(a) Contributions to the sports club for the year should be calculated in the same way as membership subscriptions. Using a T account format below, the income from contributions (for the income and expenditure account) is the balancing figure. Contributions in advance brought forward are liabilities (credit balance b/f) and contributions in arrears brought forward are assets (debit balance b/f).

CONTRIBUTIONS

		£			£
1.1.19X5	Balance in arrears b/f	778	1.1.19X5	Balance in advance b/f	398
31.12.19X5	∴ Income and expenditure	1,168	31.12.19X5	Cash	1,780
31.12.19X5	Balance in advance c/f	657	31.12.19X5	Balance in arrears c/f	425
		2,603			2,603

42.

BERLEY SPORTS CLUB - INCOME AND EXPENDITURE ACCOUNT
FOR THE YEAR ENDED 31 DECEMBER 19X5

	£	£
Income		
Contributions		1,168
Net income from bar trading		332
Income from socials: receipts	177	
less expenses	67	
		110
Miscellaneous		56
		1,666
Expenses		
Ground rent	63	
Rates	312	
Water	48	
Electricity	411	
Insurance	221	
Equipment repairs	326	
Ground maintenance	133	
Wages	140	
Telephone	69	
Loan interest	64	
Miscellaneous expenses	88	
Depreciation	498	
		(2,373)
		(707)

BERLEY SPORTS CLUB
BALANCE SHEET AS AT 31 DECEMBER 19X5

	£	£
Fixed assets		
Pavilion at NBV £(13,098 - 498)		12,600
Current assets		
Bar stock	394	
Bar debtors	50	
Contributions in arrears	425	
Prepayments £(16+76)	92	
Cash at bank	1,700	
	2,661	
Current liabilities		
Bar creditors £(901+65)	966	
Accrued charges	58	
Contributions in advance	657	
	1,681	
Net current assets		980
		13,580
Long-term liability		
Loan £(1,080-170)		(910)
		12,670
Accumulated fund		
Balance at 1 January 19X5		13,377
Less deficit for year		707
		12,670

Summary of the chapter

43.
- Income and expenditure accounts are the equivalent of profit and loss accounts for non-trading organisations. In the examination it is usually easy to recognise such questions because they always refer to the accounts of a club or society.

- In the presentation of income and expenditure accounts:

  (a) match sources of revenue with related costs to show net income from the organisation's various activities;

  (b) treat subscriptions received in advance as a current liability and (unless the question states the contrary) treat subscriptions in arrears as a current asset;

  (c) describe the result for the year as surplus or deficit, not as profit or loss;

  (d) describe the capital of the organisation as the accumulated fund but remember that capital may also include other funds such as a life membership fund.

TEST YOUR KNOWLEDGE

Numbers in brackets refer to paragraphs of this chapter

1. List three differences between the accounts of a non-trading organisation and those of a business. (2)

2. List five sources of income for a non-trading organisation. (3)

3. What is a receipts and payments account? (8)

4. Describe two ways of accounting for income from life membership fees. (22)

5. The profit or loss on the sale of a fixed asset which has been subject to depreciation charges is taken directly to the accumulated fund. True or false? (33)

Now try questions 3 and 4 at the end of this section

Chapter 21

PARTNERSHIP ACCOUNTS

The purpose of this chapter is:

- to explain the principal features of partnership accounts, and in particular the differences between the accounts of a partnership and those of a sole trader

- to illustrate the preparation of accounts for partnership businesses

---

Definition of a partnership

1. Partnership is defined by the Partnership Act 1890 as 'the relation which subsists between persons carrying on a business in common with a view of profit'. A partnership is therefore an arrangement between two or more individuals in which they undertake to share the risks and rewards of a joint business operation. The most well-known partnerships are those of professional people, such as accountants and solicitors, who are currently forbidden by the rules of their professions from taking on 'limited liability' by forming themselves into limited companies rather than partnerships.

2. An important feature of partnership is that each partner must accept full liability for the debts of the partnership. For example, if two partners sharing profits equally have capital of £5,000 each in their business, but the business becomes insolvent because of its debts:

   (a) each partner must accept full liability for the business debts, even if these exceed 2 x £5,000 = the £10,000 of capital in the business;

   (b) and what is more, if one partner is unable to pay his share of the debts in full, the other partner must take on the balance himself as his own personal liability. This is known as 'joint and several' liability.

   When a partnership 'goes broke' individual partners might be obliged to sell off their homes and personal possessions, leaving themselves destitute.

3. It is usual for a partnership to be established formally by means of a partnership agreement. However, if individuals act as though they are in partnership, even though no written agreement exists, it will be presumed in law that a partnership does exist, and that the terms of the partnership agreement are those laid down in the Partnership Act 1890.

The partnership agreement

4. The partnership agreement is a written agreement in which the terms of the partnership are set out, and in particular the financial arrangements as between partners. The items it should cover are:

    (a) *partnership capital*. Each partner puts in a share of the business capital. If there is to be an agreement on how much each partner should put in and keep in the business, as a minimum fixed amount, this should be stated;

    (b) *profit-sharing ratio*. Partners can agree to share profits in any way that they choose. For example, if there are three partners in a business, they might agree to share profits equally but on the other hand, if one partner does a greater share of the work, or has more experience and ability, or puts in more capital, the ratio of profit sharing might be different; eg 3:2:1 or 3:1:1 or 4:2:1 etc;

    (c) *interest on capital*. Partners might agree to pay themselves interest on the capital they put into the business. If they do so, the agreement will state what rate of interest is to be applied;

    (d) *partners' salaries*. Partners might also agree to pay themselves salaries. These are not salaries in the same way that an employee of the business will be paid a wage or salary because partners' salaries are an appropriation of profit, and not an expense in the profit and loss account of the business. The purpose of paying salaries is to give each partner a satisfactory basic income before the residual profits are shared out. For example, if Bill and Ben are partners sharing profit in the ratio 2:1 they might agree to pay themselves a salary of £10,000 each.

    If profits before deducting salaries are then £26,000, the income of each partner would be:

	Bill	Ben	Total
	£	£	£
Salary	10,000	10,000	20,000
Share of residual profits (ratio 2:1)	4,000	2,000	6,000
	14,000	12,000	26,000

    The partnership agreement will indicate whether or not salaries are to be paid, and if so, how much each partner should receive;

    (e) *partners' drawings*. Partners may draw out their share of profits from the business. However, they might agree to put a limit on how much they should draw out in any period. If so, this limit should be specified in the partnership agreement. To encourage partners to delay taking drawings out of the business until the financial year has ended, the agreement might also be that partners should be charged interest on their drawings during the year;

    (f) *guarantees*. If one partner guarantees that another will earn a minimum income in the business, such a guarantee should be written into the agreement.

5. If the partnership agreement does not cover any of these points, the rules laid down in section 24 of the Partnership Act 1890 are presumed to apply instead. For example, it would be presumed that:

(a) profits are shared equally;

(b) there are no partners' salaries;

(c) partners are entitled to 5% interest on any loans advanced to the business; and

(d) partners should not receive any interest on capital put into the business.

A partnership agreement illustrated

6. The terms of a partnership agreement might be as follows:

Jenner, Hall and Custer form a partnership and agree that:

(a) profits should be shared in the ratio 5:3:2;

(b) interest should be allowed on capital contributed at 8% per annum;

(c) a salary of £6,000 per annum will be paid to Custer;

(d) interest will be paid on drawings during the year, at the rate of 1% per month;

(e) Jenner has guaranteed a minimum income of £8,000 per annum to Hall, gross of interest on drawings.

This agreement will enable Jenner, Hall and Custer to work out how the profits of the business should be shared out (appropriated) between the partners.

How does accounting for partnerships differ from accounting for sole traders?

7. Partnership accounts are identical in many respects to the accounts of sole traders. In particular:

(a) the assets of a partnership are like the assets of any other business, and are accounted for in the same way. The assets side of a partnership balance sheet is no different from what has been shown in earlier chapters of this manual;

(b) the net profit of a partnership is calculated in the same way as the net profit of a sole trader. The only minor difference is that if a partner makes a loan to the business (as distinct from a capital contribution) then interest on the loan will be an expense in the profit and loss account, in the same way as interest on any other loan, from a person or organisation who is not a partner.

8. There are two respects in which partnership accounts are different, however:

(a) the funds put into the business by each partner are shown differently;

(b) the net profit must be appropriated by the partners, ie shared out according to the partnership agreement. These appropriations of profit must be shown in the partnership accounts.

Funds employed

9. Capital contributed to his business by a sole trader is recorded in his capital account; capital contributed to a partnership is recorded in a series of capital accounts, one for each partner. (Since each partner is ultimately entitled to repayment of his capital it is clearly vital to keep a record of how much is owed to whom.) The precise amount of capital contributed by each partner is a matter for general agreement and there is no question of each partner necessarily

contributing the same amount, although this does sometimes happen. The balance for the capital account will always be a brought forward credit entry in the partnership accounts, because the capital contributed by proprietors is a liability of the business.

10. In addition to a capital account, each partner normally has:
    (a) a current account; and
    (b) a drawings account.

11. The current account is an extension of the capital account, and is a record of how much extra the partner has invested in the business. The balance on the current account of a partner is therefore the profits so far retained in the business by that partner.

12. The main difference between the capital and current account in accounting for partnerships is that:

    (a) whereas the balance on the capital account remains static from year to year (with one or two exceptions);

    (b) the current account is continually fluctuating up and down, as the partnership makes profits which are shared out between the partners, and as each partner takes out drawings.

    A further difference is that when the partnership agreement provides for interest on capital, partners receive interest on the balance in their capital account, but not on the balance in their current account.

13. The drawings accounts serve exactly the same purpose as the drawings account for a sole trader. Each partner's drawings are recorded in a separate account. At the end of an accounting period, each partner's drawings are cleared to his current account, ie:

Credit	Drawings account of partner
Debit	Current account of partner

    (If the amount of the drawings exceeds the balance on a partner's current account, the current account will show a debit balance. However, in normal circumstances, we should expect to find a credit balance on the current accounts.)

14. The capital side of the partnership balance sheet will therefore consist of:

    (a) the capital accounts of each partner; and
    (b) the current accounts of each partner, net of drawings.

    This will be illustrated in an example later.

Partners' loans

15. In addition, it is sometimes the case that an existing or previous partner will make a loan to the partnership, in which case he becomes a creditor of the partnership. The main reasons why such loans tend to occur are:

(a) partnerships are often short of cash, and if existing partners do not wish to contribute further capital (which may be tied up in the business for many years) one or more of them may be prepared to enter into a formal agreement (eg for a specified period at a realistic interest rate); and

(b) when a partner retires there is often insufficient cash to pay the total balance owed to him (ie his current and capital account balances). The amount which he cannot yet be paid is usually transferred to a loan account.

16. For the purposes of balance sheet display such a loan is not included as partners' funds, but is shown separately as a long-term liability (unless repayable within twelve months). This is the case whether or not the loan creditor is also an existing partner.

However, interest on such loans will be credited to the partners' current account (if he is an existing partner.) This is administratively more convenient, especially when the partner does not particularly want to be paid the loan interest in cash immediately it becomes due.

(a) Interest on loans from a partner is accounted for as an expense in the P & L account, and not as an appropriation of profit, even though the interest is added to the current account of the partners.

(b) If there is no interest rate specified, the Partnership Act 1890 (section 24) provides for interest to be paid at 5% pa on loans by partners.

Appropriation of net profits

17. The net profit of a partnership is shared out between them according to the terms of their agreement. This sharing out is shown in a profit and loss appropriation account, which follows on from the profit and loss account itself.

The accounting entries are:

(a) *Debit*   Profit and loss account with net profit c/d
   Credit   Profit and loss appropriation account with net profit b/d

(b) *Debit*   Profit and loss appropriation account
   Credit   The current accounts of each partner with the individual share of profits for each partner.

18. The way in which profit is shared out depends on the terms of the partnership agreement. The steps to take are:

(a) establish how much the net profit is;

(b) appropriate interest on capital and salaries first. Both of these items are an appropriation of profit and are not expenses in the P & L account;

(c) if partners agree to pay interest on their drawings during the year,

   Debit   Current accounts
   Credit   Appropriation of profit account.

These nominal interest charges in effect provide an addition to the net profit, for sharing out between partners;

(d) residual profits: the difference between net profit (plus any interest charged on drawings) and appropriations for interest on capital and salaries is the residual profit. This is shared out between partners in the profit-sharing ratio;

(e) each partner's share of profits is credited to his current account;

(f) the balance on each partner's drawings account is debited to his current account;

(g) if there is a guarantee by one partner that another partner should receive a minimum annual income, and the appropriations of profit fail to provide this minimum amount, then the difference should be paid by the partner giving the guarantee, as follows:

Debit	Current account of partner giving the guarantee
Credit	Current account of partner receiving the guarantee.

19. In practice each partner's capital account will occupy a separate ledger account, as will his current account etc. For examination purposes however, it is customary to present the details of these accounts side by side, in columnar form, to save time. The examples which follow in this text use the columnar form; they might also ignore the breakdown of net assets employed (fixed, current assets, etc) to help clarify and simplify the illustrations.

First example: partnership accounts

20. Locke, Niece and Munster are in partnership with an agreement to share profits in the ratio 3:2:1. They also agree that:

(a) all three should receive interest at 12% on capital;
(b) Munster should receive a salary of £6,000 per annum;
(c) interest will be charged on drawings at the rate of 10% per annum;
(d) Locke has guaranteed Niece a minimum annual income of £8,000, gross of interest on drawings.

The balance sheet of the partnership as at 31 December 19X5 revealed the following:

	£	£
Capital accounts		
Locke	20,000	
Niece	8,000	
Munster	6,000	
		34,000
Current accounts		
Locke	3,500	
Niece	(700)	
Munster	1,800	
		4,600
Loan account (Locke)		6,000
Capital employed to finance net fixed assets and working capital		44,600

Drawings made during the year to 31 December 19X6 were:

Locke	£6,000
Niece	£4,000
Munster	£7,000

The net profit for the year to 31 December 19X6 was £24,530 before deducting loan interest.

Required: prepare the profit and loss appropriation account for the year to 31 December 19X6, and the partners' capital accounts and current accounts.

Solution

21. The interest rate on the loan by Locke is not specified and so presumably is 5% since this is the rate laid down in section 24 of the Partnership Act 1890, in the absence of any overriding agreement that a different interest rate should apply.

22. The interest payable by each partner on their drawings during the year is calculated on the assumption that the drawings were made at an even rate throughout the course of the year. Since the annual interest rate on drawings in advance of the year end is 10%, an 'average' interest rate of 5% should be applied to the total amount of drawings.

		£
Locke	5% of £6,000	300
Niece	5% of £4,000	200
Munster	5% of £7,000	350
		850

These payments are debited to the current accounts and credited to the profit and loss appropriation account.

23. We can now begin to work out the appropriation of profits.

		£	£
Net profit less loan interest (deducted in P & L a/c – £24,530 – £300)			24,230
Interest on drawings			850
			25,080
Munster salary			6,000
			19,080
Interest on capital:			
Locke	(12% of £20,000)	2,400	
Niece	(12% of £8,000)	960	
Munster	(12% of £6,000)	720	
			4,080
			15,000
Residual profits:			
Locke (3)		7,500	
Niece (2)		5,000	
Munster (1)		2,500	
			15,000

The total income of Niece's gross of interest
on drawings is:

	£
Interest on capital	960
Residual profits	5,000
	5,960

Since this is £2,040 less than the guaranteed minimum income for Niece of £8,000, Locke must pay
£2,040 to Niece. This is accomplished by means of a transfer between their current accounts.

Solution

24.

LOCKE, NIECE AND MUNSTER
PROFIT AND LOSS APPROPRIATION ACCOUNT
FOR THE YEAR ENDED 31 DECEMBER 19X6

	£	£		£	£
Salaries – Munster		6,000	Net profit b/d		24,230
Interest on capital			Interest on drawings:		
Locke	2,400		Current account of		
Niece	960		Locke	300	
Munster	720		Niece	200	
		4,080	Munster	350	
Residual profits					850
Locke	7,500				
Niece	5,000				
Munster	2,500				
		15,000			
		25,080			25,080

PARTNERS' CURRENT ACCOUNTS

	Locke £	Niece £	Munster £		Locke £	Niece £	Munster £
Balance b/f		700		Balance b/f	3,500		1,800
Interest on				Loan interest	300		
drawings	300	200	350	Interest on			
Transfer to				capital	2,400	960	720
Niece	2,040			Salary			6,000
Drawings	6,000	4,000	7,000	Residual			
Balance c/f	5,360	3,100	3,670	profits	7,500	5,000	2,500
				Transfer from			
				Locke		2,040	
	13,700	8,000	11,020		13,700	8,000	11,020

PARTNERS' CAPITAL ACCOUNTS

	Locke	Niece	Munster
Balance b/f	20,000	8,000	6,000

25. The balance sheet of the partners as at 31 December 19X6 would be:

	£	£
Capital accounts		
Locke	20,000	
Niece	8,000	
Munster	6,000	
		34,000
Current accounts		
Locke	5,360	
Niece	3,100	
Munster	3,670	
		12,130
		46,130
Net assets		
As at 31 December 19X5		44,600
Added during the year (applying the business equation, this is the difference between net profits and drawings = (£24,230 - £17,000))		7,230
Add loan interest added to Locke's current account and not paid out		300
As at 31 December 19X6		52,130
Less long term creditor - Locke (loan)		(6,000)
		46,130

A second example: changing the partnership agreement

26. It might be useful now to look at a more complete example of partnership accounts, to show how the normal accounting methods for recording assets and liabilities and computing net profit are applied. The example will also explain how changes in the terms of the partnership agreement should be dealt with.

Light and Dark have been trading in partnership for several years. Up to 30 June 19X8 the partnership agreement provided for Dark to be credited with a salary of £3,000 per annum, interest on partners' capital accounts at 5% per annum, and the balance of the net profit/loss to be divided between Light and Dark in the ratio 3:2.

However, as from 1 July 19X8, it was agreed that Dark's salary would be £4,000 per annum, interest on partners' capital accounts would be increased to 10% per annum and the balance of the net profit divided equally between Light and Dark.

The following trial balance as at 31 December 19X8 has been extracted from the books of the partnership:

	£	£
Gross profit for the year		20,000
Administrative expenses	8,000	
Capital accounts:		
Light - at 31 December 19X7		40,000
introduced 30 June 19X8		10,000
Dark - at 31 December 19X7		30,000
Current accounts - at 31 December 19X7		
Light	1,000	
Dark		4,000
Drawings: Light	3,000	
Dark	2,000	
Fixed assets - at cost	66,000	
Provision for depreciation of fixed assets at		
31 December 19X7		18,000
Stock in trade, at cost	12,300	
Trade debtors	27,000	
Balance at bank	9,700	
Trade creditors		7,000
	129,000	129,000

After preparing the above trial balance, it transpires that:

(a) The correct value of the partnership's stock in trade at 31 December 19X7 was £20,000, whilst it had been included in the accounts for the year ended 31 December 19X7 at £15,000.

(b) A loan of £10,000 to the partnership from Light on 30 June 19X8 has been credited to Light's capital account. The partners have agreed that the rate of interest applicable to the loan is 12% per annum.

(c) Effect has not been given to the decision to create a provision for doubtful debts of 2% of trade debtors as at 31 December 19X8.

(d) It is partnership policy to provide for depreciation annually at the rate of 10% on the cost of fixed assets held at the end of each financial year.

(e) It can be assumed that the following arose at a uniform rate throughout 19X8:
    (i)   gross profit;
    (ii)   administrative expense;
    (iii) depreciation expenses;
    (iv) provision for doubtful debts.

Required:

(a) The journal entries necessary to adjust for the corrected value of stock in trade at 31 December 19X7. (Narratives are required.)

(b) The partnership profit and loss appropriation account for the year ended 31 December 19X8, the partners' current accounts for the year ended 31 December 19X8 and the partnership balance sheet as at 31 December 19X8.

(c) State briefly the advantages and disadvantages of regarding the £10,000 paid into the partnership on 30 June 19X8, by Light as a loan rather than an addition to capital as far as:
(i) Light; and
(ii) Dark are concerned.

Discussion and solution

27. The net profit should be calculated first, and the appropriation of profits afterwards.

The trial balance has been prepared after completing the trading account for the year to 31 December 19X8. We know this because the trial balance includes an entry for the gross profit earned. This means that the balance on the stock account is the closing stock figure. (When a trial balance is prepared before the trading account is put together, the balance on the stock account is the opening stock figure.)

28. An error has occurred in the valuation of opening stocks, and this must be corrected. The opening stocks were undervalued by £5,000, which means that the cost of sales for 19X8 has been understated by £5,000. This in turn means that the gross profit has been overstated by £5,000.

At the same time, however, the profit of the previous year had been understated by £5,000, because the closing stocks at 31 December 19X7 were undervalued in the accounts for the year ended 31 December 19X7. In other words, the profits for 19X7 should be £5,000 higher and the profits for 19X8 £5,000 lower. The correction should be made as follows:

(a) add £5,000 to the partners' profits b/f – ie to their current accounts – thereby increasing 19X7 profits by £5,000;
(b) add £5,000 to the cost of sales in 19X8, thereby reducing 19X8 profits by £5,000.

29. The journal entry is:

	Debit £	Credit £
Cost of sales	5,000	
Current accounts:		
Light (3)		3,000
Dark (2)		2,000

The correction of an error in the stock valuation at 31 December 19X7 only discovered when preparing the 19X8 accounts.

30.   LIGHT AND DARK – PROFIT AND LOSS ACCOUNT
                    FOR THE YEAR ENDED 31 DECEMBER 19X8

	£	£
Gross profit £(20,000 – 5,000)		15,000
Administrative expenses	8,000	
Depreciation (10% of £66,000)	6,600	
Increase in provision for doubtful debts (2% of £27,000)	540	
Loan interest – Light (6 months x 12% pa x £10,000)	600	
		15,740
Net loss		(740)

31. The terms of the partnership agreement changed on 30 June 19X8 and so we must divide the loss for the year into:

    (a) profit or loss for the first 6 months to 30 June 19X8;
    (b) profit or loss for the second 6 months to 31 December 19X8.

    Of the items in the P & L account, all but loan interest on Light's new loan from 30 June 19X8 arose evenly throughout the year.

	Total	1st 6 months to 30 June		2nd 6 months to 31 December	
	£	£		£	
Gross profit	15,000	7,500		7,500	
Expenses, excluding loan interest	(15,140)	(7,570)		(7,570)	
Loan interest	(600)			(600)	
Net loss	(740)	(70)		(670)	
Dark – salary		(1,500)	(6 months)	(2,000)	(6 months)
Interest on capital					
Light (on £40,000)		(1,000)	(6 months at 5%)	(2,000)	(6 months at 10%)
Dark (on £30,000)		(750)	(6 months at 5%)	(1,500)	(6 months at 10%)
Residual loss		(3,200)		(6,170)	
Shared by Light	(3)	1,992	(1)	3,085	
Dark	(2)	1,328	(1)	3,085	
		3,320		6,170	

32. These calculations illustrate that when the terms of the partnership agreement change during the course of an accounting year:

    (a) the net profit for the year must be split pro rata between the pre-change and post-change period, according to when during the year the change occurred, but with any items of expense relating specifically to the pre-change or post-change period charged wholly to that period (as with loan interest in our example);

    (b) the appropriation of the net profit (or loss) should similarly be applied to the pre-change and post-change periods, according to the length (in months) of each period.

    Since the change occurred exactly in mid-year in this problem, the appropriation of the profit/loss is applied on a half yearly basis to the pre-change and post-change periods.

33. The profit and loss appropriation account can now be drawn up:

LIGHT AND DARK
PROFIT AND LOSS APPROPRIATION ACCOUNT
FOR THE YEAR ENDED 31 DECEMBER 19X8

	£	£		£	£
Net loss b/d		740	Residual losses		
Salary - Dark		3,500	Light £(1,992+3,085)	5,077	
Interest on capital			Dark £(1,328+3,085)	4,413	
Light	3,000				9,490
Dark	2,250				
		5,250			
		9,490			9,490

34. The partners' current accounts should include the adjustment due to the stock valuation error.

PARTNERS' CURRENT ACCOUNTS

	Light £	Dark £		Light £	Dark £
Balance b/f	1,000		Balance b/f		4,000
Residual losses	5,077	4,413	Stock valuation	3,000	2,000
Drawings	3,000	2,000	Salary		3,500
			Interest on capital	3,000	2,250
			Interest on loan	600	
Balance c/d		5,337	Balance c/d	2,477	
	9,077	11,750		9,077	11,750
Balance b/d	2,477		Balance b/d		5,337

Note: it is assumed that the interest on Light's loan is added to his current account, and not paid out separately.

35.

LIGHT AND DARK
BALANCE SHEET AS AT 31 DECEMBER 19X8

	£	£	£
Fixed assets at cost			66,000
Less provision for depreciation £(18,000 + 6,600)			24,600
			41,400
Current assets			
Stock in trade		12,300	
Trade debtors	27,000		
Less provision for doubtful debts	540		
		26,460	
Balance at bank		9,700	
		48,460	
Current liabilities			
(amounts falling due within 1 year)			
Trade creditors		7,000	
Net current assets			41,460
			82,860
Loan capital - Light			(10,000)
			72,860

	£	£
Capital accounts:		
Light	40,000	
Dark	30,000	
		70,000
Current accounts:		
Light	(2,477)	
Dark	5,337	
		2,860
		72,860

36. The significance of having a loan rather than an addition to capital is that:

   (a) if the partnership is dissolved, Light will be entitled to repayment of the loan before the partners share out any residual income from the sale of the business assets;

   (b) a different interest rate can be applied to the loan (perhaps a commercial rate) compared with the interest applied to the capital accounts of the partners.

Minimum profit shares

37. It occasionally happens that a partner is guaranteed a minimum profit share. If this exceeds the share of profit which the partner would otherwise receive, the remaining profit (after appropriation of the minimum share) is split between the remaining partners in the appropriate ratio. For example, A B and C share profits in the ratio 3:2:2 and C is entitled to a minimum share of £6,000. The current profit available for appropriation is £19,000. Of this C must have £6,000. The remaining £13,000 is split between A and B, in the ratio A:B ie 3:2. A therefore receives £7,800 and B £5,200.

Summary of the chapter

38.
> - The two examples in this chapter have been used to illustrate the preparation of partnership accounts, and especially the terms of a partnership agreement. Further practice is advisable for you, and you should attempt the illustrative questions at the end of this chapter.
>
> - Once you have understood the basic principles for appropriating profits, you might find that you can adapt your basic knowledge to deal with particular situations. You should perhaps remember in particular, however, the terms set out by the Partnership Act 1890 (section 24) in the absence of any alternative agreement, ie
>
>   (a) no salaries or interest on capital should be credited to partners;
>
>   (b) profits and losses (whether capital or revenue) should be shared equally between the partners;
>
>   (c) if a partner makes a loan to the business then interest will be at 5% per annum, and charged as an expense in the profit and loss account, not as an appropriation of profit.
>
>   You might need to remember these rules, especially (c).

TEST YOUR KNOWLEDGE

Numbers in brackets refer to paragraphs of this chapter

1. What is 'joint and several liability'?   (2)

2. Describe two ways in which the accounts of a partnership differ from those of a sole trader.   (8)

3. What are the differences between a partner's current account and his capital account?   (12)

4. Interest paid on loans made by partners to the business is an appropriation of profit. True or false?   (16)

Now try questions 5-7 at the end of this section

Chapter 22

LIMITED COMPANIES

The purpose of this chapter is:

- to describe the statutory framework regulating the accounts of limited companies

- to explain certain features peculiar to the accounts of limited companies (share capital; dividends; debentures; reserves; contingent liabilities)

- to illustrate the preparation of limited company accounts

Introduction

1. So far, this study text has dealt mainly with the accounts of businesses in general. In this chapter we shall turn our attention to the accounts of limited companies. As we should expect, the accounting rules and conventions for recording the business transactions of limited companies and then preparing their final accounts, are much the same as for sole traders. For example, companies will have a cash book, sales day book, purchase day book, journal, sales ledger, purchase ledger and nominal ledger etc. They also prepare a profit and loss account annually, and a balance sheet at the end of the accounting year.

2. There are, however, some differences in the accounts of limited companies, of which the following are perhaps the most significant.

   (a) The legislation governing the activities of limited companies is very extensive. Amongst other things, the Companies Acts define certain minimum accounting records which must be maintained by companies; they specify that the annual accounts of a company must be filed with the Registrar of Companies and so available for public inspection; and they contain detailed requirements on the minimum information which must be disclosed in a company's accounts. Businesses which are not limited companies (non-incorporated businesses) enjoy comparative freedom from statutory regulation.

   (b) The owners of a company (its *members* or *shareholders*) may be very numerous. Their capital is shown differently from that of a sole trader; and similarly the appropriation account of a company is different.

Limited liability

3. Sole traders and partnerships are, with some significant exceptions, generally fairly small concerns. The amount of capital involved may be modest, and the proprietors of the business usually participate in managing it. Their liability for the debts of the business is unlimited, which means that if the business runs up debts that it is unable to pay, the proprietors will

become personally liable for the unpaid debts, and would be required, if necessary, to sell their private possessions in order to repay them. For example, if a sole trader has some capital in his business, but the business now owes £40,000 which it cannot repay, the trader might have to sell his house to raise the money to pay off his business debts.

4. Limited companies offer limited liability to their owners. This means that the maximum amount that an owner stands to lose in the event that the company becomes insolvent and cannot pay off its debts, is the capital in the business. Thus limited liability is a major advantage of turning a business into a limited company. However, in practice, banks will normally seek personal guarantees from shareholders before making loans or granting an overdraft facility and so the advantage of limited liability is lost to a small owner managed business. There are other disadvantages too. In comparison with sole trader businesses and partnerships, there is a significantly increased administrative and financial burden. This arises from:

- compliance with the Companies Act 1985, notably in having to prepare annual accounts and have them audited, in keeping statutory registers and having to publish accounts etc;

- having to comply with all SSAPs;

- formation and annual registration costs.

5. As a business grows, it needs more capital to finance its operations, and significantly more than the people currently managing the business can provide themselves. One way of obtaining more capital is to invite investors from outside the business to invest in the ownership or equity of the business. These new co-owners would not usually be expected to help with managing the business. To such investors, limited liability is very attractive.

Investments are always risky undertakings, but with limited liability the investor knows the maximum amount that he stands to lose when he puts some capital into a company.

Public and private companies

6. There are two classes of limited company:

(a) private companies. These have the word 'limited' at the end of their name. Being private, they cannot invite members of the public to invest in their equity (ownership);

(b) public companies. These are much fewer in number than private companies, but are generally much larger in size. They have the words 'public limited company' - shortened to PLC or plc (or the Welsh language equivalent) at the end of their name. Public limited companies can invite members of the general public to invest in their equity, and the 'shares' of these companies may be traded on The Stock Exchange.

The accounting records of limited companies

7. There is a legal requirement for companies in the UK to keep accounting records which are sufficient to show and explain the company's transactions. The records should:

(a) disclose the company's current financial position at any time;

(b) contain

    (i)   day-to-day entries of money received and spent;
    (ii) a record of the company's assets and liabilities;
    (iii) where the company deals in goods:
        (1) a statement of stocks held at the year end, and supporting stocktaking sheets;
        (2) with the exception of retail sales, statements of goods bought and sold which identify the sellers and buyers of those goods;

(c) enable the directors of the company to ensure that the final accounts of the company give a true and fair view of the company's profit or loss and balance sheet position.

Registers: the statutory books

8.   A company must also keep a number of registers. These include:

(a) a register of members;
(b) a register of shareholders' 5 per cent interests;
(c) a register of charges and a register of debenture holders;
(d) a register of directors and company secretaries;
(e) a register of directors' interests (in shares or debentures of the company).

These registers are known collectively as the (non-accounting) statutory books of the company.

Register of members

9.   The members of a company are its shareholders. The register of members is a record which shows:

(a) the names and addresses of the members, the number of shares held by each member, the amount paid to the company for those shares and the nominal value of those shares;

(b) the class of shares held by the member (eg preference shares, non-voting ordinary shares etc);

(c) the date on which the member was entered in the register as a member and the date on which he acquired extra shares, where this occurs;

(d) the date on which any person ceased to be a member. Past members must be kept on the register for at least 20 years.

The transfer of shares from one person to another (eg by sales) will also be recorded in this register, showing the date of transfer and number and nominal value of the shares transferred.

The register must be kept available for public inspection, at least two hours per day during business hours, and usually at the company's registered office.

10. A company should also keep a register of members who hold more than 5% of the total issued shares with unrestricted voting rights (ie voting ordinary shares). This is a 'register of shareholders' 5% interests'. The shareholder himself is obliged to notify the company that his holding of ordinary shares exceeds 5% of the total, and the company will then enter the fact in its register. However, it is proposed in the Companies Bill 1989 to reduce this percentage to 3%.

Register of debenture holders

11. Debentures are loans. Companies might raise loans by issuing debenture stock, which would be purchased by a number of different investors. A register of debenture holders should be kept by the company.

Register of charges

12. When a company borrows money, by issuing debentures or by borrowing from a bank, it will usually be required to offer some security for the loan. For example, the security for a debenture loan might be some freehold property owned by the company, so that if the company failed to keep up its interest payments, or to pay back the loan when repayment becomes due, the lender could set in motion procedures which might end up with the sale of the property to pay back the loan. Security provided in this way gives rise to a charge on the assets which are offered as a security. A company must keep a register of any such charges on its assets.

The capital of limited companies

13. The proprietors' capital in a limited company consists of share capital. When a company is set up for the first time, it issues shares, which are paid for by investors, who then become shareholders of the company. Shares are denominated in units of 25 pence, 50 pence, £1 or whatever seems appropriate. The 'face value' of the shares is called their nominal value.

14. For example, when a company is set up with a share capital of, say, £100,000, it may be decided to issue:

     (a)   100,000 shares of £1 each nominal value; or
     (b)   200,000 shares of 50p each; or
     (c)   400,000 shares of 25p each; or
     (d)   250,000 shares of 40p each etcetera.

     The amount at which the shares are issued may exceed their nominal value. For example, a company might issue 100,000 £1 shares at a price of £1.20 each. Subscribers will then pay a total of £120,000. The issued share capital of the company would be shown in its accounts at nominal value, £100,000; the excess of £20,000 is described not as share capital, but as *share premium*.

Authorised, issued, called-up and paid-up share capital

15. A distinction must be made between authorised, issued, called-up and paid-up share capital.

     (a)   *Authorised* (or *nominal*) capital is the maximum amount of share capital that a company is empowered to issue. The amount of authorised share capital varies from company to company, and can change by agreement.

           For example, a company's authorised share capital might be 5,000,000 ordinary shares of £1 each. This would then be the maximum number of shares it could issue, unless the maximum were to be changed by agreement.

     (b)   *Issued* capital is the nominal amount of share capital that has been issued to shareholders. The amount of issued capital cannot exceed the amount of authorised capital.

Continuing the example above, the company with authorised share capital of 5,000,000 ordinary shares of £1 might have issued 4,000,000 shares. This would leave it the option to issue 1,000,000 more shares at some time in the future.

When share capital is issued, shares are allotted to shareholders. The term 'allotted' share capital means the same thing as issued share capital.

(c) *Called-up* capital. When shares are issued or allotted, a company does not always expect to be paid the full amount for the shares at once. It might instead call up only a part of the issue price, and wait until a later time before it calls up the remainder.

For example, if a company allots 400,000 ordinary shares of £1, it might call up only, say, 75 pence per share. The issued share capital would be £400,000, but the called up share capital would only be £300,000.

(d) *Paid-up* capital. Like everyone else, investors are not always prompt or reliable payers. When capital is called up, some shareholders might delay their payment (or even default on payment). Paid-up capital is the amount of called-up capital that has been paid.

For example, if a company issues 400,000 ordinary shares of £1 each, calls up 75 pence per share, and receives payments of £290,000, we would have:

Allotted or issued capital	£400,000
Called-up capital	£300,000
Paid-up capital	£290,000
Called-up capital not paid	£10,000

The balance sheet of the company would then include called up capital not paid on the assets side, as follows:

	£
Called-up capital not paid	10,000
Cash (called-up capital paid)	290,000
	300,000
Called-up share capital	
400,000 ordinary shares of £1,	
with 75p per share called up.	300,000

The board of directors

16. A company might have a large number of shareholders, or only a few. No matter how many there are, they delegate authority for the day-to-day management of the company to its directors, who are directly responsible to the shareholders for what they do. (In some companies, the directors of the company and its shareholders might be the same people.) There must also be a company secretary. Company policy is decided at regular meetings of the board of directors.

17. It is important to note that whereas the salary of a sole trader or a partner in a partnership is not a charge in the P & L account, but is an appropriation of profit, the salary of a director is a P & L account expense, even when the director is also a shareholder of the company.

18. It would be wrong to give the impression that all companies are large-scale with many shareholders. The vast majority of UK companies are in fact small and family-owned. There are many good reasons why a sole trader (say Alfred Newbegin Tools) might choose to set up his own company (Newbegin Tools Ltd). These include limited personal liability and various tax advantages. Such a company would typically have one director (Alf) and his wife (Mabel) would be the company secretary. There would be two shareholders (Alf and Mabel) and board meetings would tend to be held during the commercial breaks on television or over breakfast. In this case it would be true to say that the providers of capital would also be running the business (as is normal with a sole trader) but Alf and Mabel as individuals would now be distinct from the business, because a company is a 'person' in its own right in the eyes of the law. Alf's salary, formerly an appropriation of profit, would now be a charge against company profits.

Dividends

19. Shareholders who are also directors of their company will receive a salary as a director. They are also entitled to a share of the profits made by the company.

Profits paid out to shareholders are called dividends. Dividends are appropriations of profit after tax. A company might pay dividends in two stages during the course of their accounting year:

(a) in mid year, after the half-year financial results are known, the company might pay an interim dividend;
(b) at the end of the year, the company might pay a further final dividend.

The total dividend for the year is the sum of the interim and the final dividend. (Not all companies by any means pay an interim dividend. Interim dividends are, however, commonly paid out by public limited companies).

At the end of an accounting year, a company's directors will have proposed a final dividend payment, but this will not yet have been paid. This means that the final dividend should be appropriated out of profits and shown as a current liability in the balance sheet.

20. The terminology of dividend payments can be confusing, since they may be expressed either in the form, as 'x pence per share' or as 'y per cent'. In the latter case, the meaning is always 'y per cent of the *nominal* value of the shares in issue'. For example, suppose a company's issued share capital consists of 100,000 50p ordinary shares which were issued at a premium of 10p per share. The company's balance sheet would include the following:

Called up share capital: 100,000 50p ordinary shares   £50,000
Share premium account (100,000 x 10p)   £10,000

If the directors wish to pay a dividend of £5,000, they may propose either:

(a) a dividend of 5p per share (100,000 x 5p = £5,000); or
(b) a dividend of 10% (10% x £50,000 = £5,000).

Ordinary shares and preference shares

21. At this stage it is relevant to distinguish between the two types of shares most often encountered, preference shares and ordinary shares.

    Preference shares were until recently rather old-fashioned and rarely issued; but they are currently having one of their occasional resurgences of popularity and cumulative preference shares have been issued to fund many recent takeovers. Preference shares carry the right to a final dividend which is expressed as a percentage of their nominal value: eg a 6% £1 preference share carries a right to an annual dividend of 6p. Preference dividends have priority over ordinary dividends; in other words, if the directors of a company wish to pay a dividend (which they are not obliged to do) they must pay any preference dividend first. Otherwise, no ordinary dividend may be paid.

    The rights attaching to preference shares are set out in the company's constitution. They may vary from company to company, but typically:

    (a) preference shareholders have a priority right over ordinary shareholders to a return of their capital if the company goes into liquidation;

    (b) preference shares do not carry a right to vote;

    (c) if the preference shares are *cumulative*, it means that before a company can pay an ordinary dividend it must not only pay the current year's preference dividend, but must also make good any arrears of preference dividends unpaid in previous years.

22. *Ordinary shares* are by far the most common. They carry no right to a fixed dividend but are entitled to all profits left after payment of any preference dividend. Generally however, only a part of such remaining profits is distributed, the rest being kept in reserve (see below). The amount of ordinary dividends fluctuates although there is a general expectation that it will increase from year to year. Should the company be wound up, any surplus is shared between the ordinary shareholders. Ordinary shares normally carry voting rights.

    Ordinary shareholders are thus the effective owners of a company. They own the 'equity' of the business, and any reserves of the business (described later) belong to them. Ordinary shareholders are sometimes referred to as equity shareholders. Preference shareholders are in many ways more like creditors (although legally they are members, not creditors). It should be emphasised however that the precise rights attached to preference and ordinary shares vary from company to company; the distinctions noted above are generalisations.

Dividends, ordinary shares and preference shares: example

23. Garden Gloves Ltd has issued 50,000 ordinary shares of 50 pence each and 20,000 7% preference shares of £1 each. Its profits after taxation for the year to 30 September 19X5 were £8,400. The board of directors has decided to pay an ordinary dividend (ie a dividend on ordinary shares) which is 50% of profits after tax and preference dividend.

    Required: show the amount in total of dividends and of retained profits, and calculate the dividend per share on ordinary shares.

Solution

24. Profits after tax and preference dividend are called *earnings*, and an important measure of company performance is the *earnings per share*. Although not required by the problem, the earnings per share (EPS) is also shown below.

	£
Profit after tax	8,400
Preference dividend (7% of £1 x 20,000)	1,400
Earnings (profit after tax and preference dividend)	7,000
Earnings per share (÷ 50,000) 14 pence	
Ordinary dividend (50% of earnings)	3,500
Retained profit (also 50% of earnings)	3,500

The ordinary dividend is 7 pence per share (£3,500 ÷ 50,000 ordinary shares).

The appropriation of profit would be shown as follows:

	£	£
Profit after tax		8,400
Dividends: preference	1,400	
ordinary	3,500	
		4,900
Retained profit		3,500

The market value of shares

25. The nominal value of shares will be different from their market value, which is the price at which someone is prepared to purchase shares in the company from an existing shareholder. If Mr A owns 1,000 £1 shares in Z Ltd he may sell them to B for £1.60 each.

This transfer of existing shares does not affect A Ltd's own financial position in any way whatsoever, and apart from changing the register of members, Z Ltd does not have to bother with the sale by Mr A to Mr B at all. There are certainly no accounting entries to be made for the share sale.

26. Shares in private companies do not change hands very often, hence their market value is often hard to estimate. Public companies are usually (not always) quoted; a quoted company is one whose shares are traded on The Stock Exchange and it is the market value of the shares which is quoted.

The final accounts of limited companies

27. The preparation and publication of the final accounts of limited companies in the UK are governed by the Companies Act 1985 which consolidates, and replaces, the provisions of the Companies Acts 1948, 1967, 1976 and 1981. At this stage in your studies, you do not have to learn the detailed regulations laid down by this Act. However, the general format of the balance sheet and profit and loss account of a limited company will be shown below with some simplifications, in order to introduce certain assets and liabilities which we have not come across before in earlier chapters of this study text.

28. The format of a limited company balance sheet is shown below.

TYPICAL COMPANY LIMITED BALANCE SHEET
AS AT....

	£	£	£
Fixed assets			
Intangible assets			
Development costs		X	
Concessions, patents, licences, trademarks		X	
Goodwill		X̲	
			X
Tangible assets			
Land and buildings		X	
Plant and machinery		X	
Fixtures, fittings, tools and equipment		X	
Motor vehicles		X̲	
			X
Investments			X̲
			X
Current assets			
Stocks		X	
Debtors and prepayments		X	
Investments		X	
Cash at bank and in hand		X̲	
		X	
Creditors: amounts falling due within one year (ie current liabilities)			
Debenture loans			
(nearing their redemption date)	X		
Bank overdraft and loans	X		
Trade creditors	X		
Bills of exchange payable	X		
Taxation	X		
Accruals	X		
Proposed dividend	X̲		
		(X)	
Net current assets			X̲
Total assets less current liabilities			X
Creditors : amounts falling due after more than one year			
Debenture loans		X	
Taxation		X̲	
			(X̲)
			X̲̲

	£	£
Capital and reserves		
Called up share capital		
Ordinary shares	X	
Preference shares	X	
		X
Reserves		
Share premium account	X	
Revaluation reserve	X	
Other reserves	X	
Profit and loss account (retained profits)	X	
		X
		X

29. The profit and loss account of a company might have a format roughly similar to the one below.

TYPICAL COMPANY LIMITED
Profit and loss account for the year ended...

	£	£
Turnover		X
Cost of sales		(X)
Gross profit		X
Distribution costs	X	
Administrative expenses	X	
		(X)
		X
Other operating income	X	
Income from fixed asset investments	X	
Other interest receivable and similar income	X	
		X
		X
Interest payable		(X)
Profit before taxation		X
Tax		(X)
Profit after tax		X
Dividends: Preference	X	
Ordinary	X	
		(X)
Retained profit for the year		X
Profit and loss account as at the beginning of the year		X
Profit and loss account as at the end of the year		X

Intangible fixed assets

30. Intangible fixed assets represent amounts of money paid by a business to acquire benefits of a long-term nature. Goodwill and deferred development expenditure are two intangible assets which were discussed in detail in an earlier chapter.

31. If a company purchases some patent rights, or a concession from another business, or the right to use a trademark, the cost of the purchase can be accounted for as the purchase of an intangible fixed asset. These assets must then be amortised (depreciated) over their economic life.

Tangible fixed assets

32. As with any other type of business, tangible fixed assets are shown in the balance sheet at their net book value (ie at cost less provision for depreciation). Sometimes, a fixed asset, such as a building, might be revalued to a current market value. Depreciation would then be based on the revalued amount, and the balance sheet value of the asset would be the revalued amount less provision for depreciation on the revalued amount.

Investments

33. Investments are fixed assets if the company intends to hold on to them for a long time, and current assets if they are only likely to be held for a short time before being sold.

Current liabilities

34. The term 'creditors: amounts falling due within one year' was introduced by the Companies Act 1981 as an alternative phrase meaning 'current liabilities'. It is therefore likely that you will come across this term increasingly often as you progress through your accountancy studies.

Debenture loans

35. Limited companies may issue debenture stock (debentures) or loan stock. These are long-term liabilities described on the balance sheet as loan capital. They are different from share capital in the following ways:

   (a) shareholders are members of a company, while providers of loan capital are creditors;

   (b) shareholders receive dividends (appropriations of profit) whereas the holders of loan capital are entitled to a fixed rate of interest (an expense charged against revenue);

   (c) loan capital holders can take legal action against a company if their interest is not paid when due, whereas shareholders cannot enforce the payment of dividends;

   (d) debentures or loan stock are often secured on company assets, whereas shares are not.

36. The holder of loan capital is generally in a less risky position than the shareholder. He has greater security, although his income is fixed and cannot grow, unlike ordinary dividends. As remarked earlier, preference shares are in practice very similar to loan capital, not least because the preference dividend is normally fixed.

37. Interest is calculated on the nominal value of loan capital, regardless of its market value. If a company has £700,000 (nominal value) 12% debentures in issue, interest of £84,000 will be charged in the profit and loss account per year. Interest is usually paid half-yearly; examination questions often require an accrual to be made for interest due at the year-end.

   For example, if a company has £700,000 of 12% debentures in issue, pays interest on 30 June and 31 December each year, and ends its accounting year on 30 September, there would be an accrual of three months' unpaid interest (3/12 x £84,000) = £21,000 at the end of each accounting year that the debentures are still in issue.

Redeemable debentures

38. When a company issues debentures, it is in effect raising a loan from investors. Although some debentures are irredeemable, which means that the loan does not have to be paid back ever, most debenture stock is redeemable. Redeemable debentures are issued for a given period of time, after which the company must pay back the money it has borrowed. When they are redeemable 'at par', a repayment of £100 must be made per £100 of debentures in issue. Sometimes they are redeemable at a premium - say, £105 to be paid per £100 of debentures in issue, which would result in a premium on redemption of 5%.

The redemption date for debentures is published in a company's accounts. For example, debentures may be shown as

10% debenture stock   2000 - 2004

This means that the stock will be redeemed at any time from the year 2000 (at the option of the company) but at the latest must be redeemed in the year 2004.

As the redemption date draws near, and is less than one year away, the debentures would switch from being a long-term liability of the company to a current liability.

Taxation

39. Companies pay *corporation tax* on the profits they earn. Small companies pay tax at the rate of 25% on their taxable profits, and large companies pay 35%. Note that because a company has a separate legal personality, its tax is included in its accounts. An unincorporated business would not show income tax in its accounts, as it would not be a business expense but the personal affair of the proprietors.

(a) The charge for corporation tax on profits for the year is shown as a deduction from net profit, before appropriations.

(b) In the balance sheet, tax payable to the government is generally shown as a current liability as it is usually due nine months after the year end. However, some companies do not pay tax for over 12 months after the end of their accounting year. In these cases, the tax payable for the year just ended would be an amount falling due for payment in over one year, and so would be a long-term liability in the balance sheet. (This anomaly is currently being phased out.)

40. For example, suppose that a company incurs corporation tax as follows:

(a) For the year to 30 September 19X3   £150,000
(b) For the year to 30 September 19X4   £215,000

This company does not have to pay the tax until 1 January, 15 months after the end of its accounting year, so that

(a) the £150,000 owing for the year to 30 September 19X3 would be payable on 1 January 19X5;
(b) the £215,000 owing for the year to 30 September 19X4 would be payable on 1 January 19X6.

In the balance sheet of the company as at 30 September 19X4, there would be:

Creditors: amounts falling due within one year
    Tax (payable 1.1.X5)   £150,000

Creditors: amounts falling due after more than one year
    Tax (payable 1.1.X6)   £215,000

Overprovision of tax

41. When corporation tax on profits is calculated for the profit and loss account, the calculation is only an estimate of what the company thinks its tax liability will be. In subsequent dealings with the Inland Revenue, a different corporation tax charge might eventually be agreed.

The difference between the estimated tax on profits for one year and the actual tax charge finally agreed for the year is made an adjustment to taxation on profits in the following year.

If the tax on profits in 19X1 was:

(a) overestimated – the tax on profits in 19X2 will be reduced;
(b) underestimated – the tax on profits in 19X2 will be increased.

Overprovision of tax : example

42. Urals Ltd made a profit before tax of £150,000 in the year to 30 September 19X3 and of £180,000 in the following year (to 30 September 19X4).

The estimated corporation tax for the first year was £60,000 and in the second year was £75,000. The actual tax charge in the year to 30 September 19X3 was finally agreed with the Inland Revenue at £55,000.

Required: compute the charge for taxation in the year to 30 September 19X4.

Solution

43.

	To 30 September	
	19X3	*19X4*
	£	£
Estimate of tax on profits	60,000	75,000
Actual tax charge	55,000	
Overestimate of tax in 19X3	5,000	(5,000)
Tax charge in year to 30 September 19X4		70,000

The effect of this adjustment will be to increase profits in 19X4 by £5,000, to correct the 'error' in 19X3 when profits were reduced by £5,000 because of the overestimate of the tax charge.

Differences between the tax charge in the P & L account and tax payable in the balance sheet

44. The tax on profits in the P & L account and the tax payable in the balance sheet are not usually the same amount.

    One reason is because it can take over a year to agree the tax liability and but no under or overprovision can be calculated at the year end until the liability is agreed. For example, Bernard Ltd's accounts for the year ended 31 December 19X8 shows an estimated tax liability of £50,000. On 1 October 19X9, the company pays £45,000 to the Inland Revenue on account. This is the latest estimate of the liability. As at 31 December 19X9, the liability is not yet agreed with the Inland Revenue and so it would be imprudent to treat the £5,000 as an overprovision. It is therefore shown in the 19X9 accounts as a liability in addition to the 19X9 liability.

    Another reason for discrepancies between profit and loss account and balance sheet is worth explaining briefly at this stage in your studies. When a company pays a dividend to its shareholders, it must soon afterwards pay some tax to the Inland Revenue. This dividend-related tax is regarded as an advance payment of its corporation tax liability by the company, and it is therefore called advance corporation tax or ACT. Thus, if a company pays a dividend, and so has to pay ACT on the dividend, its corporation tax liability as at the end of the year will be the tax on profits for the year, less the ACT already *paid*. Any ACT due on a proposed dividend will be added to the corporation tax liability.

Ledger accounts and limited companies

45. Limited companies keep ledger accounts, and the only difference between the ledger accounts of companies and sole traders is the nature of some of the transactions, assets and liabilities for which accounts need to be kept.

    For example, there will be an account for each of the following items:

    (a) *Taxation*

        (i)   Tax charged against profits will be accounted for by:

                Debit   P & L account
                Credit   Taxation account.

        (ii)   The outstanding balance on the taxation account will be a liability in the balance sheet, until eventually paid, when the accounting entry would be:

                Debit   Taxation account
                Credit   Cash

    (b) *Dividends*
    A separate account will be kept for the dividends for each different class of shares (eg preference, ordinary).

        (i)   Dividends declared out of profits will be accounted for by

                Debit   P & L appropriation account
                Credit   Dividends payable account

                Dividends payable (but not yet paid) are a current liability.

(ii) When dividends are paid, we then have

Debit Dividends payable account
Credit Cash

(c) *Debenture loans*
Debenture loans being a long-term liability will be shown as a credit balance in a debenture loan account.

Interest payable on such loans is not credited to the loan account, but is credited to a separate creditors' account for interest until it is eventually paid: ie

Debit Interest account (an expense, chargeable against profits)
Credit Interest payable (creditors, and a current liability until eventually paid).

(d) *Share capital and reserves*
There will be a separate account for

(i) each different class of share capital (always a credit balance b/f);
(ii) each different type of reserve (nearly always a credit balance b/f).

We shall now turn our attention to these items in more detail.

Share capital and reserves

46. The net fixed assets of a company, plus the working capital (ie current assets minus current liabilities) minus the long-term liabilities, are 'financed' by the shareholders' capital.

47. Shareholders' capital consists of

(a) the nominal value of issued capital (minus any amounts not yet called up on issued shares); and
(b) reserves.

48. The share capital itself might consist of both ordinary shares and preference shares. All reserves, however, are owned by the ordinary shareholders, who own the 'equity' in the company.

Called-up share capital

49. A company's issued share capital is its called-up share capital, provided that there are no shares in issue which have so far only been partly called up.

This means that if a company has issued 200,000 ordinary shares of 50 pence each, and 50,000 10% preference shares of £1 each, all fully called up, the called up share capital in the balance sheet will be

	£
200,000 ordinary shares of 50p each	100,000
50,000 10% preference shares of £1 each	50,000
	150,000

Reserves

50. In the case of a sole trader, the proprietor's interest = net assets of the business, and in the case of a partnership, partners' funds = net assets. For a company the equation is:

$$\text{Shareholders' funds} = \text{net assets}$$

Furthermore:

$$\text{Shareholders' funds} = \text{share capital and reserves}$$

A company's share capital will remain fixed from year to year, unless new shares are issued. Reserves are difficult to define neatly since different reserves arise for different reasons, but it follows from the above that:

$$\text{Reserves} = \text{net assets minus share capital}$$

The total amount of reserves in a company varies, according to changes in the net assets of the business.

51. The typical balance sheet in paragraph 28 lists a number of reserves, although the list is not comprehensive.

52. A distinction should be made between:

    (a)   statutory reserves, which are reserves which a company is required to set up by law, and which are not available for the distribution of dividends;

    (b)   non-statutory reserves, which are reserves consisting of profits which are distributable as dividends, if the company so wishes.

Profit and loss reserve (retained profits)

53. The most significant non-statutory reserve is variously described as

    (a)   revenue reserve;
    (b)   retained profits;
    (c)   retained earnings;
    (d)   undistributed profits;
    (e)   profit and loss account;
    (f)   unappropriated profits.

54. These are profits earned by the company and not appropriated by dividends, taxation or transfer to another reserve account.

This reserve generally increases from year to year, as most companies do not distribute all their profits as dividends. Dividends can be paid from it: even if a loss is made in one particular year, a dividend can be paid from previous years' retained profits. For example, if a company makes a loss of £100,000 in one year, yet has unappropriated profits from previous years totalling £250,000, it can pay a dividend not exceeding £150,000. One reason for retaining some profit each year is to enable the company to pay dividends even when profits are low (or non-existent). Another reason is usually shortage of cash.

Very occasionally, you might come across a debit balance on the profit and loss account. This would indicate that the company has accumulated losses.

Other non-statutory reserves

55. The company directors may choose to set up other reserves. These may have a specific purpose (eg plant and machinery replacement reserve) or not (eg general reserve). The creation of these reserves usually indicates a general intention not to distribute the profits involved at any future date, although legally any such reserves, being non-statutory, remain available for the payment of dividends.

56. Profits are transferred to these reserves by making an appropriation out of profits, usually profits for the year. Typically, you might come across the following:

	£	£
Profit after taxation		100,000
Appropriations of profit:		
Dividend	60,000	
Transfer to general reserve	10,000	
		70,000
Retained profits for the year		30,000
Profit and loss reserve b/f		250,000
Profit and loss reserve c/f		280,000

57. There is no real significance about the creation of separate non-statutory reserves. After all, there is little difference between:

	£	£
Net assets:		3,500
Financed by		
Share capital		2,000
Reserves: General (distributable as dividend)	1,000	
Retained profits (distributable)	500	
		1,500
		3,500

and

	£
Net assets	3,500
Financed by	
Share capital	2,000
Reserves: retained profit (distributable)	1,500
	3,500

58. The establishment of a 'plant and machinery replacement reserve' (or something similar) indicates an intention by a company to keep funds in the business to replace its plant and machinery (over and above the provision for depreciation, perhaps because inflation is pushing up replacement costs). However, the reserve would still, legally, represent distributable profits, and the existence of such a reserve no more guarantees the company's ability to replace its fixed assets in the future than the depreciation charge in the P & L account, or accumulated provision for depreciation in the balance sheet.

The share premium account

59. There are a number of statutory (or capital) reserves, the most important of which at this stage is the share premium account. Section 130 of the Companies Act 1985 states that 'where a company issues shares at a premium, whether for cash or otherwise, a sum equal to.... the premiums on those shares shall be transferred to the share premium account'. By 'premium' is meant the difference between the issue price of the share and its nominal value. When a company is first incorporated (set up) the issue price of its shares will probably be the same as their nominal value and so there would be no share premium. If the company does well the market value of its shares will increase, but not the nominal value. The price of any new shares issued will be approximately their market value. The difference between cash received by the company and the nominal value of the new shares issued is transferred to the share premium account. For example, if X Ltd issues 1,000 £1 ordinary shares at £2.60 each the book entry will be:

		£	£
Debit	Cash	2,600	
Credit	Ordinary share capital		1,000
Credit	Share premium account		1,600

A share premium account only comes into being when a company issues shares at a price in excess of their nominal value. The market price of the shares, once they have been issued, has no bearing at all on the company's accounts, and so if their market price goes up or down, the share premium account would remain unaltered.

60. Once established, the share premium account constitutes capital of the company which cannot be paid out in dividends. The share premium account will increase in value if and when new shares are issued at a price above their nominal value. The share premium account can be 'used' – and so decrease in value – only in certain very limited ways, which are largely beyond the scope of your basic financial accounting syllabus. One use of the share premium account, however, is to 'finance' the issue of bonus shares, which are described later in this chapter.

61. The share premium account cannot be distributed as dividend under any circumstances. The reason for creating statutory reserves is to maintain the capital of the company. This capital 'base' provides some security for the company's creditors, bearing in mind that the liability of shareholders is limited in the event that the company cannot repay its debts. It would be most unjust – and illegal – for a company to pay its shareholders a dividend out of its base capital when it is not even able to pay back its debts.

Revaluation reserve

62. A revaluation reserve must be created when a company revalues one or more of its fixed assets. Revaluations frequently occur with freehold property, as the market value of property rises. The company's directors might wish to show a more 'reasonable' value of the asset in their balance sheet, to avoid giving a misleading impression about the financial position of the company.

63. When an asset is revalued, the difference between:

   (a) the revalued amount of the asset and
   (b) its net book value in the company's accounts before the revaluation takes place, is credited to a revaluation reserve.

Depreciation is subsequently charged on the revalued amount.

Example: revaluation reserve

64. X Ltd bought freehold land and buildings for £20,000 ten years ago; their net book value (after depreciation of the buildings) is now £19,300. A professional valuation of £390,000 has been given, and the directors wish to reflect this in the accounts.

65. The revaluation surplus is £390,000 - £19,300 = £370,700. The entry to be made is thus:

		£	£
Dr	Freehold property	370,700	
Cr	Revaluation reserve		370,700

The balance sheet will then include:

	£
Reserves	
Revaluation reserve	370,700
Fixed assets	
Freehold property (at valuation)	390,000

66. An unrealised profit (such as the £370,700 above) is generally not distributable, whereas a realised profit (ie if the property is actually sold for £390,000) usually is distributable.

Distinction between reserves and provisions

67. A reserve is an appropriation of distributable profits for a specific purpose (eg plant replacement) while a provision is an amount charged against revenue as an expense. A provision relates either to a diminution in the value of an asset (eg doubtful debtors) or a known liability (eg audit fees), the amount of which cannot be established with any accuracy. Provisions (for depreciation, doubtful debts etc) are dealt with in company accounts in the same way as in the accounts of other types of business.

Bonus issues

68. A company may wish to increase its share capital without needing to raise additional finance by issuing new shares. For example, a profitable company might expand from modest beginnings over a number of years. Its profitability would be reflected in large balances on its reserves, while its original share capital might look like that of a much smaller business.

69. It is open to such a company to re-classify some of its reserves as share capital. This is purely a paper exercise which raises no funds. Any reserve may be re-classified in this way, including a share premium account or other statutory reserve.

Example

70.
BUBBLES LIMITED
BALANCE SHEET (EXTRACT)

	£'000	£'000
Funds employed		
Share capital		
£1 ordinary shares (fully paid)		1,000
Reserves		
Share premium	500	
Undistributed profit	2,000	
		2,500
		3,500

Bubbles decided to make a '3 for 2' bonus issue (ie 3 new shares for every 2 already held).

	£'000	£'000
The double entry is		
Dr Share premium	500	
Dr Undistributed profit	1,000	
Cr Ordinary share capital		1,500

	£'000
After the issue the balance sheet is as follows:	
Share capital	
£1 ordinary shares (fully paid)	2,500
Reserves	
Undistributed profit	1,000
Shareholders' funds	3,500

71. 1,500,000 new ('bonus') shares are issued to existing shareholders, so that if Mr X previously held 20,000 shares he will now hold 50,000. The total value of his holding should theoretically remain the same however, since the net assets of the company remain unchanged and his share of those net assets remains at 2% (ie 50,000/2,500,000; previously 20,000/1,000,000).

Rights issues

72. A rights issue (unlike a bonus issue) is an issue of shares for cash. The 'rights' are offered to existing shareholders, who can sell them if they wish.

Example

73. Bubbles Ltd (above) decides to make a rights issue, shortly after the bonus issue. The terms are '1 for 5 @ £1.20' (ie one new share for every five already held, at a price of £1.20). Assuming that all shareholders take up their rights (which they are not obliged to) the double entry is:

	£'000	£'000
Dr Cash	600	
Cr Ordinary share capital		500
Cr Share premium		100

74. Mr X who previously held 50,000 shares will now hold 60,000, and the value of his holding should increase (theoretically at least) because the net assets of the company will increase. The new balance sheet will show:

	£'000	£'000
Share capital		
£1 ordinary shares		3,000
Reserves		
Share premium	100	
Undistributed profit	1,000	
		1,100
Shareholders' funds		4,100

The increase in funds of £600,000 represents the cash raised from the issue of 500,000 new shares at a price of £1.20 each.

Formation expenses

75. When a company is newly set up, formation expenses may be incurred. These can be debited to a share premium account, if there is one, otherwise they must be debited as an expense in the profit and loss account.

Interest on loans

76. Interest payable on debenture loans is at a fixed rate of interest on the nominal value of the loan, regardless of the market value of the debentures. If a company has issued £500,000 (nominal value) 10% debentures, the annual interest paid will be £50,000. The debentures might however be bought and sold on The Stock Exchange for more or less than the nominal value.

77. Interest is usually paid half yearly. At the end of an account year, there might be an accrual of interest in the balance sheet (say three month's accrued interest not yet due for payment), or six months' interest now payable but not yet paid. Accrued interest or interest payable are current liabilities.

Example: company accounts

78. We can now try to draw together several of the items described in this chapter into an illustrative example. Study it carefully: it is a typical examination-type problem.

79. The accountant (unqualified) of Wislon Ltd has prepared the following trial balance as at 31 December 19X7:

	£'000
50p ordinary shares (fully paid)	350
7% £1 preference shares (fully paid)	100
10% debentures (secured)	200
Retained profit 1.1.X7	242
General reserve 1.1.X7	171
Freehold land and buildings 1.1.X7 (cost)	430
Plant and machinery 1.1.X7 (cost)	830
Provision for depreciation:	
Freehold buildings 1.1.X7	20
Plant and machinery 1.1.X7	222
Stock 1.1.X7	190
Sales	2,695
Purchases	2,152
Preference dividend	7
Ordinary dividend (interim)	8
Debenture interest	10
Wages and salaries	254
Light and heat	31
Sundry expenses	113
Suspense account	135
Debtors	179
Creditors	195
Cash	126

Notes:

1. Sundry expenses include £9,000 paid in respect of insurance for the year ending 1 September 19X8. Light and heat does not include an invoice of £3,000 for electricity for the three months ending 2 January 19X8, which was paid in February 19X8. Light and heat also includes £20,000 relating to salesmen's commission.

2. The suspense account is in respect of the following items:

	£'000
Proceeds from the issue of 100,000 ordinary shares	120
Proceeds from the sale of plant	300
	420
Less consideration for the acquisition of Mary & Co	285
	135

3. The net assets of Mary & Co were purchased on 3 March 19X7. Assets were valued as follows:

	£'000
Investments	230
Stock	34
	264

All the stock acquired was sold during 19X7. The investments were still held by Wislon at 31.12.X7.

4. The freehold property was acquired some years ago. The buildings element of the cost was estimated at £100,000 and the estimated useful life of the assets was fifty years at the time of purchase. As at 31 December 19X7 the property is to be revalued at £800,000.

5. The plant which was sold had cost £350,000 and had a net book value of £274,000 as on 1.1.X7. £36,000 depreciation is to be charged on plant and machinery for 19X7.

6. The debentures have been in issue for some years. The 50p ordinary shares all rank for dividends at the end of the year.

7. The directors wish to provide for:

   (i) debenture interest due;

   (ii) a final ordinary dividend of 2p per share;

   (iii) a transfer to general reserve of £16,000;

   (iv) audit fees of £4,000.

8. Stock as at 31 December 19X7 was valued at £220,000 (cost).

9. Taxation is to be ignored.

Required: prepare the final accounts of Wislon Ltd.

Approach and suggested solution

80. (a) Normal adjustments are needed for accruals and prepayments (insurance, light and heat, debenture interest and audit fees). The debenture interest accrued is calculated as follows:

	£'000
Charge needed in P & L account (10% x £200,000)	20
Amount paid so far, as shown in trial balance	10
Accrual - presumably six months' interest now payable	10

The accrued expenses shown in the balance sheet comprise:	£'000
Debenture interest	10
Light and heat	3
Audit fee	4
	17

   (b) The misposting of £20,000 to light and heat is also adjusted, by reducing the light and heat expense, but charging £20,000 to salesmen's commission.

   (c) Depreciation on the freehold building is calculated as $\frac{£100,000}{50} = £2,000$.

   The NBV of the freehold property is then £430,000 - £20,000 - £2,000 = £408,000 at the end of the year. When the property is revalued a reserve of £800,000 - £408,000 = £392,000 is then created.

   (d) The profit on disposal of plant is calculated as proceeds £300,000 (per suspense account) less NBV £274,000 ie £26,000. The cost of the remaining plant is calculated at £830,000 - £350,000 = £480,000. The depreciation provision at the year end is:

	£'000
Balance 1.1.X7	222
Charge for 19X7	36
Less depreciation on disposals (350 - 274)	(76)
	182

(e) Goodwill arising on the purchase of Mary & Co is: £'000

Consideration (per suspense account)	285
Assets at valuation	264
Goodwill	21

In the absence of other instructions, this is shown as an asset on the balance sheet. The investments, being owned by Wislon at the year end, are also shown on the balance sheet, whereas Mary's stock, acquired and then sold, is added to the purchases figure for the year.

(f) The other item in the suspense account is dealt with as follows: £'000

Proceeds of issue of 100,000 ordinary shares	120
Less nominal value 100,000 x 50p	50
Excess of consideration over nominal value (= share premium)	70

(g) Appropriations of profit must be considered. The final ordinary dividend, shown as a current liability in the balance sheet, is

$$(700,000 + 100,000 \text{ ordinary shares}) \times 2p = £16,000$$

(h) The transfer to general reserve increases that reserve to £171,000 + £16,000 = £187,000.

81.

WISLON LTD
TRADING AND PROFIT AND LOSS ACCOUNT
FOR THE YEAR ENDING 31 DECEMBER 19X7

	£'000	£'000	£'000
Sales			2,695
Less cost of sales			
Opening stock		190	
Purchases		2,186	
		2,376	
Less closing stock		220	
			2,156
Gross profit			539
Profit on disposal of plant			26
			565
Less expenses			
Wages, salaries and commission		274	
Sundry expenses		107	
Light and heat		14	
Depreciation: freehold buildings		2	
plant		36	
Audit fees		4	
Debenture interest		20	
			457
Net profit			108
Appropriations			
Transfer to general reserve		16	
Dividends:			
preference (paid)	7		
ordinary: interim (paid)	8		
final (proposed)	16		
		31	
			47
Retained profit for the year			61
Retained profit brought forward			242
Retained profit carried forward			303

82.

WISLON LTD
BALANCE SHEET
AS AT 31 DECEMBER 19X7

	Cost/ val'n £'000	Dep'n £'000	£'000
Fixed assets			
Intangible assets			
Goodwill			21
Tangible assets			
Freehold property	800	–	800
Plant and machinery	480	182	298
	1,280	182	
Investments			230
			1,349
Current assets			
Stock		220	
Debtors		179	
Prepayment		6	
Cash		126	
		531	
Creditors: amounts falling due *within one year*			
Creditors	195		
Accrued expenses	17		
Proposed dividend	16		
	228		
Net current assets			303
Total assets less current liabilities			1,652
Creditors: amounts falling due *after more than one year*			
10% debentures (secured)			(200)
			1,452
Capital and reserves			
Called up share capital			
50p ordinary shares		400	
7% £1 preference shares		100	
			500
Reserves			
Share premium		70	
Revaluation reserve		392	
General reserve		187	
Profit and loss account		303	
			952
			1,452

Contingent liabilities

83. A contingency is 'a condition which exists at the balance sheet date, where the outcome will be confirmed only on the occurrence or non-occurrence of one or more uncertain events'. At the balance sheet date of a business, there will be some transactions or events that might or might not happen in the future, and the happening or non-happening of the event will affect the financial situation of the business. Some examples might help to explain contingencies more clearly.

    (a) At the balance sheet date a business is likely to have some debtors who owe it money. Some of these outstanding debts might eventually turn out to be bad, but at the balance sheet date the business cannot say for certain whether they will or will not be bad.

    (b) A company might be acting as the guarantor of a loan from a bank to someone else. (For reasons we need not worry about here, one company might guarantee the repayment of a loan with interest which has been made by a lender such as a bank to another company). If the borrower defaults on his repayments, the bank might call on the guarantee provided by the company, so that the company becomes obliged to repay the loan on the borrower's behalf. This would only happen, of course, if the borrower defaults. It is a contingency.

    (c) A company might receive a bill of exchange from a customer, as payment for goods sold. If the company then sells the bill to a bank (ie discounts the bill) to obtain immediate cash, the bank will insist on a promise by the company that it will repay the bank the full value of the bill in the event that it is dishonoured (ie not paid) by the customer when payment becomes due.

84. If a contingency eventually happens, the company might stand to gain or to lose. In other words, there will be a contingent gain or a contingent loss. In the accounts of a business, it is generally prudent to ignore contingent gains. However, it is also prudent not to ignore liabilities which potentially exist in relation to contingent losses. These are called contingent liabilities.

85. Both the Companies Act 1985 and SSAP 18 *Accounting for contingencies* require contingent liabilities to be dealt with in the accounts of a company, except where the possibility of the loss occurring is remote.

    (a) SSAP 18 states that 'a material contingent loss should be accrued in financial statements where it is probable that a future event will confirm a loss which can be estimated with reasonable accuracy'. In other words, if there is a contingent loss which is substantial in amount ('material') the loss should be charged against the profits of the current period ('accrued') and shown as a liability in the balance sheet. For example, a *provision* can be made against doubtful debts, if it is reasonably likely that a material loss from bad debts will arise. The provision is a liability in the balance sheet, set off as we have seen against the total value of debtors.

    (b) The Companies Act requires companies to give deails, in a *note* to their balance sheet rather than in the balance sheet itself, of any charge on assets of the company (eg mortgaged property) or any guarantees given by the company. Where the loss is a possible event but not a probable one, there is no need to make a charge in the P & L account or to create a balance sheet liability. A descriptive note to the accounts is sufficient, stating the nature of the contingency and the amount of the potential loss.

Example

86. You are required to state *briefly* how you would deal with each of the following when preparing a company's profit and loss account and balance sheet.

    (a) The company is defending in the court an action for damages due to alleged breach of contract.

    (b) The goods received records show that various items, properly ordered, have been received in the financial year, but no invoice has yet been received.

    (c) The company sells articles which it guarantees to repair, free of charge, during the six months from the date of sale. A large number of such articles has been sold during the last six months.

Solution

87. (a) There is a contingency to provide for, in the event that the company loses the court action. It is assumed that the potential damages are material.

        (i) If it is probable that the company will lose the action, a provision for the loss should be accrued in the accounts, by charging the provision against profits of the current period, and showing the provision as a liability in the balance sheet.

        (ii) If it is not thought probable that the company will lose the action, a note to its balance sheet should give details of the contingent liability, and an estimate of the potential loss.

    (b) It is certain that the company will be invoiced for the goods. There is no contingency. The receipt of the goods should be accounted for by the entries:

        Debit   Purchases
        Credit   Accruals

    When the invoice is eventually received, the accruals account will be cleared by:

        Debit   Accruals
        Credit   Creditors

    (c) The company will almost certainly be called on to repair some of the articles it has sold. That being so, it should make a *provision* for repair costs, charge the provision against the profits for the six months just ended, and show the provision as a current liability in the balance sheet.

Summary of the chapter

88.
- This chapter has explained some important differences between the accounts of a limited company and those of sole traders or partnership.

- The accounts records and financial statements of a limited company are strictly regulated by statute.

- A company is recognised in law as a person, with its own identity quite separate from that of its owners. One important consequence of this is the concept of limited liability: a company's shareholders have no liability for the company's debts, beyond what they have contributed as capital.

- In the case of a sole trader or partnership, day-to-day management of the business is usually in the hands of the owner(s). With companies, the owners (members or shareholders) appoint directors to be responsible for management. The fact that in small companies shareholders and directors are often the same people should not obscure the legal distinction between the two roles: if a director receives a salary, that is an employee payroll cost chargeable as an expense against profit; if he is also a shareholder and receives a dividend, that is an appropriation of profit.

- Except for certain professional practices, a partnership must not have more than 20 partners. The amount of capital that 20 people can provide may not be great, and this makes it difficult for partnerships to expand. There is no limit on the number of people who can subscribe capital to acquire shares in a limited company.

TEST YOUR KNOWLEDGE
Numbers in brackets refer to paragraphs of this chapter

1. What is the meaning of limited liability? (3)

2. List four of the statutory books which companies must maintain. (8)

3. What is the difference between issued capital and called-up capital? (15)

4. What are the differences between ordinary shares and preference shares? (21)

5. What are the differences between debentures and share capital? (35)

6. What is ACT? (44)

7. How does a share premium account arise? (59)

8. Distinguish between a bonus issue and a rights issue. (68, 72)

9. Give two examples of contingent liabilities. (83)

Now try questions 8-9 at the end of this section

Chapter 23

MANUFACTURING ACCOUNTS

The purpose of this chapter is:

- to explain the difference between financial accounts and cost and management accounts

- to illustrate the preparation of manufacturing accounts

Introduction

1. A manufacturing account might be prepared by a manufacturing company, in order to establish the cost of the work it has produced during a period of time. When a manufacturing account is prepared, it precedes the trading, profit and loss account, so that there is:

    (a) a manufacturing account, to establish the cost of goods produced;

    (b) a trading account, to establish the cost of goods sold and gross profit;

    (c) and a profit and loss account, to establish the net profit, before appropriations for corporation tax and dividends etc.

2. Manufacturing accounts are not obligatory for manufacturing companies, because they can prepare a trading, profit and loss account without a manufacturing account if they wish to do so. However, a manufacturing account is needed if management want to know what the cost of producing goods has been, for 'internal' information.

Cost and management accounts

3. Most of the financial accounts that we have examined so far have as their aim the provision of summarised information about the progress or state of a business as a whole. Such information is generally of limited use for those who manage the business, because it is retrospective and does not distinguish between different sections of the same business. Therefore most large businesses also produce internal accounts for the purposes of management control. Such accounts are generally referred to as 'management accounts' and are an important practical aspect of accounting, especially in larger organisations where managers tend to need more regular formal reports to learn what is happening in business operations.

4. There is no obligation to produce management accounts and no set layout; they are solely for internal consumption and are produced in whatever format is convenient. The main reasons for producing such accounts are:

    (a)   to generate up-to-date information for management purposes (because if a business is making a loss action must be taken soon, not six months after the end of the accounting period, when the profit and loss account is published); and

    (b)   to provide analysis of results from various sections of the business (because some sections might be profitable and others not).

5.   Because these accounts are primarily concerned with the analysis of costs they are also known as 'cost accounts' and the person who produces them is sometimes referred to as a 'cost accountant'. Costing is an extremely important topic but in this study text we will confine ourselves to one aspect of cost accounts, the manufacturing account.

Component elements in the manufacturing process

6.   A manufacturing account is basically a list of the costs of producing the work in a factory, or in several factories, during a period. These costs consist of:

    (a)   the cost of raw materials and components that are used to make up the products. These are called 'direct materials';

    (b)   the cost of the labour that makes the products. Labour that is directly involved in producing an item of output is called 'direct labour';

    (c)   other costs incurred in the factory, which cannot be attributed to the production of any specific output but which are incurred to keep the factory running. These 'indirect costs', or overheads, include the salaries of supervisors, factory rent, depreciation of the factory building, depreciation of plant and machinery, factory rates, cleaning materials and other general expenses relating to the factory.

7.
> The total direct costs of production are known as prime cost, and the total of direct costs plus overheads is known as *factory cost* or *works cost*.

8.   A further distinction is often made between:

    (a)   *variable costs*. These are costs that vary with the number of goods produced, or the number of hours worked. For example, if a unit of production has a variable cost of £10, the total variable cost of 10 such units would be £100, and the total variable cost of 20 such units would be £200 etc;

    (b)   *fixed costs*. These are the costs which are the same total amount for a period of time, regardless of the number of units produced or the number of hours worked. Factory rent and rates, and depreciation of factory premises are examples of fixed costs.

9.   In general, direct costs are variable costs. Most overhead costs, or even all overhead costs, are regarded as fixed costs, although there are often some variable overhead costs too.

Opening and closing stocks

10. When a company engages in the manufacture of goods, it will have three different types of stock or inventory:

    (a) raw materials and components, purchased from suppliers and held in store, but not yet used for producing any manufactured goods;

    (b) work in progress or work in process (WIP), which is partly-manufactured output, not yet completed and still being worked on in the factory at the end of the period;

    (c) finished goods, not yet sold and so held in store.

11. It may help to think about stocks of raw materials, work in progress and finished goods in the following terms:

    (a) to manufacture goods, a business must first of all purchase raw materials;

    (b) raw materials are then issued to the production department, where they become a part of work in progress. Direct labour and overhead costs are added to the cost of raw materials to build up the cost of this work in progress;

    (c) when production is completed, the finished goods are put into a finished goods store;

    (d) when these finished goods are eventually sold, their cost is added to the cost of goods sold.

12. In calculating the cost of production during a period, account must be taken of the opening and closing stock levels both of raw materials and components, and also of work in progress.

13. For example, suppose that on 1 July 19X5, a factory has raw material stocks valued at £400, and unfinished work in progress valued at £250. During June:

    (a) purchases of raw materials amounted to £750;
    (b) labour costs and factory overheads amounted to £600.

At 30 June 19X5, closing stocks of raw materials were valued at £150 and unfinished work in progress at £400.

14. The cost of production during June 19X5 would be calculated as follows:

MANUFACTURING ACCOUNT FOR JUNE 19X5

	£	£	£
Opening stock, raw materials		400	
Purchases		750	
		1,150	
Closing stock, raw materials		150	
Cost of raw materials used in production		1,000	
Labour and factory overheads		600	
		1,600	
Add cost of opening WIP	250		Transfer to trading
Less cost of closing WIP	(400)		account (note 1) 1,450
Increase in cost of WIP		(150)	
Cost of finished goods produced		1,450	1,450

Notes

1. The manufacturing account is part of the double entry book-keeping system, and is a ledger account in the nominal ledger.

2. Costs of raw materials used in June, and labour and overhead costs in June, should be added to the value of opening WIP to arrive at the total value of production, both finished and unfinished. The value of closing WIP must then be subtracted to arrive at a value for the cost of finished goods produced and transferred to the finished goods stores, awaiting sale.

Putting a value to work in progress and finished goods

15. One of the vexing problems in accounting is deciding on the most suitable way of putting a value to manufactured goods, both unfinished WIP and also finished goods. The problem exists because there are a number of different ways to value output, and none of them is obviously 'better' than the others. The differences are that:

(a) WIP and finished goods might be valued at their variable cost (also known as direct cost or 'marginal' cost) or at a full factory cost that includes both direct costs and a share of factory overheads. Although SSAP 9 requires that WIP and finished goods should be valued at full factory cost in published financial accounts, internal 'management' accounts often value them at variable cost. The Companies Act 1985 states that either full factory cost or variable cost would be a legally acceptable method for valuing stocks in the published accounts of limited companies.

(b) If stocks are valued at full factory cost, some abritrary method must be selected for sharing out factory overheads between different types of product made in the factory.

16. A detailed analysis of these problems is more appropriate to a study of cost accounting than to financial accounting. However, though we shall not dwell here on the difficulties in establishing a suitable and 'fair' method for sharing out overhead costs, we do need to take a look at the 'mechanics' of the method. Sharing out overhead costs in a fair manner is known as 'apportionment' of overheads.

Apportionment of overheads

17. There are two main reasons for apportioning overheads, given that the closing stocks of WIP and finished goods are to be valued at full factory cost. The two reasons are that:

    (a) some items of expense relate not only to manufacturing, but also to selling and administration. These items of shared expense must be apportioned between manufacturing overhead and selling and administration;

    (b) when a company makes two or more different product items perhaps in two or more different production departments, manufacturing overheads must be apportioned:

        (i)   firstly, between different production departments;
        (ii) and secondly, within each production department, between the different items of product made there.

18. Items of expense which are sometimes shared between manufacturing overhead, selling expenses and administration expenses might include the following:

    (a) rent and rates of premises, where the same building is used as a factory, administration office and sales office;

    (b) heating and lighting of shared premises, and similarly canteen costs and telephone expenses (unless telephones are separately metered and invoiced).

First example: apportionment of overheads

19. A manufacturing company has its factory and offices at the same site. Its results for the year to 31 December 19X5 were as follows:

	£
Sales	179,000
Purchases	60,000
Direct labour	70,000
Depreciation of equipment	10,000
Local authority rates	5,000
Depreciation of building	2,000
Heating and lighting	3,000
Telephone	2,000
Other manufacturing overheads	2,300
Other administration expenses	2,550
Other selling expenses	1,150

Shared overhead costs are to be apportioned as follows:

	Manufacturing	Administration	Selling
Depreciation of equipment	80%	5%	15%
Rates	50%	30%	20%
Depreciation of building	50%	30%	20%
Heating and lighting	40%	35%	25%
Telephone	–	40%	60%

The values of stocks are as follows:

	At 1 January 19X5 £	At 31 December 19X5 £
Raw materials	5,000	3,000
Work in progress	4,000	3,000
Finished goods	16,000	18,000

Required:

Prepare the manufacturing, trading and profit and loss account of the company for the period to 31 December 19X5.

Solution

20. MANUFACTURING ACCOUNT FOR THE YEAR ENDED 31 DECEMBER 19X5

	£	£
Opening stock of raw materials		5,000
Purchases		60,000
		65,000
Closing stock of raw materials		3,000
Raw materials used in production		62,000
Direct labour		70,000
Prime cost		132,000
Manufacturing overheads:		
Depreciation of equipment (80% of £10,000)	8,000	
Rates (50% of £5,000)	2,500	
Depreciation of buildings (50% of £2,000)	1,000	
Heating and lighting (40% of £3,000)	1,200	
Other expenses	2,300	
		15,000
Manufacturing costs during the year		147,000
Add opening stock of WIP	4,000	
Less closing stock of WIP	(3,000)	
Reduction in stock of WIP		1,000
Cost of finished goods fully produced, transferred to trading account		148,000

TRADING AND PROFIT AND LOSS ACCOUNT
FOR THE YEAR ENDED 31 DECEMBER 19X5

	£	£	£
Sales			179,000
Opening stock of finished goods		16,000	
Cost of finished goods produced		148,000	
		164,000	
Closing stock of finished goods		18,000	
Cost of goods sold			146,000
Gross profit			33,000
Selling expenses			
Depreciation of equipment (15% of £10,000)	1,500		
Rates (20% of £5,000)	1,000		
Depreciation of building (20% of £2,000)	400		
Heating and lighting (25% of £3,000)	750		
Telephone (60% of £2,000)	1,200		
Other expenses	1,150		
		6,000	
Administration expenses			
Depreciation of equipment (5% of £10,000)	500		
Rates (30% of £5,000)	1,500		
Depreciation of building (30% of £2,000)	600		
Heating and lighting (35% of £3,000)	1,050		
Telephone (40% of £2,000)	800		
Other expenses	2,550		
		7,000	
			13,000
Net profit			20,000

Second example: apportionment of overheads

21. Bracedep Ltd has two production departments, which both do work on three products, sirks, varks, and zooks.

(a) Wages costs in each department for the year to 31 December 19X7 were:

	£
Assembly department	70,000
Finishing department	30,000
	100,000

(b) Manufacturing overheads in total for the year were £150,000. These are to be apportioned between departments in proportion to wages costs incurred during the year.

(c) Departmental overhead costs are to be apportioned between products as follows:

	Assembly dept	Finishing dept
Sirks	30%	50%
Varks	40%	10%
Zooks	30%	40%

Required: calculate the overhead cost attributable to each product during the year.

Solution

22.		Assembly Dept		Finishing Dept		Total
Manufacturing overhead	(70%)	105,000	(30%)	45,000		150,000
Apportioned as follows:						
Sirks	(30%)	31,500	(50%)	22,500		54,000
Varks	(40%)	42,000	(10%)	4,500		46,500
Zooks	(30%)	31,500	(40%)	18,000		49,500
		105,000		45,000		150,000

Profit centres and transfer pricing

23. In some businesses, management establish 'profit centres' of operations, with each centre held accountable for making a profit, and the manager of the centre made responsible for its good or bad results. When a production department is established as a profit centre, it makes a 'profit' on the output it makes and transfers out, either to finished goods store or to another profit centre. However, production departments do not sell goods, they only make them; and so if a production department is a profit centre, its 'income' must come from the goods it makes, not the goods sold. This is achieved, in profit centre accounting, by creating an 'artificial' selling price for goods produced and transferred. This artificial, or 'internal' selling price is called a transfer price.

24. The value of goods transferred out of the production department, at transfer price value, is

   (a) a cost to the department (eg stores) receiving the goods, and
   (b) 'income' to the production department. The production department's profit is therefore its income from goods made, less the cost of those goods.

25. The concept of profit centre accounting is not necessarily an easy one to understand. Remember that accounts are prepared both for 'external' publication, and also for 'internal' management information. Profit centres are established so that managers can judge how profitable is each different part of their organisation's operations. Transfer pricing is therefore a 'management accounting' aspect of manufacturing accounts.

26. Since the production department will earn a 'profit' on the goods it produces, but the business as a whole will only make a profit on what it sells, a discrepancy will arise in the calculation of:

   (a) the production department profit; and
   (b) the overall profit of the business;

   in periods when production volumes and sales volumes differ. Dealing with this discrepancy will be illustrated by means of the example below. This example is quite lengthy, and you should follow it carefully.

Example: profit centres

27. Alf, Bert and Charlie are in partnership retailing widgets which they manufacture themselves. Alf is responsible for manufacturing the widgets (in the factory), Bert for selling and distribution (from the warehouse) and Charlie is responsible for running the office and general administration. Overall business is profitable but no detailed analysis of costs and efficiency has ever been made. A manufacturing account is now to be drawn up, and combined with a trading and profit and loss account, in order to see how costs are spread between the three different departments. The factory is to be made a profit centre, with a transfer price for its output.

During 19X6 Alf, Bert and Charlie have produced and sold many widgets. Their total costs have been as follows:

	£
Purchases	133,700
Light and heat	4,000
Depreciation of freehold premises	1,100
General expenses	9,000
Factory wages	215,000
Salaries	73,000
Repairs and maintenance of plant and machinery	4,200
Manufacturing expenses	111,000
Advertising	4,000
Salesmens' commission	19,000
Carriage outwards	8,000
Depreciation on plant and machinery	7,000
Power	5,500

Additional information:

1. Stock on hand was as follows:

	1.1.X6	31.12.X6
	£	£
Raw materials	21,000	15,000
Work in progress	19,000	22,000
Finished widgets	70,000	80,000

   The above figures represent the cost to the partnership, and ignore any internal 'profit' element due to transfer pricing (see note 2).

2. Ten widgets cost 10p to produce, on average. To buy the same number of identical widgets from an external supplier would cost 11p. The valuation of stocks of finished widgets is therefore to be inflated by 10% for internal purposes.

3. Sales during 19X6 were £600,000.

4. The depreciation charge on the freehold premises is to be apportioned on the basis of area:

	Sq feet
Factory	2,100
Warehouse	1,400
General office	350

5. It has been agreed that the light and heat charge will be split as follows:

Factory	$\frac{1}{2}$
Warehouse	$\frac{1}{4}$
General office	$\frac{1}{4}$

6. The charge for salaries is analysed as follows:

	£
Factory supervisor	8,000
Salesmen	49,000
General administration	16,000
	73,000

7. The costs are listed after taking account of accruals and prepayments and before partners' salaries, interest and drawings.

You are required to prepare the manufacturing account for the factory for 19X6, and a trading and profit and loss account for the partnership as a whole.

Approach

28. The technique required by this type of question is organisation. The various costs have to be arranged in a meaningful way; ie split between the production, selling and administrative functions.

29. The manufacturing account comes first, listing all production expenses. The direct expenses, raw materials and factory wages, constitute the prime cost. Factory overheads must then be added with an apportionment of costs shared between the factory, warehouse and general office.

30. The total of costs listed so far (£493,000 in the answer) of course represents total production costs for the year but generally some items are unfinished at the year end, as in this question, so an adjustment has to be made for work in progress. By subtracting the increase in work in progress from the total production costs, we arrive at the factory cost of finished goods produced. This is the cost of widgets finished during the year and passed to the warehouse for sale.

31. To take account of the fact that it is cheaper to make widgets than to buy them from outside a notional 'factory profit' is calculated and added to the factory cost to produce the 'transfer price of finished goods'. The transfer price represents the approximate price the warehouse would have had to pay to external suppliers if the business had purchased widgets instead of manufacturing them.

32. The factory therefore makes a profit on the goods it has completed.

The double entry in the accounts for the transfer of finished goods is

Credit Manufacturing account - production at transfer price;
Debit Trading account - cost of finished goods produced, at transfer price.

Opening and closing stocks would also be valued at transfer price, which in this example is cost plus 10%.

33. The gross profit in the trading account is calculated with opening finished goods stock, the cost of finished output and closing finished goods stock all at their transfer price value. Since this value is higher than their cost (by 10%) the gross profit in the trading account will be understated, because the cost of sales will be overstated.

34. To the gross profit calculated in the trading account must be added the factory profit included in the transfer price and 'realised' in the manufacturing account. The extra detail here enables us to say that if they had merely been trading in widgets bought from outside, Alf, Bert and Charlie would have made a gross profit of £72,000. However, since they have manufactured their own widgets they have made an additional gross profit of £48,000.

35. Some of the finished goods produced during the year have not been sold, and so far as the business as a whole is concerned, the manufacturing 'profit' on goods made but not sold cannot be included in the P & L account.

    The 'profit' on the goods made but not yet sold is an unrealised profit, and must be excluded from the final accounts. This is done by creating a provision for unrealised profits.

    (a) The profit element in closing stocks of finished goods sold is removed from the P & L account of the business by means of the double entry

    Debit   P & L account
    Credit   Provision for unrealised profit,

    with the unrealised profit element in closing stock values.

    (b) In the balance sheet, stocks of finished goods are valued as follows:

	£
Gross value (including profit)	X
Less provision for unrealised profit	(X)
Cost	X

    (c) The reverse transaction is required for opening stocks; ie

    Debit   Provision for unrealised profit
    Credit   P & L account

    with the profit element in opening stocks, sold during the period.

    (d) The provision for unrealised profit on opening stocks and closing stocks of finished goods can be set off against each other, and so we need to record only the increase (cost to P & L account) in the provision for unrealised profit during the period.

    These lengthy explanations will now be illustrated in the following solution to the example.

Solution

36.

ALF, BERT AND CHARLIE
MANUFACTURING ACCOUNT
FOR THE YEAR ENDED 31 DECEMBER 19X6

	£	£
Raw materials		
Balance at 1.1.X6	21,000	
Purchases	133,700	
	154,700	
Less balance at 31.12.X6	15,000	
		139,700
Factory wages		215,000
Prime cost		354,700
Indirect factory expenses		
Manufacturing expenses	111,000	
Repair and maintenance of plant and machinery	4,200	
Depreciation – factory	600	
– plant and machinery	7,000	
Supervisor's salary	8,000	
Power	5,500	
Light and heat	2,000	
		138,300
		493,000
Work in progress		
Balance at 1.1.X6	19,000	
Less balance at 31.12.X6	22,000	
Increase in WIP		(3,000)
Factory cost of goods produced		490,000
Factory profit (10% of cost of goods produced)		49,000
Transfer price of finished goods produced		539,000

TRADING AND PROFIT AND LOSS ACCOUNT
FOR THE YEAR ENDED 31 DECEMBER 19X6

	£	£	£
Sales			600,000
Less cost of goods sold			
Balance 1.1.X6 (at transfer price)		77,000	
Transfer price of finished goods produced		539,000	
		616,000	
Less balance at 31.12.X6 (at transfer price)		88,000	
			528,000
Gross profit			72,000
Factory profit (transferred from manufacturing account)			49,000
			121,000
Less increase in provision for unrealised profit on closing stock (note 1 below)		1,000	
Selling and distribution expenses			
Salaries and commissions	68,000		
Carriage outwards	8,000		
Advertising	4,000		
Light and heat	1,000		
Depreciation on warehouse	400		
		81,400	
Administration expenses			
Salaries	16,000		
General expenses	9,000		
Light and heat	1,000		
Depreciation on general office	100		
		26,100	
			108,500
Net profit available for appropriation			12,500

Note 1

	£
Provision for unrealised profit needed 31.12.X6, closing stock of finished goods 1/11 x £88,000	8,000
Less provision brought forward 1.1.X6, opening stock of finished goods 1/11 x £77,000	7,000
Increase needed	1,000

Since profit is 10% on cost, the transfer price is 110% of cost, and profit is 10/110 of the transfer price.

37. Certain points should be emphasised:

(a) the double entry for the factory profit is:

Debit   Manufacturing account
Credit   P & L account

(b) the movement on the provision for unrealised profit on stock is calculated in exactly the same way as a movement on a provision for doubtful debts;

(c) once the net profit for the year is found it is appropriated by the partners (or the company) in the normal manner;

(d) stock would be displayed on the balance sheet as follows:

	£	£
Current assets		
Stock		
Raw materials		15,000
Work in progress		22,000
Finished goods	88,000	
Less provision	8,000	
		80,000
		117,000
Debtors etc		

(c) If you are not convinced that the partnership's net profit for the period is really £12,500, recalculate a trading and P & L account ignoring transfer prices altogether. Your net profit should still come out as £12,500.

38. Examination of the trading and profit and loss account for Alf, Bert and Charlie reveals that the profit is due to the fact that the partners manufacture their own widgets. Gross profit from this is £48,000. The net profit is relatively low (£12,500). This seems to be due partly to high selling and distribution expenses. It would seem that the manufacturing side of the partnership is probably more efficient than the selling side (although Bert might dispute this).

Work in progress valued at prime cost

39. Work in progress in the example above was valued at full factory cost, ie at prime cost plus a proportion of the indirect factory expenses. If it had been valued at prime cost only, the adjustment for the increase or decrease in work in progress would have appeared in the manufacturing account before listing factory overhead expenses.

Summary of the chapter

40.

- Manufacturing accounts are prepared for internal management use only. Their purpose is to distinguish between the costs and profitability associated with manufacturing operations and those associated with trading (which are shown in the trading account).

- Manufacturing accounts highlight:

  o *prime cost* - the cost of raw materials and direct labour employed in production;

  o *factory cost of goods produced* - equal to prime cost plus indirect factory expenses and plus or minus any movement over the period in the cost of work in progress;

  o *factory profit* - a notional profit earned in the manufacturing operation, reflecting the relative cheapness of manufacturing goods compared with buying them in from outside suppliers;

  o *transfer price of finished goods produced* - equal to factory cost plus factory profit. This transfer price appears in the trading account as part of the cost of goods sold.

TEST YOUR KNOWLEDGE

Numbers in brackets refer to paragraphs of this chapter

1. What is the purpose of producing internal management accounts? (3,4)

2. What types of cost are included in a manufacturing account? (6)

3. What is 'prime cost'? What is factory cost? (7)

4. What is the purpose of apportioning overheads? (17)

5. What is a profit centre? (23)

Now try questions 10 and 11 at the end of this section

1. **HIGHTON**

   A Highton is in business as a general retailer. He does not keep a full set of accounting records; however it has been possible to extract the following details from the few records that are available:

	1 April 19X1	31 March 19X2
	£	£
Freehold land and buildings at cost	10,000	10,000
Motor vehicle (cost £3,000)	2,250	
Stock, at cost	3,500	4,000
Trade debtors	500	1,000
Prepayments: motor vehicle expenses	200	300
property insurance	50	100
Cash at bank	550	950
Cash in hand	100	450
Loan from Highton's father	10,000	
Trade creditors	1,500	1,800
Accruals: electricity	200	400
motor vehicle expenses	200	100

   Extract from a rough cash book for the year to 31 March 19X2

	£
Receipts	
Cash sales	80,400

	£
Payments	
Cash purchases	17,000
Drawings	7,000
General shop expenses	100
Telephone	100
Wages	3,000

   Extract from the bank pass sheets for the year to 31 March 19X2

	£
Receipts	
Cash banked	52,850
Cheques from trade debtors	8,750

	£
Payments	
Cheques to suppliers	47,200
Loan repayment (including interest)	10,100
Electricity	400
Motor vehicle expenses	1,000
Property insurance	150
Rates	300
Telephone	300
Drawings	1,750

   Note: depreciation is to be provided on the motor vehicle at a rate of 25% per annum on cost.

   You are required to prepare a trading and profit and loss account for the year to 31 March 19X2, and a balance sheet as at that date.

SECTION 3: ILLUSTRATIVE QUESTIONS

2. CHURCH

The summarised balance sheet of Richard Church, photographic retailer, as at 31 March 19X2, is as follows:

	£		£	£
Capital account: R Church	32,400	Shop equipment and		
		fittings at cost	15,000	
		Less depreciation	3,000	
				12,000
Loan – S Chappell	3,000	Motor vehicle at cost	6,000	
		Less depreciation	1,500	
				4,500
Trade creditors	4,740	Stock at or below cost		10,420
Accrued expenses – heating		Trade debtors		6,260
and lighting	380	Rent paid in advance		650
		Bank		6,690
	40,520			40,520

Despite professional advice, Richard Church has not maintained an accounting system, but produces the following information regarding the financial year ended 31 March 19X3:

(i) Total sales and sales returns were £152,600 and £3,500 respectively. An average gross profit to sales ratio of 30 per cent is maintained during the year.

(ii) The trade debtors figure at 31 March 19X3 was £5,620, on which figure it has been decided to make a provision for doubtful debts of 5 per cent at the year end. During the course of the financial year trade debts amounting to £470 had been written off.

(iii) The trade creditors figure at 31 March 19X3 was £6,390. Discounts received from suppliers amounted to £760 in the financial year.

(iv) Stock, at or below cost at 31 March 19X3, indicates an increased investment of £4,000 in stock over that one year earlier. Drawings from stock by Richard Church during the year amounted to £600 and were included in payments made to suppliers; otherwise no records of these drawings were made.

(v) Payments for shop salaries for the year were £15,840, and for heating, lighting, rent and rates and other administration expenses amounted to £3,460. At 31 March 19X3 rent paid in advance amounted to £480, and heating bills outstanding were £310.

(vi) Shop fittings acquired during the year, and paid for, amounted to £2,000. Depreciation on shop equipment and fittings is provided annually at the rate of 10 per cent on the original cost of assets held at the financial year end. Similarly, depreciation on the motor vehicle is to be provided at the rate of 25% on original cost.

(vii) On 31 March 19X3 the loan from S Chappell was repaid.

(viii) Cash drawings during the financial period by Richard Church amounted to £9,000.

Required:

(a) Trading and profit and loss account for the year ended 31 March 19X3.
(b) Balance sheet in respect of the above year end.

3. SWALLOW

As the accountant of the Swallow Bowling Club you have been presented with the following information for the year to 30 September 19X3:

Receipts	£	*Payments*	£
Cash in hand at 1.10.X2	20	Club running expenses	770
Cash at bank at 1.10.X2	1,200	Cost of refreshments	180
Subscriptions	2,050	Christmas dance expenses	500
Bar receipts	3,600	Bar purchases	1,750
Christmas dance ticket sales	650	Lawn mower	600
Refreshment sales	320	Cash in hand at 30.9.X3	30
		Cash at bank at 30.9.X3	4,010
	7,840		7,840

Notes:

1	Subscriptions	*In arrears* £	*In advance* £
	At 1.10.X2	100	50
	At 30.9.X3	200	75

2	Fixed assets	*At 1.10.X2* £	*At 30.9.X3* £
	Club premises, at cost	50,000	50,000
	Less depreciation	35,000	37,500
		15,000	12,500

Depreciation is to be charged on the lawn mower at a rate of 15% per annum on cost.

3   Bar stock was valued at £150 at 30 September 19X2 and £200 at 30 September 19X3.

4	Outstanding expenses	*At 1.10.X2* £	*At 30.9.X3* £
	Bar purchases	300	400
	Club expenses	250	200

5   Rates paid in advance at 30 September 19X2 and at 30 September 19X3 amounted to £200 and £300 respectively.

You are required to prepare the club's income and expenditure account for the year to 30 September 19X3 and a balance sheet as at that date.

4. IMPROVIDENT ACTUARIES

The following balances were taken from the books of the Improvident Actuaries Society Golf Club as at 1 January 19X5:

	£	£
Course at cost		70,000
Clubhouse at cost		15,000
Building fund – represented by investments:		
£20,000 4% consolidated stock	7,400	
Deposit with building society	10,000	
		17,400
Subscriptions in advance (19X5)		400
Creditors for bar supplies		350
Life membership fund		4,000
Subscriptions in arrear		600
Bar stock		4,800
Clubhouse equipment at cost		3,200
Cash in hand	100	
Cash at bank	850	
		950

An analysis of the bank account operated by the club showed the following summary of receipts and payments during the year ended 31 December 19X5:

	£
Receipts:	
Subscriptions	25,000
Life members	2,000
Sale of instruction manuals	700
Green fees	300
Sale of old carpet from clubhouse	22
Bar takings	28,500
Consolidated stock interest	800

	£
Payments:	
Upkeep of course	16,150
General clubhouse expenses (including bar wages of £4,200)	12,150
Petty cash (expenses paid to treasurer)	1,550
Bar supplies	23,150
Purchase of instruction manuals	250
Piano	500
Deposited with building society	800
Replacement carpet for clubhouse	1,260

The following information is significant for the preparation of the club's accounts:

(a) the club maintains a building fund separate from the capital fund and life membership fund. The building fund is invested in consolidated stock and a building society, whilst the capital fund and life membership fund are represented by the general assets of the club;

(b) the building society has been instructed to credit the interest on the club's account direct to the account at each half year. The society computes interest half yearly on 30 June and 31 December. This year the interest amounted to £740. Interest paid on the consolidated stock is also added to the building fund by paying it into the building society account;

(c) there were four life members at the beginning of the year, one of whom has since died. Two other life members have however joined the club;

(d) renewals of clubhouse furnishings are to be treated as revenue expenditure;

(e) outstanding at 31 December 19X5 were:

	£
Creditors for bar supplies	1,600
Subscriptions in advance (19X6)	900
Subscriptions in arrear (19X5)	300
Bar chits not yet settled	35

(f) bar stocks at 31 December 19X5 were valued at £4,300;

(g) it is a rule of the club that a cash float of £100 shall be maintained in the treasurer's hands. To this end an imprest petty cash account is operated;

(h) an insurance premium of £480 has been paid by cheque during 19X5 for the year to 31 March 19X6.

You are required to prepare:

(a) an income and expenditure account for the year ended 31 December 19X5; and
(b) a balance sheet as at that date.

5. ADAMS BROWN AND CARTER

Adams, Brown and Carter are in partnership sharing profits and losses on the basis of 2:1:1. Their net profit for the year ended 28 February 19X4 is £9,530, before taking into consideration the following matters.

The capital accounts of the partners have been fixed for the past year at the following figures:

Adams	£10,000
Brown	£6,000
Carter	£4,000

The partners are entitled to interest on their capital accounts at the rate of 8% per annum. In addition, partnership salaries are due as follows:

Brown £1,500 : Carter £1,100

The partners' total drawings for the year ended 28 February 19X4 have been as follows:

Adams	£2,000
Brown	£1,800
Carter	£1,600

Since the drawings have been made at various times during the year, it is agreed that the partners should be charged interest at the fixed rate of 5% on their total drawings.

The partners' current account balances at 1 March 19X3, were:

Adams	£1,800
Brown	£1,200
Carter	£300

Required: prepare the appropriation account and current accounts of the partnership for the year ended 28 February 19X4.

(LCCI Spring 1984)

6. NORTH AND SOUTH

North and South are in partnership sharing profits and losses in the ratio 2:1. The following trial balance was extracted from their books at the close of business on 28 February 19X3:

	Dr £	Cr £
Capital accounts 1 March 19X2		
North		2,800
South		1,500
Drawings:		
North	2,900	
South	1,450	
Bank overdraft		310
Cash	70	
Purchases and sales	8,260	17,350
Discounts	510	190
Stock at 1 March 19X2	1,870	
Debtors and creditors	3,920	1,750
Wages and salaries	2,160	1,750
Rent and rates	390	
Fixtures and fittings	500	
Delivery van	700	
Van running expenses	420	
Current accounts 1 March 19X2		
North		270
South		240
Bad debts written off	170	
General expenses	1,090	
	24,410	24,410

Notes

1 Stock 28 February 19X3 - £2,280.
2 Rent prepaid 28 February 19X3 - £30.
3 Wages accrued 28 February 19X3 - £60.
4 Provide for depreciation as follows:
    Fixtures and fittings £50: Delivery van £70.
5 No interest is to be allowed on the capital accounts
6 The capital accounts are to remain fixed at the figures shown in the trial balance. Entries concerning drawings and share of profit are to be passed through the current accounts.

Required:

Prepare the trading and profit and loss accounts for the year ended 28 February 19X3 together with a balance sheet as at that date.

(LCCI Winter 1983)

7. BEN, KEN AND LEN

Ben, Ken and Len are in partnership sharing profits and losses in the ratio 3:2:1. The following is the trial balance of the partnership as at 30 September 19X3:

	£	£
Bad debts provision (at 1 October 19X2)		1,000
Bank and cash in hand	2,500	
Capital accounts:		
Ben		18,000
Ken		12,000
Len		6,000
Current accounts:		
Ben		700
Ken	500	
Len		300
Debtors and creditors	23,000	35,000
Depreciation (at 1 October 19X2)		
Land and buildings		12,000
Motor vehicles		8,000
Drawings:		
Ben	4,000	
Ken	3,000	
Len	3,000	
Land and buildings at cost	60,000	
Motor vehicles at cost	20,000	
Office expenses	4,000	
Purchases	85,000	
Rates	4,000	
Sales		150,000
Selling expenses	14,000	
Stock (at 1 October 19X2)	20,000	
	243,000	243,000

You are provided with the following additional information:

1   Stock at 30 September 19X3 was valued at £30,000.
2   Fixed assets are written off at the following rates: Land and buildings 5% per annum on cost; Motor vehicles 20% per annum on cost.
3   At 30 September 19X3 an amount of £1,775 was owing for selling expenses.
4   Rates were prepaid by £2,000 as at 30 September 19X3.
5   A certain bad debt of £500 is to be written off.
6   The bad debts provision is to be 5% of outstanding debtors as at 30 September 19X3.
7   The partnership agreement covers the following appropriations:
   (a)   Len is to be allowed a salary of £6,000 per annum.
   (b)   Interest of 10% per annum is allowed on the partners' capital account balances.
   (c)   No interest is allowed on the partners' current accounts.
   (d)   No interest is charged on the partners' drawings.

You are required to:
(a)   prepare the partners' trading, profit and loss and profit and loss appropriation accounts for the year to 30 September 19X3;
(b)   write up the partners' current accounts for the year to 30 September 19X3, and bring down the balances as at 1 October 19X3; and
(c)   prepare the partnership balance sheet at 30 September 19X3.

(AAT December 1983)

8. NOCTURNE

The following balances appeared in the books of Nocturne Ltd as at 30 September 19X4:

	£
Sales	120,000
Purchases	65,700
Creditors	9,450
Furniture and equipment at cost	33,000
Freehold premises at cost	84,000
Depreciation – furniture and equipment	15,000
– freehold premises	9,000
Debtors	19,044
Provision for doubtful debts	1,224
Bad debts	1,014
Sales returns	1,450
Wages and salaries	12,108
Administration expenses	4,686
Selling and distribution expenses	2,844
Financial expenses	654
Discounts received	2,646
Debenture interest (six months to 31 March 19X4)	600
8% debentures	15,000
Interim dividend on preference shares	900
10% £1 preference shares	18,000
£1 ordinary shares called up and fully paid	50,000
General reserve	7,500
Share premium	10,000
Retained profits at 1 October 19X3	11,000
Stock at 1 October 19X3	18,872
Cash at bank	9,000
Cash in hand	948
Goodwill at cost	14,000

Additional information relevant to the year ended 30 September 19X4 is as follows:

(i) The provision for doubtful debts is to be revised at 5% of debtors.
(ii) Bank charges of £120 are outstanding at 30 September 19X4, as is £1,100 for accrued wages and salaries, and £350 for computer services.
(iii) Stock at 30 September 19X4 was £22,654.
(iv) Depreciation is to be provided of £1,000 on freehold premises, and at 10% on the written down value of furniture and equipment. Goodwill is to be amortised evenly over four years.
(v) A final preference share dividend is to be declared and an ordinary share dividend of 6p per share is proposed for the year ended 30 September 19X4.
(vi) Taxation on the 19X3/X4 profits is estimated at £15,000.

Required:

(a) The trading and profit and loss statements for the year ended 30 September 19X4.
(b) The balance sheet as at 30 September 19X4, indicating the shareholders' funds employed and the working capital figure.

9. HOWTON

The following list of balances was extracted from the books of Howton Co Ltd at 31 December 19X4:

	£	£
£1 ordinary shares		150,000
8% £1 preference shares		50,000
7% debentures		100,000
General reserve		65,000
Land at cost	111,000	
Plant and machinery at cost	382,000	
Undistributed profit at 1 January 19X4		35,000
Share premium account		20,000
Stock at 1 January 19X4	35,000	
Sales		290,000
Discount allowed and received	3,200	4,600
Debtors and creditors	48,000	27,000
Provision for depreciation on plant and machinery at 1 January 19X4		85,500
Bank	7,500	
Carriage inwards	1,100	
Purchases	165,000	
Suspense account		400
Wages	23,500	
Lighting and heating	2,900	
Office salaries	8,600	
Debenture interest	7,000	
Directors' fees	12,800	
Interim dividends:		
Ordinary (5%)	7,500	
Preference (4%)	2,000	
Provision for doubtful debts		1,500
General expenses	11,900	
	829,000	829,000

Inspection of the books and records of the company yields the following additional information.

(a) On 31 December 19X4 the company issued bonus shares to the ordinary shareholders on a 1 for 10 basis. No entry relating to this has yet been made in the books.

(b) The authorised share capital of the company is 200,000 £1 ordinary shares and 50,000 8% £1 preference shares.

(c) Stock at 31 December 19X4 was valued at £41,000.

(d) The suspense account (£400) relates to cash received for the sale of some machinery on 1 January 19X4. This machinery cost £2,000 and the depreciation accumulated thereon amounted to £1,500.

(e) The directors, on the advice of an independent valuer, wish to revalue the land at £180,000 thus bringing the value into line with current prices.

(f) Wages owing at 31 December 19X4 amount to £150.

(g) Depreciation is to be provided on plant and machinery at 10% on cost.

(h) General expenses (£11,900) includes an insurance premium (£200) which relates to the period 1 April 19X4 to 31 March 19X5.

(i) The provision for doubtful debts is to be reduced to $2\frac{1}{2}$% of debtors.

(j)   The directors wish to provide for:

    (i)   a final ordinary dividend of 5%;
    (ii)   a final preference dividend;
    (iii) a transfer to general reserve of £5,000.

You are required to prepare the trading and profit and loss accounts of the Howton Co Ltd for the period ended 31 December 19X4 and a balance sheet as at that date. Ignore taxation.

10. MARSDEN

The following information has been extracted from the books of account of the Marsden Manufacturing Company for the year to 30 September 19X4:

	£
Advertising	2,000
Depreciation for the year to 30 September 19X4:	
Factory equipment	7,000
Office equipment	4,000
Direct wages	40,000
Factory: Insurance	1,000
Heat	15,000
Indirect materials	5,000
Power	20,000
Salaries	25,000
Finished goods (at 1 October 19X3)	24,000
Office: electricity	15,000
general expenses	9,000
postage and telephones	2,900
salaries	70,000
Raw material purchases	202,000
Raw material stock (at 1 October 19X3)	8,000
Sales	512,400
Work in progress (at 1 October 19X3)	12,000

Notes:

1.   At 30 September 19X4, the following stocks were on hand:

	£
Raw materials	10,000
Work in progress	9,000
Finished goods	30,000

2.   At 30 September 19X4, there was an accrual for advertising of £1,000, and it was estimated that £1,500 had been paid in advance for electricity. These items had not been included in the books of account for the year to 30 September 19X4.

3.   The finished goods are transferred from the factory at the manufacturing cost of production plus an addition of 10% for factory profit.

You are required to prepare Marsden's manufacturing, trading and profit and loss account for the year to 30 September 19X4.

(AAT December 1984)

11. SNIPPING LIMITED

Snipping Limited is in business to make and sell small components for the motor trade. The company operates from a small factory. A trial balance extracted from the books on 30 June 19X5 was as follows:

	£	£
Share capital – 100,000 ordinary shares of 50p each		50,000
General reserve		44,000
Profit and loss a/c – unappropriated profit		881
Interim dividend paid	3,200	
Cash at bank and in hand	6,714	
Sundry trade debtors and creditors	26,409	11,647
Freehold property, at cost (land £15,000)	25,000	
Plant, at cost	26,000	
Plant depreciation		12,400
Vehicles, at cost	10,600	
Vehicle depreciation		6,100
Fixtures and fittings, at cost	7,941	
Fixtures and fittings depreciation		2,358
Stock 1 July 19X4 – Material	6,811	
– Work in progress	11,532	
– Finished goods	21,669	
Provision for doubtful debts		1,381
Bad debts	979	
Rates and insurance	1,843	
Wages	21,674	
Factory power	4,512	
Light and heat	3,256	
Maintenance	2,194	
Salaries	18,000	
Returns inwards and outwards	269	634
Advertising	1,716	
Transport expenses	4,609	
Bank charges	585	
Sundry expenses	5,830	
Purchases, sales	183,476	244,925
15% debentures		20,000
Discounts received		493
	394,819	394,819

The following notes are relevant:

1. Provision for doubtful debts is to be adjusted to a figure equal to 8% of debtors.

2. Depreciation is to be provided for the year using the reducing balance method and applying rates of 15% on plant, 25% on vehicles and 10% on fixtures and fittings, and treated as factory overhead, selling overhead and administrative overhead for plant, vehicles and fixtures and fittings respectively.

3. Buildings are to be depreciated using the straight line method, over a fifty year life commencing this year. This expense is considered to be a factory overhead.

403

4.   At 30 June 19X5:

Electricity (light and heat) accrued was £154
Insurance prepaid was £48
Rates prepaid were £150

Stocks were valued at:	Raw material	£27,851
	Work in progress	£16,490
	Finished goods	£24,627

5.   Light and heat, insurance, rates and sundry expenses are to be apportioned in the ratio 4:1 between factory and administrative overheads. An amount of £6,000 posted to the wages account concerns the salary of the factory manager.

6.   Some components which cost £541 have been charged out to a customer with a profit margin of £17 added, but the customer has indicated that he intends to return them since they are not what he ordered.

7.   Debenture interest has not yet been paid this year.

8.   The directors wish to provide for a final dividend which will bring the dividend for the year up to 5p a share.

You are required to prepare in good form a manufacturing, trading and profit and loss account for the year ended 30 June 19X5 and a balance sheet as at that date.

1. **HIGHTON**

TRADING, PROFIT AND LOSS ACCOUNT FOR THE YEAR ENDED 31 MARCH 19X2

	£	£
Sales: cash	80,400	
credit (Working 1)	9,250	
		89,650
Cost of sales:		
Opening stock	3,500	
Purchases: cash	17,000	
credit (Working 2)	47,500	
	68,000	
Less closing stock	4,000	
		64,000
Gross profit		25,650
Expenses:		
Depreciation of motor vehicle (25% x £3,000)	750	
Motor vehicle expenses (Working 3)	800	
Property insurance £(50 + 150 − 100)	100	
Loan interest	100	
Electricity £(400 + 400 − 200)	600	
General shop expenses	100	
Telephone £(100 + 300)	400	
Wages	3,000	
Rates	300	
		6,150
Net profit		19,500

BALANCE SHEET AS AT 31 MARCH 19X2

	£	£
Fixed assets		
Freehold land and buildings at cost		10,000
Motor vehicle: cost	3,000	
accumulated depreciation	1,500	
		1,500
		11,500
Current assets		
Stock	4,000	
Trade debtors	1,000	
Prepayments	400	
Cash at bank	950	
Cash in hand	450	
	6,800	
Current liabilities		
Trade creditors	1,800	
Accruals	500	
	2,300	
Net current assets		4,500
		16,000
Proprietor's capital		
At 1 April 19X4 (Working 4)*		5,250
Net profit for the year	19,500	
Less drawings £(7,000 + 1,750)	8,750	
Profit retained in business		10,750
		16,000

*The opening capital could be inserted as a balancing figure: working 4 is included merely to prove the figure.

Workings

1.

DEBTORS CONTROL ACCOUNT

	£		£
Opening balance	500	Bank	8,750
∴ Credit sales	9,250	Closing balance	1,000
	9,750		9,750

2.

CREDITORS CONTROL ACCOUNT

	£		£
Bank	47,200	Opening balance	1,500
Closing balance	1,800	∴ Credit purchases	47,500
	49,000		49,000

3.

MOTOR VEHICLE EXPENSES

	£		£
Prepayment b/f	200	Accrual b/f	200
Bank	1,000	∴ P & L account	800
Accrual b/f	100	Prepayment c/f	300
	1,300		1,300

4. PROPRIETOR'S CAPITAL AT 1 APRIL 19X1

	£	£
Assets		
Freehold land and buildings	10,000	
Motor vehicle	2,250	
Stock	3,500	
Debtors and prepayments	750	
Cash at bank and in hand	650	
		17,150
Liabilities		
Loan	10,000	
Creditors and accruals	1,900	
		11,900
		5,250

2. CHURCH

(a)
TRADING, PROFIT AND LOSS ACCOUNT
FOR THE YEAR ENDED 31 MARCH 19X3

	£	£
Sales (less returns)		149,100
Opening stock	10,420	
Purchases (balancing figure)	108,370	
	118,790	
Closing stock £(10,420 + 4,000)	14,420	
Cost of goods sold		104,370
Gross profit (30% x £149,100)		44,730
Add discounts received		760
		45,490
Expenses:		
Bad debts	470	
Provision for doubtful debts (5% x £5,620)	281	
Salaries	15,840	
Heat, light etc (W5)	3,560	
Depreciation:		
Shop fittings 10% x £(15,000 + 2,000)	1,700	
Motor vehicle 25% x £6,000	1,500	
		3,351
Net profit		22,139

(b)
BALANCE SHEET AS AT 31 MARCH 19X3

	Cost £	Depreciation £	Net £
Fixed assets			
Shop equipment and fittings	17,000	4,700	12,300
Motor vehicle	6,000	3,000	3,000
	23,000	7,700	15,300
Current assets			
Stock		14,420	
Trade debtors less provision		5,339	
Rent paid in advance		480	
Bank		16,100	
		36,339	
Current liabilities			
Trade creditors		6,390	
Accrued expenses		310	
		6,700	
Net current assets			29,639
			44,939
Proprietor's capital			
Balance at 31 March 19X2			32,400
Profit for year		22,139	
Less drawings £(9,000 + 600)		9,600	
			12,539
			44,939

Workings
Tutorial note: no distinction is made in the question between cash transactions and bank transactions. A 'total cash account' must therefore be constructed instead of the more usual columnar bank and cash account.

1.
TOTAL CASH ACCOUNT

	£		£
Balance b/f	6,690	Creditors (Working 3)	106,560
Debtors (Working 2)	149,270	Salaries	15,840
		Heat, light etc	3,460
		Shop fittings	2,000
		Loan – repayment	3,000
		Drawings	9,000
		Balance c/d	16,100
	155,960		155,960
Balance b/d	16,100		

2.
TOTAL DEBTORS ACCOUNT

	£		£
Balance b/f	6,260	Bad debts	470
Sales	152,600	Returns inwards	3,500
		Cash (balancing figure)	149,270
		Balance c/d	5,620
	158,860		158,860
Balance b/d	5,620		

3.
TOTAL CREDITORS ACCOUNT

	£		£
Discounts received	760	Balance b/f	4,740
Cash (balancing figure)	106,560	Purchases (Working 4)	108,970
Balance c/d	6,390		
	113,710		113,710
		Balance b/d	6,390

4.
PURCHASES ACCOUNT

	£		£
Creditors	108,970	Trading account	108,370
		Drawings	600
	108,970		108,970

5. *Heat, light etc*

	£	£
Amounts paid in year		3,460
Add: rent prepayment at 31.3.X2	650	
heating accrual at 31.3.X3	310	
		960
		4,420
Less: rent prepayment at 31.3.X3	480	
heating accrual at 31.3.X2	380	
		860
P & L charge for year		3,560

3. **SWALLOW**

INCOME AND EXPENDITURE ACCOUNT
FOR THE YEAR ENDED 30 SEPTEMBER 19X3

	£	£
Income		
Gross profit from bar (Working 1)		1,800
Subscriptions (Working 2)		2,125
Christmas dance:		
ticket sales	650	
less expenses	500	
		150
Refreshment sales:		
receipts	320	
less cost of refreshments	180	
		140
		4,215
Expenditure		
Club running expenses (Working 3)	620	
Depreciation:		
premises	2,500	
lawn mower (15% x £600)	90	
		3,210
Net surplus for year		1,005

BALANCE SHEET AS AT 30 SEPTEMBER 19X3

	Cost £	Dep'n £	Net £
Fixed assets			
Club premises	50,000	37,500	12,500
Lawn mower	600	90	510
	50,600	37,590	13,010
Current assets			
Bar stocks		200	
Subscriptions in arrears		200	
Rates prepayment		300	
Cash at bank and in hand		4,040	
		4,740	
Current liabilities			
Creditors for bar purchases		400	
Subscriptions received in advance		75	
Accrued expenses		200	
		675	
Net current assets			4,065
			17,075
Accumulated fund			
Balance at 1 October 19X2 (Working 4)			16,070
Surplus for year			1,005
			17,075

SECTION 3: SUGGESTED SOLUTIONS

Workings

1   Bar trading account

		£	£
Sales (= cash receipts)			3,600
Less cost of sales:			
Opening stock		150	
Purchases £(1,750 + 400 - 300)		1,850	
		2,000	
Less closing stock		200	
			1,800
Gross profit transferred to I & E account			1,800

2   <center>SUBSCRIPTIONS ACCOUNT</center>

	£		£
Arrears b/f	100	Subs in advance b/f	50
I & E a/c (bal. fig)	2,125	Cash	2,050
Subs in advance c/f	75	Arrears c/f	200
	2,300		2,300

3   <center>CLUB RUNNING EXPENSES *</center>

	£		£
Rates prepayment b/f	200	Expenses accrual b/f	250
Cash	770	I & E a/c (bal. fig)	620
Expenses accrual c/f	200	Rates prepayment c/f	300
	1,170		1,170

* Club running expenses are assumed to include rates, since no separate rates payment is listed in the receipts and payments information.

4   Accumulated fund at 1 October 19X2

	£	£
Assets		
Premises at NBV		15,000
Stock		150
Subscriptions in arrears		100
Rates prepayment		200
Cash at bank and in hand		1,220
		16,670
Liabilities		
Creditors for bar purchases	300	
Subscriptions received in advance	50	
Accrued expenses	250	
		(600)
Accumulated fund		16,070

Note: in the examination it would be sufficient to enter the figure of £16,070 in the balance sheet simply as a balancing figure. Working 4 is presented here for reference only.

4. IMPROVIDENT ACTUARIES

(a) *Tutorial note and workings:*
This question involves a bar trading account, membership subscriptions, life membership with a member dying, and a building fund. These items should be dealt with one at a time.

(i) *Bar trading account.* We must first of all calculate bar sales and bar purchases.

	£
Bar takings	28,500
Bar chits not yet settled at 31 December	35
	28,535
Bar chits unsettled as at start of year	0
Bar sales	28,535
Creditors for bar supplies as at 31 December	1,600
Cash payments for bar supplies	23,150
	24,750
Creditors for bar supplies as at start of year	350
Purchases of bar supplies	24,400

BAR TRADING ACCOUNT FOR THE YEAR TO 31 DECEMBER 19X5

	£		£
Opening stocks	4,800	Sales	28,535
Purchases	24,400		
	29,200		
Less closing stocks	4,300		
	24,900	Loss on bar trading	
Wages	4,200	(to I & E account)	565
	29,100		29,100

(ii) ### ANNUAL SUBSCRIPTIONS

	£		£
Subscriptions in arrears b/f 1 Jan	600	Subscriptions in advance b/f 1 Jan	400
∴ Subscriptions income (I & E account)	24,200	Cash (subscriptions received)	25,000
Subscriptions in advance c/d 31 Dec	900	Subscriptions in arrears c/d 31 Dec	300
	25,700		25,700
Subscriptions in arrears b/d	300	Subscriptions in advance b/d	900

(If you do this calculation by the T account method, as shown above, you need to remember that subscriptions in arrears are debtors, and so a debit balance b/f, just as subscriptions in advance are liabilities of the club and so a credit balance b/f.)

(iii) *Life membership.* Presumably, the method of accounting for life membership here is to keep all payments in a life membership fund until a life member dies, when his or her contributions should be transferred direct to the accumulated fund. Since there were four life members at the start of the year, and the life membership fund stood at £4,000, £1,000 will be transferred from this fund to the accumulated fund.

LIFE MEMBERSHIP FUND

	£		£
Accumulated fund (death of member)	1,000	Balance b/f	4,000
Balance c/d	5,000	Cash (new members)	2,000
	6,000		6,000
		Balance b/d	5,000

(iv) *The building fund.* The building fund is a capital fund of the club, and it is represented directly by investments in consolidated stock and a building society account, which are assets (investments) of the club. The accounts for these assets, shown below in T account form, are a mirror image of the building fund (capital) and we should always expect the balance on the building fund account to be equal to the combined balance on the accounts of the two investments.

BUILDING SOCIETY ACCOUNT
(INVESTMENT = ASSET OF CLUB)

	£		£
Balance b/f	10,000		
Cash (new deposits with building society during year)	800		
Interest (added to account)	740	Balance c/f	11,540
	11,540		11,540

Presumably the £800 paid into the building society during the year is the interest on the consolidated stock, amounting to 4% of £20,000 = £800 (see note (b) of question).

4% CONSOLIDATED STOCK
(INVESTMENT = ASSET)

Balance b/f	7,400	Balance c/f	7,400

This account is unchanged, because no new stock is bought during the year, and no stock has been sold. (*Note:* the consolidated stock will be a government security, on which a fixed rate of interest (here 4%) is paid on the nominal or face value of the stock, here £20,000.)

The building fund is a mirror image of these investment accounts.

BUILDING FUND

	£		£
		Balance b/f £(10,000+7,400)	17,400
		Cash paid into building society	800
Balance c/f	18,940	Building society interest	740
	18,940		18,940

412

(v) *General expenses.* A few further figures have still to be calculated in order to prepare a full solution.

	£
Club house expenses (£12,150 - £4,200)	7,950
Petty cash	1,550
	9,500
Less insurance prepayment (one quarter of £480)	120
	9,380

(vi) *Accumulated fund.* The balance b/f at the start of the year will be the difference between club assets and liabilities, minus the sum of the life membership fund and the building fund.

	£	£
Assets as at 1 January 19X5		
£(70,000+15,000+17,400+600+4,800+3,200+950)		111,950
Less current liabilities (400 + 350)	750	
Life membership fund	4,000	
Building fund	17,400	
		22,150
		89,800

(vii) *Cash at bank*

	£
Cash at bank, 1 January	850
Total receipts in year	57,322
	58,172
Total payments in year	55,810
Cash at bank, 31 December	2,362

(viii) We now have the basic information to prepare an income and expenditure account and balance sheet. It is assumed that the piano bought during the year is a fixed asset. Unusually, we are given no information about depreciation of the club equipment or club house itself, and so depreciation should be ignored.

(b)
INCOME AND EXPENDITURE ACCOUNT
YEAR ENDED 31 DECEMBER 19X5

	£	£	£
Income			
Subscriptions			24,200
Green fees			300
Profit on manuals £(700 - 250)			450
			24,950
Expenditure			
Course upkeep		16,150	
General expenses		9,380	
Renewals of club furniture *		1,238	
Bar loss:			
Cost of sales	24,900		
Wages	4,200		
	29,100		
Takings	28,535		
		565	
			27,333
Deficit for year taken to accumulated fund			2,383

* *Note:* net cost of renewals is a revenue expenditure = £1,260 - £22 (from sale of old carpet).

413

(c)

IMPROVIDENT ACTUARIES
BALANCE SHEET AS AT 31 DECEMBER 19X5

	£	£
Fixed assets		
Course at cost		70,000
Clubhouse at cost		15,000
Clubhouse equipment at cost	3,200	
Additions – piano	500	
		3,700
Investments (also fixed assets)		
Building fund:		
£20,000 4% consolidated stock at cost	7,400	
Deposit with building society	11,540	
		18,940
Current assets		
Bar stocks	4,300	
Subscriptions in arrears	300	
Prepayment of insurance premium	120	
Debtors (bar chits unsettled)	35	
Bank	2,362	
Cash in hand (petty cash)	100	
	7,217	
Current liabilities		
Subscriptions in advance	900	
Creditors	1,600	
	2,500	
		4,717
		112,357
Funds employed		
Accumulated fund as at 1 January		89,800
Transfer from life membership fund		1,000
		90,800
Less deficit for the year		2,383
Accumulated fund as at 31 December		88,417
Life membership fund as at 1 January	4,000	
Less transfer to capital fund	(1,000)	
Add new life members	2,000	
Life membership fund as at 31 December		5,000
Building fund as at 1 January	17,400	
Add interest:		
Consolidated stock	800	
Building society	740	
Building fund as at 31 December		18,940
Funds employed		112,357

5. ADAMS BROWN AND CARTER

APPROPRIATION ACCOUNT
FOR THE YEAR ENDED 28 FEBRUARY 19X5

	£		£
Interest on capital - current account of:		Net profit b/f	9,530
Adams (8% x £10,000)	800	Interest on drawings - current account of:	
Brown (8% x £6,000)	480	Adams (5% x £2,000)	100
Carter (8% x £4,000)	320	Brown (5% x £1,800)	90
Salaries - current account of:		Carter (5% x £1,600)	80
Brown	1,500		
Carter	1,100		
Residual profits - current account of:			
Adams (2/4)	2,800		
Brown (1/4)	1,400		
Carter (1/4)	1,400		
	9,800		9,800

PARTNERS' CURRENT ACCOUNTS

	Adams £	Brown £	Carter £		Adams £	Brown £	Carter £
Drawings	2,000	1,800	1,600	Balance b/f	1,800	1,200	300
Interest on drawings	100	90	80	Interest on capital	800	480	320
Balances c/d	3,300	2,690	1,440	Salaries		1,500	1,100
				Profit share	2,800	1,400	1,400
	5,400	4,580	3,120		5,400	4,580	3,120
				Balances b/d	3,300	2,690	1,440

6.   NORTH AND SOUTH

NORTH AND SOUTH
TRADING AND PROFIT AND LOSS ACCOUNT
FOR THE YEAR ENDED 28 FEBRUARY 19X3

	£	£
Sales		17,350
Less cost of goods sold:		
Opening stock	1,870	
Purchases	8,260	
	10,130	
Less closing stock	2,280	
		7,850
Gross profit		9,500
Add discounts received		190
		9,690
Expenses:		
Discounts allowed	510	
Wages and salaries £(2,160 + 60)	2,220	
Rent and rates £(390 - 30)	360	
Depreciation:		
Fixtures and fittings	50	
Delivery van	70	
Van running expenses	420	
Bad debts written off	170	
General expenses	1,090	
		4,890
Net profit available for appropriation		4,800
Appropriations:		
North (2/3)	3,200	
South (1/3)	1,600	
		4,800

NORTH AND SOUTH
BALANCE SHEET
AS AT 28 FEBRUARY 19X3

	£	£
Fixed assets		
Fixtures and fittings £(500-50)	450	
Delivery van £(700-70)	630	
		1,080
Current assets		
Stock	2,280	
Debtors and prepayment £(3,920 + 30)	3,950	
Cash	70	
	6,300	
Current liabilities		
Bank overdraft	310	
Creditors and accrual £(1,750 + 60)	1,810	
	2,120	
Net current assets		4,180
		5,260

PARTNERS' ACCOUNTS

	North £	South £	Total £
Capital accounts	2,800	1,500	4,300
Current accounts (see below)	570	390	960
	3,370	1,890	5,260

Working

PARTNERS' CURRENT ACCOUNTS

	North £	South £		North £	South £
Drawings	2,900	1,450	Balances b/f	270	240
Balances c/d	570	390	Profit share	3,200	1,600
	3,470	1,840		3,470	1,840
			Balances b/d	570	390

7. BEN KEN AND LEN

(a)

BEN, KEN AND LEN
TRADING, PROFIT AND LOSS AND APPROPRIATION ACCOUNTS
FOR THE YEAR ENDED 30 SEPTEMBER 19X3

	£	£
Sales		150,000
Less cost of goods sold:		
Opening stock	20,000	
Purchases	85,000	
	105,000	
Less closing stock	30,000	
		75,000
Gross profit		75,000
Expenses:		
Depreciation: land and buildings (5% x £60,000)	3,000	
motor vehicles (20% x £20,000)	4,000	
Office expenses	4,000	
Rates £(4,000-2,000)	2,000	
Selling expenses £(14,000 + 1,775)	15,775	
Bad debts	500	
Increase in provision for doubtful debts		
5% x £(23,000 - 500) - £1,000	125	
		29,400
Net profit available for appropriation		45,600
Appropriations:		
Salary – Len	6,000	
Interest on capital: Ben	1,800	
Ken	1,200	
Len	600	
	9,600	
Residual profit: Ben (3/6)	18,000	
Ken (2/6)	12,000	
Len (1/6)	6,000	
		45,600

(b)   PARTNERS' CURRENT ACCOUNTS

	Ben £	Ken £	Len £		Ben £	Ken £	Len £
Balance b/f		500		Balances b/f	700		300
Drawings	4,000	3,000	3,000	Appropriation			
Balances c/d	16,500	9,700	9,900	a/c:			
				Salary			6,000
				Int on capital	1,800	1,200	600
				Profit share	18,000	12,000	6,000
	20,500	13,200	12,900		20,500	13,200	12,900
				Balances b/d	16,500	9,700	9,900

(c)   BEN, KEN AND LEN
                                       BALANCE SHEET
                                       AS AT 30 SEPTEMBER 19X3

	Cost £	Dep'n £	Net £
Fixed assets			
Land and buildings	60,000	15,000	45,000
Motor vehicles	20,000	12,000	8,000
	80,000	27,000	53,000
Current assets			
Stock		30,000	
Debtors less provision £(23,00 – 500 – 1,125)		21,375	
Prepayment		2,000	
Cash at bank and in hand		2,500	
		55,875	
Current liabilities			
Creditors		35,000	
Accrual		1,775	
		36,775	
Net current assets			19,100
			72,100

PARTNERS' ACCOUNTS

	Ben £	Ken £	Len £	Total £
Capital accounts	18,000	12,000	6,000	36,000
Current accounts	16,500	9,700	9,900	36,100
	34,500	21,700	15,900	72,100

8. NOCTURNE

(a)   TRADING, PROFIT AND LOSS ACCOUNT
FOR THE YEAR ENDED 30 SEPTEMBER 19X4

	£	£
Sales (net of returns)		118,550
Less cost of goods sold:		
Opening stock	18,872	
Purchases	65,700	
	84,572	
Less closing stock	22,654	
		61,918
Gross profit		56,632
Add: decrease in provision for doubtful debts		
£1,224 - (5% x £19,044)		272
discounts received		2,646
		59,550
Expenses:		
Administration expenses £(4,686 + 350)	5,036	
Selling and distribution expenses	2,844	
Financial expenses £(654 + 120)	774	
Wages and salaries £(12,108 + 1,100)	13,208	
Bad debts	1,014	
Debenture interest (8% x £15,000)	1,200	
depreciation - premises	1,000	
furniture and equipment		
10% x £(33,000 - 15,000)	1,800	
Amortisation of goodwill	3,500	
		30,376
Profit before taxation		29,174
Taxation		15,000
Profit after taxation		14,174
Dividends: preference - interim paid	900	
- final proposed	900	
ordinary - final proposed (50,000 x 6p)	3,000	
		4,800
Retained profit for the year		9,374
Retained profits brought forward		11,000
Retained profits carried forward		20,374

(b)

BALANCE SHEET
AS AT 30 SEPTEMBER 19X4

	Cost £	Dep'n £	Net £
Fixed assets			
Goodwill	14,000	3,500	10,500
Freehold premises	84,000	10,000	74,000
Furniture and equipment	33,000	16,800	16,200
	131,000	30,300	100,700
Current assets			
Stock		22,654	
Debtors less provision £(19,044 - 952)		18,092	
Cash at bank and in hand		9,948	
		50,694	
Current liabilities			
Creditors		9,450	
Accruals £(120 + 1,100 + 350 + (deb.int.) 600)		2,170	
Taxation payable		15,000	
Proposed dividends		3,900	
		30,520	
Working capital			20,174
			120,874
Long-term liability			
8% debentures			(15,000)
			105,874
Capital and reserves			
Called up share capital			
10% £1 preference shares		18,000	
£1 ordinary shares		50,000	
			68,000
Reserves			
Share premium account		10,000	
General reserve		7,500	
Profit and loss account		20,374	
			37,874
			105,874

9. HOWTON

Notes

1. The bonus share issue of 1/10 x 150,000 shares can be made out of the share premium: ie
   Debit Share premium account   £15,000
   Credit Ordinary shares account   £15,000

   The issued share capital is now £165,000 and share premium £5,000.

2. The sale of the plant and machinery has not yet been entered in the accounts, since the cash received has been debited to cash, but credited to a suspense account.

DISPOSAL OF PLANT AND MACHINERY

	£		£
Plant and machinery a/c: cost of plant and machinery sold	2,000	Suspense account - sale price Depreciation on plant and machinery	400 1,500 100
	2,000		2,000

3. Plant and machinery at cost is now £382,000 - £2,000 sold = £380,000

4. Depreciation for the year on plant and machinery 10% of £380,000 = £38,000
   Accumulated provision for depreciation

	£
Per trial balance	85,500
Less depreciation on plant and machinery sold	1,500
	84,000
Add depreciation for the year	38,000
	122,000

5.
	£
Land at revalued amount	180,000
Land at cost* (per trial balance)	111,000
Credit to revaluation reserve	69,000

   * The land is not depreciated so there is no net book value to consider.

6. The insurance premium paid includes a prepayment of $\frac{3}{12}$ x £200 = £50, and so general expenses in the P & L account will be £11,900 - £50 = £11,850.

7.
Debtors	£48,000
Provision for doubtful debts	£1,200
Provision per trial balance	£1,500
Reduction in provision (credit P & L account)	£300

8. Since debenture interest (7% of £100,000) = £7,000 is included in the trial balance in full, this means that it must already have been paid for the year, and accounted for by:

   Debit Debenture interest   £7,000
   Credit Cash   £7,000

HOWTON LIMITED
TRADING AND PROFIT AND LOSS ACCOUNT
FOR THE PERIOD ENDED 31 DECEMBER 19X4

	£	£	£
Sales			290,000
Less cost of sales			
Opening stock		35,000	
Purchases		165,000	
Carriage inward		1,100	
		201,100	
Less closing stock		41,000	
			160,100
Gross profit			129,900
Provision for doubtful debts no longer required			300
Discounts received			4,600
			134,800
Less expenses			
Wages £(23,500 + 150 accrued)		23,650	
Office salaries		8,600	
Directors' fees		12,800	
General expenses		11,850	
Light and heating		2,900	
Depreciation on machinery		38,000	
Loss on sale of machinery		100	
Discounts allowed		3,200	
Debenture interest		7,000	
			108,100
Net profit available for appropriation			26,700
Appropriations			
Dividends paid (interim)			
5% ordinary	7,500		
8% preference x 6 months	2,000		
		9,500	
Dividends proposed			
5% final ordinary (on nominal value £165,000)	8,250		
8% final preference x 6 months	2,000		
		10,250	
General reserve		5,000	
			24,750
			1,950
Undistributed profit at 1 January 19X4			35,000
Undistributed profit at 31 December 19X4			36,950

HOWTON LIMITED
BALANCE SHEET
AS AT 31 DECEMBER 19X4

	£	£	£
Fixed assets			
Land (at valuation)			180,000
Plant and machinery: cost		380,000	
depreciation		122,000	
			258,000
			438,000
Current assets			
Stock		41,000	
Debtors and prepayments (less provision)		46,850	
Bank		7,500	
		95,350	
Creditors: amounts falling due within			
one year			
Creditors and accruals	27,150		
Dividends proposed:			
5% ordinary	8,250		
8% preference (6 months)	2,000		
		37,400	
Net current assets			57,950
Total assets less current liabilities			495,950
Creditors: amounts falling due after			
more than one year			
7% debentures			(100,000)
			395,950
Capital and reserves			
Called up share capital			
165,000 £1 ordinary shares		165,000	
50,000 8% preference shares		50,000	
			215,000
Reserves			
Share premium		5,000	
Revaluation reserve		69,000	
General reserve £(65,000 + 5,000)		70,000	
Undistributed profit		36,950	
			180,950
			395,950

10. MARSDEN

MANUFACTURING, TRADING AND PROFIT AND LOSS ACCOUNT
FOR THE YEAR ENDED 30 SEPTEMBER 19X4

	£	£
Raw materials		
Opening stock	8,000	
Purchases	202,000	
	210,000	
Less closing stock	10,000	
		200,000
Factory wages		40,000
Prime cost		240,000
Indirect factory expenses		
Insurance	1,000	
Heat	15,000	
Indirect materials	5,000	
Power	20,000	
Salaries	25,000	
Depreciation of factory equipment	7,000	
		73,000
		313,000
Work in progress		
Opening stock	12,000	
Less closing stock	9,000	
		3,000
Factory cost of goods produced		316,000
Factory profit		31,600
Transfer price of goods produced		347,600
Sales		512,400
Less cost of goods sold:		
Opening stock of finished goods	24,000	
Transfer price of finished goods produced	347,600	
	371,600	
Less closing stock of finished goods	30,000	
		341,600
Gross profit from trading		170,800
Factory profit		31,600
		202,400
Increase in provision for unrealised profit		
(1/11 x £30,000) - (1/11 x £24,000)*	545	
Expenses:		
Advertising £(2,000 + 1,000)	3,000	
Depreciation of office equipment	4,000	
Electricity £(15,000 - 1,500)	13,500	
General expenses	9,000	
Postage and telephones	2,900	
Salaries	70,000	
		102,945
Net profit		99,455

* It is assumed that the finished goods valuations are at transfer price from the factory, not at cost.

11. SNIPPING LIMITED

Tutorial note: you might find the following comments helpful in preparing a solution.

(1) The trial balance shows figures before adjustments are made to the provision for doubtful debts, depreciation, the return of components by the customer, debenture interest and the final dividend. The stocks in the trial balance are those at the beginning of the year.

(2) Adjustments must obviously be made for the items listed in notes 1-8. You must also be able to distinguish between profit and loss account items (revenue) and balance sheet items (capital) in the trial balance.

(3) It is assumed that the components sold (note 6 in the question) are items of raw material stock rather than finished goods, although the question is not entirely clear about this.

Solution

(a) The provision for doubtful debts is to be 8% of debtors.

	£
Debtors in the trial balance	26,409
Less sales value of components to be returned £(541 + 57)	598
(presumably, the customer has not yet paid for them)	
Adjusted debtors figure	25,811

	£
Provision for doubtful debts (8%)	2,065
Provision in the trial balance (ie as at the start of the year)	1,381
Increase in provision in the year (P & L account item)	684

(b) Depreciation

	Plant £	Vehicles £	Fixtures & fittings £	Buildings £
Net book value as at start of year	13,600	4,500	5,583	10,000 (cost)
Depreciation in year				
15% of reducing balance	2,040 *			
25% of reducing balance		1,125 *		
10% of reducing balance			558 *	
2% of cost				200 *
Accumulated depreciation to start of year	12,400	6,100	2,358	0
Accumulated depreciation as at end of year	14,440	7,225	2,916	200
	*Factory overhead	*Selling overhead	*Admin overhead	*Factory overhead

(c) Adjustments to light and heat, insurance, rates and stocks

	Light and heat £	Rates and insurance £	Raw material stocks £
As in the trial balance	3,256	1,843	
As at the year end			27,851
Light and heat: expenses accrued (note 1)	154		
Insurance: prepaid (note2)		(48)	
Rates: prepaid (note 2)		(150)	
Stocks due to be returned, at cost (note 3)			541
Adjusted values	3,410	1,645	28,392

Notes

1. An accrued expense means that there has not yet been an invoice of payment for costs incurred. The accrued electricity charge should therefore be added to the light and heat costs already recorded as exenses in the trial balance.

2. A prepayment means that money has been paid (or an invoiced debt is owed) for an item whose costs relate to a later period. The prepaid insurance and rates are included in the trial balance, but should not be charged against the current year's profits. Prepayments appear as a current asset in the balance sheet.

3. The components to be returned by the customer will be added back to the raw materials stock (at cost). This item of stock in transit has been added to the value of stocks to appear in the balance sheet.

(d) Apportionment of costs

Item	Total cost £	Factory overheads (80%) £	Admin overheads (20%) £
Light and heat	3,410	2,728	682
Rates and insurance	1,645	1,316	329
Sundry expenses	5,830	4,664	1,166

Factory wages (£21,674) should be reduced by £6,000, the factory manager's salary. This salary is more properly a factory overhead, rather than a direct wages cost.

(e) Return of components. The sales figure of £244,925 should be reduced by
   (i)   the components sold for £(541 + 57) = £598 but about to be returned;
   (ii) other returns (ie returns inwards) given in the trial balance as £269.

	£	£
Sales		244,925
Less:		
components returned	598	
other returns inwards	269	
		867
Adjusted figure for sales		244,058

(f) Debenture interest for the year is 15% of £20,000 = £3,000. This is a charge to P & L, and will appear as a current liability in the balance sheet, since the interest has not yet been paid. (We know this, since there is no expense account in the trial balance for debenture interest.)

(g) Final dividend. Total dividend for the year is 100,000 shares x 5p = £5,000. This is an appropriation of profit. Since the interim dividend already paid is £3,200, the proposed final dividend must be £1,800.

(h) Cost of sales. The cost of sales will be calculated in the manufacturing, trading and P & L account below. However, it is first of all necessary to calculate raw material purchases, allowing for returns.

	£
Purchases (as in trial balance)	183,476
Returns outwards	634
Net purchases	182,842

SNIPPING LIMITED
MANUFACTURING ACCOUNT
FOR THE YEAR ENDED 30 JUNE 19X5

	£	£
Raw materials		
Opening stock	6,811	
Purchases, net of returns	182,84	
	189,653	
Less closing stock	28,392	
		161,261
Factory wages		15,674
Prime cost		176,935
Factory overhead		
Factory power	4,512	
Plant depreciation	2,040	
Plant maintenance	2,194	
Rates and insurance	1,316	
Light and heat	2,728	
Sundry expenses	4,664	
Factory manager's salary	6,000	
Building depreciation	200	
		23,654
Factory cost of resources consumed		200,589
Work in progress: opening stocks	11,532	
closing stocks	(16,490)	
Increase in work in progress stocks		(4,958)
Factory cost of finished goods produced		195,631

SNIPPING LIMITED
TRADING AND PROFIT AND LOSS ACCOUNT
FOR THE YEAR ENDED 30 JUNE 19X5

	£	£
Sales, net of returns		244,058
Less cost of sales:		
Opening stock of finished goods	21,669	
Factory cost of finished goods produced	195,631	
	217,300	
Less closing stock of finished goods	24,627	
		192,673
Gross profit		51,385
Administration expenses		
Rates and insurance	329	
Light and heat	682	
Sundry expenses	1,166	
Salaries	18,000	
Depreciation of fixtures and fittings	558	
	20,735	
Selling expenses		
Advertising	1,716	
Transport	4,609	
Vehicle depreciation	1,125	
Bad debts written off	979	
Increase in provision for doubtful debts	684	
	9,113	
Financial items		
Loan interest	3,000	
Bank charges	585	
	3,585	
Discounts received	(493)	
Net cost	3,092	
		32,940
Net profit		18,445
Appropriation of profit		
Interim dividend paid	1,800	
Final dividend proposed	3,200	
		5,000
Retained profit for the year		13,445
Retained profit brought forward		881
Retained profit carried forward		14,326

SNIPPING LIMITED
BALANCE SHEET
AS AT 30 JUNE 19X5

	Cost £	Dep'n £	Net £
Fixed assets			
Freehold property	25,000	200	24,800
Plant	26,000	14,440	11,560
Vehicles	10,600	7,225	3,375
Fixtures and fittings	7,941	2,916	5,025
	69,541	24,781	44,760
Current assets			
Stocks: raw materials		28,392	
work in progress		16,490	
finished goods		24,627	
Debtors	25,811		
Less provision for doubtful debts	2,065		
		23,746	
Prepayments (rent and insurance)		198	
Cash		6,714	
		100,167	
Creditors: amounts falling due within one year			
Trade creditors	11,647		
Accruals (light and heat)	154		
Loan interest payable	3,000		
Proposed dividend	1,800		
		16,601	
Net current assets			83,566
			128,326
Creditors: amounts falling due after more than one year			
15% debentures			(20,000)
			108,326
Capital and reserves			
Share capital (50,000 shares of £1)			50,000
General reserve			44,000
Profit and loss account			14,326
			108,326

SECTION 4

INTERPRETATION OF FINANCIAL STATEMENTS

Chapter 24

INTERPRETATION OF FINANCIAL STATEMENTS

The purpose of this chapter is:

- to introduce the principles of interpreting financial statements

- to explain the main accounting ratios derived from financial statements

---

Introduction

1. The profit and loss account and the balance sheet are both sources of useful information about the condition of a business. The analysis and interpretation of these statements can be done by calculating certain ratios, between one item and another, and then using the ratios for comparison, either:

   (a) between one year and the next for a particular business, in order to identify any trends, or significantly better or worse results than before; or

   (b) between one business and another, to establish which business has performed better, and in what ways.

2. The most important ratios are described in this and the following chapter.

Profit margin, asset turnover and return on capital employed

3. There are three principal ratios which can be used to measure how efficiently the operations of a business have been managed. These are:

   (a) profit margin;
   (b) asset turnover;
   (c) return on capital employed.

4. *Profit margin* is the ratio of profit to sales, and may also be called 'profit percentage'. For example, if a company makes a profit of £20,000 on sales of £100,000 its profit percentage or profit margin is 20%. This also means that its costs are 80% of sales. A high profit margin indicates that:

(a) either costs are being kept well under control because if the ratio of costs to sales goes down, the profit margin will automatically go up. For example, if the cost:sales ratio changes from 80% to 75%, the profit margin will go up from 20% to 25%;

(b) or sales prices are high. For example, if a company sells goods for £100,000 and makes a profit of £16,000 costs would be £84,000 and the profit margin 16%. Now if the company can raise selling prices by 20% to £120,000 without affecting the volume of goods sold or their costs, profits would rise by the amount of revenue increase (£20,000) to £36,000 and the profit margin would also rise (from 16% to 30%).

5. *Asset turnover* is the ratio of sales turnover in a year to the amount of capital employed. For example, if a company has sales in 19X4 of £720,000 and has assets of £360,000, the asset turnover will be:

$$\frac{£720,000}{£360,000} = 2 \text{ times}$$

This means that for every £1 of assets employed, the company can generate sales turnover of £2 per annum. To utilise assets more efficiently, managers should try to create a higher volume of sales and a higher asset turnover ratio. For example, suppose that our firm with assets of £360,000 can increase its sales turnover from £720,000 to £900,000 per annum. The asset turnover would improve to:

$$\frac{£900,000}{£360,000} = 2.5 \text{ times}$$

The significance of this improvement is that if a business can create more sales turnover from the same amount of assets it should make larger profits (because of the increase in sales) without having to increase the size of its investment.

Return on capital employed (ROCE)

6. *Return on capital employed* (ROCE) is the amount of profit as a percentage of capital employed. If a company makes a profit of £30,000, we do not know how good or bad the result is until we look at the amount of capital which has been invested to achieve the profit. £30,000 might be a good sized profit for a small firm, but it would not be good enough for a 'giant' firm such as Marks and Spencer, say. For this reason, it is helpful to measure performance by relating profits to capital employed, and because this seems to be the only satisfactory ratio or percentage which judges profits in relation to the size of business, it is sometimes called the primary ratio in financial analysis.

7. You may already have realised that there is a mathematical connection between return on capital employed, profit margin and asset turnover:

$$\frac{\text{Profit}}{\text{Capital employed}} = \frac{\text{Profit}}{\text{Sales}} \times \frac{\text{Sales}}{\text{Capital employed}}$$

$$\text{ROCE} = \text{Profit margin} \times \text{Asset turnover}$$

This is important. If we accept that ROCE is the single most important measure of business performance, comparing profit with the amount of capital invested, we can go on to say that business performance is dependent on two separate 'subsidiary' factors, each of which contributes to ROCE:

(a) profit margin;
(b) asset turnover.

For this reason, just as ROCE is sometimes called the primary ratio, the profit margin and asset turnover ratios are sometimes called the secondary ratios.

8. The implications of this relationship must be understood. Suppose that a return on capital employed of 20% is thought to be a good level of business performance in the retail trade for electrical goods:

(a) company A might decide to sell its products at a fairly high price and make a profit margin on sales of 10%. It would then need only an asset turnover of 2.0 times to achieve a ROCE of 20%;

(b) company B might decide to cut its prices so that its profit margin is only 2½%. Provided that it can achieve an asset turnover of 8 times a year, attracting more customers with its lower prices, it will still make a ROCE of 2½% x 8 = 20%.

9. Company A might be a department store and company B a discount warehouse. Each will have a different selling price policy, but each, in its own way, can be effective in achieving a target ROCE. In this example, if we supposed that both companies had capital employed of £100,000 and a target return of 20% or £20,000:

(a) company A would need annual sales of £200,000 to give a profit margin of 10% and an asset turnover of 2 times;

(b) company B would need annual sales of £800,000 to give a profit margin of only 2½% but an asset turnover of 8 times.

The inter-relationship between profit margin and asset turnover

10. A higher return on capital employed can be obtained by increasing the profit margin or the asset turnover ratio. The profit margin can be increased by reducing costs or by raising selling prices.

However, if selling prices are raised, it is likely that sales demand will fall, with the possible consequences that the asset turnover will also decline. If higher prices mean lower sales turnover, the increase in profit margin might be offset by the fall in asset turnover, so that total return on capital employed might not improve.

Example

11. Suppose that Swings and Roundabouts Ltd achieved the following results in 19X6:

Sales	£100,000
Profit	£5,000
Capital employed	£20,000

The company's management wish to decide whether to raise its selling prices. They think that if they do so, they can raise the profit margin to 10% and by introducing extra capital of £55,000, sales turnover could be increased to £150,000.

Required: evaluate the decision in terms of the effect on ROCE, profit margin and asset turnover.

Solution

12. At present, ratios are:

Profit margin	5%
Asset turnover	5 times
ROCE (5/20)	25%

With the proposed changes, the profit would be 10% x £150,000 = £15,000, and the asset turnover would be:

$$\frac{£150,000}{£\ 75,000} = 2 \text{ times, so that the ratios might be:}$$

Profit margin   x   Asset turnover   =   ROCE

10%   x   2 times   =   20% $(\frac{£15,000}{£75,000})$

In spite of increasing the profit margin and raising the total volume of sales, the extra assets required (£55,000) only raise total profits by £(15,000 - 5,000) = £10,000.

The return on capital employed falls from 25% to 20% because of the sharp fall in asset turnover from 5 times to 2 times.

Whose return and whose capital employed?

13. Most of the providers of finance to a business expect some return on their investment:

(a) trade creditors and other current liabilities merely expect to be paid what they are owed;

(b) a bank charges interest on overdrafts;

(c) interest must be paid to the holders of loan stock and debentures;

(d) preference shareholders expect a dividend at a fixed percentage rate of the nominal value of their shares;

(e) ordinary shareholders also expect a dividend. However, any retained profits kept in the business also represent funds 'owned' or 'provided' by them.

14. So when we refer to 'return' we must be clear in our mind about which providers of finance we are concerned with, and we should relate the return earned for those providers of finance to the amount of capital they are providing.

   (a) If 'return' is profit after tax, it is return earned by ordinary and preference shareholders. The capital employed by these investors is:

      (i)   the nominal value of preference shares;
      (ii)   the nominal value of ordinary shares;
      (iii) the amount in various reserves, because reserves are surpluses or profits retained in a business and 'owned' by the equity investors - ie the ordinary shareholders in a company.

   (b) If 'return' is profit after tax and preference dividend, the left-over return is for ordinary shareholders, and is called 'earnings'. The return on equity capital is:

$$\frac{\text{Earnings}}{\text{Ordinary share capital plus reserves}}$$

   (c) If we prefer to consider the business as a whole, then the fixed assets and net current assets are financed by long-term capital which may include loan creditors as well as shareholders. The fund available to satisfy the claims of all these providers of finance is the profit before interest payments and taxation. In this case ROCE may be calculated as:

$$\frac{\text{Profit before interest and tax (PBIT)}}{\text{Loan capital plus share capital plus reserves}}$$

which equals

$$\frac{\text{PBIT}}{\text{Fixed assets plus net current assets}}$$

Example

15. Suppose that Draught Limited reports the following figures:

PROFIT AND LOSS ACCOUNT FOR 19X4 (EXTRACT)

	£
Profit before interest and tax	120,000
Interest	(20,000)
Profit before tax	100,000
Taxation	(40,000)
Profit after tax	60,000
Preference dividend	(1,000)
Profit available for ordinary shareholders (= earnings)	59,000
Ordinary dividend	(49,000)
Retained profits	10,000

BALANCE SHEET AT 31 DECEMBER 19X4

	£	£
Fixed assets: tangible assets		350,000
Current assets	400,000	
Less current liabilities	150,000	
Net current assets		250,000
Total assets less current liabilities		600,000
Creditors: amounts falling due after more than one year:		
10% debenture loans		200,000
		400,000
Capital and reserves:		
Called up share capital:		
5% preference shares	20,000	
ordinary shares	80,000	
		100,000
Profit and loss account		300,000
		400,000

16. Using the three alternatives described in paragraph 14, ROCE might be calculated in any of the following ways:

(a) *Return on shareholders' capital*

$$\frac{\text{Profit after tax}}{\text{Share capital plus reserves}} = \frac{£60,000}{£400,000} = 15\%$$

(b) *Return on equity capital*

$$\frac{\text{Profit after tax and preference dividend (earnings)}}{\text{Ordinary share capital plus reserves}} = \frac{£59,000}{£380,000} = 15.5\%$$

(c) *Return on total long-term capital*

$$\frac{\text{Profit before interest and tax}}{\text{Loan capital plus share capital plus reserves}} = \frac{£120,000}{£600,000} = 20\%$$

Earnings per share

17. In the previous example it is possible to calculate the return on each ordinary share in the year. This is the earnings per share (EPS). Earnings are profits after tax and preference dividend, which can either be paid out as a dividend to ordinary shareholders or retained in the business. Earnings are the total return for ordinary shareholders and for Draught Ltd in 19X4, the EPS is:

$$\frac{£60,000}{100,000 \text{ shares}} = 60 \text{ pence}$$

In practice, there are usually further complications in calculating the EPS but fortunately these are outside your syllabus!

Gearing

18. We have now seen that a company is financed by different types of capital and that each type expects a return in the form of interest or dividend.

    Gearing is a method of comparing how much of the long-term capital of a business is provided by equity (ordinary shares and reserves) and how much is provided by investors who are entitled to interest or dividend before ordinary shareholders can have a dividend themselves. These sources of capital are loans and preference shares, and are sometimes known collectively as 'prior charge capital'.

19. The two most usual methods of measuring gearing are:

    (a) $\dfrac{\text{Prior charge capital (long-term loans and preference shares)}}{\text{Equity (ordinary shares plus reserves)}} \times 100\%$

        (i)   a business is low-geared if the gearing is less than 100%;
        (ii) it is neutrally-geared if the gearing is exactly 100%;
        (iii) it is high-geared if the gearing is more than 100%;

    (b) $\dfrac{\text{Prior charge capital (long-term loans and preference shares)}}{\text{Total long-term capital}}$

    A business is now low-geared if gearing is less than 50% (calculated under method (b)), neutrally-geared if gearing is exactly 50% and high-geared if it exceeds 50%.

20. Low gearing means that there is more equity finance in the business than there is prior charge capital. High gearing means the opposite - ie that prior charge capital exceeds the amount of equity.

21. A numerical example might be helpful:

    Draught Limited, the company in paragraph 15, has a gearing of:

    (a) $\dfrac{£220,000}{£380,000}$ (debenture loans plus preference shares) $\times 100\% = 57.9\%$ or
                        (ordinary shares plus reserves)

    (b) $\dfrac{£220,000}{£600,000}$ (debenture loans plus preference shares) $\times 100\% = 36.7\%$
                        (total long-term capital)

Why is gearing important?

22. Gearing can be important when a company wants to raise extra capital, because if its gearing is already too high, we might find that it is difficult to raise a loan. Would-be lenders might take the view that ordinary shareholders should provide a fair proportion of the total capital for the business and that at the moment they are not doing so. Unless ordinary shareholders are prepared to put in more money themselves (either by issuing new shares or by retaining more profits), the company might be viewed as a bad business risk.

23. If excessive gearing indicates that more loans should not be made to a company, we must now ask the question "what is excessive gearing?"

Unfortunately, there is no hard and fast answer to this question. The 'acceptable' level of gearing varies according to the country (eg average gearing is higher among companies in Japan than in Britain), the industry, and the size and status of the individual company within the industry. The more stable the company is, the more 'safe' higher gearing should be.

24. The advantages of gearing (ie of using debt capital) are as follows:

    (a) debt capital is cheaper, because:

        (i)   the reward (interest or preference dividend) is fixed permanently, and therefore diminishes in real terms if there is inflation. Ordinary shareholders, on the other hand, usually expect dividend growth;

        (ii) the reward required by debt-holders is usually lower than that required by equity holders, because debt capital is often secured on company assets, whereas ordinary share capital is a more risky investment;

        (iii) payments of interest attract tax relief, whereas ordinary (or preference) dividends do not;

    (b) debt capital does not normally carry voting rights, but ordinary shares usually do. The issue of debt capital therefore leaves pre-existing voting rights unchanged;

    (c) if profits are rising, ordinary shareholders will benefit from gearing (see example below).

25. The main disadvantage of gearing is that if profits fall even slightly, the profit available to shareholders will fall at a greater rate.

Gearing and earnings

26. One of the reasons why high gearing might be considered risky for lenders is that the more loan capital a business has, the bigger becomes the size of profit before interest and tax (PBIT) which is necessary to meet demands for interest payments.

Example: gearing and earnings per share

27. A numerical example might help to illustrate this point. Suppose that there are two companies, Nogear Ltd and Highgear Ltd, which have the following long-term capital structures:

	Nogear Ltd £	Highgear Ltd £
Ordinary shares of £1	10,000	4,000
10% loans	0	6,000
Total long-term capital	10,000	10,000

Required:
What are the earnings per share for each company if profits before interest and tax are:
(a) £500;
(b) £1,000;
(c) £1,500?

Assume that taxation on profits (after deducting interest) is 50%.

Solution

28.

		Nogear Ltd £	*Highgear Ltd* £
(a)	*PBIT = £500:*		
	PBIT	500	500
	Interest	-	600
	Profit/(loss) before tax	500	(100)
	Tax (50%)	250	-
	Earnings	250	-
	Number of shares	10,000	4,000
	Earnings per share	2.5 pence	Nil
(b)	*PBIT = £1,000*	£	£
	PBIT	1,000	1,000
	Interest	-	600
	Profit before tax	1,000	400
	Tax (50%)	500	200
	Earnings	500	200
	Number of shares	10,000	4,000
	Earnings per share	5 pence	5 pence
(c)	*PBIT = £1,500*	£	£
	PBIT	1,500	1,500
	Interest	0	600
	Profit before tax	1,500	900
	Tax (50%)	750	450
	Earnings	750	450
	Number of shares	10,000	4,000
	Earnings per share	7.5 pence	11.25 pence

29. In a high-geared company, profits before interest and tax might be insufficient to pay interest charges. However, once profits get larger the earnings per share grow at a much faster rate than a low-geared company. (The term 'gearing' is derived from this rate of change in earnings per share, which is slow in low-gear and fast in high-gear.)

30. In our example, when PBIT is £500, Highgear makes a loss, whereas Nogear makes earnings of 2.5p per share. When profits double to £1,000 before interest and tax, the earnings per share in Highgear have 'caught up' and are equal to the EPS in Nogear. With PBIT in excess of £1,000, the earnings per share of Highgear overtake those of Nogear, and the difference gets bigger as profits go up.

Interest cover

31. We have now looked at 'risk' implications of gearing. There is a view that as a company's gearing gets bigger and exceeds a certain limit, it becomes a bad risk for more loans, and the company might also be in danger of failing to earn enough returns to pay the interest charges.

32. One way of measuring this gearing risk is to look at the interest cover a company provides. This is:

$$\frac{\text{Profit before interest and tax}}{\text{Interest paid in the year}}$$

33. If this ratio is less than 1, it means that the company has not earned enough to cover its interest charges, and has made a loss. A ratio of not much more than 1 would show that the company was able to make a profit after paying interest, but only just, and it must be regarded as a risky investment. A 'safe' ratio for interest cover is thought to be 3 at the very minimum. If the ratio is less than 3, the company probably has too high a gearing for the size of profits that it makes.

34. For example, in the case of Draught Ltd, in paragraph 15, interest cover is:

$$\frac{120,000}{£20,000} = 6 \text{ times}$$

This would be regarded as 'safe'.

Stock market ratios

35. Certain measures are widely used in investment analysis. They will be illustrated using the following example:

DESMOND LIMITED
PROFIT AND LOSS APPROPRIATION ACCOUNT
FOR THE YEAR ENDING 31 DECEMBER 19X9

	£'000	£'000
Net profit		107
Appropriations:		
Dividends – Preference (paid)	21	
– Ordinary (paid)	50	
	71	
Transfer to general reserve	14	
		85
Net profit retained for the year		22

Desmond Ltd has 2,000 50p ordinary shares in issue, with a current market value of 94p each.

Price/earnings (P/E) ratio

36. This is a comparison of the current market value of a share and the earnings per share (EPS). The calculation of EPS has already been illustrated. In Desmond's case, EPS is £(107–21)/2,000 = 4.3p.

Desmond's P/E ratio is therefore 94p/4.3p = 21.9.

The price/earnings ratio varies from company to company, depending on two factors:

(a) market expectations of particular companies' growth rates. For example, the market expects Marks and Spencer profits to grow, and is prepared to pay more for their shares. Therefore M & S have a higher P/E ratio than Woolworths, from whom more sluggish growth is expected;

(b) the area in which the company operates. Retail stores have P/E ratio averages of about 10, for example, while property companies have an average in the area of 35. Hence Desmond Ltd might be an exceptionally high-growth retail store, or a rather mediocre property company.

Dividend yield

37. This relates dividends (the shareholders' reward) to the market price of the shares.

$$\frac{\text{Dividend per share}}{\text{Market price per share}} \quad \text{x} \quad 100\%$$

Desmond's net dividend per share is

$$\frac{£50,000}{2,000,000} \quad = \quad 2.5p$$

Net dividend yield is therefore:

$$\frac{2.5p}{94p} \quad \text{x} \quad 100\% \quad\quad = \quad 2.7\%$$

38. It follows from the above that changes in the market price cause changes in the dividend yield. If annual dividends are halved and the market price drops by 50%, the dividend yield will remain the same.

Dividend cover

39. This measures the relationship between profits available for distribution to equity and dividends actually declared:

$$\frac{\text{Profits after interest (and after taxation) and preference dividend}}{\text{Ordinary dividend}}$$

In Desmond's case this is $\dfrac{107,000 - 21,000}{50,000}$

$$= \quad 1.72$$

40. Ordinary dividend cover is generally much lower than interest cover or preference dividend cover. 2 is widely considered acceptable, and in cases where dividends are paid from retained profits the cover will be negative.

Summary of the chapter

41.

> * In this chapter, we have looked at the primary accounting ratio, ROCE, and at ratios analysing profitability and asset turnover, and the significance of the ratios has been explained.
>
> * Gearing as a feature of capital structure has also been introduced.
>
> * A number of ratios important to investment analysis have been explained.

In the next chapter, we shall go on to look at working capital more closely.

TEST YOUR KNOWLEDGE

Numbers in brackets refer to paragraphs of this chapter

1. Define 'profit margin' and 'asset turnover'. (4, 5)

2. What is the relationship which links ROCE, profit margin and asset turnover? (7)

3. How is the ratio 'return on total long-term capital' calculated? (16(c))

4. Describe two methods of calculating a gearing ratio. (19)

5. List three advantages of debt capital over equity capital. (24)

6. Define 'interest cover'. (32)

7. Define 'price earnings ratio'. (36)

Chapter 25

THE OPERATING CYCLE
AND WORKING CAPITAL RATIOS

The purpose of this chapter is:

- to explain the importance of working capital in the operations of a business

- to explain the considerations involved in fixing a level of working capital

- to illustrate certain accounting ratios related to working capital and liquidity

---

Introduction

1. Working capital is the difference between current assets (mainly stocks, debtors and cash) and current liabilities (such as trade creditors and a bank overdraft).

    Current assets are items which are either cash already, or which will soon lead to the receipt of cash. Stocks will be sold to customers and create debtors; and debtors will soon pay in cash for their purchases.

    Current liabilities are items which will soon have to be paid for with cash. Trade creditors will have to be paid and bank overdraft is usually regarded as a short- term borrowing which may need to be repaid fairly quickly.

    In published balance sheets, the word 'current' is applied to stocks, debtors, short-term investments and cash (current assets) and amounts due for payment within one year's time (current liabilities).

Working capital and trading operations

2. Current assets and current liabilities are a necessary feature of a firm's trading operations. There is a repeated cycle of buying and selling which is carried on all the time. For example, suppose that on 1 April a firm has the following items:

	£
Stocks	3,000
Debtors	0
Cash	2,000
	5,000
Creditors	0
Working capital	5,000

3. It might sell all the stocks for £4,500, and at the same time obtain more stock from suppliers at a cost of £3,500. The balance sheet items would now be:

	£
Stocks	3,500
Debtors	4,500
Cash	2,000
	10,000
Creditors	3,500
Working capital	6,500

(The increase in working capital to £6,500 from £5,000 is caused by the profit of £1,500 on the sale of the stocks.)

4. The debtors for £4,500 will eventually pay in cash and the creditors for £3,500 must also be paid. This would give us:

	£
Stocks	3,500
Debtors	0
Cash (2,000 + 4,500 - 3,500)	3,000
	6,500
Creditors	0
Working capital	6,500

5. However, if the stocks are sold on credit for £5,500 and further purchases of stock costing £6,000 are made, the cycle of trading will continue as follows:

	£
Stocks	6,000
Debtors	5,500
Cash	3,000
	14,500
Creditors	6,000
Working capital (boosted by further profit of £2,000)	8,500

From this basic example you might be able to see that working capital items are part of a continuous flow of trading operations. Purchases add to stocks and creditors at the same time, creditors must be paid and debtors will pay for their goods. The cycle of operations always eventually comes back to cash receipts and cash payments.

The operating cycle or cash cycle

6. The operating cycle (or cash cycle) is a term used to describe the connection between working capital and cash movements in and out. The cycle is usually measured in days or months.

7. A firm buys raw materials, probably on credit. The raw materials might be held for some time in stores before being issued to the production department and turned into an item of finished goods. The finished goods might be kept in a warehouse for some time before they are eventually sold to customers. By this time, the firm will probably have paid for the raw materials purchased. If customers buy the goods on credit, it will be some time before the cash from the sales is eventually received.

8.   The cash cycle, or operating cycle, measures the period of time:

   (a) between the purchase of raw materials and the receipt of cash from debtors for goods sold; and
   (b) between the time cash is paid out for raw materials and the time cash is received in from debtors.

9.   This cycle of repeating events may be shown in either of two ways:

   (a)
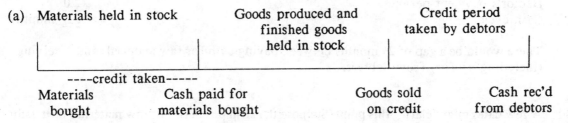

| Materials held in stock | Goods produced and finished goods held in stock | Credit period taken by debtors |

----credit taken-----

| Materials bought | Cash paid for materials bought | Goods sold on credit | Cash rec'd from debtors |

   The thick horizontal line represents the passage of time. The operating cycle starts with the purchase of materials and ends with the receipt of cash from debtors. Cash is not paid when materials are bought because credit is taken from suppliers.

   (b)

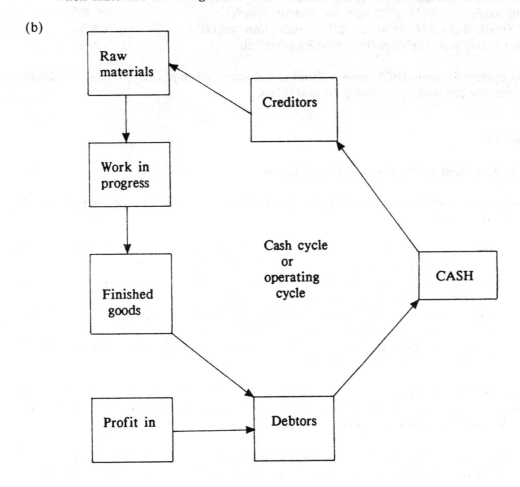

447

10. Suppose that a firm buys raw materials on 1½ months' credit, holds them in store for 1 month and then issues them to the production department. The production cycle is very short, but finished goods are held for 1 month before they are sold. Debtors take two months' credit. The cash cycle would be:

	months
Raw material stock turnover period	1.0
Less credit taken from suppliers	(1.5)
Finished goods stock turnover period	1.0
Debtor's payment period	2.0
Cash cycle	2.5 months

There would be a gap of 2½ months between paying cash for raw materials and receiving cash (including profits) from debtors.

11. A few dates might clarify this point. Suppose the firm purchases its raw materials on 1 January. The sequence of events would then be as follows:

	Date
Purchase of raw materials	1 Jan
Issue of materials to production (one month after purchase)	1 Feb
Payment made to suppliers (1½ months after purchase)	15 Feb
Sale of finished goods (one month after production begins)	1 Mar
Receipt of cash from debtors (two months after sale)	1 May

The cash cycle is the period of 2½ months from 15 February, when payment is made to suppliers, until 1 May, when cash is received from debtors.

Turnover periods

12. A 'turnover' period is an (average) length of time.

   (a) In the case of stock turnover, it is the length of time an item of stock is held in stores before it is used:

      (i) a raw materials stock turnover period is the length of time raw materials are held before being issued to the production department;

      (ii) a work in progress turnover period is the length of time it takes to turn raw materials into finished goods in the factory;

      (iii) a finished goods stock turnover period is the length of time that finished goods are held in a warehouse before they are sold;

      (iv) when a firm buys goods and re-sells them at a profit, the stock turnover period is the time between their purchase and their resale.

   (b) The debtors turnover period, or debt collection period, is the length of the credit period taken by customers - ie it is the time between the sale of an item and the receipt of cash for the sale from the customer.

   (c) Similarly, the creditors turnover period, or period of credit taken from suppliers, is the length of time between the purchase of materials and the payment to suppliers.

13. Turnover periods can be calculated from information in a firm's profit and loss account and balance sheet.

Stock turnover periods are calculated as follows:

(a) Raw materials: $\dfrac{\text{(Average) raw material stocks held}}{\text{Total raw materials consumed in one year}}$ x 12 months

(b) Work in progress (the length of the production period):

$\dfrac{\text{(Average) finished goods stocks held}}{\text{Total cost of production in the year}}$ x 12 months

(c) Finished goods: $\dfrac{\text{(Average) stocks}}{\text{Total cost of goods sold in one year}}$ x 12 months

(d) Stocks of items bought for re-sale:

$\dfrac{\text{(Average) stocks}}{\substack{\text{Total (materials) cost of goods} \\ \text{bought and sold in one year.}}}$ x 12 months

The word 'average' is put in brackets because although it is strictly correct to use average values, it is more common to use the value of stocks shown in a balance sheet - ie at one point in time - to estimate the turnover periods.

14. For example, if a company buys goods costing £620,000 in one year but uses goods costing £600,000 in production (in regular monthly quantities) and the cost of material in stock at 1 January is £100,000, the stock turnover period could be calculated as:

$\dfrac{£100,000}{£600,000}$ x 12 months = 2 months

In other words, stocks are bought two months before they are eventually re-sold.

15. The debt collection period is calculated as:

$\dfrac{\text{Average debtors}}{\text{Annual credit sales}}$ x 12 months

For example, if a company sells goods for £1,200,000 per annum in regular monthly quantities, and if debtors in the balance sheet are £150,000, the debt collection period is:

$\dfrac{£150,000}{£1,200,000}$ x 12 months = 1.5 months

In other words, debtors will pay for goods 1½ months on average after the time of sale.

16. The period of credit taken from suppliers is calculated as:

$\dfrac{\text{Average trade creditors}}{\text{Total purchases in one year}}$ x 12 months

(Notice that the creditors are compared with materials bought whereas for raw material stock turnover, raw material stocks are compared with materials used in production. This is a small, but significant difference.)

For example, if a company sells goods for £600,000 and makes a gross profit of 40% on sales, and if the amount of trade creditors in the balance sheet is £30,000, the period of credit taken from the suppliers is:

$$\frac{£30,000}{(60\% \text{ of } £600,000)} \text{ x 12 months} = 1 \text{ month}$$

In other words, suppliers are paid in the month following the purchase of goods.

Example: calculating the cash cycle

17. The profit and loss account of Legion Ltd for the year to 30 June 19X4 and the balance sheet of the company as at 30 June 19X4 are as follows:

PROFIT AND LOSS ACCOUNT

	£	£
Sales		360,000
Cost of goods sold	180,000	
Wages and salaries	80,000	
Depreciation	20,000	
Other expenses	60,000	
		340,000
Profit		20,000

BALANCE SHEET

	£	£
Fixed assets at cost less depreciation		180,000
Stocks	30,000	
Debtors	75,000	
Cash	10,000	
	115,000	
Trade creditors	45,000	
		70,000
		250,000
Share capital and reserves		250,000

Required: calculate the length of the cash cycle.

Solution

18.
Stock turnover	Debt collection period	Credit taken from suppliers
$\frac{30,000}{180,000}$ x 12	$\frac{75,000}{360,000}$ x 12	$\frac{45,000}{180,000}$ x 12
= 2 months	= 2½ months	= 3 months

The cash cycle is:

	months
Stock turnover period	2
Credit taken from suppliers	(3)
Debt collection period	2.5
Cash cycle	1.5 months

In this example, Legion Ltd pays its suppliers one month after the stocks have been sold, since the stock turnover is 2 months but credit taken is three months.

Turnover periods and the total amount of working capital

19. If the stock turnover period gets longer or if the debt collection period gets longer, the total amount of stocks held or of debtors will increase. Similarly, if the period of credit taken from the suppliers gets shorter, the amount of creditors will become smaller. The effect of these changes would be to increase the size of working capital (ignoring bank balances or overdrafts).

20. Suppose that a company has annual sales of £480,000 (in regular monthly quantities, all on credit) and a materials cost of sales of £300,000. (Note: a 'materials cost of sales' is the cost of materials in the cost of sales.)

    (a) If the stock turnover period is 2 months, the debt collection period 1 month and the period of credit taken from suppliers is 2 months, the company's working capital (ignoring cash) would be:

		£
Stocks	(2/12 x £300,000)	50,000
Debtors	(1/12 x £480,000)	40,000
		90,000
Creditors	(2/12 x £300,000)	(50,000)
		40,000

    The cash cycle would be (2 + 1 - 2) = 1 month.

    (b) Now if the stock turnover period is extended to 3 months and the debt collection period to 2 months, and if the payment period for purchases from suppliers is reduced to one month, the company's working capital (ignoring cash) would be:

		£
Stocks	(3/12 x £300,000)	75,000
Debtors	(2/12 x £480,000)	80,000
		155,000
Creditors	(1/12 x £300,000)	(25,000)
		130,000

    and the cash cycle would be (3 + 2 - 1) = 4 months.

21. If we ignore the possible effects on the bank balance or bank overdraft, (which are themselves included in working capital) it should be seen that a lengthening of the cash cycle will result in a larger volume of working capital.

22. If the volume of working capital required by a business varies with the length of the cash cycle, it is worth asking the question: "Is there an ideal length of cash cycle and an ideal volume of working capital?"

23. Obviously, stocks, debtors and creditors should be managed efficiently, and:

    (a) stocks should be sufficiently large to meet the demand for stock items when they are needed, but they should not be allowed to become excessive;

    (b) debtors should be allowed a reasonable credit period, but overdue payments should be 'chased up';

    (c) suppliers should be asked to allow a reasonable period of credit and the firm should make use of the credit periods offered by them.

24. Another important aspect of the size of working capital, however, is liquidity.

Liquidity

25. The word 'liquid' means 'readily converted into cash' and a firm's liquidity is its ability to convert its assets into cash to meet all the demands for payments when they fall due.

26. The most liquid asset, of course, is cash itself (or a bank balance). The next most liquid assets are short-term investments (stocks and shares) because these can be sold quickly for cash should this be necessary. Debtors are fairly liquid assets because they should be expected to pay their bills in the near future. Stocks are the least liquid current asset because they must first be sold (perhaps on credit) and the customers given a credit period in which to pay before they can be converted into cash.

27. Current liabilities are items which must be paid for in the near future. When payment becomes due, enough cash must be available. The managers of a business must therefore make sure that a regular supply of cash comes in (from current assets) at all times to meet the regular flow of payments it is necessary to provide for.

Liquidity ratios

28. There are two common liquidity ratios:

    (a) the current ratio or working capital ratio;
    (b) the quick ratio or liquidity ratio.

29. The *current ratio* or *working capital ratio* is the more commonly used and is the ratio of current assets to current liabilities.

    A 'prudent' current ratio is sometimes said to be 2:1. In other words, current assets should be twice the size of current liabilities. This is a rather simplistic view of the matter, because particular attention needs to be paid to certain matters:

    (a) bank overdrafts: these are technically repayable on demand, and therefore must be classified as current liabilities. However, many companies have semi-permanent overdrafts in which case the likelihood of their having to be repaid in the near future is remote. It would also often be relevant to know a company's overdraft limit - this may give a truer indication of liquidity than a current or quick ratio;

(b) whether the year-end figures are typical of the year as a whole. This is particularly relevant in the case of seasonal businesses. For example, many large retail companies choose an accounting year end following soon after the January sales and their balance sheets show a higher level of cash than would be usual at any other time in the year.

30. In practice, many businesses operate with a much lower current ratio and in these cases, the best way to judge their liquidity would be to look at the current ratio at different dates over a period of time. If the trend is towards a lower current ratio, we would judge that the liquidity position is getting steadily worse.

For example, if the liquidity ratios of two firms A and B are as follows:

	1 Jan	1 Apr	1 July	1 Oct
Firm A	1.2 : 1	1.2 : 1	1.2 : 1	1.2 : 1
Firm B	1.3 : 1	1.2 : 1	1.1 : 1	1.0 : 1

we could say that firm A is maintaining a stable liquidity position, whereas firm B's liquidity is deteriorating. We would then begin to question firm B's continuing ability to pay its bills. A bank for instance, would need to think carefully before granting any request from firm B for an extended overdraft facility.

31. The *quick ratio* is used when we take the view that stocks take a long time to get ready for sale, and then there may be some delay in getting them sold, so that stocks are not particularly liquid assets. If this is the case, a firm's liquidity depends more heavily on the amount of debtors, short-term investments and cash that it has to match its current liabilities. The quick ratio is the ratio of current assets excluding stocks to current liabilities.

32. A 'prudent' quick ratio is 1 : 1. In practice, many businesses have a lower quick ratio (eg 0.5 : 1), and the best way of judging a firm's liquidity would be to look at the trend in the quick ratio over a period of time. The quick ratio is also known as the *liquidity ratio* and as the *acid test ratio*.

33. You may find that an examination question defines a liquidity ratio for you which is slightly different from either of the two above. For example, you may be asked to measure the liquidity ratio as:

$$\frac{\text{debtors}}{\text{current liabilities}}$$

Obviously, you should read the question carefully to get your definition correct.

Increases in working capital tie up cash

34. An increase in stocks and debtors, or a decrease in creditors, will have the effect of reducing the cash surplus we would otherwise expect. An example might illustrate this point.

35. At 1 January, Cottontail Ltd had stocks of £2,000, no debtors or cash, and creditors of £1,000. During the month, stocks costing £15,000 were purchased and goods costing £14,000 were sold for £20,000. At 31 January, creditors were £500, and debtors £3,000.

The gross profit in January was £6,000, ie:

	£
Sales	20,000
Cost of sales	14,000
Gross profit	6,000

36. Cottontail should expect a cash surplus of £6,000 from these sales, but the cash balance at 31 January will not be as high as £6,000. This is because Cottontail has increased its investment in the other items of working capital (ie other than cash).

	£
Increase in stocks held (15,000 - 14,000)	1,000
Increase in debtors (3,000 - 0)	3,000
Decrease in creditors (1,000 - 500)	500
Increase in other items of working capital	4,500
Profit in January	6,000
Increase in cash (balance)	1,500

37. This can be proved as follows:

	£	£
Creditors at 1 January	1,000	
Purchases	15,000	
	16,000	
Creditors at 31 January	(500)	
Payments to creditors in January		15,500
Debtors at 1 January	0	
Sales in January	20,000	
	20,000	
Debtors at 31 January	(3,000)	
Receipts from debtors in January		17,000
Net receipts of cash in January		1,500

38. This example is intended to illustrate that an increase in stocks and debtors or a decrease in creditors will tie up cash, so that cash receipts during a period of time will be less than the cash profits earned. (Similarly, a decrease in stocks and debtors or an increase in creditors will have the opposite effect of releasing cash, so that cash receipts during a period will exceed the cash profits earned).

39. An example now completes this chapter. Attempt your own calculations and analysis before reading the solution given here.

Example

40. The cash balance of Wing Ltd has declined significantly over the last 12 months. The following financial information is provided:

	Year to 31 December	
	19X2	19X3
	£	£
Sales	573,000	643,000
Purchases of raw materials	215,000	264,000
Raw materials consumed	210,000	256,400
Cost of goods manufactured	435,000	515,000
Cost of goods sold	420,000	460,000

	Balance at 31 December	
	19X2	19X3
	£	£
Debtors	97,100	121,500
Creditors	23,900	32,500
Stocks: Raw materials	22,400	30,000
Work in progress	29,000	34,300
Finished goods	70,000	125,000

All purchases and sales were made on credit.

Required:

(a) an analysis of the above information, which should include calculations of the cash operating cycle (ie the time lag between making payment to suppliers and collecting cash from customers) for 19X2 and 19X3;

(b) a brief report on the implications of the changes which have occurred between 19X2 and 19X3.

Notes:

1. Assume a 360 day year for the purpose of your calculations and that all transactions take place at an even rate.
2. All calculations are to be made to the nearest day.

Suggested solution

41. (a) The information should be analysed in as many ways as possible, and you should not omit any important items. The relevant calculations would seem to be as follows:

(i)	19X2	19X3
	£	£
Sales	573,000	643,000
Cost of goods sold	420,000	460,000
Gross profit	153,000	183,000

(ii)   Size of working capital and liquidity ratios, ignoring cash/bank overdrafts:

		£	£
Debtors		97,100	121,500
Stocks:	Raw materials	22,400	30,000
	Work in progress	29,000	34,300
	Finished goods	70,000	125,000
		218,500	310,800
Creditors		23,900	32,500
Working capital (ignoring cash or overdraft)		194,600	278,300
Current ratio		218,500	310,800
		23,900	32,500
		= 9.1:1	= 9.6:1

(iii) Turnover periods:

	19X2				19X3			
			days				days	
Raw materials in stock	$\frac{22,400}{210,000}$	x 360	=	38.4	$\frac{30,000}{256,400}$	x 360	=	42.1
Work in progress (production period)	$\frac{29,000}{435,000}$	x 360	=	24	$\frac{34,300}{515,000}$	x 360	=	23.9
Finished goods stock	$\frac{70,000}{420,000}$	x 360	=	60	$\frac{125,000}{460,000}$	x 360	=	97.8
Debtors' collection period	$\frac{97,100}{573,000}$	x 360	=	61	$\frac{121,500}{643,000}$	x 360	=	68
Creditors' payment period	$\frac{23,900}{215,000}$	x 360	=	(40)	$\frac{32,500}{264,000}$	x 360	=	(44.3)
Cash cycle				143.4				188.5

(b)   Sales were about 12% higher in 19X3 than in 19X2 and the cost of sales was about 9% higher. The investments in stocks and debtors minus creditors rose from £194,600 to £287,300, ie by £83,700 or nearly 44%. This is completely out of proportion to the volume of increase in trade, which indicates that working capital turnover periods are not being properly controlled.

The increase in working capital of £83,700 means that the net cash receipts from profits in 19X3 were £83,700 less than they would have been if there had been no increase at all in stocks and debtors (less creditors) during 19X3. The company might therefore have an unnecessary bank overdraft, although we are not given enough information to comment on this point fully.

Current assets must be financed by a combination of long-term funds and current liabilities. Working capital (current assets minus current liabilities) is the amount of this finance provided by long-term funds. A large and unnecessary increase in working capital will mean that too many long-term funds are invested in current assets (and they